PRESCOTT

CLINICAL ASSESSMENT OF MALINGERING AND DECEPTION

Clinical Assessment of Malingering and Deception

Edited by
RICHARD ROGERS
Metropolitan Toronto Forensic Service,
Clarke Institute of Psychiatry and
University of Toronto

The Guilford Press
New York   London

Printed in the United States of America

Last digit is print number 9 8 7 6 5 4 3

Library of Congress Cataloging in Publication Data

Clinical assessment of malingering and deception.

   Includes bibliographies and index.
   1. Malingering—Diagnosis. 2. Deception. I. Rogers,
Richard, 1950–   . [DNLM: 1. Malingering—diagnosis.
W 783 C641]
RA1146.C57 1988   616.85′2   88-11212
ISBN 0-89862-721-4

Contributors

Jason Brandt, PhD, is an assistant professor of psychiatry at Johns Hopkins University School of Medicine, where he holds a joint appointment in the department of psychology. His clinical specialization is human neuropsychology with extensive research on memory disorders. Recently, Dr. Brandt has investigated the application of neuropsychological knowledge to dissimulation.

Charles R. Clark, PhD, is director of psychology at the Center for Forensic Psychiatry in Ann Arbor, Michigan. Under his able leadership the center's large forensic psychology staff enjoys a national reputation for the high quality of their clinical assessments. Dr. Clark has a continued interest in the assessment of malingering in individuals facing criminal charges.

Alan J. Cunnien, MD, is a consultant in psychiatry at the Mayo Clinic, Scottsdale, Arizona, and instructor in psychiatry at the Mayo Medical School in Rochester, Minnesota. His clinical and professional experience include being a Mayo Foundation Scholar at Rush-Presbyterian-St. Luke's Medical Center and coordinator of psychiatric education at the Mayo Medical School. He is well known for his scholarly reviews, particularly on topics of forensic psychiatry.

Roger L. Greene, PhD, is associate professor of psychology at Texas Tech University. He is internationally known for the high quality of his research on the MMPI. His book, *The MMPI: An Interpretive Manual*, is widely regarded as the standard text for MMPI interpretation.

William G. Iacono, PhD, is an associate professor of psychology at the University of Minnesota. Dr. Iacono received the Distinguished Scientific Award for his early career contributions to psychophysiology both from the Society for Psychophysiological Research and from the American Psychological Association. He has been a consultant to the Office of Technology Assessment of the U.S. Congress on the scientific status of polygraph testing and has frequently testified as an expert witness on the polygraph.

Ron Langevin, PhD, is director of research psychology at the Clarke Institute of Psychiatry and associate professor of psychiatry at the University of Toronto. He is widely respected for his extensive phallometric and neuropsychological research with sexually anomalous males. Dr. Langevin is the author of two highly regarded books on this topic: *Erotic Preference, Gender Identity, and Aggression in Men: New Research Studies*, and *Sexual Strands: Understanding and Treating Sexual Anomalies in Men.*

Robert D. Miller, MD, PhD, is training director of the Forensic Center at the Mendota Mental Health Institute, Madison, Wisconsin. He is also associate clinical professor of psychiatry and lecturer in law at the University of Wisconsin–Madison, and clinical associate professor of psychiatry at the Medical College of Wisconsin in Milwaukee. He is experienced in the use of hypnosis in both clinical and forensic contexts, and has written articles and testified in court as an expert witness on the use of hypnosis to enhance memories.

Loren Pankratz, PhD, is a clinical psychologist at the Portland V.A. Medical Center and associate professor in the Departments of Medical Psychology and Psychiatry at the Oregon Health Sciences University. His consultation work on medical and surgical services has been the source of many articles on malingering and factitious disorders. Dr. Pankratz is best known for his development of symptom validity testing.

Christopher J. Patrick, PhD, completed his doctorate in clinical psychology at the University of British Columbia in 1987. He is presently a postdoctoral fellow in the Department of Clinical and Health Psychology, University of Florida, Gainesville. He has a sustained research interest in the detection of deception.

Kathleen M. Quinn, MD, is an assistant professor of psychiatry at the Case Western Reserve School of Medicine. In addition, she is a psychiatric consultant to the Cuyahoga County criminal and domestic relations courts. She has written and taught extensively on the assessment of sexual abuse and malingering.

Phillip J. Resnick, MD, is professor of psychiatry at Case Western Reserve University and director of their forensic psychiatry program. Dr. Resnick, former president of the American Academy of Psychiatry and Law, is nationally known for his training workshops on the assessment of malingering.

Richard Rogers, PhD, is senior psychologist and coordinator of research at the Metropolitan Toronto Forensic Service (METFORS), Clarke Institute of Psychiatry. He is an associate professor of psychiatry and special lecturer in psychology at the University of Toronto. Dr. Rogers is editor of *Behavioral Sciences and the Law* and the first recipient of the Distinguished Contributions to Forensic Psychology Award from the American Academy of Forensic Psychologists. One of his major research interests is the clinical assessment of malingering.

Lawrence J. Stava, PhD, is a unit chief on the Forensic Rehabilitation Services at the Forensic Center at the Mendota Mental Health Institute, Madison, Wisconsin. He has used hypnosis extensively in his clinical practice and has published and taught courses on hypnosis and related subjects. Dr. Stava is a member of the Society for Clinical and Experimental Hypnosis.

Lana Stermac, PhD, is research coordinator of the Forensic Service, Clarke Institute of Psychiatry, and lecturer at the Ontario Institute for Studies in Education and the Department of Psychiatry, University of Toronto. Her clinical interests focus on the assessment of special populations. Her current research centers on clinical interventions with sexually violent individuals.

Robert M. Wettstein, MD, is assistant professor of psychiatry at the University of Pittsburgh and a faculty member of the Law and Psychiatry Program. He has written widely on clinical and forensic psychiatry, including the use of sodium amytal interviews. Dr. Wettstein is currently coeditor of *Behavioral Sciences and the Law*.

Preface

Malingering and deception, although long recognized as critical issues in the clinical assessment of psychiatric patients, have yet to be systematically addressed. Clinicians and applied researchers alike lack a single integrative source for the practice and study of dissimulation. *Clinical Assessment of Malingering and Deception* was written to address this need. From the perspective of the practitioner, this book provides a thorough review of the available clinical methods and their usefulness in identifying malingering and defensive patients. When clinically feasible, each chapter offers a *threshold model* (i.e., when should the issue be investigated?) and a *clinical decision model* (i.e., what are the criteria for reaching a definite conclusion?) in the evaluation of dissimulation. From the perspective of the applied researcher, this book critiques current research designs and suggests methodological improvements. In addition, prospective researchers are encouraged to combine these research methods and create a new generation of dissimulation research.

Assessing malingering and other deceptive response styles has a rich and diverse background, including case studies of malingerers, psychometric studies of malingering and defensiveness, social-psychological research on the detection of deception, and psychophysiological studies of dissimulation. Such diversity has yielded a fragmented literature and nonstandardized criteria for evaluating dissimulation. This book, through its introductory and summary chapters, proposes (1) standardized terms and definitions, and (2) a model for establishing gradations of malingering and defensiveness. Such standardization is imperative in satisfying the twin roles of improved clinical practice and more systematic research.

The intended audience of the book is divided evenly between practitioners, who are likely to find this handbook a useful adjunct to their general clinical assessment, and applied researchers, for whom it offers a critique of current research models and suggested avenues for further research. The contributors, again reflecting the diversity of the topic, address both audiences.

I want to thank publicly the contributors for their energy and commitment to writing this book. This is more a pro forma acknowledgment; each contributor manifested patience and tenacity in dealing with my obsessiveness through a minimum of three drafts. I genuinely appreciate the very useful editorial efforts of two members of my research staff, Roy Gillis and Susan Dickens. Finally, this book would not have been possible without the superb secretarial efforts of Yvonne Kornelson, Margaret James, Gladys Chan, and Kim Yoshiki. Kim deserves particular mention for her undaunted cheerfulness in undertaking the monumental task of organizing and integrating the reference material.

Richard Rogers

Table of Contents

1

Introduction

RICHARD ROGERS

A fundamental issue for mental health professionals in their clinical assessment of psychiatric patients is the careful investigation of malingering and other forms of dissimulation. Diagnoses of mental disorders rely heavily on the honesty, accuracy, and completeness of patients' self-report; distortions, both intentional and unintentional, complicate greatly the assessment process. This book is devoted to a systematic examination of dissimulation, integrating a distillation of research findings with a discussion of their clinical applications.

This chapter describes how changes in the delivery of mental health services may affect patients' honesty and propensity to dissimulate. It also discusses the overall format and chapter organization. In addition, the chapter provides the basic working tools necessary for a critical reading of the text. These tools include (1) general terminology, (2) gradations of malingering and defensiveness, and (3) an overview of research designs in dissimulatioṇ research.

Traditional practice has often assumed the veracity of psychiatric patients in describing their psychological impairment. This assumption, given the complex delivery system for mental health services, may well be naive. The clinician–patient relationship is complicated by a spectrum of sociolegal issues that extend far beyond psychological treatment. Even patients contemplating outpatient psychotherapy (often considered the bastion of voluntary treatment) are aware of the limitations on confidentiality, issues of insurance reimbursability, and the social implications of seeking treatment (Halleck, 1971; Robitcher, 1980). As noted by Rogers and Cavanaugh (1983), consumers of mental health services are increasingly aware of the far-reaching implications of their participation and of clinicians' often divided loyalties.

A second assumption found particularly in psychotherapy practice is that the veracity of patients' self-report is of only secondary importance, since the primary focus of treatment is on process and not content issues. From such a perspective, it is not essential to assess the truthfulness and completeness of patients' presenting complaints. In contrast to this ap-

Richard Rogers, Metropolitan Toronto Forensic Service (METFORS), Clarke Institute of Psychiatry, and University of Toronto, Toronto, Ontario, Canada.

proach, however, mental health systems have placed an increasing importance on assessment as a precondition or determining factor in establishing what treatment modality, if any, is offered to patients. From this latter perspective, the assessment of patients' honesty and accuracy is crucial. Towards that end, clinicians must be aware of and be able to evaluate thoroughly dissimulation or deliberate distortions in patients' self-report.

The book has as a basic assumption that the honesty, accuracy, and completeness of each patient's self-report should be considered an integral element of clinical assessment. Available research literature has demonstrated consistently that intentional and unintentional distortions occur in patients' presentations on a range of diagnostic cases. For example, Sierles (1984) found a considerable proportion of psychiatric patients who admitted to malingering an illness. He found that patients with symptoms of sociopathic behavior and/or substance abuse were most likely to engage in deception. Lorei (1970) in an extensive survey of 12,054 staff members from 12 veteran's administration hospitals found the determination of malingering was considered the second most important clinical issue (after dangerousness) in determining a patient's level of adjustment and readiness to be discharged. From a forensic perspective, Rogers (1986a) found that 20.8% of the criminal defendants being assessed for insanity engaged in suspected or definite malingering, with an additional 5.2% having unintentional distortions in their self-report. These studies, although exemplifying the importance of malingering in clinical assessment, do not adequately represent the wide range of psychiatric patients and treatment settings. In addition, these reports are limited to malingering and do not address other forms of dissimulation such as defensiveness and irrelevant responding. Therefore, clinicians are encouraged to address the honesty and accuracy of patients' presentations and, where possible, to standardize their assessments.

This book has two primary objectives, which I consider to be of equal importance. The first is to offer a clear and succinct summary of current research on malingering and deception as it applies to psychological impairment. Inherent in this discussion is the encouragement of more sophisticated research and the careful application of research findings to clinical practice. The second and related objective is the development of an empirically based conceptual model for the evaluation of malingering and deception. At present, clinical assessment of dissimulation is based largely on idiosyncratic and unvalidated approaches. The goal of the second objective is to standardize diagnostic evaluations and provide a meaningful framework for clinical decision making.

The scope of this book was determined in part by current clinical methods and available applied research and its focus became primarily dissimulation as it relates to psychological and not physical disorders. Thus, although factitious disorders and Munchausen syndrome are discussed, no attempt is made to explore dissimulation of purely physical disorders (e.g., malingered deafness). In addition, several topics are not addressed since their clinical relevance is limited. For example, a large research literature exists (see, for example, Rogers, 1987) on interpersonal variables as they relate to deception. No attempt is made to comprehensively review this vast array of studies because of their limited applicability to psychiatric patients in clinical settings. Such research has questionable usefulness, since it addresses how nonprofessionals detect unspecified deception in nonpsychiatric subjects under highly controlled experimental conditions. The scope of the book is therefore focused on clinical research and its applications in the assessment of psychiatric populations.

Format for the Book

This book is organized into four major sections: Diagnostic Issues, Psychometric Approaches, Specialized Methods, and Synthesis. Section I, Diagnostic Issues, addresses (1) specific syndromes associated with dissimulation, (2) assessment of malingering and deception with special populations, namely sociopaths and children, (3) differential diagnosis between malingering and commonly feigned disorders, such as psychosis and posttraumatic stress disorders, and (4) the evaluation of feigned amnesia and memory impairment. Section II, Psychometric Approaches, comprises chapters on objective personality measures, projective testing, and intellectual and neuropsychological measures. The purpose of these three chapters is a careful review of current research findings with the twin goals of improving clinical methods for assessing dissimulation and discarding ineffective traditional techniques.

Section III, Specialized Methods, examines an array of investigative techniques in the assessment of dissimulation. Three such techniques are hypnosis, polygraphy, and drug-assisted interviews, which are often employed to assess nonspecific deception. Plethysmography, or phallometric methods of assessing sexual arousal, is reviewed in the light of frequent defensiveness and denial among men who engage in aberrant sexual activity. Finally, the usefulness of structured interviews in the identification of dissimulation is discussed, including a review of the Schedule of Affective Disorders and Schizophrenia (SADS) (Spitzer & Endicott, 1978) and an experimental measure of malingering referred to as the Structured Interview of Reported Symptoms (SIRS) (Rogers, 1986b).

Section IV, Synthesis, provides an interesting integration of clinical methods and research data. These related chapters summarize the important clinical and research issues on the assessment of dissimulation for both practitioners and applied researchers. The clinical methods chapter discusses how clinical procedures should be employed and proposes a preliminary model for their clinical applications. The research chapter explores four basic research designs (case study, psychometric, social-psychological, and psychophysiological), their present status, and their future directions in the applied study of dissimulation.

The format for each chapter allows considerable flexibility, given the breadth and diversity of topics. However, each chapter incorporates a distillation of research findings on malingering and deception with a conceptual understanding and heuristic (i.e., empirically untested but clinically accepted) approaches to the assessment of dissimulation. Whenever possible, each chapter offers, on the basis of research data, two decision paradigms: the *threshold model* and the *clinical decision model*. The threshold model addresses the issue of *when* clinicians should thoroughly investigate suspected dissimulation through the use of specific methods. This model employs explicit criteria for establishing at what point sufficient concern is raised (i.e., threshold) to warrant further assessment. The clinical decision model addresses the issue of *how* clinicians arrive at their conclusions. This model presents explicit criteria for making the clinical determination of malingering and defensiveness. A survey of the chapters demonstrates the inherent difficulties of establishing these models where relevant research is limited. As a result, many chapters are missing one or both models or address less precise issues, such as patients' unreliabiliity.

Terms and Definitions

The diversity of clinical and research interests in the assessment of dissimulation among psychiatric patients has militated against consistent definitions and agreed-upon terms for describing psychological deception. The definitions presented below represent one useful step in the standardization of this terminology. These definitions will be used uniformly throughout the book.

Response Styles

The vast bulk of clinical literature on dissimulation focuses exclusively on malingering. Of importance to clinical practice and applied research are other deceptive response styles that are frequently overlooked or deemphasized. Listed below are six distinct response styles of dissimulation.

1. Malingering (American Psychiatric Association, 1980) refers to the conscious fabrication or gross exaggeration of physical and/or psychological symptoms. It is distinguished from factitious disorders in that the malingered presentation extends beyond a patient role and is understandable in light of the individual's circumstances.

2. Defensiveness (Rogers, 1984a) is the polar opposite term of malingering. It refers to the conscious denial or gross minimization of physical and/or psychological symptoms. This term is derived from extensive psychometric research on patients who present themselves in the most favorable light. Care must be taken to distinguish this term from *ego defenses*, which involve intrapsychic processes that distort perception.

3. *Irrelevant responding* refers to a response style in which the individual does not become psychologically engaged in the assessment process (Rogers, 1984a). The responses given are not necessarily related to the content of the clinical inquiry. This process of disengagement, although most prevalent in psychological testing, is also observed in clinical interviews when a particular patient makes no effort to respond accurately to clinical inquiry.

4. *Random responding* is a subset of irrelevant responding where a random pattern can be identified. This response style (see Chapter 8) is seen almost exclusively on objective personality measures, such as the MMPI.

5. *Honest responding* refers to a response pattern reflecting a patient's sincere attempt to be accurate in his or her responses. Factual inaccuracies must therefore be evaluated in light of the patient's understanding and perceptions.

6. *Hybrid responding* (Rogers, 1984a) refers to any combination of the above response styles. Although clinically observed, the incidence of hybrid response styles remains completely unknown. An example of hybrid responding drawn from forensic evaluations is the pedophile who is honest about questions of psychopathology and highly defensive with respect to his sexual behavior.

Other Terms

1. *Dissimulation* is a general term to describe an individual who is deliberately distorting or misrepresenting his or her psychological symptoms. Dissimulation may incorporate any of the above response styles with, of course, the exception of honest responding.

2. *Deception* is an all-encompassing term to describe any and all attempts by an individual to distort or misrepresent his or her self-report. This term includes both dissimulation as well as all other forms of dishonesty. For example, some patients are dishonest about their past and current behavior, attitudes or perceptions. Such deception may be totally separate from the patient's described psychological functioning (i.e., dissimulation).

3. *Unreliability* is a nonspecific term used to describe clinically the characteristics of an individual whose response style is not honest and self-disclosing, yet where no further clarification can be made with respect to his or her intention.

4. *Self-disclosure* refers to how much an individual reveals about himself or herself (Jourard, 1971). A person is considered to have high self-disclosure when he or she evidences an honest response style in addition to a high degree of openness.

5. *Simulation–malingering paradox* (Rogers & Cavanaugh, 1983) refers to the research problem exemplified by simulation studies of dissimulation in which subjects are asked to comply with instructions to fake (e.g., problems or symptoms) in order to study patients who fake symptoms when asked to comply with their psychological or medical assessment.

Gradations of Malingering and Defensiveness

Malingering and defensiveness have traditionally been treated as if they were dichotomous variables. For example, research on the Minnesota Multiphasic Personality Inventory (MMPI) has attempted to establish "fake bad" profiles with optimal cut-off scores for establishing the presence of malingering. Although such research is valuable, it does not address the pressing clinical need for established gradations of dissimulation. For diagnostic purposes, it is of critical importance that an individual who is mildly defensive can be differentiated from others who are engaging in gross denial. Similarly, gradations of malingering may be of considerable importance in addressing dispositional issues or making treatment recommendations. The gradations provided in Table 1.1 represent a refinement of previous theoret-

Table 1.1. Gradations of Malingering and Defensiveness

Unreliability
1. *Self-report with limited reliability:* The patient answers most inquiries with a fair degree of accuracy, but volunteers little or nothing and may distort or evade on circumscribed topics.
2. *Self-report without reliability:* The patient, through guardedness, exaggeration, or denial of symptoms, convinces the clinician that his or her responses are inaccurate. Such cases may be suspected of malingering or defensiveness, although the patient's intent cannot be unequivocally established.

Malingering
1. *Mild malingering:* There is unequivocal evidence that the patient is attempting to malinger, primarily through exaggeration. The degree of distortion is minimal and plays only a minor role in differential diagnosis.
2. *Moderate malingering:* The patient, either through exaggeration or fabrication, attempts to present himself or herself as considerably more disturbed than is the case. These distortions may be limited to either a few critical symptoms (e.g., the fabrication of command hallucinations) or represent an array of lesser distortions.
3. *Severe malingering:* The patient is extreme in his or her fabrication of symptoms to the point that the presentation is fantastic or preposterous.

Defensiveness
1. *Mild defensiveness:* There is unequivocal evidence that the patient is attempting to minimize the severity but not the presence of his or her psychological problems. These distortions are minimal in degree and of secondary importance in establishing a differential diagnosis.
2. *Moderate defensiveness:* The patient minimizes or denies substantial psychological impairment. This defensiveness may be limited to either a few critical symptoms (e.g., pedophilic interest) or represent lesser distortions across an array of symptomatology.
3. *Severe defensiveness:* The patient denies the existence of any psychological problems or symptoms. This categorical denial includes common foibles and minor emotional difficulties that most healthy individuals have experienced and would acknowledge.

ical work (Rogers, 1984b, 1987) for establishing gradations of dissimulation. In this model, both the terms malingering and defensiveness are reserved for cases where there is unequivocal evidence of deliberate dissimulation. In contrast, cases where intentionality is in doubt would be characterized by the two gradations of unreliability.

The differentiations between malingering and defensiveness discussed above should be viewed as preliminary, since they have not been tested empirically with psychiatric populations and suspected dissimulators. Research with forensic patients (Rogers, 1984b) has demonstrated that clinicians are able to make reliable discriminations for gradations of malingering. This conceptualization does, however, highlight the need for establishing consistent gradations of dissimulation both with respect to clinical practice and more sophisticated research designs.

Examination of dissimulation studies is likewise hampered by the absence of any systematic schema for establishing the degree of certainty in either clinical conclusions or research findings. *Degree of certainty* refers to the level of empirical support and theoretical basis for justifying a diagnostic conclusion. The absence of such standardization is an important limiting factor in assessing the clinical usefulness of applied research in general, as well as its particular applications to dissimulation. As an alternative, Rogers (1986a) has suggested a descriptive ranking of psychological data based on the degree of certainty established in clinical research. This paradigm is presented in Table 1.2.

Implications of this paradigm to clinical assessment are far reaching since many important diagnostic conclusions are based on relatively little empirical data. Germane to the study of malingering and deception, these

Table 1.2. Degree of Certainty in Clinical Findings

Level of Certainty	Clinical Criteria
Unsupported	Nonsignificant or conflicting research findings
Speculative	Conclusions that are consistent with accepted theory and supported by one or two studies of limited generalizability
Tentative	Research studies consistently show statistical significance in the expected direction, but have little or no practical value in classifying subjects
Probable	Research studies consistently establish statistical significance in which cutting scores, measures of central tendency, or a similar statistic accurately differentiate between at least 75% of the criterion groups
Definite	Accurate classification of 90% or more of individual subjects based on extensive, cross-validated research. Findings are congruent with accepted theory

Note. Adapted from Rogers (1986).

descriptive rankings allow for a more systematic comparison of research findings as well as offer a greater degree of standardization in the evaluation of dissimulation. These rankings should therefore be applied in the critical analysis of dissimulation in both research findings and clinical applications. A general concern echoed throughout this book is the use of clinical indicators of speculative or tentative certainty as a primary basis for the determination of malingering or defensiveness.

Research Designs in the Study of Dissimulation

The research literature on dissimulation is richly diverse, drawn from case studies, psychometric, social-psychological, and psychophysiological research. Each design has methodological advantages and limitations in the study of dissimulation. The next paragraphs briefly outline these basic research approaches to enable the reader to better understand the subsequent chapters. In addition, a detailed analysis of these designs and potential methodological innovations will be presented in Chapter 17.

The case study approach has been applied primarily to the study of malingering and specific syndromes associated with dissimulation. This approach is essentially naturalistic research in the examination of one or more cases where the issue of dissimulation must be evaluated on clinical grounds. As an idiographic approach, case studies may offer a broad range of clinical observations that may, in turn, be the stimulus for more systematic research.

Psychometric research examines a broad range of dissimulative styles including malingering, defensiveness, and irrelevant and random responding. This type of research is based primarily on a simulation design in which subjects are asked to comply with instructions to dissimulate. Such a design examines the responses of primarily nonpsychiatric samples on standardized measures, which are then compared across experimental conditions.

Social-psychological research has focused almost exclusively on the study of deception in general populations. Such research employs confederates under specific experimental conditions with nonprofessional subjects being asked to assess the honesty/deception of the confederates. Relevance of this research to actual clinical practice has only recently been explored (Rogers, 1984a).

Psychophysiological approaches have focused on deception primarily in their applications to polygraph techniques. Under optimal research designs, systematic comparisons of physiological measures are made under deceptive and honest conditions by researchers blind to the design. In actual practice, however, the techniques employed are more heuristic than empirical.

Conclusion

The traditional practitioner–patient relationship has eroded gradually in the face of competing demands such as the limits of confidentiality, insurance reimbursability, questions of divided loyalty, and burgeoning legal issues associated with patients' rights and professional malpractice. Given these fundamental changes in the professional relationship, clinicians can no longer assume, if they ever could, that patients will not deliberately distort their clinical presentations. Assessment of patients' response styles should therefore be an integral component of most clinical assessments.

Both clinical practice and applied research on dissimulation require greater standardization in (1) the use of descriptive terms and (2) the establishment of gradations of malingering and defensiveness. Degrees of deliberate distortion are important in clinical decision making, for providing treatment recommendations, and in addressing relevant psycholegal issues. Assessment of dissimulation, because of its important consequences to patients and mental health services, requires careful investigation employing a variety of well-validated clinical techniques and, wherever possible, empirically based decision models.

PART ONE

DIAGNOSTIC ISSUES

2

Psychiatric and Medical Syndromes Associated with Deception

ALAN J. CUNNIEN

By design or by inference, the American Psychiatric Association's *Diagnostic and Statistical Manual of Mental Disorders* (DSM-III) delimits a number of syndromes whose diagnostic criteria include features of malingering, defensiveness, or other varieties of consciously or unconsciously based deception. Most obvious are factitious disorders and malingering, although clinical experience illustrates prominent elements of deception in substance abuse-disorders, eating disorders, and several personality disorders. This chapter will describe DSM-III and proposed DSM-III-R criteria for major syndromes associated with deception, assess the clinical and theoretical validity of each syndrome, and provide clinical and threshold criteria for each diagnosis. A number of other syndromes or symptoms not described in DSM-III will be reviewed to assess their relationship to deception: Munchausen syndrome by proxy, compensation neurosis, confabulation, pathological lying and *pseudologia fantastica*, and acts of imposture.

Whether in clinical or forensic settings, practitioners encounter great difficulty maintaining neutrality and a spirit of scientific inquiry when confronted with obvious or presumed deceit, self-induced disease, or other patient-generated varieties of interference with evaluation and treatment (Fras, 1978). Practitioners' often-incorrect assumptions about patients' purely conscious intention to deceive have produced a plethora of pejorative terms describing such patients: *malingering, compensation neurosis, functional overlay, psychogenic pain, medical care abuse, hospital addiction,* and so on. Irritation with difficult patients may force clinicians into making untestable or overgeneralized conclusions, for example, that improvement of pain after financial settlement indicates malingering (Hyler & Spitzer, 1978) or that the deception and truculence of the Munchausen patient serve only the conscious goal of defeating the physician. By evaluat-

Alan J. Cunnien, Mayo Clinic, Scottsdale, Arizona, and Mayo Medical School, Rochester, Minnesota.

ing current knowledge about the contributions of conscious motivations and actions to disorders associated with deception, this chapter will enable clinicians to take a more circumspect view of causality and treatability in this group of often "hateful patients" (Groves, 1978). Diagnostic and clinical accuracy will improve as clinicians learn to avoid personalizing the apparently personal effrontery of deceptive patients.

DSM-III and DSM-III-R require clinicians to formulate judgments about a patient's intentionality and goal-orientation in order to discriminate, for example, between malingering and factitious disorder. For example, the patient who simulates pain in order to obtain drugs is a malingerer, and the patient who simulates pain in order to draw attention to a difficult home situation is factitiously ill. An act may be so clearly deceptive as to obviate any debate about its veracity, but motivations for deceptive acts are highly complex and are not amenable to simple categorizations of conscious versus unconscious or environmental versus internal and psychological.

The following discussion of syndromes and diagnostic criteria will include assessment of deficiencies in current descriptive and psychodynamic diagnostic schemes. Jonas and Pope (1985) suggested that the impossible questions of voluntariness and degree of consciousness be set aside in favor of longitudinal, phenomenological studies of biological, genetic, treatment, and outcome characteristics in dissimulating patients. Their preliminary studies showed striking similarities among patients with conversion illness, malingering, and factitious illness regardless of age, sex distribution, course of illness, family history, or response to treatment. Jonas and Pope highlighted the current deficiencies in diagnosis and treatment of deceptive disorders: (1) "forcing" of patients into diagnostic categories based on the inference of consciousness and goal orientation, (2) unfair dichotomization of consciousness and unconsciousness or malingering and nonmalingering (see also Rogers, 1986a), (3) overlapping of syndromes not permitted by the narrow schema of DSM-III, and (4) inadequate genetic, biological, dynamic, and characterologic data founded in part on societal and medical disinterest in individuals or patients who deceive.

Although factitious illness was known to Hippocrates, and despite attempts to categorize it in the early 19th century (Gavin, 1834), DSM-II gave recognition only to the ill-defined Ganser syndrome and included it as an "adjustment disorder of adult life" (American Psychiatric Association, 1968, p. 49). DSM-III provided criteria for factitious disorders of three types: factitious disorder with psychological symptoms, chronic factitious disorder with physical symptoms, and atypical factitious disorder with physical symptoms. The essential features of all factitious disorders is the voluntary production of physical or psychological symptoms with the apparent goal of assuming the role of patient. The goal is "not otherwise understandable in light of the individual's environmental circumstances" (American Psychiatric Association, 1980, p. 287), and factitious disorders are thus distinguished from malingering with its easily recognized external goals.

The voluntary or intentional production or exaggeration of any symptom is not readily discernible. The best available criteria to date for assessment of voluntary control of symptoms were defined by Pope, Jonas, and Jones (1982, p. 181) as the presence of any two of the following: admission by the patient of voluntary control; unconventional, fantastic, or nonstereotypical symptoms; or unconventional symptom response to pharmacological or environmental changes. DSM-III, unfortunately, provides the clinician only with behavioral concomitants of factitious illness (e.g., approximate answers, lying, eagerness to undergo medical tests) and omits even rudimentary clinical criteria for assessing voluntariness. In addition, most human behavior serves both conscious and unconscious goals and is undertaken with mixed intentions. A patient might simulate pain to serve several simultaneous functions: to satisfy narcotic dependency, to avoid traumatic marital conflict, and to identify with an ill parent. Current diagnostic terminology would force the classification of such a patient as a malingerer, overlooking sensitive psychological precipitants and denying needed psychological treatment.

Factitious Disorder with Psychological Symptoms

Factitious disorder with psychological symptoms (FDPS) is often viewed incorrectly as synonymous with Ganser syndrome, pseudopsychosis, hysterical psychosis, and pseudodementia. Table 2.1 lists DSM-III criteria for FDPS; of note is the fact that it is appropriate to diagnose FDPS in the presence of an underlying mental disorder. Thus, it is acceptable to find that a depressed patient fabricates a superimposed factitious psychotic disorder or that a schizophrenic patient grieves for a factitiously mourned loved one. The proposed draft of DSM-III-R in development (American Psychiatric

Table 2.1. DSM-III Diagnostic Criteria for Factitious Disorder with Psychological Symptoms

A. The production of psychological symptoms is apparently under the individual's voluntary control.
B. The symptoms produced are not explained by another mental disorder (although they may be superimposed on one).
C. The individual's goal is apparently to assume the "patient" role and is not otherwise understandable in light of the individual's environmental circumstances (as is the case in malingering).

Note. From *Diagnostic and statistical manual of mental disorders* (3rd ed.) (p. 287), 1980, Washington, D.C.: American Psychiatric Association. Copyright 1980 by the American Psychiatric Association. Reprinted by permission.

Association, 1986) would not allow the diagnosis of any physical or psychiatric factitious disorder in the presence of another Axis I diagnosis; this is an unfair extension of the law of parsimony and one which might result in the omission of significant psychosocial elements in patient diagnosis and management. This chapter will also review several syndromes not explicitly defined in DSM-III but which may be subsumed under the diagnosis of FDPS: factitious posttraumatic stress disorder, factitious bereavement, and factitious child abuse or neglect.

Ganser Syndrome

In 1897, Ganser described a syndrome of transient psychosis and clouding of consciousness in three male prisoners. Classic Ganser syndrome is narrowly defined: sudden onset of psychosis with prominent hallucinations, sensory changes of conversion type, clouding of consciousness with resultant amnesia for the episode, concrete or approximate answers (*vorbeireden*), and sudden resolution with complete return to normal mental functioning (F. A. Whitlock, 1967). Although the possibility of malingering has been raised in light of the number of reports of Ganser syndrome in prisoners, clouding of consciousness and rapid symptom resolution are inconsistent with malingering (Rieger & Billings, 1978) as are the ludicrous and childlike approximate answers (Ingraham & Moriarty, 1967). In contrast, Resnick's (1984) opinion that Ganser syndrome represented a form of malingered mental disorder was based on the approximate answers given by normal subjects attempting to simulate mental illness. Case reviews by others (de la Fuente, Hanson, & Duncan, 1980; Cocores, Santa, & Patel, 1984) gave clear evidence of occurrence of the syndrome in nonprisoners and during the course of other mental illness, head trauma, or family conflict. No author has demonstrated Ganser symptoms to be under voluntary control.

F. A. Whitlock (1967) noted the similarity of approximate answers to those found in schizophrenic thought disorder, nominal aphasia, and toxic/organic confusional states; he placed more emphasis on the randomness of answers than on their approximate nature and concluded that Ganser syndrome was a stress-related psychotic disorder. The precise etiology and nosology of Ganser syndrome are unknown. Ganser-like patients without psychotic symptoms best fit DSM-III criteria for atypical dissociative disorder. Classic Ganser syndrome would best be classified as a brief reactive psychosis even if dissociative mechanisms are present (Kiloh, 1961). The occurrence of approximate answers has been reported in other psychiatric illnesses and should not, in and of itself, be interpreted as evidence of Ganser syndrome (Scott, 1965). Ganser syndrome has not been demonstrated to be voluntary in nature and should be removed from classification as a factitious disorder.

Pseudopsychosis

No consensus exists in the literature or clinical practice as to the definition of pseudopsychosis; however, it is used in DSM-III as synonymous with FDPS. As used in clinical practice it subsumes a number of functional psychoses: malingered, reactive, "hysterical," and truly factitious. Malingered psychoses will be reviewed briefly in a subsequent section and in detail in Chapter 3.

The incidence of factitious psychosis meeting DSM-III criteria for FDPS is unknown but probably rare. In an excellent study of 9 cases of factitious psychosis culled from 219 consecutive psychotic admissions, Pope *et al.* (1982) performed the only published analysis of epidemiological, phenomenological, and outcome parameters. Seven of nine patients were female, all demonstrated severe borderline or histrionic personalities, and none had family histories of psychosis. Most impressive were long-term (four- to seven-year) follow-up data suggesting that, compared with schizophrenic and manic patients, patients with factitious psychosis fared *more poorly* on measures of global assessment, social function, and freedom from residual symptoms. The authors' criteria for voluntariness were consistent with the spirit of DSM-III and are detailed in the introduction to this chapter. Twelve patients with factitious psychosis were described by Ritson and Forrest (1970); some had past diagnoses of schizophrenia serving as models for current symptoms. The remainder demonstrated personality disorders. Although presenting little epidemiological information, the authors provided helpful advice for management. They recommended the use of a "contract conference" at which staff present the patient with the fact that symptoms are not genuine and offer to help understand and treat underlying adjustment problems. The widely reported poor prognosis of factitious psychosis is probably a testament to the nature of the severe underlying personality disorder noted in DSM-III (American Psychiatric Association, 1980, p. 286).

In reviewing 56 cases of pseudopsychosis, Bishop and Holt (1980) noted the following consistent features: prominent psychotic symptoms, preservation of affect, temporal relationship between meaningful events and symptom onset, symptoms allowing the avoidance of unpleasant activity, and a history of hysterical symptoms such as sensory loss or amnesia. The authors suggested that pseudopsychosis is analogous to somatoform disorders in etiology and presentation. It is logical to consider that some patients employ conversion mechanisms to produce physical symptoms, whereas others produce psychiatric manifestations. It is reasonable to restrict use of the term *pseudopsychosis* to the entity narrowly defined by Bishop and Holt; in contrast, the use of the term *hysterical psychosis* is discouraged since it lacks clear phenomenological description.

In describing six patients feigning psychosis, Hay (1983) noted that five of the six developed overt schizophrenia during follow-up assessments. He argued that the diagnosis of simulated psychosis should be made with caution and with the implied obligation to follow such patients carefully. In describing a form of feigned psychosis characterized by situationally based ego dissolution, Hollender and Hirsch (1964) were apparently defining a syndrome most compatible with brief reactive psychosis.

It is reasonable to conclude that the incidence of factitious psychosis, compatible with DSM-III criteria for FDPS, is very low. As delineated by Pope *et al.* (1982), this disorder has a poor prognosis and is indicative of severe underlying character pathology. Other varieties of simulated psychosis, reflective of conversion mechanisms or ego dissolution, are best classified as brief reactive psychoses although this nosology provides no information about clinical course, treatment options, or prognosis. Either because of its brief course or due to pessimism about attendant character pathology, no authors have offered comprehensive advice on pharmacological or psychotherapeutic treatment of factitious psychosis.

Pseudodementia

In a classic treatise on pseudodementia, Kiloh (1961) used the term to refer to apparent dementia in patients with underlying affective or other psychiatric illness, and noted reversal of cognitive impairment after treatment of the primary disease. The term has also been used to refer to patients in whom conversion mechanisms produce a "caricature of dementia" (McAllister, 1983). No author has systematically described dementing symptoms of a voluntary nature, raising questions about including pseudodementia as a category of FDPS.

Caine (1981) provided the most accurate working definition for pseudodementia: (1) the intellectual impairment occurs in a patient with a primary psychiatric disorder; (2) the features of the neuropsychological abnormality resembled, at least in part, the presentation of a neuropathologically induced cognitive deficit; (3) the intellectual disorder was reversible; and (4) the patient had no apparent primary neuropathological process that led to the genesis of the disturbance (p. 1361). Wells (1979) provided an exhaustive list of differences between demented and pseudodemented subjects. The latter group more often demonstrated easily dated symptom onset, rapid progression, history of psychiatric illness, complaints about cognitive deficits, lack of effort on examination, behavior incongruent with level of cognitive dysfunction, preservation of concentration, equal impairment of recent and remote memories, and no nocturnal aggravation.

Factitious Posttraumatic Stress Disorder

Introduction of new disorders into psychiatric nomenclature provided potential deceivers with ready avenues for personal, financial and psychological gains. The introduction of posttraumatic stress disorder (PTSD) into

DSM-III was no exception. Sparr and Pankratz (1983) provided the first in-depth analysis of simulated PTSD symptoms in five men claiming to have served in Vietnam; four had never been overseas and two had never seen military service. Investigation revealed that one patient was malingering, two qualified for diagnosis of FDPS, and that the other two had elements of Munchausen syndrome. A similar array of conscious and unconscious contributions to simulated PTSD were noted in seven cases described by Lynn and Belza (1984). All authors emphasized the paramount importance of documenting alleged military histories.

In Chapter 6, Resnick will detail methods for differentiating simulated from true PTSD. The cases previously cited raise several general points of interest. First, simulated PTSD (or any simulated mental illness) presents along varied lines of consciousness and intention and with varied goals; that is, it may be malingered, factitious, delusional, or some combination of the three. Second, factitious PTSD qualifies for inclusion as a factitious disorder with psychological symptoms even though its etiology, incidence, course, and prognosis have yet to be determined with systematic studies. Third, and as noted by Eisendrath (1984), reductionistic DSM-III terminology is of limited utility in factitious PTSD and other factitious disorders. The boundaries of factitious PTSD with malingering, Munchausen syndrome, and psychotic illnesses are blurred; neither DSM-III terminology nor the small number of psychodynamic case studies permit clinicians to differentiate among these disorders with any degree of certainty.

Factitious Bereavement

Two available studies of patients feigning bereavement provide more important information about the blurred boundaries between malingering, factitious disorders, and Munchausen syndrome. Snowdon, Solomons, and Druce (1978) reported 12 simulating patients whose chief complaint was the alleged loss of a loved one. Most were depressed and suicidal; 11 of the 12 were male. Nine had used aliases in the past, six had past symptoms of Munchausen syndrome, and most left the hospital suddenly. Despite the presence of *pseudologia fantastica* and other symptoms of Munchausen syndrome, several patients' mourning appeared truly factitious (i.e., it was under voluntary control and had as its only apparent purpose the assumption of the patient role). Half of patients effectively prevented treatment by discharging themselves against medical advice; psychotherapy of unreported benefit was prescribed for the remainder.

In a second study, Phillips, Ward, and Ries (1983) described 20 patients who falsely reported the death of a loved one in a dramatic and unverifiable fashion. Again, the patients were predominantly male and complained of depression and suicidal ideation. Interestingly, 15 of the 20 had histories of factitious physical symptoms, 4 had used aliases, and 12 demonstrated patterns of sociopathy. The authors stressed the great difficulty of assessing conscious intent and concluded that patients are never purely conscious or unconscious of their motivation but, rather, "more or less conscious of it" (p. 423). The authors discouraged viewing factitious bereavement as a specific diagnostic entity, perceiving it as a specific pathological behavior designed to elicit care and nurturance.

Despite the disclaimer of Phillips *et al.*, some types of simulated mourning appear to merit the broad diagnosis of FDPS. More importantly, however, the clinician is encouraged to be aware of the fluidity of factitious symptoms across somatic and emotional boundaries and of the fact that mixed levels of conscious awareness of behavior make the pure diagnosis of malingering or factitious disorder unlikely.

Factitious Child Abuse or Neglect

Goodwin, Cauthorne, and Rada (1980) described a "Cinderella syndrome" (p. 1223) in three adopted girls who claimed that their adoptive parents were neglectful and dressed them in rags; all intentionally changed into shabby clothes for public show or attributed benign bruises to parental abuse. The factitious (rather than malingered) nature of the complaints became obvious when the authors found common psychological themes: actual histories of previous abuse, early loss of a maternal figure, and current emotional abuse; the manufactured symptoms were thus "cries for help."

Goodwin, Sahd, and Rada (1978) earlier described incest hoaxes perpetrated by alleged victims or by angry spouses; they also noted that persistent emphasis on Freudian seduction theory causes authorities and therapists to underestimate the actual incidence of incest. Nondelusional false claims of incest by any party were ascribed to opportunistic lying in the service of revenge or fantasy fulfillment and would qualify for the diagnosis of FDPS.

Schuman (1986) noted that false allegations of abuse by a vengeful parent may represent a form of factitious disorder by proxy. All authors stressed the importance of thorough investigation of alleged abuse and adequate understanding of personal motives for factitious claims of abuse or neglect.

Chronic Factitious Disorder with Physical Symptoms

The medical profession's chronic frustration in dealing with Munchausen syndrome and milder forms of contrived physical disease was well reflected in a twist of Churchill's words: "Never in the history of medicine have so many been so much annoyed by so few" (Asher, 1972, p. 154). Review of pertinent literature will illustrate another of the profession's responses to these complex diseases: "Never in the history of medicine have so many written so much about so little." Voluminous case reports and analyses leave the discerning reader with grave uncertainties as to the etiology, spectrum, treatment, and course of physical factitial illness.

DSM-III defined two varieties of factitious physical disorder: chronic factitious disorder with physical symptoms (CFDPS) and atypical factitious disorder with physical symptoms (AFDPS); criteria for CFDPS are listed in Table 2.2. The atypical disorder is considered a residual category for factitious physical disorders not meeting full criteria for CFDPS. The essential feature of either category is that the patient has produced (or claims to demonstrate) physical symptoms that are under voluntary control and that serve a goal understandable only in light of the individual's psychological need to be a patient. The presence of an external, easily recognizable goal mandates the diagnosis of malingering. The following sections will describe varieties of physical factitial illness, the spectrum of actions and motivations observed, psychological formulations, and treatment options. The reader will discern that narrow DSM-III criteria cannot approximate the complexity and breadth of factitious physical illness, that psychodynamic formulations are based on isolated case reports, and that future diagnostic schemes will need to incorporate, as yet, undiscovered information about causality and intentionality in factitious illness.

Although DSM-III equates CFDPS with the epithet "Munchausen syndrome," the latter is apparently only a rare, extreme, and archetypical form of chronic factitious physical illness (Asher, 1961). The syndrome has no established diagnostic criteria and significantly overlaps malingering and conversion disorder (Cramer, Gershberg, & Stern, 1971). Even such fundamental data such as sex distribution of Munchausen syndrome is debated, presumably due to its indistinct clinical boundaries (Folks & Freeman, 1985). The classic patient is admitted to the hospital with a dramatic and superficially plausible story of acute abdominal, haematological, or neurological illness. Personal historical details reminiscent of *pseudologia fantastica* are evident and the patient's manner is evasive and belligerent; there are no family or visitors to confirm background data and the patient will resist establishment of such contacts. There are often multiple scars and the

Table 2.2. DSM-III Diagnostic Criteria for Chronic Factitious Disorder with Physical Symptoms

---

A. Plausible presentation of physical symptoms that are apparently under the individual's voluntary control to such a degree that there are multiple hospitalizations.

B. The individual's goal is apparently to assume the "patient" role and is not otherwise understandable in light of the individual's environmental circumstances (as is the case in malingering).

Note. From *Diagnostic and statistical manual of mental disorders* (3rd ed.) (p. 290), 1980, Washington, D.C.: American Psychiatric Association. Copyright 1980 by the American Psychiatric Association. Reprinted by permission.

patient may demand another procedure if not first discovered in the act of producing disease—by injecting pathogens, by inducing blood loss, by ingesting thyroid or other medications, by feigning epilepsy, or by consciously producing any other of a host of artifactual or true physical symptoms. Other characteristics include: (1) previous admissions, sometimes with the use of aliases, (2) demands for drugs or special attention that result in staff conflict, and (3) a patient who may seem seriously ill yet does not cooperate with well-intentioned care. Patients often discharge themselves against medical advice or threaten litigation; curiously, there has been only one reported case of a malpractice action by a Munchausen patient (Lipsitt, 1986).

Striking terms were coined for main presentations of the syndrome; *laparotomophilia migrans, haemorrhagica histrionica,* and *neurologica diabolica*; these reflect the combined amusement and wrath such perplexing patients engender. Early dismissals and physician anger account for much of the lack of organized clinical and therapeutic information about this and other factitial illnesses.

Psychological formulations of motivations for such contrived disease have shared common themes for over 50 years. Even before Asher's naming of Munchausen syndrome, Menninger (1934) noted that polysurgical addiction was characterized by intense aggression against the self and by its projection onto the perceived sadistic parent as symbolized by the physician. Spiro's (1968) seminal case report and dynamic formulation suggested that overriding character pathology determined the course of the syndrome. He noted the results of such primitive organization: (1) imposture based upon early deprivation, incomplete ego development, superego defects, and abortive attempts at mastery of early trauma; (2) selection of the hospital as the stage upon which to enact masochism and imposture because of its ready supply of primitive elements of caretaking and control; (3) wanderlust as symbolic of a simultaneous search for intimacy and inability to accept it; and (4) masochism in two forms: identification with a hostile and pain-inflicting doctor, and institutional transference reenactment of the early hostile relationship with the parent.

Bursten (1965) noted the curious counterphobic nature of the Munchausen patient, that is, his futile attempt to rise above earlier rejection by masochistically re-creating his experience in the hospital environment. Cramer *et al.* (1971) found a high incidence of previous significant relationships with a physician as parent or lover; factitious patients, including those who suffer from Munchausen syndrome, have a notoriously high frequency of employment as nurses or laboratory technicians, again reflecting conflicting wishes for union with caretaking figures represented by physicians. Hyler and Sussman (1981) enumerated other predisposing factors: (1) significant physical illness as a child, (2) anger against doctors for perceived past mismanagement, (3) and a history of parents who falsified medical histories or otherwise modeled medical deceit. Stone (1977) reaffirmed the unconsciously based need for medical care in combination with the perverse pleasure consciously derived from duping physicians.

Munchausen syndrome with its frequent hospitalizations, production of serious disease, *pseudologia fantastica*, and inevitable sudden discharge is undoubtedly "the ultimate factitious disorder" (Folks & Freeman, 1985) although even its incidence rates are unknown. Although psychiatric treatment for any type of factitious disease may be ineffective, most authors have not taken into account the wide individual variations in severity and frequency of factitious symptoms and of attendant disability. Nadelson (1979) divided Munchausen syndrome into two groups based on severity. The prototypical patient is committed to a life of disease production, deception, and drifting as described by Asher (1951); pathology is believed to be borderline or schizophrenic. In contrast, nonprototypical or "working Munchausen" patients often simulate life-threatening disease and demonstrate severe character pathology but show more geographic and occupational stability and often seek medical employment. The latter group is more common and perhaps less detectable because of better cooperation with medical care, the presence of family and visitors, and their own medical sophistication. Examples of nonprototypical cases in the literature include those with hyper- or hypometabolic states (Gorman, Wahner, & Tauxe, 1970), 32 cases of factitious fever and self-induced infection described by Aduan, Fauci, Dale, Herzberg, and Wolff (1979), and 21 cases of self-induced hypoglycemia via insulin injection (Moore, McBurney, & Service, 1973).

Atypical Factitious Disorder with Physical Symptoms

DSM-III (American Psychiatric Association, 1980) decribes AFDPS as a residual category for patients who do not meet full criteria for chronic factitious disorder with physical symptoms; no diagnostic criteria are provided. It is unknown whether this category represents a *forme fruste* of Munchausen syndrome or other, diverse entities. Nadelson (1979) argued the latter, contrasting the occasional producer of factitious disease with two varieties of Munchausen syndrome described above. Occasional factitial actions are most often reactions to specific stressors, trivial in presentation, rarely life-threatening, and not reflective of severe character pathology. Scoggin's "simple factitious illness" (1983) may represent the same entity—a group of patients predisposed to acting out specific conflicts via physical simulation yet not prone to other severe life disruptions.

Pseudoseizures (Riley & Roy, 1982) are a common form of limited factitious illness, often occurring under stress in 5–20% of patients with known organic seizures and in others with family symptom models. Such seizures are often bizarre and uncoordinated, lacking in tonic components, long in duration, more common when observed, and lacking in physical injury or postictal confusion (Ramani, Quesney, Olson, & Gumnit, 1980).

Definitive detection occurs via video-monitored EEG (Poulose & Shaw, 1977). Treatment is often successful by avoiding overuse of anticonvulsants and offering insight into symptom models and stress reduction.

King and Chalmers (1984) coined the term *dermatitis simulata* to describe a common but generally innocuous factitial practice: intentional skin irritation by physical or chemical means. Although extreme cases requiring digital amputation (Brough, 1977) or multiple amputations for factitious gangrene (Prosser Thomas, 1937) have been reported, most represent mild dermatoses amenable to local treatment without need for psychotherapy.

A host of other varieties of less severe factitial behavior have been described: factitious arrhythmia (Sturmann, Shoen, and Filiberti, 1985), pancreatitis simulated by placing saliva in urine (Robison, Gitlin, Morrelli, & Mann, 1982), pheochromocytoma simulated by addition of epinephrine to urine (Brandenburg *et al.*, 1979), and factitious hypoglycemia (Moore *et al.*, 1973). The ingenuity of such deceptive patients is illimitable.

Malingering

"The pride of a doctor who has caught a malingerer is akin to that of a fisherman who has landed an enormous fish" (Asher, 1972, p. 145); the pleasure doctors take in apprehending the malingerer stems not only from the fact that deceit is taken as an effrontery to the clinician but also from mistaken perceptions that the sole purpose of malingering is financial gain (Menninger, 1935). Menninger also speculated that physician anger at malingerers arose from the naive misperception that any behavior could have purely external and conscious motives.

This section will briefly review knowledge about the definition, causation, and varieties of malingering. Subsequent chapters in this volume, by Resnick, Clark, and Brandt (Chapters 3–6), will review malingering and its relationship to specific disorders in adults.

DSM-III defines malingering as "the voluntary production and presentation of false or grossly exaggerated physical or psychological symptoms. The symptoms are produced in pursuit of a goal that is easily recognizable with an understanding of the individual's circumstances rather than of his or her individual psychology" (American Psychiatric Association, 1980, p. 331). Obtaining drugs, avoiding military or combat duty, avoiding work or prison, and attainment of monetary compensation are obvious examples of such goals.

Bleuler (1944) suggested that simulation of insanity, regardless of motivation, reflected mental illness. The inclusion of malingering as a "V Code for Conditions not Attributable to a Mental Disorder" in DSM-III indicates that malingering is not a diagnosis in and of itself, but merely a condition or response set to be distinguished from true illness. Gorman (1982) defined malingering as an illegal act in contrast to a mental status, implying that it be removed from diagnostic nomenclature. Rogers and Cavanaugh (1983) viewed malingering as a coping strategy and suggested that clinicians reassess common attitudes that it is pathological or immoral to tell an untruth. Szasz (1956) viewed the diagnosis of malingering as social condemnation and not as a legitimate condition since it carries no scientific power and always bears moral overtones.

Rogers (1986a) cautioned that malingering not be considered an all-or-nothing or dichotomous variable and that the threshold for the diagnosis on forensic cases be rather high. The same should be true in the clinical realm, where mention of the term could have drastic effects on insurance coverage, disability payment, or employability; Parker (1979) noted the lethal effects of the diagnosis in a man who killed two physicians and then committed suicide (autopsy proved that the doctors were unfortunately correct in calling the man a malingerer!).

DSM-III assumes that motivation for malingering is purely environmental and makes a distinction between malingering and factitious disorders. Travin and Potter (1984) preferred to view malingering as a process which has both individually identifiable internal (psychological) influences and more obvious external goals. Travin and Potter, like Gorman (1982) posited that malingering can coexist with disorders such as Munchausen syndrome, conversion disorder, and various personality disorders. Nadelson (1979) advocated that disorders of deception be classified along a spectrum from purely unconscious motivation (conversion disorder) to partial consciousness (malingering) motivation.

Any psychiatric disorder may be malingered or exaggerated: schizophrenic syndromes, depression, posttraumatic stress disorder, mental retardation, amnesia, and so forth. Neurologic malingering appears to be the most "popular" among those who choose to simulate physical illness. Gorman (1984) reviewed detection of the most common syndromes: impaired consciousness and coma, seizures, deafness, visual acuity changes, and peripheral motor or sensory defects. Other commonly malingered complaints to obtain drugs or hospitalization include pain of any type, urinary stones, and bleeding from alimentary or respiratory tracts. Although the incidence of malingering is unknown, Sierles (1984) noted that malingered behaviors were roughly equivalent in psychiatric, medical, or surgical patients and that an increased incidence of such behavior was associated with sociopathy, alcoholism, and drug abuse.

Disorders with Dissimulation as a Common Feature

Substance Use Disorders

Anyone can attest to the fact that alcoholics and drug addicts practice persistent deception: denying or minimizing use, hiding supplies to avoid detection, and projecting blame onto others. Defensiveness on clinical examination is a primary, but unstandardized, sign of addiction. Naish (1979) went so far as to describe alcoholics as "notorious liars and deceivers" (p. 140). Surprisingly, DSM-III criteria for substance dependence do not include any measure of deception or denial, factors important in detection of the disease and in its treatment.

Bejerot (1972) believed that the unreliability and simulation characteristic of addicts served as defenses to promote drive satisfaction. Johnson (1973) felt that rationalization to the self and projection were tantamount to unconscious defenses (akin to use of those terms in psychoanalytic literature); there is no proof of such inaccessibility to consciousness, however, and all clinicians are aware of the fragile veneer of defensiveness in the chemically dependent—one which is susceptible to strong confrontation or family intervention and which therefore does not approximate an ego defense in the classic sense. "The patient is defensive" may be more palatable than "the patient is lying," particularly if clinicians believe in the disease concept of chemical dependency.

Eating Disorders

Although DSM-III criteria for anorexia nervosa and bulimia exclude elements of deceptive food behaviors, clinicians are aware of a host of everyday deceptive tactics including hiding and quartering of food, lying about food intake, secretive laxative and diuretic abuse, lying about body weight, denying hunger or fatigue, and manipulations of weight such as ingestion of water or sewing heavy objects into clothing prior to weighing. Although Bruch (1966) claimed the distortion of body image in anorectics to be delusional or nearly so, there is no evidence that it is anything other than a conscious manipulation to defend the wish to become thinner.

Deception in eating disorders may serve the same purpose as Bejerot (1972) described in addictive disorders, that is, allowing uninterrupted pleasure in the "addiction" to thinness. Reduction of deceptive behavior in addictive and eating disorders often parallels clinical improvement; further inquiry into the nature of deceptive practices might have beneficial effects on diagnosis and monitoring of both conditions.

Other Syndromes Characterized by Deception

Munchausen Syndrome by Proxy

Meadow (1977) coined the term *Munchausen syndrome by proxy* to describe a condition in which parents or other caretakers systematically provided factitious information about a child's health or manipulated the child's condition by production of seizures, injection of pathogens, injection of insulin, feeding of poisons, or neglect of true physical illness. In both of Meadow's cases, the mothers had histories of altering their own medical records or conditions. Analogous to Munchausen syndrome proper, the parent may find that the child's physical illness is the only avenue to meet dependency or other psychological needs in the caretaker—and what better place than the nurturing pediatrics ward?

Palmer and Yoshimura (1984) reviewed usual clinical indicators: (1) unusual calm in the parent, (2) symptoms worsening during or after parental visits, (3) no response to normally effective treatment, (4) parents in a paramedical field, and (5) frequent comparison of the child's medical problems to those of the parents. Frequent dynamics include avoidance of parental responsibility, entry into a caregiving milieu, and symbolic reenactment of previous losses.

Compensation Neurosis

The origin of the pejorative term of *compensation neurosis* is unclear. In clinical usage, it has come to refer to (1) disability persisting long after expected recovery from an injury, and (2) to subjective symptoms exceeding physical findings. The term is only used for litigants and is reflective of clinicians' misperceptions that pecuniary gain is the prime motivator for symptom maintenance. Compensation neurosis is usually diagnosed after closed head injury and in the course of worker's compensation or other civil actions.

Little objective information is available about this "syndrome" so as to make intelligent review impossible. Miller (1961a) implied that the syndrome constituted an intentional (therefore, malingered) attempt at freeloading and described usual symptoms of headache, depression, nervousness, irritability and restlessness, insomnia, and pain. In following 200 cases after compensation, he found that two-thirds were male and that symptom severity was inversely proportional to the original severity of injury. In a closer examination of 50 cases, he found that 45 returned to work within 2 years of settlement and erroneously concluded that symptoms improved after financial gain was secured. An equally plausible hypothesis was that the impoverished worker eventually returned to work despite persistent symptoms.

Compensation neurosis may exist as an entity and represent either a true neurotic reaction to unsatisfactory employment, malingering, improperly diagnosed physical illness, or some combination of the three. Until research with better samples and prospective orientation (Weighill, 1983) is available, the term compensation neurosis has no validity (Mendelson, 1985) and should be replaced by accepted DSM-III classifications such as malingering, factitious disorder, or conversion disorder.

Confabulation

Confabulation, the apparent fabrication of mundane or fantastic historical material revealed after questioning the amnestic or Korsakoff patient, has classically been attributed to conscious attempts to disguise memory deficits. F. A. Whitlock (1981) reviewed previous hypotheses and put forth explanations which did not require the assumption of deception. First, he noted that the incorrect replies of densely amnestic patients represented true memories from the distant past which were displaced by defective recall mechanisms. He described patients as truly unaware of the memory disturbance and noted that confabulation was rarely spontaneous but occurred mainly in response to questioning—further reducing the likelihood of intent to deceive. Mercer, Wapner, Gardner, and Banson (1977) found that 95% of confabulated data occurred upon testing of recent memory and that confabulation resolved as recent memory improved. He noted organic defects in self-monitoring and inability to provide verbal self-correction, concluding that confabulation was an organically based epiphenomenon of amnestic illness.

Recent studies suggest that confabulation is only purposeful or deceptive in the eyes of the examiner, that it bears direct relationship to the severity of amnesia, and that it should not be considered deceptive in nature.

Pseudologia Fantastica *and Pathological Lying*

Pseudologia fantastica and its synonyms—pathological lying, mendacity, mythomania—are used in clinical parlance to refer to repetitive, "compulsive," and often patently ridiculous lies of uncertain motivation. Although *pseudologia fantastica* may be a preferable term when story-telling is particularly egregious, there is no reason (other than linguistic aesthetics) to choose one term over another.

In a classic paper, Deutsch (1982) opined that *pseudologia fantastica* reflected reactivation of unconscious memory traces of a former real experience and thus that it reflected an elaborated, condensed, and symbolized "truth" of earlier life reactivated to accommodate present libidinal conflicts. Regardless of the origin of the falsehood, Deutsch considered the patient aware of the deception. Hoyer (1959) remarked upon three dynamic traits in the pathological liar: (1) unresolved Oedipal conflicts and castration anxiety, (2) a primitive desire to ridicule or get revenge upon adults, and (3) a need to lie to maintain or bolster self-esteem. Similar dynamics were described above in Munchausen syndrome, and interestingly, fantastic lying is also common in that condition.

Snyder (1986) described *pseudologia fantastica* in borderline patients and noted that mendacity appeared related to psychological factors of need for narcissistic gratification, low self-esteem, and the splitting off of the all-bad self and object representations. In this more primitive population, fantastic lying may represent a variety of projective identification (Ogden, 1979) in which unwanted aspects of the self are split off, projected onto the recipient of the lie, and recovered in a modified version after injection of reality by the therapist/recipient.

Pseudologia fantastica and its synonyms are marked by conspicuously conscious attempts to engage the observer by apparent loss of reality testing, although most authorities speculate that the pseudologue is aware of deceit and is therefore lying. Fantastic lies may exist either in isolation or on the presence of another entity such as Munchausen syndrome or severe character pathology; they should be considered as primarily representative of underlying pathology rather than as necessarily indicative of a freestanding syndrome of lying.

Imposture

Imposture, or pretending to be someone other than oneself in physical or psychological terms, is not of necessity a pathological exercise—witness, for example, the widespread enjoyment of costume parties on Halloween (Wells, 1986). Other impostures of various severity were delimited by Wells: (1) imposture for gain (e.g., fraud or claims of false identity), (2) Munchausen syndrome, (3) hoaxes and literary impostures, (4) transvestism, (5) selected cases of anorexia nervosa, and (6) limited, nonpathological types.

In practice, many impostors of the limited type (frauds, cons), will deal solely with the legal system and demonstrate primary antisocial traits. Sophisticated impostors (malingerers, Munchausen patients) demonstrate more primitive combinations of narcissistic and borderline pathology and will likely be refractory to legal or therapeutic interventions. Imposture is not to be considered a psychiatric syndrome in and of itself, but rather a varied clinical response to characterological and neurotic needs for applause and appreciation.

Clinical Applications

The following section contains a number of models for clinical consideration and diagnosis of major syndromes associated with deception. The threshold and clinical decision models are not intended to supplant DSM-III criteria nor are the models inconsistent with current diagnostic nomenclature. Rather, they are an amplification upon DSM-III criteria and acknowledge the nonexclusivity of certain disorders and the possibility of multiple levels of intentionality and voluntariness. In addition, they highlight the complexity of syndromes associated with deception and reflect

Table 2.3. Threshold Model for Consideration of Factitious Disorders with Psychological Symptoms (FDPS)

Suggested Criteria for all forms of FDPS (all must be present)
1. Suspicion of voluntary control over symptomatology:
   a. symptoms worsen when observed, or
   b. symptoms are bizarre or ridiculous, or
   c. symptoms wax and wane with environmental events
2. Evidence of desire to assume the patient role:
   a. prominent recent environmental stressor, or
   b. chronic, severe conflicts in job or personal life
3. Evidence of a severe personality disorder

Suggested additional criteria for specific varieties of FDPS:
A. Factitious psychosis should be suspected when general criteria for FDPS have been met and when prominent psychotic symptoms are associated with any of the following:
   1. rapid onset of symptoms after a psychological stress, or
   2. approximate or random answers, or
   3. history of factitious physical or psychiatric symptoms
B. Factitious posttraumatic stress disorder should be suspected when general criteria for FDPS have been met and when prominent, readily volunteered symptoms of PTSD are associated with any of the following:
   1. unconfirmed history of military service, or
   2. history of factitious physical or psychiatric symptoms
C. Factitious bereavement or depression should be suspected when general criteria for FDPS have been met and when prominent depressive symptoms are associated with any of the following:
   1. dramatic, unconfirmed claim of recent loss or death, or
   2. symptoms grossly out of proportion to actual loss or death, or
   3. history of factitious physical or psychiatric symptoms

---

awareness that neither untestable psychodynamic formulations nor DSM-III criteria alone provide a reasonable level of diagnostic certainty. Several current "syndromes" or terminologies should not be considered as disorders of deception: Ganser syndrome, pseudodementia, confabulation, compensation neurosis, *pseudologia fantastica*, and imposture. These will not need to be examined further.

Table 2.3 presents a threshold model with criteria which should alert the clinician to the possibility that psychotic, anxiety, or depressive symptoms may be factitious in nature. Note that factors other than suspicion about voluntary symptoms may first alert the clinician to the need for further investigation; the plausible presentation of symptoms by many factitial patients obliges the clinician to pay attention to such ancillary features as past history, character disturbance, and nature of symptom onset. It is sugested that all criteria in Table 2.4 be met before making a diagnosis of FDPS. The criteria for voluntariness are modeled after those of Pope *et al.* (1982). Note that FDPS should not be diagnosed (for legal and ethical reasons) until investigation demonstrates clear motivation to assume the role of patient. Even if some element of this motivation is conscious, the absence of clear environmental goals eliminates the diagnosis of malinger-

Table 2.4. Clinical Decision Model for Establishing Factitious Disorder with Psychological Symptoms

---

All of the following must be present:
A. Psychotic, depressive, or posttraumatic symptoms[a] are clearly under voluntary control as manifested by at least one of the following:
  1. patient acknowledgment of voluntary control, or
  2. clearly ridiculous or bizarre symptoms, or
  3. symptom remission after minor environmental manipulation
B. Clear evidence of desire to assume the patient role:
  1. documented severe recent psychological stress, or
  2. documented severe job or personal conflicts
C. Another mental disorder, if present, cannot explain current symptoms.
D. Malingering, if present, cannot explain current symptoms.

---

[a]Adapted from Pope *et al.* (1982).

ing. However, it would be reasonable to make a concurrent diagnosis of malingering (which DSM-III will not allow) if external incentives and psychological motivators appear of approximately equal strength.

Because of common behavioral features in patients with physical factitious disease of any type of severity, Table 2.5 incorporates clinical findings for a threshold model to alert clinicians to the presence of any of these disorders. Behavioral, historical, and characterological features are given equal weight in raising the suspicion of factitious illness. Table 2.6 provides

Table 2.5. Threshold Model for Consideration of Chronic or Atypical Factitious Disorder with Physical Symptoms

---

Factitious disorder with physical symptoms should be suspected when the plausible history or finding of physical illness is accompanied by any three of the following:
A. History of multiple hospitalizations
B. Refusal to allow access to old medical records
C. Use of an alias
D. *Pseudologia fantastica*
E. Evidence of chronic wandering
F. Extreme belligerence or evasiveness
G. Demand for medication or hospitalization
H. Evidence of voluntary control over symptoms:
  1. symptoms inconsistent with known physical illness, or
  2. discovery of paraphernalia or medications which explain symptoms, or
  3. laboratory results consistent with factitious illness
I. Evidence of desire to assume the patient role:
  1. prominent recent environmental stress, or
  2. chronic, severe conflicts in job or personal life
J. Evidence of a severe personality disorder
K. History of factitious physical or psychological symptoms

Table 2.6. Clinical Decision Model for Establishing Factitious Disorder with Physical Symptoms

A. Chronic factitious disorder with physical symptoms (all of the following must be present):
   1. Physical complaints or symptoms are clearly under voluntary control as manifested by at least one of the following:
      a. patient acknowledgment of voluntary control, or
      b. discovery of paraphernalia or medications which explain symptoms, or
      c. confirmatory laboratory testing
   2. Clear evidence of need to assume the patient role:
      a. strong interest in medical diseases as they pertain to the patient, or
      b. acknowledgment of dependency needs which are gratified by medical attention
   3. Another physical disorder, if present, cannot explain current symptoms.
   4. Malingering, if present, cannot explain current symptoms.
   5. History of multiple hospitalizations
B. Atypical factitious disorder with physical symptoms
   1. Meets above criteria 1 through 4 for chronic factitious disorder with physical symptoms
C. Munchausen syndrome (all of the following must be present):
   1. Meets all above criteria for CFDPS
   2. Chronic wandering
   3. *Pseudologia fantastica*
   4. Evidence of multiple surgeries
   5. Extreme belligerence and evasiveness

a clinical decision model for diagnosis of CFDPS, Munchausen syndrome (as a special subtype of CFDPS), and atypical factitious disorder with physical symptoms. Because there is good reason to believe that severity of illness corresponds to prognosis and functional capacity (Nadelson, 1979), such a trichtomy appears justified. In deference to the opinions of Travin and Potter (1984) and Gorman (1982) that malingering and factitious disease may coexist because of multiple, simultaneous levels of causation and intention, Table 2.6 allows for dual diagnosis.

Tables 2.7 and 2.8 provide similar criteria for threshold and clinical decision models in detection and diagnosis of malingered physical or psy-

Table 2.7. Threshold Model for Consideration of Malingering

Malingering should be suspected when physical or psychiatric symptoms are accompanied by any of the following:
A. Involvement in civil or criminal legal action
B. Potential for combat duty
C. Lack of cooperation with examination and recommendations
D. Complaints grossly in excess of physical findings
E. Apparent environmental incentive for simulation of illness (e.g., obtaining drugs or avoiding work)
F. Suspicion of voluntary control over symptomatology:
   1. symptoms worsen when observed, or
   2. bizarre or ridiculous symptoms, or
   3. symptoms fail to respond to customary treatment

Table 2.8. Clinical Decision Model for Establishing Malingering

---

All of the following must be present:

A. Physical or psychiatric symptoms are clearly under voluntary control as manifested by at least one of the following
   1. patient acknowledgment of voluntary control, or
   2. direct observation of illness production, or
   3. observed failure to cooperate with treatment, or
   4. rapid remission of illness when environmental incentives are removed or achieved
B. Obvious causal relationship between illness production and environmental incentives:
   1. avoidance of work, military service, or incarceration, or
   2. financial gain, or
   3. avoidance of prosecution or execution, or
   4. acquisition of drugs
C. Evidence of intrapsychic need to assume the patient role, if present, is overshadowed by environmental incentives
D.. Another mental or physical disorder, if present, cannot explain current symptoms

---

chological illness. Because of its apparently low predictive value, the presence of antisocial personality disorder should not alert the clinician to suspect malingering. This is consistent with changes in DSM-III-R (American Psychiatric Association, 1986).

Note that the degree of consciousness of behavior or degree of consciousness about intention are not included as factors in clinical assessment. Although consciousness of motivation certainly increases across the spectrum of disease from conversion disorder to malingering (Nadelson, 1979), there are simply no behavioral or clinical concomitants from which to assess conscious intention. The related factor of voluntariness of behavior may be assessed more directly (Pope *et al.*, 1982) but should not be considered as tantamount to determination of the degree of conscious or unconscious motivation.

Summary

None of the classic psychiatric and medical syndromes associated with malingering and deception have been subjected to rigorous population-based phenomenological studies, genetic research, dynamic formulations beyond the case study method, biological evaluations, or well-controlled studies of outcome and prognosis. Whether or not the accurate clinical assessment of intentionality ever becomes available, such demographic and outcome data would provide clinicians with more effective diagnostic and management strategies. The present criteria, although preliminary, must suffice in evaluating and treating the deceptive patient.

3

Malingered Psychosis

PHILLIP J. RESNICK

"Though this be madeness, yet there is method in it."
—Shakespeare, *Hamlet*

The incidence of feigned psychosis is unknown. Hay (1983) found 5 cases out of 12,000 admissions, 4 of whom subsequently developed schizophrenia. In one series of 320 murderers, 3 feigned psychosis and remained "sane" after a 10-year follow-up (Hay, 1983). Rogers (1986a) found a 4.5% incidence of definite malingering and a 20% frequency of moderate deception or suspected malingering in defendants evaluated for insanity but judged sane. The accuracy of such prevalence estimates is highly questionable because individuals who successfully fake psychosis are never included in the statistics. The apparent low incidence in nonforensic populations is probably due to a combination of the failure of clinicians to suspect malingering and the lack of motive to malinger psychosis prior to the recent trend towards deinstitutionalization.

Malingered psychosis is likely to increase. Since the deinstitutionalization movement, thousands of the chronically mentally ill, who would rather be in the stable environment of a psychiatric hospital, are living in marginal circumstances in the community (Travin & Protter, 1984). Schizophrenic patients have shown the ability to present themselves as sick or healthy, depending on their goals (Braginsky & Braginsky, 1967). Society's disfranchised individuals are starting to shift coping strategies from somatic to psychiatric symptoms. This shift can be attributed to lack of precision in psychiatric diagnosis, widespread availability of mental health services, and the decreased stigma of mental illness (Bishop & Holt, 1980).

Defining the Problem

Many authors, especially when psychoanalytic influence was at its peak, labeled malingering a form of mental disease. Eissler (1951), for example,

Phillip J. Resnick, Division of Forensic Psychiatry, Case Western Reserve University, Cleveland, Ohio.

stated, "It can be rightly claimed that malingering is always a sign of a disease often more severe than a neurotic disorder because it concerns an arrest of development at an early phase" (p. 252). Others have pointed out the irrationality of this view. Wertham (1949) noted, "There is a strange, entirely unfounded superstition even among psychiatrists that if a man simulates insanity there must be something mentally wrong with him in the first place. As if a sane man would not grasp at any straw if his life were endangered by the electric chair" (p. 49).

Malingering is listed in the Diagnostic and Statistical Manual of Mental Disorders (DSM-III-R), as a condition not attributable to a mental disorder. It is defined as the intentional production of false or grossly exaggerated physical or psychological symptoms, motivated by external incentives (American Psychiatric Association, 1987). Thus, malingering requires a deceitful state of mind. No other syndrome is so easy to define, but so difficult to diagnose.

Persons usually malinger psychosis for one of the following five purposes: First, criminals may seek to avoid punishment by pretending to be incompetent to stand trial, insane at the time of the crime, worthy of mitigation at sentencing, or incompetent to be executed. Second, malingerers may seek to avoid conscription into the military, be relieved from undesirable military assignments, or avoid combat. Third, malingerers may fake psychosis to seek financial gain from social security disability, veterans' benefits, workers' compensation, or damages for alleged psychological injury. Fourth, prisoners may malinger to obtain drugs, or to be transferred to a psychiatric hospital in order to facilitate escape or do "easier time." Finally, malingerers may seek admission to a psychiatric hospital to avoid arrest or to obtain free room and board, known colloquially as "three hots and a cot."

One 14-year-old girl feigned hallucinations in order to be hospitalized to escape from sexual harassment by her mother's new boyfriend (reported in Greenfeld, 1987). She had previously observed an older cousin's psychotic episode. When her family situation again became chaotic, she was institutionalized a second time on the basis of a feigned psychosis. It was only when the hospital staff told her they would be placing her infant with the baby's father that she volunteered that she had faked her psychotic symptoms.

Several authors (Berney, 1973; Bustamante & Ford, 1977; Folks & Freeman, 1985; Hay, 1983; Pope, Jonas, & Jones, 1982; Schneck, 1970) have suggested that pseudomalingering should be carefully considered before making a diagnosis of malingering. In Leonid Andreyev's (1902) novel, *The Dilemma*, a physician committed murder with a premeditated plan to appear insane (Schneck). When the physician later began to have true hallucinations, he realized that his insanity was genuine. The idea of someone becoming mentally ill after malingering insanity in order to escape criminal responsibility has great popular appeal in mystery stories, but it is extremely rare in forensic practice. Schneck suggested that pseudomalingering is a mechanism to maintain an intact self-image, which would be marred by acknowledging psychological problems that cannot be consciously mastered.

Pope *et al.* (1982) found 9 patients with factitious psychosis out of 219 consecutive admissions to their research ward. Their 7-year follow-up study revealed that all nine patients met DSM-III criteria for either borderline or histrionic personality. None of the patients went on to develop a typical psychotic disorder, but eight of the nine displayed intermittent or continuous factitious symptoms. The researchers concluded that factitious psychotic symptoms were a grave prognostic sign. In fact, Hay (1983) has suggested that the simulation of schizophrenia is usually the prodromal phase of genuine illness.

Research on Malingered Psychosis

The research literature on detecting malingered psychosis is sparse. No research has demonstrated the ability of clinicians to accurately detect malingered psychosis. In Rosenhan's (1973) classic study, eight pseudopatients were admitted to psychiatric hospitals, all alleging that they heard voices. Although they stopped claiming symptoms once they were admitted, their hospital stays ranged from 9 to 52 days. All the subjects were diagnosed as schizophrenic. Rosenhan concluded that mental health professionals were unable to distinguish normality from mental illness.

Anderson, Trethowan, and Kenna (1959) had 18 normal subjects simulate mental disease in order to study the phenomenon of *vorbeireden* (the approximate answer), a central symptom in the Ganser syndrome. The malingerers were compared with three control groups: (1) normal volunteers, (2) patients with organic dementia, and (3) patients with pseudodementia (primarily hysterics with conversion symptoms). The malingerers most often chose to feign depression or paranoid disorders; their efforts did not closely resemble well-defined psychiatric disorders. Two sought to pretend mental retardation by maintaining an air of obtuseness, vagueness, and poverty of content. The malingerers experienced difficulty, however, in suppressing correct answers to questions because they felt the "pull of reality" throughout the interviews. Increasing fatigue caused replies to become increasingly normal.

Many malingerers in the Anderson *et al.* (1959) study gave approximate answers to questions because they felt they should not give the right answers. To avoid the impression of spuriousness, they gave nearly correct answers in contrast to patients with actual dementia who usually made more discrepant errors. In the patients with organic dementia, perseveration was a striking feature; it was evident when progressing from one question to the next and during serial-seven subtraction. In contrast, no significant perseveration was apparent in malingerers. The authors concluded that the presence of perseveration is a strong indication of true, rather than simulated, organic impairment. The fact that approximate or "near miss" answers were given by all groups lends support to the theory that the Ganser syndrome is a form of malingering.

Sherman, Trief, and Sprafkin (1975) had a group of Veterans Administration (V.A.) day-care psychiatric patients present themselves as (1) severely mentally ill individuals, and (2) normal mentally healthy individuals. The more disturbed patients showed greater differences between the two interviews. In their "malingered" interviews, patients claimed that they had recurrent senseless thoughts, hallucinated noises, and had suicidal ideas. The primary differences were in their statements about symptoms, rather than in their interview styles or behavior.

Hallucinations

Persons alleging suspicious hallucinations should be questioned in great detail (see Table 3.1) regarding what content they manifest, how vivid they seem, and whether they occur alone or with others (Seigel & West, 1975). Before discussing the effect of hallucinations on current functioning, patients should be asked to describe past hallucinations and their response to them. Detailed knowledge about actual hallucinations is the clinician's greatest asset in recognizing simulated hallucinations.

Both psychotic (Goodwin, Alderson, & Rosenthal, 1971) and acute schizophrenic patients (Mott, Small, & Andersen, 1965; Small, Small, & Andersen, 1966) show a 76% rate of hallucinations in at least one sensory modality. The incidence of auditory hallucinations in schizophrenics is 66% (Mott et al.; Small et al.). Sixty-four percent of hallucinating patients reported hallucinations in more than one modality (Small et al.); the incidence of visual hallucinations in psychotics is estimated at 24% (Mott et al.) to 30% (Small et al.). Hallucinations are usually (88%) associated with delusions (Lewinsohn, 1970).

The Goodwin et al. (1971) study of 116 hallucinating patients provides very helpful data for determining authenticity. Hallucinations were generally intermittent, rather than continuous. When schizophrenics were asked if their hallucinations could have been due to their imaginations, 56% responded affirmatively.

Auditory Hallucinations

Goodwin et al. (1971) described the following characteristics of auditory hallucinations. Both male and female voices were heard by 75% of the patients. The message was usually clear; it was vague only 7% of the time.

Table 3.1. Areas of Inquiry about Auditory Hallucinations

Content
Clarity
Loudness
Duration and frequency
Continuous or intermittent
Single or multiple voices
Male or female
Inside or outside head
Tone of voice of hallucinations
Voices speak in second or third person
Insight into unreality of voices
Belief that others could hear the voices
Familiar or unfamiliar voices
Relationship to person speaking
Associated hallucinations of other senses
Converse with voices
Ability to put the voices out of mind
Relationship to delusions
Patient's reaction to the voices
Strategies to diminish voices
Directions to do things by voices
Effort not to obey voices

The hallucinations were accusatory about one-third of the time. They reported that hallucinations contained both familiar and unfamiliar voices and were most often (88%) perceived as originating outside the patient's head.

Small *et al.* (1966) reported that the major themes in auditory hallucinations of schizophrenics were persecution or instructions. Schizophrenics reported auditory hallucinations as seemingly coming from outside their heads in 50% (Junginger & Frame, 1985) to 76% of cases (Goodwin *et al.*, 1971). Estimates of how many patients talk back to their hallucinations range from 30% (Goodwin *et al.*) to 60% (Mott *et al.*, 1965).

Command hallucinations are auditory hallucinations that instruct a person to act in a certain manner. They are easy to make up in order to support an insanity defense, as for example in the case of *People v. Schmidt* (1915). Hellerstein, Frosch, and Koenigsberg (1987) found in a retrospective chart review that 38.4% of all patients with auditory hallucinations reported commands. Studies of schizophrenic auditory hallucinations found that 30 to 64% included commands or instructions (Goodwin *et al.*, 1971; Hellerstein *et al.*; and Mott *et al.*, 1965; Small *et al.*, 1966). Command hallucinations occurred in 30% (Goodwin, *et al.*) to 40% (Mott *et al.*) of alcoholic withdrawal hallucinations. Patients with affective disorders reported that 46% of hallucinations were commands (Goodwin *et al.*).

Hellerstein *et al.* (1987) found that the content of command hallucinations was 51.7% suicide, 5.2% homicide, 12.1% nonlethal injury of self or others, 13.8% nonviolent acts, and 17.2% unspecified. The research method of reviewing charts, rather than making direct inquiries, probably increased the relative proportion of violent commands since these are more likely to be charted. Interestingly, there was no significant difference in the number of assaultive acts performed by psychotic patients with and without command hallucinations. Research suggests that hallucinatory commands are generally ignored by patients (Goodwin *et al.*, 1971; Hellerstein *et al.*).

Malingerers sometimes report that their auditory command hallucinations contained stilted language. For example, one malingerer charged with attempted rape stated that the voices said, "Go commit a sex offense." Other malingerers describe far-fetched commands, such as a robber who alleged that (malingered) voices kept screaming, "Stick up, stick up, stick up!"

Persons suspected of feigning auditory hallucinations should be asked what they do to make the voices go away. Frequent coping strategies among actual schizophrenics are: (1) specific activities (working, watching TV), (2) changes in posture (lie down or walk), (3) seeking out interpersonal contact, and (4) taking medication (Falloon & Talbot, 1981; Kanas & Barr, 1984). Schizophrenic hallucinations tend to diminish when patients are involved in activities (Goodwin *et al.*, 1971).

Visual Hallucinations

Visual hallucinations are usually of normal-sized people, and are seen in color (Goodwin *et al.*, 1971). Visual hallucinations in psychotic disorders appear suddenly and typically without prodromata (Assad & Shapiro, 1986). Psychotic hallucinations do not change if the eyes are closed or open. In contrast, drug-induced hallucinations are more readily seen with the eyes closed or in darkened surroundings (Assad & Shapiro).

Dramatic, atypical visual hallucinations should arouse suspicions of malingering. One defendant, who was charged with attempted murder, claimed visual hallucinations of a "green laughing devil, a god with a flowing white beard, a black doberman pinscher dog, and President Ronald Reagan." When he was asked detailed questions, he frequently replied, "I don't know." He subsequently admitted to malingering.

Hallucinations in Specific Disorders

Alcoholic hallucinosis, following the cessation or reduction of alcohol intake, often involves quite vivid hallucinations. Although the hallucinations are usually voices, the likelihood of noise, music or unintelligible voices is greater than in schizophrenia. The patient's actions are practically never the result of command hallucinations, but are motivated by the desire to avoid disgrace, injury, or other consequences of the voices' threats (American Psychiatric Association, 1980). Patients will discuss alcohol-induced hallucinations more easily than schizophrenic hallucinations (Alpert & Silvers, 1970).

Mott et al. (1965) found that persons hospitalized for alcoholism had an 84% incidence of hallucinations (75% auditory and 70% visual). Auditory hallucinations, almost invariably perceived as originating from outside the patient's head, may address the individual directly, but more commonly discuss him or her in the third person. The major themes in alcoholic hallucinations were spirituality, persecution, and instructions concerning the management of everyday affairs. A majority of alcoholics thought the hallucinations were real at the time, but later recognized their unreality; 40% never accepted them as real. Alcoholics are typically frightened by their hallucinations. In contrast, schizophrenics are often frightened in the early stages of their illness, but become more comfortable as the illness progresses (Mott et al.).

In multiple personality disorders, auditory hallucinations are perceived as originating from within the head more often than from outside the head. The message may be faint or inaudible, due to barriers among the alter personalities. The content of the hallucinations is often related to dynamics among the personalities. Although patients usually resist command hallucinations at first, they may give in due to exhaustion or fear of threats made by alter personalities. Somatic hallucinations are common in multiple personality disorders (R. P. Kluft, July 19, 1984; personal communication).

Malingered Mutism

Malingered mutism may occur as a solitary symptom or as part of a malingered psychosis. Giving up speech for a prolonged time is not an easy sacrifice, and is not usually attempted unless a person is facing a very severe penalty or anticipating a very large award (Davidson, 1952).

Altshuler, Cummings, and Mills (1986) found that 39% of outpatients presenting with mutism were likely to have an affective disorder, 29% some form of schizophrenia, 17% organic brain syndrome, 9% character disorders, and 6% uncertain diagnoses. Mutism occurring as a part of catatonic stupor is recognized by the presence of generalized catatonia, posturing, negativism, automatic obedience, waxy flexibility, and other typical schizophrenic features. Patients with extreme psychomotor retardation, as seen in depressive stupor, are likely to show universal motor inhibition in addition to mutism.

Mutism may occur in patients with or without catatonia. Mutism without catatonia may be seen in paranoid schizophrenic patients unwilling to communicate because of paranoid distrust, and in chronic schizophrenic patients isolated in long-term settings. Corticosteroids and antihypertensive agents have also produced mutism without catatonia (Altshuler *et al.*, 1986).

Mutism with catatonia is observed not only in catatonic schizophrenia, but also in other types of schizophrenia, depression, mania, and brief dissociative states. Mutism with catatonia can be caused by drugs, such as PCP; and such neurological conditions as head injuries, herpes encephalitis, teritiary syphilis, frontal lobe lesions, the postictal phase of epilepsy, akinetic mutism, and Wernicke's encephalopathy. Altshuler *et al.* (1986) found that one-half of the mute patients with neurological diagnoses were misdiagnosed on initial evaluation as having psychiatric disorders. Medical conditions reported to produce mutism with catatonia include hyperparathyroidism, diabetic ketosis, myxedema, and Addison's disease.

The catatonic condition of waxy flexibility is difficult to maintain for a prolonged period. The genuineness of insensitivity to pain can be appraised by noting whether the patient reacts (by pupillary changes or muscle reflexes) to an unexpected pinprick in the back. The catatonic will respond in the same way whether or not he or she sees the painful stimulus coming. In contrast, malingerers will respond differently, depending on whether or not they anticipate the painful stimulus. If a malingerer sees the examiner approaching with a pin, he or she will show little reaction other than preliminary tensing of the muscles. If malingerers are pricked in the back without warning, however, they are likely to show reflex muscle contraction and pupillary dilatation (Davidson, 1952).

The most difficult differential diagnosis of mutism is between a conversion disorder and malingering. The critical distinction is whether or not mutism is under the person's voluntary control. The exact details of when the patient stopped speaking are critical; the onset of a conversion disorder may have occurred after a crime that involved "unspeakable horror" or upon arrest, which may also have been traumatic. The person with mutism due to a conversion disorder is likely to have a history of past conversion symptoms, display evidence of repression and dissociative phenomena, have mutism as a solitary symptom, and be suggestible and easily hypnotized. The malingerer is more likely to have a history of prior antisocial conduct, lying, past malingering, and a criminal record.

Another important discriminator is that individuals suffering from genuine mutism seek to convey their wishes by noises and signs, whereas malingerers frequently make no effort at all. Feigned mutism may sometimes be exposed by suddenly arousing the patient from a deep sleep and immediately asking some simple question. The malingerer may reply before he or she remembers to be mute (Davidson, 1952; East, 1927).

The use of a sodium amobarbital (or pentobarbital) interview may be helpful in the differential diagnosis of mutism. Neurological symptoms, such as disorientation or confabulation, may become worse. Depressed patients may show depressed speech content. Catatonic schizophrenic patients may have a lucid interval or show schizophrenic speech patterns (Altshuler *et al.*, 1986). Narcoanalysis cannot be considered highly reliable in ascertaining whether the defendant had been consciously or unconsciously choosing not to speak (see Chapter 11). One-half of the subjects in one study were able to maintain a lie under the influence of sodium amobarbital (Redlich, Ravitz, & Dession, 1951).

Daniel and Resnick (1987) provide a good example of the successful use of narcoanalysis to detect malingered mutism. A 53-year-old man was charged with raping and murdering an 11-year-old girl. The day after the crime, he voluntarily admitted himself to a state hospital and complained of hearing voices. He stopped talking completely upon being told that he was charged with murder. In his room, he would lay curled up, not respond to any questions, and avoid eye contact with the clinician. When he did not know he was being observed, he appeared to initiate conversations with fellow patients. No signs of catatonia or depression were observed; complete neurological and laboratory examinations were negative. With the permission of the defendant and his attorney, a sodium amobarbital interview was done. The defendant described the offense and spoke for about 90 minutes, but did not utter a word afterwards. He showed a pattern of voluntarily admitting himself to psychiatric hospitals after several prior offenses and having the charges against him dismissed.

Malingering of Other Syndromes

An individual feigning depression may go so far as to refuse food for months, and even endure tube feedings. He or she may assume the face of melancholia with some fidelity when in the presence of observers, concentrating on dysphoric expression of the mouth, but the forehead is likely to remain unwrinkled. Although the bodily movements may be purposely slowed, the malingerer does not usually adopt the forward inclination of the head and trunk, and flexed hips and knees prominent in major depression with melancholia. Genuine sufferers from depression often find their gloom worst in the early morning, but malingerers are unlikely to know this (East, 1927). Persons feigning depression do not show the physical signs of slowing, such as constipation. Suicide attempts are sometimes made, but as a rule they are clumsy and obviously planned for their effect on others (Singer & Krohn, 1924).

Feigned mania is difficult to successfully maintain for any length of time because it is hard to continue the rapid flight of ideas, incoherent speech, motor excitement, and insomnia present in the true disorder (East, 1927). A premature ending of the excited period due to fatigue suggests malingering (Davidson, 1952). A "therapeutic" response to lithium or anti-psychotics is likely to occur "too quickly" in malingerers to be a true response to medication.

An individual suspected of malingering a multiple-personality disorder should not be approached with a skeptical attitude, since this may precipitate frantic efforts to prove the disorder in genuine cases. Both malingerers and true multiple-personality disorder patients occasionally appear "very phony" when trying to defend themselves. Extended interviews may be useful because unforced dissociation most often occurs between 2½ and 4 hours after beginning an interview. It is very difficult for the malingerer to be consistent in the assumed personality's voice (exclusive of accent), movement characteristics, and memory (Kluft, 1987).

Clinical Assessment of Malingered Psychoses

The clinician should be particularly careful to ask open-ended questions of suspected malingerers and let the patient tell the complete story with few interruptions. Details can be clarified later with specific questions. Inquiries about hallucinations should be carefully phrased to avoid giving clues about the nature of true hallucinations. The clinician should try to ascertain whether the patient has ever had the opportunity to observe psychotics (e.g., during prior employment). Clinicians may feel irritation at being deceived, but any expression of irritation or incredulity is likely to make the malingerer more adamant (Miller & Cartlidge, 1972).

Clinicians may modify their interview style when patients are suspected of malingering psychosis. The interview may be prolonged since fatigue diminishes the malingerer's ability to maintain a counterfeit account (Andersen et al., 1959). Rapid firing of questions increases the likelihood of getting contradictory replies from malingerers, but it may also create confusion among mentally impaired persons. The clinician may get additional clues by asking leading questions that emphasize a different psychosis than the malingerer is trying to portray (Ossipov, 1944). Questions about improbable symptoms may be asked to see if the malingerer will endorse them. For example, "Have you ever believed that automobiles are members of organized religion?" (Rogers, 1986b). Another device is to mention, within earshot of the suspected malingerer, some easily imitated symptom that is not present. The sudden appearance of the symptom suggests malingering.

Psychological testing should be obtained in suspected malingerers. Although some malingerers may successfully feign psychosis on specific tests, the majority will reveal some confirmatory evidence (see Chapters 8, 9 and 10). The M test, a brief test for measuring malingering of schizophrenia, contains true–false items describing actual symptoms of schizophrenia, bizarre attitudes and beliefs, and improbable symptoms. An initial study

(See Chapter 8) suggested its potential usefulness at discriminating schizophrenic from malingering subjects (Beaber, Martson, Michelli, & Mills, 1985).

Inpatient assessment should be considered in difficult cases of suspected malingering. Feigned psychotic symptoms are difficult to maintain 24 hours a day. Ray (1871, p. 455) suggested that suspected malingerers be secretly observed so that "in their moments of forgetfulness or fancied security they may be seen laying aside their false colors and suddenly assuming their natural manners." Sometimes a malingerer will only assume a slumped posture and expression of detachment when clinicians approach, resuming a more natural, laughing, appearance on their departure (MacDonald, 1976). Hospitalized psychiatric patients are quire skillful at detecting a malingerer in their midst (Rosenhan, 1973); they have been known to tell malingerers to stop play-acting (Ritson & Forrest, 1970).

After completing a detailed examination, the clinician may decide to confront a patient with his or her suspicions. The suspected malingerer should be given every opportunity to save face. Once malingering is denied, there is a risk that it will be harder to admit later. It is better to say, "You haven't told me the whole truth," than, "You have been lying to me" (Inbau & Reid, 1967).

Clinical Indicators of Malingered Psychoses

All malingerers are actors who portray their psychoses as they understand them (Ossipov, 1944), often overacting their part (Wachspress, Berenberg, & Jacobson, 1953). Malingerers sometimes mistakenly believe that the more bizarrely they behave, the more psychotic they will appear. The malingerer "sees less than the blind, he hears less than the deaf, and he is more lame than the paralyzed. Determined that his insanity shall not lack multiple and obvious signs, he, so to speak, crowds the canvas, piles symptom upon symptom and so outstrips madness itself, attaining to a but clumsy caricature of his assumed role" (Jones & Llewellyn, 1917, p. 80).

Malingerers are eager to call attention to their illnesses in contrast to schizophrenics, who are often reluctant to discuss their symptoms (Ritson & Forrest, 1970). Some malingerers limit their symptoms to repeatedly volunteering one or two blatant "delusions" (MacDonald, 1976). One malingerer stated that he was an "insane lunatic" when he killed his parents at the behest of hallucinations that "told me to kill in my demented state."

It is more difficult for malingerers to successfully imitate the form than the content of schizophrenic thinking (Sherman, Trief, & Sprafkin, 1975). Derailment, neologisms, and incoherent word salads are rarely simulated. Common errors made by malingerers include the beliefs that nothing must be remembered correctly, and that the more inconsistent and absurd the discourse, the better the deception. If the malingerer is asked to repeat an idea, he or she may do it quite exactly, whereas the genuine schizophrenic will often go off on a tangent. Some malingerers give the appearance of profound concentration before they give absurd answers (MacDonald, 1976).

Malingerers are unlikely to show the subtle signs of residual schizophrenia, such as impaired relatedness, blunted affect, concreteness, digressive speech, or peculiar thinking. It is rare for malingerers to show perseveration. The presence of perseveration suggests actual organic damage or an extremely well-prepared malingerer. Malingerers' symptoms may fit no known diagnostic entity. Symptoms may have been selected from various psychoses. Malingering should always be considered before invoking a diagnosis of atypical psychosis.

Malingerers may claim the sudden onset of a delusion. In reality, systematic delusions usually take several weeks to develop. Abrupt renunciation of a delusion is also suspicious. The content of feigned delusions are generally persecutory, occasionally grandiose, but seldom self-depreciatory (Davidson, 1952; East, 1927). Malingerers' behavior usually does not conform to their alleged delusions; acute schizophrenic behavior usually does. However, "burned out" schizophrenics may no longer behave in a manner consistent with their delusions.

Malingerers are likely to have contradictions in their accounts of their illness. The contradictions may be evident within the story itself, or between the malingerer's version and other evidence. When malingerers are caught in contradictions, they may either sulk or laugh with embarrassment (MacDonald, 1976).

Malingerers are more likely to answer "I don't know" to questions about psychotic symptoms, such as hallucinations and delusions. It may simply mean that they do not know what to say when queried about the details of their alleged delusions and hallucinations. When asked whether an alleged voice was male or female, one malingerer replied, "It was *probably* a man's voice." Malingerers are more likely to repeat questions or answer questions slowly, to give themselves more time to make up answers.

Malingerers are likely to have nonpsychotic alternative motives for their behavior, such as killing to settle a grievance or seeking shelter in a V.A. hospital. A crime without apparent motive, such as killing a stranger, lends credence to the presence of true mental disease. Genuine psychotic explanations for rape, robbery, or check forging are unusual.

Malingerers may try to take control of the interview and behave in an intimidating, bizarre manner. The clinician should avoid the temptation to terminate such an interview prematurely. Malingerers sometimes accuse clinicians of regarding them as faking. Such behavior is extremely rare in genuinely psychotic persons.

Persons who have true schizophrenia may malinger additional symptoms to escape criminal responsibility or seek an increase in disability compensation. These are the most difficult cases to accurately assess. Clinicians have a lower index of suspicion for malingering because of the history of psychiatric hospitalizations and the presence of residual schizophrenic symptoms. These malingerers are able to draw upon their prior experience with hallucinations and their observations of other psychotics. They know what questions to expect from clinicians. If they spend time in a forensic psychiatric hospital, they are likely to learn how to modify their story to fit the exact criteria for an insanity defense.

The following case illustrates a number of these points. Mr. B., a 36-year-old man charged with murdering his brother, was referred by his attorney for evaluation of an insanity defense. The defendant had his brother killed because he felt that his brother had betrayed the family and violated his honor. He reported no psychiatric history or unusual beliefs about his brother. I informed the attorney that I found no basis for an insanity defense. When the defense attorney referred him for a second psychiatric evaluation, Mr. B. said, "Some people who wanted to see the family business destroyed replaced my brother with a robot." He claimed that he believed "springs and wires would pop out" when his brother was destroyed. A second defense psychiatrist accepted the robot story at face value.

The defendant told the same robot story to the psychiatrist employed by the prosecution. Interviews with the coconspirators revealed that the defendant had never told them his brother had been replaced by a robot. Upon arrest, the defendant denied any involvement in his brother's killing, and made no mention of the robot story.

The prosecution psychiatrist had several reasons for concluding that the defendant was malingering. First, there was no past history of mental illness, unusual beliefs, or hallucinations. Second, the "robot belief" was an atypical delusion. Third, anger and greed were rational alternative motives for the killing. Fourth, during the time the defendant allegedly believed his brother was a robot, the defendant carried out his usual duties. Fifth, the defendant had contradictions in his story. Sixth, his symptoms fit no known diagnostic entity. Seventh, his behavior was not consistent with his alleged delusions. Finally, he did not show any residual signs of schizophrenia. Indeed, the defendant's alleged "delusion" stood alone, unsupported by any corroborating evidence. A jury found Mr. B. guilty of murder.

Clinical Applications

Malingering must be suspected in the assessment of all patients. Otherwise, separate small clues of dissimulation that would lead to a more detailed investigation may be overlooked. In cases of suspected psychosis, the clini-

cian should inquire about the characteristics of hallucinations and delusions, since the typical characteristics of these symptoms have been well
researched. Table 3.2 provides a threshold model for the identification of
suspicious hallucinations and delusions.

A major focus of this book is the development of clinical decision
models for establishing when a particular disorder is malingered. Table 3.3
offers such a model for malingered psychosis. Before a conclusion is made
with respect to malingering, the clinician must first establish that the patient's motivation is both conscious and serves some recognizable goal
(other than maintaining a sick role). To make a firm determination of
malingered psychosis, the clinician must observe (1) variability in presentation, (2) improbable or incongruous clinical presentation, and (3) corroborative data. These criteria are presented in Table 3.3.

Forensic Applications

Concern about defendants' faking mental illness to avoid criminal responsibility dates back to at least the 10th century (Brittain, 1966; Collinson, 1812;
"Shamming Insanity," 1881; Resnick, 1984). By the 1880s, many Americans
considered physicians a generally impious, mercenary, and cynical lot who
might participate in the "insanity dodge" (Rosenberg, 1968). After the
Hinckley verdict, columnist Carl Rowan (1982, p. 10B) stated, "It is about
time we faced the truth that the 'insanity' defense is mostly last gasp legal
maneuvering, often hoaxes, in cases where a person obviously has done
something terrible."

Table 3.2. Threshold Model for the Assessment of Hallucinations
and Delusions

Malingering should be suspected if any of the following are observed:
A. Hallucinations
    1. Continuous rather than intermittent hallucinations
    2. Vague or inaudible hallucinations
    3. Hallucinations not associated with delusions
    4. Stilted language reported in hallucinations
    5. Inability to state strategies to diminish voices
    6. Self-report that all command hallucinations were obeyed
B. Delusions
    1. Abrupt onset or termination
    2. Eagerness to call attention to delusions
    3. Conduct not consistent with delusions
    4. Bizarre content without disordered thinking

Table 3.3. Clinical Decision Model for the Assessment of Malingered Psychosis

---

Meet the following criteria:

A. Understandable motive to malinger
B. Variability of presentation as observed in at least one of the following:
   1. Marked discrepancies in interview and noninterview behavior
   2. Inconsistencies in reported psychotic symptoms
   3. Contradictions between reported prior episodes and documented psychiatric history
C. Improbable psychiatric symptoms as evidenced by at least one of the following:
   1. Reporting elaborate psychiatric symptoms which lack common paranoid, grandiose, or religious themes
   2. Sudden emergence of purported psychotic symptoms to explain antisocial behavior
   3. Atypical hallucinations or delusions (see Table 3.2)
D. Confirmation of malingered psychosis by either:
   1. Admission of malingering following confrontation
   2. Presence of strong corroborative information such as psychometric data or past history of dissimulation

---

Clinical Assessment of Criminal Defendants

Prior to seeing a defendant, the clinician should be equipped with as much background information as possible: for example, police reports, witness statements, autopsy findings, past psychiatric records, statements of the defendant, and observations of the correctional staff. It is often helpful if a social worker can interview family members prior to the clinician's examination.

The clinician should attempt to learn some relevant information about the defendant or crime that the defendant is unaware the clinician knows. One reliable method of assessing veracity is to compare the defendant's self-report with known past information. For example, does he or she honestly report past criminal activity as recorded on the "rap sheet"? How does the defendant's version of the offense compare with the victim's account? (Hall, 1982)

Any defendant who may subsequently raise psychiatric issues should be seen as soon as possible after the crime. If a clinician is employed by a defense attorney, it is often possible to evaluate the defendant within a few days of the crime; requests from judges and prosecutors are usually not received until 1 or 2 months later. Early evaluation reduces the likelihood that the defendant will have been coached about the legal criteria for insanity by other prisoners or the occasional unethical attorney. The more quickly defendants are seen, the less time they have to plan deception, work out a consistent story, and rehearse their lies. Prompt examination also enhances the clinician's credibility in court.

The defendant must be told at the outset about the purpose of the examination, the disposition of the report, and the lack of confidentiality. More complete information will be elicited if the clinician behaves in an empathic, supportive manner. Stone (1984) points out the ethical dilemma engendered by having clinicians "seduce" defendants into revealing information that may hurt their cases. Despite proper warnings, the illusion of the doctor as healer commonly persists. The ethical issue is beyond the scope of this chapter, but good rapport is helpful in gathering material to detect malingering.

When defendants present with a mixed picture of schizophrenia and antisocial features, countertransference feelings may cause mental health professionals to focus on the antisocial traits and ignore the underlying illness (Travin & Protter, 1984). The clinician must guard against any temptation to either accept a psychotic version at face value or to dismiss it out of hand.

The far-sighted clinician will record in detail the defendant's early account of the crime, even if he or she is not competent to stand trial. Once defendants are placed in a maximum security hospital, they are likely to learn how to modify their story to avoid criminal responsibility. Recording the early version also reduces the likelihood of being misled later by a defendant's unconscious memory distortions.

The clinician should take a careful history of past psychiatric illnesses, including details of prior hallucinations, before eliciting an account of the current crime. Malingerers are less likely to be on guard because they infrequently fully anticipate the relevance of such information to the current insanity issue. If defendants should subsequently fake hallucinations to explain their criminal conduct, it will be too late to falsify past symptoms to lend credence to the deception. Reports of prior hallucinations should be confirmed in past hospital records.

Malingering Incompetence to Stand Trial

The following example provides an unusual opportunity to see the detailed thinking of someone who repeatedly faked psychosis for the explicit purpose of avoiding trial. Mr. K., a 30-year-old, single, white man, charged with aggravated robbery, had charges dropped on three prior occasions because he was found incompetent to stand trial.

Observations of Mr. K. by jailers and arresting officers showed no abnormal behavior. During the psychiatric evaluation, however, the defendant rocked back and forth and sang songs. He spoke rapidly and repeatedly interrupted the evaluator. Mr. K. immediately reported that he had ESP powers and was being tormented by the government as a political prisoner. He answered nearly all questions with questions, and often refused to explain his symptoms. When the clinician left the room, he stopped rocking and was quiet. He alleged that all courtroom personnel were against him due to a government plot. He stated explicitly that he was too sick to stand trial and should be hospitalized.

Several letters that he had written to his jailed girlfriend (a codefendant) were available for review. The following excerpts advise his girlfriend on how to malinger incompetence.

> When the doctors see you, they only hold you for a little while. All the time you are with them, don't hold a normal conversation with them. When they start asking you a question, interrupt them before they can finish asking. You can always use scriptures from the Bible to interrupt them with; make up your own scriptures, stare a lot at the floor, turn your head away from them and mumble to yourself.
>
> Start talking about any and everything. Keep changing subjects. Don't complete sentences with them. You don't know the judge from the bailiff or prosecutor. You don't fully understand what you are charged with. You never see eye to eye with your lawyer. Accuse him of being a communist. You don't understand the regular courtroom procedures; the voices told you that the courtroom was like a circus or zoo. . . . Talk stupid, dumb, and crazy to even your social worker. . . . Maybe this time next month you could be in a *nice* mental hospital. Stay there a year and they will drop all your charges.
>
> Let me give you a real life example. Today, a doctor talked to me for an hour and a half. During my competency test, the psychiatrist said I would make a good actor. He just made remarks to see how I would respond. My reply was more mumbling to myself and saying things he didn't understand. You just have to act like most of the time you're in your own little world. Just make like a real baby, meaning you don't even know the English language. You just answer like you think a crazy woman would. No matter how many times someone calls you a con or a fake, just keep up the act (K. M. Quinn, September 10, 1985; personal communication).

Several clues were observed in ascertaining that this man was malingering. He overacted his part and was eager to call attention to his illness. He showed no subtle signs of schizophrenia. He did not maintain his crazy behavior 24 hours a day. He answered many questions, "I don't know," and refused to give details.

Malingering Insanity

In assessing defendants for criminal responsibility, clinicians must determine whether they are malingering, both with respect to what they report about their psychotic behavior at the time of the act, and with respect to their symptoms at the time of the examination (Hall, 1982) (see Table 3.4). The importance of the differentiation was demonstrated by using the Schedule of Affective Disorders and Schizophrenia (SADS) Diagnostic Interview (Rogers, Thatcher, & Cavanaugh, 1984). Although the SADS successfully differentiated between sane and insane defendants at the time of their crimes, no significant differences were found in the SADS summary scales of the defendants at the time of their evaluations. Some malingerers mistakenly believe that they must show ongoing symptoms of psychosis in order to

Table 3.4. Malingered Psychosis during the Crime

A. Faking psychosis while actually committing the crime (rare)
B. Faking "psychosis during the crime" at the time of the evaluation, and either:
  1. Claiming to be well now
  2. Still faking psychosis
C. Actually psychotic during the crime, but superimposing faked exculpatory symptoms at the evaluation. Either:
  1. Still psychotic at the evaluation
  2. No longer psychotic at the evaluation

---

succeed with an insanity defense. When defendants present with current psychiatric symptoms, the clinician has the opportunity to see whether the symptoms are consistent with psychological testing.

Several clues can assist clinicians in the detection of fraudulent insanity defenses (see Table 3.5). A psychotic explanation for a crime should be questioned if the crime fits the same pattern as previous convictions. Malingering should be suspected in defendants pleading insanity if a partner was involved in the crime. Most accomplices of normal intelligence will not participate in psychotically motivated crimes. The clinician may explore the validity of such a claim by questioning the codefendant. A malingerer may tell a far-fetched story to fit the facts of a crime into a mental disease model. One malingerer with prior armed robbery convictions claimed that he robbed only upon the commands of auditory hallucinations, and gave away all the stolen money.

If a defendant is alleging an irresistible impulse, malingering should carefully be considered. The clinician should be skeptical of an impulse that is not a frequent symptom in a recognized mental disease. If a defendant denies any previous knowledge of an impulse, lying should be suspected. Experience shows that it is extremely improbable for an obsessional impulse to be uncontrollable at its first appearance (East, 1927).

Table 3.5. Threshold Model for the Assessment of Psychosis in Defendants Pleading Insanity

---

Malingering should be suspected if any of the following are present:
1. Nonpsychotic, alternative, rational motive for the crime
2. Suspicious hallucinations or delusions (see Table 3.2)
3. Current crime fits a pattern of prior criminal conduct
4. Absence of any active or subtle signs of psychosis at the evaluation
5. Report of a sudden irresistible impulse
6. Presence of a partner in the crime
7. Double denial of responsibility
8. Far-fetched story of psychosis to explain the crime

Malingering defendants tend to present themselves as blameless within their feigned illness. This tendency was demonstrated by a man who pled insanity to a charge of stabbing an 11-year-old boy 60 times with an icepick. He reported that for one week prior to the homicide, he was constantly pursued by an "indistinct, humanlike, black blob." He stated that he was sexually excited and intended to force homosexual acts on the victim, but abandoned his plan when the boy began to cry. When he started to leave, ten faces in the bushes began chanting, "Kill him, kill him, kill him." He yelled, "No," and struck out at the faces with an icepick. The next thing he knew, "the victim was covered with blood." The autopsy showed a cluster of stab wounds in the victim's head and neck—which was inconsistent with the defendant's claim that he struck out randomly at multiple faces in the bushes. His version showed a double avoidance of responsibility: (1) the faces told him to kill, and (2) he claimed to have attacked the faces, not the victim. After his conviction, he confessed to six unsolved sadistic homosexual killings.

Defensiveness after Psychotic Crimes

Injustice may also result from the simulation of sanity (see Table 3.6). Denial of psychiatric symptoms is not uncommon in persons who have committed crimes (Diamond, 1956). Defendants often find the stigma and consequences of mental illness far worse than that of criminality (Halleck, 1975). In addition, persons who are genuinely mentally ill may feel more in control of their illness by alleging that earlier symptoms were malingered. Defendants may retrospectively distort accounts of their acts due to amnesia, an acute confusional state, or a current desire simply to have past behavior make sense. Collateral information from witnesses is therefore invaluable.

Since the burden of raising the issue of insanity lies with the defendant, a grave miscarriage of justice may occur if the defendant chooses not to reveal his or her mental illness. This places a heavy responsibility on clinicians to uncover any evidence of mental unsoundness. Diamond (1986) elicited relevant psychopathology through the use of hypnosis in the trial of

Table 3.6. Defensiveness regarding Psychosis during the Crime

A. Faking well during the act itself (no motive)
B. Unconscious retrospective falsification to appear "well during the act" in the evaluation
   1. Still psychotic at the evaluation
   2. No longer psychotic at the evaluation
C. Consciously claiming to be "well during the act" in the evaluation
   1. Still psychotic at the evaluation
   2. No longer psychotic at the evaluation

Sirhan Sirhan for the assassination of Robert Kennedy. Even after listening to the tape recording of the hypnotic interviews, Sirhan alleged that the tapes were faked and denied any significant psychological impairment. Sirhan, who may have been mentally disordered, was convicted of first degree murder with the recommendation of the death penalty.

Conclusion

The detection of malingered psychosis is sometimes quite difficult. The decision that an individual is malingering is made by assembling all of the clues from a thorough evaluation of a patient's past and current functioning with corroboration from clinical records and other people. Although the identification of a person malingering psychosis may be viewed as a distasteful chore, it is important in treating patients in general, and critical in forensic assessments. Indeed, clinicians bear a heavy responsibility to assist society in differentiating true psychosis from malingered madness.

4

Sociopathy, Malingering, and Defensiveness

CHARLES R. CLARK

The relationship between sociopathy and malingering is an issue about which much is assumed and little understood. Clearly, the recommendation of DSM III-R (American Psychiatric Association, 1987), that malingering should be strongly suspected in a number of circumstances if the presence of an antisocial personality disorder is established, is intuitively correct. Sociopaths, designated as antisocial personality disorder in the formal nosology of DSM III-R, are widely understood to be prone to presenting "false or grossly exaggerated physical or psychological symptoms" (p. 360). An older view, that malingering may be a symptom of genuine mental illness acting as a defense against the disintegration of the very condition which is feigned (Eissler, 1951), finds little current support. On the other hand, few advances have been made in empirically defining the actual incidence of malingering among sociopaths and, perhaps more importantly, the frequency of sociopathy among malingerers. The distinguishing characteristics of the malingered presentations of sociopaths, the influences of situational factors, and other associated features have been poorly researched. As an exploration of the relationship between sociopathy and malingering will show, the presence of antisocial personality characteristics, in itself, poses special challenges to the clinical assessment of malingering.

The terminology used to describe sociopathy has undergone considerable changes, as has the conceptualization of the condition itself (Guttmacher & Weihofen, 1952; Hare, 1970; Mednick & Christiansen, 1977). In this regard, malingering has not played a central role in the conceptualization of sociopathy, although such considerations are logically related to a condition marked by an absence of moral constraints in which the rights of others are violated. Although malingering may be as ancient as mental illness itself (Resnick, 1984), present-day malingering—and its frequency, motivation, and phenomenology—is largely a product of a modern, humanistic society which provides special rewards, services, and compensation for

Charles R. Clark, Center for Forensic Psychiatry, Ann Arbor, Michigan.

those viewed as sick or otherwise disabled. Indeed, the present possibilities for malingering may simply be the latest "targets of opportunity" for enterprising sociopaths.

DSM III-R (American Psychiatric Association, 1987) has articulated the current diagnostic thinking that lying or untruthfulness is a possible, but not necessary, component of antisocial personality disorder. Comprehensive discussions of sociopathy, however, have always included prominent explorations of lying as an essential component of this disorder. Cleckley (1976) and Doren (1987) have emphasized the sociopath's propensity for untruthfulness and insincerity; they view such deception as one of the defining characteristics of the disorder. Yochelson and Samenow (1976), in their extensive examination of what they term the criminal personality, similarly view this tendency to lie as central to the condition. They note that, historically, insincerity or untruthfulness has almost always been identified as an essential characteristic of sociopathy. Yochelson and Samenow point out that lying is a fundamental pattern of life for sociopathic individuals and an essential precondition of their criminality; to choose a criminal lifestyle necessitates lying for purposes of self-preservation. When apprehended, sociopaths may act on the rational view that it is only sensible to create any deception which will reduce their own personal accountability. Their "stories" will be crafted to conform to whatever the sociopaths judge will fit society's view of what constitutes a good excuse or an understandable motive.

Research on the prevalence of deception in antisocial and conduct-disordered youth provide empirical support to the less rigorous clinical reports on adults (e.g., Cleckley, 1976; Yochelson & Samenow, 1976, 1977). Stouthamer-Loeber (1986), in her review of seven studies, found that conduct-disordered youth displayed chronic or problem lying at a prevalence rate of 49% or two and one-half times greater than normal samples. This finding is consistent across sources of clinical data; it holds for parental observations (e.g., Patterson, 1982), teacher ratings (e.g., Behar, 1977; Ferguson, Partyka, & Lester, 1974), and inpatient and outpatient settings (e.g., Rutter, Tizard, & Whitmore, 1970; Stewart & DeBlois, 1984).

Sociopathy in Malingerers

Research data on the incidence of sociopathy among malingerers are at best scattered. Sierles (1984) reported an attempt to assess, among other diagnostic variables, the frequency of sociopathy among malingerers. Although his research methodology (i.e., a survey of Veterans Administration inpatients and medical student controls) permits little generalizability, Sierles reported a significant correlation between self-report indices of malingering and sociopathy. Similarly, Guttmacher and Weihofen (1952) reported studies made during World War II which revealed that a large percentage of servicemen assessed as malingerers were also diagnosed as psychopaths. In the absence of a methodological description, it is unknown whether the diagnosis of psychopathy was not often invoked simply as an explanation for the observed malingering. In a review of the malingering literature, Yudofsky (1985) noted that the most commonly associated feature of malingering in the adult population is the presence of an antisocial personality disorder. Although some level of association between malingering and sociopathy is likely to exist, the research literature does not provide an accurate estimation of the degree of association, or of the frequency of malingering among sociopaths.

Data on the incidence of malingering among various diagnostic groups are not available, nor are basic demographic data regarding its frequency beyond the observations of Yudofsky (1985) that malingering seems to occur more often in men between young adulthood and middle age. From the author's observations, relatively few individuals who warrant the diagnosis of antisocial personality disorder attempt to malinger despite a potentially adversarial setting and a pending trial. Thus, malingering appears to be a relatively unpopular option even among sociopaths, despite the fact that a disproportionate number of malingerers may also be sociopaths.

Differences in Malingered Presentations

Controlled studies have yet to be conducted on the question of whether malingering by sociopaths differs qualitively from that in other diagnostic groups. On a commonsense basis, it would appear likely that sociopaths would have more occasion to malinger or to be defensive than other groups, so as to escape the consequences of their criminal actions. From this perspective, sociopaths frequently dissimulate within the context of criminal prosecution or incarceration. In contrast, it has been observed that sociopaths rarely seek treatment on their own initiative and often are coerced into treatment by the criminal justice system (Cavanaugh, Rogers, & Wasyliw, 1981). It may therefore be concluded that sociopaths would be underrepresented in voluntary treatment settings and have little motivation (except perhaps personal injury suits and disability claims) to dissimulate in these settings.

Socialized sociopaths are certainly more likely than are others to be adept at lying and dissimulation of all types. The successful assessment of their malingering requires considerable understanding of sociopathy on the part of the examiner. A naive clinician might be convinced that a sociopath's outpouring of tears and sobbing are necessarily evidence of genuine distress. Although dysphoria is common among sociopaths (Reid, 1978), a dramatic presentation of remorse or depression should raise the index of suspicion regarding the validity of a sociopath's self-report. It should be borne in mind, however, that not all colorful and extravagant presentations of malingering are made by sociopathic individuals, and that sociopaths may provide lackluster performances.

Research is not available on the question of whether there are stylistic differences in how sociopaths and others malinger. Resnick (1984) has held that criminal defendants most often feign auditory hallucinations. In addition, he has observed that criminal defendants often fabricate symptoms which appear superficially organic but are incongruous in their presentation. As I have observed, these cases usually include a presentation of gross confusion, disorientation, and attention–concentration deficits of such extreme severity as to strain credibility.

Certain highly motivated sociopaths tend to be more persistent in their malingering than others, who may lack the determination to sustain the appearance of mental illness for weeks or months. However, this observation is not uniformly true, since many sociopaths with much to gain from feigning mental illness fail to persist in their presentations long enough to satisfy thorough evaluations. Indeed, many of the presentations that appear the most disturbed, such as fecal smearing, gross confusion, mutism, or severe depression, prove particularly difficult to sustain. In the author's experience, many sociopaths with well-constructed and rehearsed presentations abandon malingering once it becomes clear that the clinician is unconvinced.

In summary, empirical differences between the malingering by sociopaths and by others have yet to be demonstrated. In the final analysis, the form of malingering, its frequency, and its duration may have far more to do with the context of the malingering than with personality variables. Diagnostic differences among malingerers may be relevant to malingering only to the extent that they give rise to a reason or a perceived need to malinger. An exploration of how sociopathic malingering varies according to the context would provide the basis for a systematic approach to the detection of malingering among sociopaths.

Malingering and the Criminal Justice System

Sociopaths are most likely to be identified in the criminal justice system since many engage repetitively in criminal behavior. In feigning mental illness, the sociopath is often looking for mental health alternatives to incarceration (e.g., being found incompetent to stand trial or insane). Although the malingerer will be concentrating on presenting a believable disorder, it will also be important to recognize that he or she often exercises a certain degree of defensiveness in avoiding genuine self-revelation, particularly with respect to his or her criminal behavior. Such defensiveness may extend to minimizing prior criminal conduct and denial of antisocial symptoms. Sociopathy, as a diagnostic concept, reflects an antisocial pattern of behavior which is largely identified by history. Sociopaths feigning mental illness may attempt to hide their antisocial qualities if they want to seek a mental health alternative to incarceration.

One malingered presentation frequently seen in the criminal justice setting, but little mentioned in the clinical literature, is a superficially "organic" presentation; this may or may not include symptoms which, on their face, would be evidence of functional psychosis. The presentation of "organicity" confers certain clear advantages to a defendant who is eager to delay the court disposition, perhaps indefinitely. The gross cognitive deficits presented (i.e., disorientation, confusion, memory impairment, reduced intellectual functioning, and regressive speech) would, if genuine, result in unfitness to stand trial and might also prevent any exploration of the defendant's antisocial history.

Case Studies

Conclusions from available research would suggest that (1) the incidence of malingering among sociopaths and (2) the clinical characteristics of malingering sociopaths have yet to be established. In the absence of empirical studies, this chapter will offer a distillation of six case studies exemplifying the diversity of malingered presentations among sociopaths. No claims are made regarding the representativeness of these cases, each of which were drawn from the author's own clinical files.

A. N., 26, was referred for an evaluation of criminal responsibility for a serious sexual offense. He identified himself as "Dr. Aaronson" and convinced an 11-year-old girl to be undressed and fondled. When evaluated, A. N. proved to be completely unresponsive to questions about the occurrence of the offense, claiming that he was unable to understand the charge or the allegations. Throughout the interview, he seemed absorbed with a bandage on his right wrist and avoided making eye contact with the clinician throughout the interview. He offered few spontaneous comments aside from repeatedly telling the clinician that he was certain the clinician was either laughing or was angry at him. His responses to even the simplest of questions elicited long pauses before a response and frequent hesitations while responding. He affected deep and puzzled concentration over such questions as his home phone number, on which he pondered for almost four minutes before indicating that he could not recall it. He presented himself as disoriented to time; he could not "even guess" how long he had been in jail, the current date, or even the season of the year. Importantly, no indications of confusion or other cognitive disturbance were observed prior to his arrest.

A. N.'s clinical presentation was guarded and circumspect. When given the opportunity to endorse various unlikely symptoms that might confirm malingering, he proceeded cautiously and vaguely. For example, asked whether he had ever seen people change color, he indicated that he had not seen people change color but had witnessed this happening to ceilings. The chief thrust of A. N.'s presentation appeared to be that he was too confused and cognitively impaired to appreciate his surroundings or circumstances.

B. D., 29, was charged with prolonged incestuous relations with his 7-year-old daughter. Although he first denied the charges, he made a full confession when confronted with his polygraph results. B. D. presented to jail personnel a picture of global amnesia and generalized confusion and disorientation. His presentation at the time of the evaluation was remarkable. He appeared puzzled and confused, and smiled constantly in a somewhat silly manner. He continually looked around the interview room, as though not comprehending his surroundings. He appeared unable to state his last name, report the date, or recall his present location (i.e., city and state). His speech was delivered in the telegraphic style reminiscent of the Hollywood Indian stereotype and with a breathless stutter, which he stopped when instructed to do so.

C. R., 27, was charged with the rape and aggravated assault of a 70-year-old woman. He presented as mute with a coarse tremor of the upper extremities and a staggering gait. He appeared to have no comprehension of his surroundings. When hospitalized, his trembling and gait disturbance disappeared, yet he maintained the appearance of complete disorientation, amnesia, and confusion. He could not recall where he had been born and raised, that he had gone to school, or that he was married with four children. C. R.'s speech tended to be minimal and monosyllabic and was seldom spontaneously delivered. Long pauses preceded his responses to even simple questions. He claimed to hear "voices" which included, always in the same sequence, two people arguing about him, children crying, and the sound of bells ringing. These "voices," he said, occurred "constantly" and kept him awake each night. Incongruously, these purported hallucinations did not occur in the context of any delusional ideas. He also claimed that he would occasionally see Jesus "just pop up" to express words of comfort to him. As a result of his organic-like presentation, C. R. was referred for extensive neurological and neuropsychological evaluations; these assessments yielded results inconsistent with genuine organic pathology.

C. R. found it difficult to maintain his basic presentation. Despite his confusion and disorientation, he had learned to play cards proficiently with the night staff. His claims to a complete inability to remember day-to-day events was belied by his timely inquiries about money placed in his patient account and similar events for which his memory was obviously intact.

D. A., 22, was charged with armed robbery for his alleged hold-up of a convenience store at knife point. When apprehended, the defendant confessed that he had only committed the robbery to feed his destitute family. It was later established that he had no family and was previously arrested for thefts, drug trafficking, and pimping.

At the time of the evaluation, D. A. claimed that all his antisocial activity had been due entirely to Lucius, a "siamese twin brother" who lived inside his body and who enjoyed drinking, using drugs, gambling, and other illegal activities. He expressed great anxiety that the clinician would laugh at him. D. A. reported internal dialogues with Lucius who had been sleeping for the last several weeks. Asked how he knew when Lucius was awake, he responded, "He lets me know that. I hear him moving around, get up, yawn and stuff." He inquired about getting an operation "to get us separated." Since all of his problems stemmed from Lucius, D. A. stated that he did not consider it fair that he was the one who would have to be punished for alleged misdeeds. D. A. was not able to sustain his claim that he was "not himself" when he performed various antisocial acts. Although ascribing all of his illegal activity to Lucius, he frequently slipped and referred to himself as the agent of these acts. These results, including an MMPI fake-bad profile, added to his unlikely symptoms, supported the conclusion that D. A. was feigning a mental disorder.

E. E., a 50-year-old white man, was accused of lying in wait for his black foreman, against whom he had a number of grievances, and fatally running him down with a truck. At the time of his evaluation, his hygiene and grooming were quite poor, and he had not bathed for several weeks. He was accompanied during the evaluation by "Sam," which he identified as "my doggie," and who was invisible to the clinician. E. E. was unsurprised that the examiner could not see his dog and helpfully indicated that Sam was a mixed breed, and brown and white in color. E. E. presented himself as confused and disorientated, being incapable of identifying himself or his circumstances, or of remembering any of the events connected with his arrest. It was concluded from this evaluation, based on his improbable presentation, that the defendant was malingering. However, E. E. was referred for a second evaluation some months later because of his bizarre, apparently paranoid behavior in the courtroom. On this occasion, he appeared eager to cooperate with the clinician to the point of being obsequious. His speech was quite pressured and became derailed at numerous points. He was convinced that he was "the son of the devil" and the "anti-Christ."

E. E. made numerous references to small inconsistencies in various police and court records relating to his case. This was evidence, he asserted, that his lawyer was "cutting a deal" with the prosecution behind his back. He went into extensive complaints of similar plots by others around him to deprive him of his rights. Despite these protests, he was at pains to indicate complete responsibility for the offense with which he was charged. Moreover, he acknowledged malingering in his first evaluation. He related that he had been attempting to "play crazy" only because others in court had deceived him and tried to take away his rights. E. E. was admitted to the hospital where the genuineness of his psychotic presentation was rapidly confirmed; he required prolonged treatment before even minimal remission was obtained.

F. D., 28, was charged with fondling two children. The offense occurred while babysitting his neighbor's family. Although he at first denied the offense, he was advised of his polygraph results and subsequently provided a complete confession. He readily reported that he was hearing voices, sometimes friendly and sometimes frightening. He reported visual hallucinations including his cat, his deceased father, and "a creature with horns of a goat, tail of a serpent, and he's black." He told the clinician that this "creature" was standing in the corner of the interview room, but did not seem alarmed by this vision, and paid more attention to the clinician's reactions than to the "creature." Given the unconvincing nature of his reported symptomatology, F. D. was asked, and answered affirmatively, a number of other questions about symptoms seldom reported by psychotic patients (e.g., his hands changing in size, faces changing colors, and gustatory hallucinations).

Perhaps the most striking observation garnered from these six studies is the amount of general deception seen in sociopaths, in addition to their malingering. A. N. employed an elaborately planned deception to secure sexual satisfaction while posing as a physician. B. D. and F. D. falsely denied their charges until confronted with failed polygraph tests. D. A., although he confessed to his crime, concocted a heart-wrenching story of his starving family. Certainly, evidence of any deception should provoke suspicion of malingering or defensiveness.

Malingering in the criminal justice system requires the simulation of severe impairment in order to achieve the defendants' objectives (e.g., avoid incarceration). This need on the part of sociopaths to appear severely disturbed is often their downfall. Feigning of marked cognitive impairment is extremely difficult to maintain for any extended period, since malingerers experience a "reality pull" (see Chapter 10). Similarly, sociopaths appear no more effective than others in presenting plausible symptoms. In four of the case studies, sociopaths presented preposterous symptoms including a breathless stutter which stops on direction, a siamese twin inside, an invisible but friendly dog, and a serpent-like creature who sits in the office.

As noted in Chapter 2, sociopaths, like all other dissimulators, elude straightforward diagnostic categorization. Sociopathy offers no immunity to Axis I disorders, substance abuse, or complicating medical conditions. E. E. was schizophrenic, although he was also a malingerer and was sociopathic. In addition, it is entirely possible that F. D. and A. D. had paraphiliac disorders about which they responded defensively. Needless to say, such complex diagnostic cases necessitate extended inpatient assessments to evaluate each possible disorder in depth.

Clinical Applications

The great majority of individuals with antisocial personality disorders are not self-referred for treatment (Reid, 1981) but are sent for clinical assessment by the criminal justice system. Within this context, the likelihood of malingering or other forms of dissimulation is naturally increased. As noted above, sociopathy does not exclude diagnoses of schizophrenia or other major mental illness; the most problematic evaluation is that of a defendant who (1) has an Axis I diagnosis superimposed on an antisocial personality disorder and (2) is being assessed within an adversarial context.

The dearth of empirical data on sociopathic malingerers, complicated by the inherent problems of assessing sociopathy among malingerers, militates against a well-defined clinical decision model. However, indications of sociopathy, together with an unusual presentation of mental disturbance, would warrant increasing levels of suspicion that the disorder is malingered. Table 4.1 outlines a threshold model for assessing malingering among sociopaths. As presented here, the threshold criteria are necessarily low,

Table 4.1. A Threshold Model of Sociopathy and Malingering

Threshold criteria require A in combination with B or C.

A. Clinical indicators of sociopathy, as observed in either of the following:
  1. The individual presenting mental disorder can be diagnosed with an Antisocial Personality Disorder or has a known history which is strongly suggestive of sociopathy.
  2. In the absence of a known history of sociopathy, the individual presenting a mental disorder is being charged with an offense which, if true, would itself suggest sociopathy. Elements of such an offense might include cruelty or other indications of a lack of empathic concern, lack of any indication of remorse or moral compunction, and the apparent presence of such common "criminal" motivations as money, nonconsensual sexual gratification, anger and revenge.

B. Clinical indicators of malingering as observed in any of the following:
  1. The mental disorder presented is anomalous or unique and does not correspond to recognized disorders (e.g., by the extreme nature of the impairment or by an unexpected combination of symptoms).
  2. The individual presenting a mental disorder has not or does not behave in ways consistent with the disturbance presented. Suspicion should be aroused, for example, when the person requesting help for a long-standing disorder has not sought treatment in the past, or when the clinical presentation is markedly inconsistent with the results of psychological testing.
  3. The presentation of the mental disorder is highly variable over time.

C. Understandable motivation: The presentation of the mental disorder occurs in a context in which there is some clear advantage to being seen as disturbed.

suggesting that the majority of individuals who are diagnosed as sociopathic should be closely evaluated for malingering.

The threshold model does not in any way suggest that most sociopaths are malingerers, or conversely, that most malingerers are sociopaths. It does, however, recommend that in forensic or other adversarial contexts, individuals with a diagnosis of Antisocial Personality Disorder should also be investigated for dissimulation.

Responses of the suspected malingerer to psychological measures can often contribute significantly to an assessment of malingering. An important clinical issue is whether sociopaths are more successful at malingering than their nonsociopathic counterparts. This question has been partially addressed with respect to two methods: the MMPI and the polygraph.

Research has demonstrated the susceptibility of the MMPI to manipulation by sociopaths. Scale 4 may be manipulated in either malingered or defensive directions (Lawton, 1963; Lawton & Kleban, 1965). In addition, Gendreau, Irvine, and Knight (1973) studied 24 inmates' MMPI responses under three instructional sets (honest, malingering, and defensive). They found that, although the inmates were successful at manipulating Scale 4, they were easily detectable by employing the F and the F-K index for malingering, and the F-K and the positive malingering (Mp) scale for defensiveness. Such findings have led Rogers (1984a) to conclude that sociopaths may well manipulate their antisocial characteristics, but that such dissimulation is no more effective than that found in other populations. Although more research is clearly needed, the above studies would suggest that commonly employed validity indicators of the MMPI are likely to be equally effective with sociopathic individuals.

The usefulness of polygraph technique with sociopathic versus nonsociopathic individuals is not clear. As illustrated by the cases of B. D. and F. D., the announcement by a polygraph examiner that the subject's responses to the procedure were untruthful may trigger a confession, regardless of the validity of the technique. Although the general usefulness of the polygraph is seriously questioned in Chapter 9, an early study (Raskin & Hare, 1978) would suggest that sociopaths at least are no more effective at undetected deception than are other populations. Although the study has methological limitations (see Lykken, 1978), there is no contrary evidence to suggest that sociopaths are any more adept at dissimulation on the polygraph.

Conclusion

More thorough investigations are needed with respect to specific psychological measures and their ability to effectively identify sociopaths who engage in malingering and other forms of dissimulation. The available research would suggest that sociopathic individuals are no more effective than others in their clinical presentation. Clinicians are strongly recommended to use standardized clinical indicators, including the MMPI, the M test, and structured interviews. Finally, the clinician may be well justified in complicated assessments for the court in describing the suspected dissimulation, but leaving unanswered the referral question when the dissimulation sufficiently obscures the psycholegal issues (Rogers, 1986a).

5

Malingered Amnesia

JASON BRANDT

Complaints of impaired memory are extraordinarily common (Harris & Morris, 1984). Otherwise healthy, normal people quite readily admit to deficits in memory, a fact that sets this aspect of cognitive functioning apart from most others. Memory deficits are also extremely common in neuropathological and psychopathological conditions (see Squire & Butters, 1984; Whitty & Zangwill, 1977). Probably every practicing clinician has evaluated at least one patient whose primary presenting symptom was impaired memory. Occasionally, such a patient will display memory deficits of a type or severity that is not understandable in terms of his or her clinical history. On these occasions, the possibility of malingering or purposeful exaggeration of memory loss is often raised, especially when there appear to be incentives to the patient for engaging in such deception.

Claims of amnesia may be particularly common in the context of forensic evaluations. Defendants in criminal cases have often entered pleas based on amnesia in order to prove incompetency to stand trial (Cocklin, 1980; Gibbens & Williams, 1977; Koson & Robey, 1973; Roesch & Golding, 1986; Sadoff, 1974), or to negate legal responsibility for criminal offenses (Hermann, 1986; Rogers, 1986a; Schacter, 1986a). Estimates of the frequency with which claims of amnesia are made in criminal cases vary, but are thought to be particularly high in homicide cases, ranging from 30% (Guttmacher, 1955) to 55% (Bradford & Smith, 1979). Claims of amnesia are also common in civil cases involving personal injury (Guthkelch, 1980), and in Social Security and disability hearings, where an incapacitating memory impairment may form the basis for substantial monetary awards.

A widespread belief among judges, jurors, and hearing officers, as well as the lay public, is that amnesia can be easily faked and is practically impossible to disprove (Comment, 1967; Kiersch, 1962; Rubinsky & Brandt,

Jason Brandt, Johns Hopkins University School of Medicine, Baltimore, Maryland.

This chapter was supported in part by NIH grants MH38387, AG05146, and NS16375. The author is grateful to Elizabeth Wiggins for her collaboration on some of the research reported herein and Milton Strauss and Richard Rogers for their helpful comments on the manuscript.

1986). The assumptions are that the criminal defendant may be claiming amnesia simply to avoid prosecution or punishment and that the plaintiff in the civil case is seeking greater monetary award than he or she is entitled. Given these considerations, it would clearly be of benefit to the legal community and to practitioners of the forensic sciences to be able to distinguish malingered amnesia from genuine amnesia.

The reason why it is so widely believed that disordered memory is particularly vulnerable to malingering is itself an interesting question. One reason may be the belief that it is actually easier to feign convincingly a behavioral deficit than a positive symptom. The malingered amnesic who succeeds in his or her deception does so by withholding normal behavior, rather than by producing new behaviors. Thus, to fake amnesia, one might simply do less of something that we all have experience doing (i.e., remembering). Whether simply withholding memories accurately mimics amnesic states, or whether psychological techniques can distinguish the malingerer from the genuine amnesic, are empirical questions to be addressed in this chapter.

Suspiciousness about claims of amnesia is also related to the fact that, to both the layperson and many legal experts, amnesia is often seen as a normal state of affairs, rather than as a pathological condition (Rubinsky & Brandt, 1986). Some courts have ruled, for example, that since everyone has experienced episodes of forgetfulness "everyone is amnesic to some degree" (*State v. McClendon*, 1968). Such an argument, however, is a gross misuse of the term *amnesia* as a neuropsychological construct. It reflects an ignorance of the syndromal aspects of pathologically impaired memory and neglects decades of experimental and clinical research on the nature, severity, and heterogeneity of amnesia.

Heterogeneity of Amnesic Syndromes

Research into the cognitive characteristics of amnesic syndromes have experienced very rapid growth in the past few years (Cermak, 1982; Kihlstrom & Evans, 1979; Squire & Butters, 1984; Whitty & Zangwill, 1977). Perhaps the most thoroughly studied amnesic state, and that upon which most theories of amnesia are based, is that of *chronic global amnesia*. This condition is a severe and permanent inability to record ongoing events and learn new information (i.e., anterograde amnesia) in spite of normal intelligence. The defect applies to the learning of both verbal and nonverbal material and is independent of stimulus modality. Patients with this syndrome also have varying degrees of difficulty in recalling events that occurred prior to the onset of the amnesic condition (i.e., retrograde amnesia). Chronic global amnesia is associated with a wide variety of neurological conditions, including alcoholic Korsakoff syndrome (Butters & Cermak, 1980), herpes simplex encephalitis (Cermak, 1976; Starr & Phillips, 1970), cerebral hypoxia (Whitty, Stores, & Lishman, 1977), bilateral medial temporal lobe lesions (Scoville & Milner, 1957), and strokes involving the medial thalamus or basal forebrain (Alexander & Freedman, 1984; Damasio, Graff-Radford, Eslinger, Damasio, & Kassel, 1985; Speedie & Heilman, 1982; Talland, Sweet, & Ballantine, 1967; Winocur, Oxbury, Roberts, Agnetti, & Davis, 1984). Although global amnesia is also a component of many dementing illnesses, such as Alzheimer disease (Corkin, 1982; Schacter, 1983; Weingartner et al. 1982) and Huntington's disease (Brandt & Butters, 1986; Butters, 1984; Weingartner, Caine, & Ebert, 1979), memory loss in these conditions is part of a more pervasive cognitive decline.

The cognitive characteristics of chronic global amnesia are variable, depending at least partially on the etiology of the amnesia and locus of the brain lesion (Butters, Miliotis, Albert, & Sax, 1984; Parkin, 1984; Squire, 1982a, 1982b; Weingartner, Grafman, Boutelle, Kaye, & Martin, 1983; but cf., Corkin et al., 1985). In a recent review, however, Hirst (1982) suggested that a "core" organic amnesic syndrome exists and is characterized by rapid forgetting of new information, normal short-term memory capacity (e.g., normal digit span), responsiveness to recognition probes and retrieval cues, increased sensitivity to proactive interference, and preserved skill learning. Parkin (1984) added normal intelligence and some degree of retrograde amnesia to this list. However, many of these features are task-dependent, and are clearly not seen in every amnesic patient (Butters et al., 1984; Moss, Albert, Butters, & Payne, 1986). In fact, it is doubtful whether a single amnesic syndrome exists. This conclusion makes it all the more important to differentiate the amnesias by etiology, locus of pathology, and information-processing characteristics.

Although most is known about the psychological characteristics of chronic global amnesia, questions of malingering rarely arise for this disorder. Patients with chronic global amnesia are typically unambiguously "brain-damaged." These patients often have other clinical signs which point to their abnormal brain functioning, and neurodiagnostic tests (e.g., CT [computerized tomography] or MRI [magnetic resonance imaging] scans, EEGs) frequently indicate the site and type of brain pathology. The issue of potential malingering arises more frequently in the context of evaluations of limited organic amnesia, temporary amnesia, or psychogenic amnesia.

Patients suffering from *limited organic amnesia* may not appear, on cursory clinical examination, to have a significant memory disorder, yet they have genuine difficulties in learning new information and in recalling events of the past. This condition also has a variety of etiologies, including head trauma (Levin, Benton, & Grossman, 1982; Schacter & Crovitz, 1977), strokes, tumors, and metabolic disorders (Brierley, 1977; Whitty et al., 1977). These memory disorders are often specific to the type of information processing required. For example, the processing of verbal material will be impaired with brain lesions of the dominant (usually left) hemisphere, whereas spatial memory disorders are seen after nondominant hemisphere lesions.

Temporary amnesia is a condition in which one or more time-limited events are not recalled, often due to acute alterations of consciousness. Drug and alcohol intoxication and epileptic seizures are examples of conditions which can cause a temporary amnesia. It should be noted, however, that these conditions are marked by alterations of consciousness (i.e., impaired attention), as well as failure to store ongoing events. In *transient global amnesia* (Bender, 1956; Gordon & Marin, 1979; Whitty, 1977; Wilson, Koller, & Kelly, 1980), there is an acute onset of anterograde amnesia, normal immediate memory, and patchy retrograde amnesia. The episode lasts no more than a few hours and leaves no residual symptoms. It is generally believed that the episodes are of vascular origin (i.e., local cerebral ischemia).

Psychogenic or functional amnesia (Abeles & Schilder, 1935; Schacter, Wang, Tulving, & Freedman, 1982) is a relatively uncommon form of memory disorder and is presumably the result of emotionally traumatic material, rather than to neurological damage. Psychodynamic formulations hold that this type of amnesia is a symbolic flight from an intolerable situation (Pratt, 1977). Although relatively little is known about the cognitive characteristics of psychogenic amnesia (Abeles & Schilder, 1935; Pratt, 1977), case studies indicate that autobiographical information and personal identity are lost, yet the ability to learn new information and access general factual knowledge remain intact. Schacter and colleagues (1982) have shown, by a series of experiments in a single case, that retrograde amnesia with "islands" of preserved memory is characteristic of psychogenic amnesia, and that general semantic knowledge is intact. This case also demonstrated that the termination of the amnesic episode is abrupt. These features make psychogenic amnesia very different from the organic amnesias.

In neither psychogenic amnesia nor malingered amnesia is there evidence of neurological dysfunction underlying the poor memory performance. There is presumed to be a strong motive for the observed deficits in both conditions. The two variables that distinguish them are (1) the extent to which the patient is aware of his or her motives, and (2) the extent to which he or she intends to deceive the examiner. Thus, the purposefulness of the patient's behavior forms the critical discriminating variable. Although clinicians may occasionally be successful in determining whether an individual really "knows" a piece of information, they are notoriously poor in determining the extent to which that individual is actually conscious of that knowledge (i.e., whether the person knows that he or she knows it) and is purposely deceiving the examiner. If the individual were actually aware of the knowledge, he or she would be diagnosed as a malingerer; if the individual were not fully aware of the knowledge, he or she would be diagnosed as a psychogenic amnesic. The criterion level of awareness and intentionality that serve as the boundary between these conditions is, unfortunately, virtually impossible to specify.

A summary of some of the major characteristics of amnesic syndromes appears in Table 5.1. It is essential to keep in mind that brain-damaged amnesic patients are quite variable in their presentation, and the precise type and locus of neuropathology are important determinants of the clinical picture in any individual case.

Obstacles to the Detection of Malingered Amnesia

A major roadblock to the study of malingered amnesia is the marked constraints on the verifiability of memory complaints. Unless an individual eventually admits that he or she has been intentionally deceptive, the clinician can never establish with confidence whether he or she has been malingering. Individuals willing to step forward and acknowledge their deceitfulness are rarely, under any circumstances, available. As a result, malingerers usually cannot be identified independently of the outcome measures (i.e., the clinical tests or experimental procedures) being evaluated.

To cope with this dilemma, investigators have often attempted to model malingered amnesia by instructing normal subjects to mimic or simulate amnesia. The basic assumption underlying most studies of simulated cognitive deficit is that the average person has either limited or

Table 5.1. Characteristics of Amnesic Syndromes

Characteristics	Organic Amnesias			Psychogenic (functional) amnesia
	Chronic global amnesia	Limited organic amnesia	Temporary amnesia	
Onset	Acute or progressive	Acute or progressive	Acute	Acute
Personal identity	Preserved	Preserved	Preserved	Lost
Anterograde memory defect	Severe	Mild to moderate	Severe	Mild
Retrograde memory defect	Mild to moderate	Mild	Patchy	Severe
Insight	Variable	Variable	Variable	Poor
Termination	Permanent	Variable	Abrupt	Abrupt

inaccurate knowledge about the disorder in question. Thus, when either severity measures or qualitative features of the simulator's performance are compared with that of individuals with genuine neuropsychological deficits, differences emerge. Studies by many research teams (Benton & Spreen, 1961; Bruhn & Reed, 1975; Goebel, 1983; Heaton, Smith, Lehman, & Vogt, 1978) have revealed that simulators perform qualitatively differently from brain-damaged patients on a variety of widely used neuropsychological tests (see Chapter 10). Although this line of research has yielded much information on the lay public's conceptualization of cognitive disorders, the extent to which experimental simulation approximates malingering as it appears in clinical or forensic settings remains questionable. Clearly, the criminal defendant who is malingering may be presumed to have a much stronger motive for doing so than the normal student given course credit or paid a small sum of money for his or her research participation.

Another obstacle to the detection of malingered amnesia is the concomitant presence of real neurocognitive impairment. Clinicians are often confronted with patients who undeniably have genuine memory deficits but who are also suspected of exaggerating their impairments. For example, one can easily imagine how a litigant in a personal-injury suit with a mild, limited organic amnesia might purposely fail memory test items in an effort to increase the monetary award. Knowing which symptoms are real and which are feigned in an individual patient requires a thorough understanding of the variety of symptoms in genuine amnesia based on the etiology in question. In addition, there are no doubt cases where truly memory-disordered patients perform less than optimally on neuropsychological assessments due to psychological motives of which they are not fully conscious (see Chapter 2). Whether these patients are seen as being malingerers or having "hysterical overlays" depends on the examiner's judgment of the patient's level of awareness and intention.

Approaches to Detecting Malingered Amnesia

Clinical Case Studies

The most common method of identifying malingered amnesia in a clinical context is through the lack of internal consistency in presented deficits. When the data available from history, interview, and neuropsychological testing fail to converge on a coherent clinical pattern and hence do not "make sense," the possibility of malingering should be considered. Discrepancies between the patient's performance across similar tests, discrepancies between his or her verbal report and observed behavior, and discrepancies between reported symptoms and clinical findings may all support the suspicion of malingering. The following case illustrates these issues.

C. R., a 45-year-old, right-handed, divorced man, reported being in his usual state of health until he was physically assaulted by a police officer during an altercation. The patient claimed to have been struck on the right side of his head, and suffered lacerations of his scalp and mouth. Since the time of that incident, 4 months prior to the evaluation, Mr. R. has complained of difficulties concentrating, episodes of disorientation, tremulousness, depression, and severe memory difficulties. He has filed suit against the police department for battery.

Two EEGs, a CT scan, and an MRI scan were all negative. Brainstem evoked potentials were reported to be abnormal, and visual nystagmus was noted on lateral gaze. He drinks alcohol and at times had been a daily drinker.

On examination, the patient was withholding and guarded. At several times during the evaluation, it appeared as if he was not performing at his best. Twice during the assessment, Mr. R. experienced "spells"; he would start to complain of feeling depressed, hyperventilate, hold his hands to his forehead, sob, and pound the table in frustration. No tears were ever observed, and the patient was able to continue conversing throughout these episodes. There was no indication of alteration of consciousness during these spells.

On self-report inventories, the patient described himself as being in severe psychological distress. He endorsed a great many symptoms of psychopathology and cognitive inefficiency. On a short-form of the Wechsler Adult Intelligence Scale (WAIS-R), Mr. R. obtained an estimated IQ of 96. This is within the average range of intellectual abilities and is consistent with his educational history (high-school graduate) and occupational status (salesman). However, it may be a slight underestimate of his true potential, as one subtest had to be discontinued due to the patient's "spells."

On the Wechsler Memory Scale, C. R. obtained a Memory Quotient of 103. This is also within the average range, and consistent with his IQ. However, there was very extreme scatter between subtests. Mr. R.'s immediate recall of text passages read to him was extremely poor, at approximately the second percentile of normal individuals his age (Crosson, Hughes, Roth, & Monkowski, 1984; Osborne & Davis, 1978). At the same time, his immediate reproduction of geometric designs was excellent, at approximately the 98th percentile. A discrepancy of this magnitude is extremely unlikely in a patient without a gross lesion of the dominant hemisphere. In addition, the patient failed to remember very easy word pairs (e.g., fruit–apple, rose–flower) on trial two of the Associate Learning subtest, after having just reported them correctly on trial one. Again, all but the most amnesic, demented, or delirious patients can typically do this.

Although this patient presented with some neurological symptoms, there was little in his cognitive profile that can be attributed specifically to brain dysfunction. The "spells" observed were qualitatively unlike those of neurological etiology (i.e., epileptic seizures) and were judged to be probably motivated by secondary gain. Whether they were intentionally staged or of emotional etiology and outside the patient's conscious control (e.g., conversion symptoms) is unclear. However, the possibility that at least some of Mr. R.'s memory symptoms were malingered had to be considered, especially in light of the fact that he was seeking monetary compensation for neuropsychological damages.

Recently, Wiggins and Brandt (1988) have demonstrated that specific questions in a clinical interview may help distinguish genuine from malingered amnesia. A group of four organic amnesics (of mixed etiologies) and a group of 27 normal young adults were asked a series of autobiographical questions. The questions, listed in Table 5.1, were judged to be very simple for even moderately impaired amnesics. These same questions were asked of 27 normal young adults who were asked to simulate amnesia. The responses were categorized as either (1) correct or plausible, or (2) incorrect or implausible (including statements such as "I don't know"). As can be seen in Table 5.2, the malingerers gave incorrect or implausible answers much more

Table 5.2. Wiggins and Brandt Personal History Interview

	Percentage of Subjects Giving Incorrect/Implausible Answers		
Interview Questions	Simulators ($n = 27$)	Amnesics ($n = 4$)	Nonsimulating Controls ($n = 27$)
"What is your . . .			
name?"	25	0	0
age?"	35	0	0
birthdate?"	42	0	0
telephone number?"	42	0	0
address?"	12	0	0
social security number?"	48	25	4
mother's first name?"	17	0	0
mother's maiden name?"	29	0	0
father's first name?"	17	0	0
brother's and/or sister's name?"	23	0	0
"What did you have for . . .			
breakfast this morning?"	25	0	0
dinner last night?"	42	25	0
"What is my (the interviewer's) . . . name?" (Asked on Day 2)			
Recall	37	50	0
Recognition, given 4 choices (if not recalled)	10	0	n/a

frequently than either of the other two groups. The brain-damaged amnesics were able to recall virtually all items of personal identity.

The clinical detection of malingering has often been accomplished by noting inconsistencies among the patient's verbal statements or behaviors (e.g., Kiersch, 1962; Price & Terhune, 1919). The assumption is that if the patient can respond appropriately at one point during the examination, his or her failure to respond appropriately at another is an indication of malingering. Although this approach might make intuitive sense, recent research findings on patients with chronic global amnesia may mitigate against its nonselective use in clinical examinations. It has been demonstrated, for example, that subtle differences in the way that a question is asked or in the task demands can make a striking difference in the performance of genuine amnesics (e.g., Graf, Squire, & Mandler, 1984). The clinical examiner who is not aware of the importance of these variables may err in diagnosing malingering in a large number of real amnesics.

Electrophysiological Approaches

A few studies have used autonomic nervous system responses to evaluate amnesic patients. The assumption of these studies is that a discrepancy between the patient's verbal report and his or her physiological arousal may reveal a feigned memory deficit. Wiggins, Lombard, Brennan, and Heckel (1964) studied a male patient with a dense time-limited retrograde memory loss that seems to be best described as psychogenic amnesia. The patient was asked both neutral and emotional questions (the latter concerning events during the period of amnesia) while his galvanic skin response (GSR) was recorded. No difference was observed in the magnitude of his GSR to these two types of questions, even though it was demonstrated that deliberate lying would result in a greater amplitude autonomic response in this patient. Thus, there was no indication that the autonomic nervous system "knew" more than the patient verbalized, suggesting, perhaps, that the memory disorder was outside his conscious control. Lynch and Bradford (1980) studied the polygraph examinations of 22 criminal defendants who claimed amnesia. The subjects were classified as having either complete ($N = 2$), "patchy" ($N = 15$), or "hazy" amnesia ($N = 5$) based on interviews, and as either "truthful" ($N = 9$), "indefinite" ($N = 4$), or "deceptive" ($N = 9$) based on the polygraph. In general, the less severe the amnesia being presented ("hazy" being the least severe), the less definitive was the polygraph. Lynch and Bradford also found that deceptive subjects were more likely to have significant personality disorders, as well as less significant histories of alcohol use, than did truthful (genuinely amnesic) subjects. An important limitation on these findings, however, was the absence of any independent criterion for determining whether a given subject was a malingerer or an actual amnesic. Given the very substantial interpretive difficulties inherent in polygraph examinations (Kleinmuntz & Szucko, 1984b; Saxe, Dougherty, & Cross, 1985; see also Chapter 12), the most we can conclude from this study is that some relationship exists between physiological responses, verbal reports, and psychopathological features. Whether any of these sets of variables is related to dissimulation cannot be determined.

Group Studies of Suspected Malingerers

Several investigators have attempted to address the problem of distinguishing genuine from malingering amnesia by examining the psychological differences between groups of suspected malingerers and genuinely amnesic patients. In an early clinical study, Hopwood and Snell (1933) reviewed the case histories of 100 male inmates of a criminal asylum who had pled amnesia at their trials. Based on poorly described criteria, the authors designated 14 of these men as malingerers and 8 as "doubtful" cases. These 22 fraudulent cases were said to be characterized by their youth (19 were under age 40), their ability to recall trivial events surrounding their crimes, and a sudden return of memory. However, it is not clear that these characteristics were determined independent of the criteria used to assign these patients to the fraudulent group.

Kiersch (1962) studied 98 individuals who presented to military hospitals with the primary complaint of amnesia. The patients were given extensive examinations, psychological testing, and interviews under hypnosis and sodium amytal. Forty-one of these individuals admitted to be lying under hypnosis or amytal, and 25 went on to admit their deception in the normal state. This study also identified 24 organic amnesics, 20 psychogenic amnesics, and 13 "mixed" amnesics. The feigned amnesic group differed from the other groups in having: (1) a much higher incidence of court-martial cases (66%), (2) a higher incidence of inconsistency in reported history, both between examiners and to the same examiner at different times (36%), (3) a trend toward more frequent character and behavior disorders, and (4) very rapid recovery (92% of the admitted malingerers).

A recent study by Parwatikar, Holcomb, and Menninger (1985) examined two groups of alleged murderers: 24 men who claimed amnesia for their crimes but did not deny committing the crimes, and 50 men who confessed to their crimes. The MMPIs and clinical histories of these two groups of subjects were compared. The authors reported that the subjects claiming amnesia had higher elevations on scales 1 (Hs), 2 (D) and 3 (Hy) of the MMPI than those who confessed to their crimes. Eighty-seven percent of those who claimed amnesia were intoxicated at the time of the alleged murders, compared to 42% of the confessed murderers. The data were then subjected to a stepwise discriminant function analysis, which classified subjects as either amnesic or confessed. The two variables of intoxication and MMPI scale 3 correctly classified 45 of the 50 confessed murders and 17 of the 24 self-proclaimed amnesics. The authors then made the unjustifiable assumption that the 7 self-proclaimed amnesics who were misclassified by the discriminant function analysis were actually malingerers. Although all these suspected malingerers were intoxicated at the time of their offenses, they had low scores on scale 3 of the MMPI. (Interestingly, these malingerers were younger than the genuine amnesics—see Hopwood & Snell, 1933.) This study by Parwatikar et al. suffers from the same interpretive problem as Lynch and Bradford's (1980) polygraph study, since none of the subjects in this study admitted that they had feigned their memory disorders. Conclusions from either study are unjustified in the absence of independent confirming evidence of malingering. Clearly, research in this field would be furthered greatly by the study of self-proclaimed amnesics who eventually confess their deceitfulness.

Newer Experimental Approaches

Research psychologists have recently begun to apply laboratory-based experimental paradigms to the problem of uncovering malingered amnesia. These procedures are generally based on the premise that the malingerer who is naive to the phenomenology of genuine amnesia will "overplay" the role and perform memory tasks more poorly than true amnesics. Occasionally, these studies have found that the presumed malingerers will perform at a level below that expected by chance (i.e., if the subject had absolutely no knowledge of the material and simply guessed). The two-alternative, forced-choice procedure appears to be particularly useful for these studies (Theodor & Mandelcorn, 1973). Since the baseline probability of success by guessing is 50% with this procedure, an individual with absolutely no knowledge at all of the material in question (i.e., a severe global amnesic) should perform at 50% accuracy. Any performance significantly below this level of accuracy (determined by reference to the binomial distribution) indicates a deliberate withholding of knowledge. With enough trials, the would-be malingerer finds it difficult to conform his or her responses to the statistical requirements of ignorance.

Pankratz and associates (Pankratz, 1979; Pankratz, Fausti, & Peed, 1975) have developed a Symptom Validity Test (see Chapter 10) which has been useful in both the detection and treatment of psychogenic or malingered symptoms. The basic paradigm involves presenting the subject with many discrete trials in which a target stimulus is present half of the time. Absolute ignorance of, or insensitivity to, the stimulus would yield very close to 50% accuracy, given a sufficient number of trials. In 1983, Pankratz studied three patients suspected of malingered amnesia with a memory version of his test. The task required the subjects to remember for 15 seconds which of two colored lights had been illuminated. After only 10 trials, a suspected malingerer who had been performing at chance began to perform at 100% accuracy. Next, a more difficult task was used, requiring memory of a three-digit number. The patient was then successful in recognizing the target number in 15 out of 15 trials. Apparently, the relatively nonthreatening task allowed the patient to give up his symptoms (Pankratz, 1983).

In a recent pilot study, Brandt, Rubinsky, and Lassen (1985) adapted Pankratz's procedure to a verbal memory paradigm, which was then administered to limited organic amnesics, normal individuals, and normal persons asked to simulate amnesia. First, a list of 20 words was read to each subject and free-recall was obtained. Next, a two-alternative, forced-choice recognition test was administered. Each target word was presented to the subject along with a distractor word. The subject's task was to recognize the target word. The 95% confidence interval for chance performance on the recognition test ranges from 6 to 14 correct. Although all of the normal individuals performed better than chance and 6 of the 19 amnesics performed at chance (the rest performing better than chance), 3 of the 10 malingerers performed *worse* than chance. Performance significantly worse than chance clearly indicates that, at some level of awareness, the target items are "known."

An attempted replication of this pilot study was recently undertaken (Wiggins & Brandt, 1988). University students and community volunteers were paid to simulate amnesia due to head trauma, emotional trauma, or of unspecified etiology. Their performances were compared with those of patients with neurologically based memory disorders (mostly limited organic amnesia due to head trauma) and normal, nonsimulating controls. Each subject was read one of two lists of concrete nouns. Immediately thereafter, free recall was obtained. The simulators performed better than the amnesics and worse than the normal individuals. The three subgroups of malingerers did not differ according to their assigned etiology. Next, each target word was paired with a distractor from the nonpresented list, and two-alternative, forced-choice recognition was obtained. Here, the simulators performed worse than both the amnesics and the normal persons (see Figure 5.1). In this study, none of the subjects performed below what chance would predict (6 to 14 correct recognitions). However, 21% of the simulators performed *at* chance, compared with only 8% of the amnesics and 2% of the normal individuals. Apparently, malingerers believe that the recognition memory of amnesics is much poorer than it actually is. Further research will be needed to determine whether a criterion score for recognition performance has sufficient predictive value to be used as a test of malingering.

Experimental research in the past decade has been particularly productive in illustrating that even patients with the most severe chronic global amnesia can learn new information and display the effects of learning experiences when tested appropriately (Warrington & Weiskrantz, 1974; Moscovitch, 1984). Globally amnesic patients display their memory deficits most strikingly on tasks which require them to remember explicitly, in the

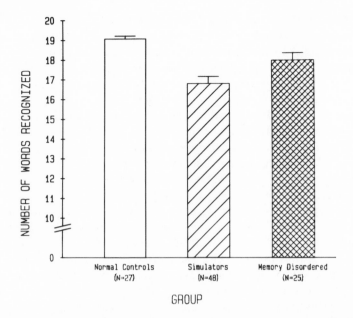

Figure 5.1. Number of words recognized on two-alternative, forced-choice recognition (from Wiggins & Brandt, 1988).

ordinary sense of recollecting, information with which they have been presented. However, they typically perform much better, and often at normal levels, on tests of *implicit memory*. These are tasks which, on the surface, do not ask subjects to remember an event, but where a prior learning experience facilitates subsequent performance. Thus, chronic global amnesics are often able to learn and retain a variety of motor, perceptual, and cognitive skills, even while they have no recollection of the learning episodes themselves, and may be unaware of having learned something new (Corkin, 1965, 1968; Moscovitch, 1982, 1984; Warrington & Weiskrantz, 1968). Korsakoff amnesics, for example, can learn and retain the skill of reading mirror-reversed words without explicitly remembering the words themselves (Cohen, 1984). This phenomenon, however, may be particular to certain patient populations (see Martone, Butters, Payne, Becker, & Sax, 1984).

Another illustration of preserved implicit memory in organic amnesics is provided by the phenomena of priming (Diamond & Rozin, 1984). Amnesic subjects asked to memorize test stimuli (e.g., words) will typically perform poorly on a variety of explicit tests of retention. However, these same subjects will display their acquisition and storage of the stimuli on tasks that are seemingly unrelated to memory. For example, Graf and associates (1984) tested the ability of amnesics and normal subjects to remember a word list under four testing conditions: (1) free-recall, (2) yes/ no recognition, (3) cued recall, where the subjects were provided with the first three letters of each of the target words and asked to use this cue to assist them in remembering the words, and (4) wordstem completion. In this fourth condition, subjects were shown the first three letters of the target words, but were asked simply to complete each wordstem with the first word that came to mind. No suggestion was given that the wordstems serve as cues for remembering the items on the word list. The amnesic subjects in this study performed more poorly than the normal individuals on the first three measures, all of which are explicit tests of memory. However, they performed as well as the normal subjects on the wordstem completion task, a test which requires memory only implicitly.

Wiggins and Brandt (1988) recently attempted to distinguish simulated from genuine amnesia by exploiting the assumption that the average layperson would have little knowledge of the retained implicit memory of amnesics and would thus overplay the role and perform implicit memory tasks much more poorly than genuine amnesics. In these experiments, all of which involved the learning of word lists, an additional qualitative feature of memory performance was also examined. In remembering lists of items, normal individuals typically display a serial position effect in free recall (Murdock, 1962). Items at the beginning and at the end of the list are more often recalled than words in the middle. That is, normal subjects display both a primacy (beginning of list) and a recency (end of list) effect in free recall. Chronic organic amnesics of several etiologies typically exhibit a relatively normal recency effect but a very attenuated primacy effect (Baddeley & Warrington, 1970; Milner, 1978). The authors predicted that the average malingerer would not be aware of this qualitative feature of organic amnesia and so would generate a normal serial position curve, rather than one without a primacy component, in his or her free recall of word lists.

Wiggins and Brandt (1988) gave 48 normal subjects instructions to simulate amnesias of varying etiologies. The malingerers were given no instructions about the severity of the memory disorders they were to feign nor any information about amnesic syndromes. This malingering group was compared with a group of 27 nonsimulating normal controls and with a group of 4 chronic amnesics of varying neurological etiologies on two verbal memory tasks. The first was a wordstem completion task similar to that of Graf et al. (1984). Subjects attempted free recall of a 20-word list and then (in an ostensibly unrelated task) completed 40 wordstems, half of which could be completed with the target words. It was predicted that the malingerers would purposely inhibit the tendency to complete the wordstem with the target word and so would not display the normal priming effect that even genuine amnesics produce. The following day, the wordstem completion task was readministered to all subjects.

The second task was a word association test. A set of 40 words and their most frequent associations (according to published norms) was constructed. Subjects were read a list of 20 of the associates (i.e., the response words) for free recall. Then, the 40 stimulus words were read to the subjects whose task it was to respond with the first word that came to mind. Subjects who respond with the previously heard associate words more often than with the not previously heard associates demonstrate a priming effect and, hence, implicit memory.

On the wordstem completion task, the normal controls displayed both a primacy and a recency effect in free recall, whereas the amnesics, as expected, displayed only a recency effect. The simulators, however, showed a normal serial position effect in free recall, similar to the normal controls and unlike the organic amnesics (see Figure 5.2). Contrary to prediction, however, the simulators, like the amnesics and normal controls, exhibited a priming effect. On both Days 1 and 2, they tended to complete the wordstems with target words.

On the free recall portion of the word association test, the simulators performed as poorly as the amnesics. Again, however, the simulators generated a normal serial position curve, whereas the genuine amnesics had a grossly abnormal primacy portion (see Figure 5.3). A small priming effect

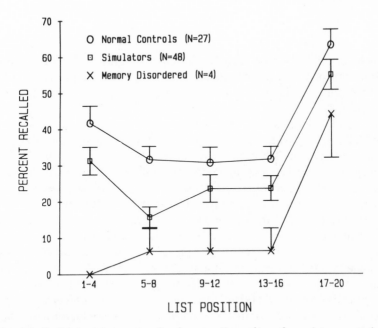

Figure 5.2. Serial position curves for free recall portion of wordstem completion task (from Wiggins & Brandt, 1988).

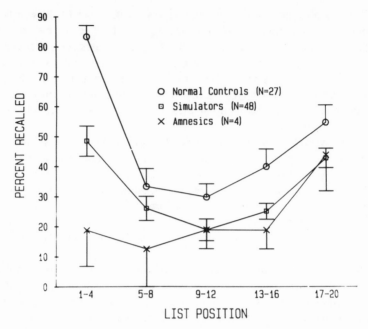

Figure 5.3. Serial position curves for free recall portion of word association task (from Wiggins & Brandt, 1988).

was found in all three groups on the word association portion. In retrospect, the selection of more distant associates might have been preferable to the most frequent associates for producing a priming effect and eliciting group differences.

Normal individuals faking amnesia are apparently not aware of the free-recall serial position phenomenon in amnesia and therefore fail to perform as expected. These data also suggest, however, that tests of implicit memory (e.g., wordstem completion or word association) may not be as useful as initially expected for the detection of malingered amnesia. Simulators perform these tasks normally. At least two possible explanations for this can be offered. First, priming and activation may fall outside the domain of what most people consider "memory" and hence are not deemed appropriate to be faked when one plays at being amnesic. Alternately, priming and activation may be relatively automatic and largely unconscious memory processes that can not be disengaged by deliberate faking.

Recently, Schacter (1986b) has used memory confidence ratings to discriminate genuine from simulated amnesia. In one study, normal subjects were shown videotapes of complex events and subsequently interrogated about individual events that were nearly impossible to recall. One group of subjects was supplied the correct answers and instructed to simulate amnesia for the remainder of the experiment. A second group did not receive this information. A different experimenter then interviewed all the subjects and asked them to rate the likelihood that they could remember the event in question under each of three conditions: (1) if they were given more time to do so, (2) if they were provided with hints, and (3) if they were given a multiple-choice recognition test. Although both groups gave their highest rating to the multiple-choice recognition procedure and their lowest rating to being given more time, the simulators gave overall lower ratings than the nonsimulators. That is, the simulators expressed lower confidence that they would ever be able to remember the event. These data are encouraging in suggesting that self-assessment of memory may aid in the identification of feigned ignorance. However, the nonsimulators in Schacter's study were uninformed of the critical event and not truly "amnesic" in the clinical sense. It is likely that these individuals never encoded the critical information due to normal inattention, rather than having forgotten it due to a pathological condition.

Future Research Directions

One avenue of research which remains relatively unexplored in the detection of faked amnesia is that of the chronometric analysis of behavior. As several authors have observed (Resnick, 1984), malingerers are more likely to have long latencies in responding to questions. This may be especially true of malingered amnesics, since they may be first inhibiting a correct response and then fabricating an alternative one. As reviewed by Rogers (1987), stalling, hedging, and requests for repetition of questions may be typical of malingerers in a variety of contexts.

Another approach to the uncovering of malingered amnesia that has not yet been subjected to careful, scientific consideration is an examination of the quality of erroneous responses. Several authors have suggested that individuals faking amnesia may give a large number of Ganser-type responses (Anderson, Trethowan, & Kenna, 1959; Bash & Alpert, 1980; Pankratz, 1983). These responses are near-miss or approximate answers, which often have a ridiculous quality to them (such as saying that the colors of the American flag are red, white, and green).

Clinical Applications

At the present time, there are no scientifically valid and reliable clinical techniques for determining with certainty whether an individual is feigning amnesia. Although the newer cognitive psychological procedures may reveal some significant differences among groups of normal individuals, amnesics, and normal persons simulating amnesia, they are clearly not of a sensitivity, specificity, or predictive value that would make them useful for clinical decision-making in individual cases. The distributions of performances of simulating and amnesic groups on virtually all clinical tests and experimental tasks overlap considerably. Thus, deviant performances may raise the question of intentional malingering, but do not provide incontrovertible proof of such. A threshold model is presented in Table 5.3, which summarizes the features that should alert the clinician to the possibility of malingered amnesia. The more of these features present, the more likely it may be that the patient is deceitful in his or her purported memory deficits.

Table 5.3 offers a synthesis of presenting complaints and clinical characteristics which should raise the index of suspicion for malingered amnesia. A complicating factor in investigating suspected amnesia is the possibility of mixed etiologies and the coexistence of organic, functional, and simulated symptoms.

A major thrust of this text is the development of clinical decision models for the determination of malingered disorders. Unfortunately, the empirical studies of simulated amnesia do not provide adequate clinical indicators for achieving reliable discriminations needed for such a model. In cases of suspected amnesia, a broad array of clinical methods should be employed, including neurological consultations and neuropsychological assessment. Finally, patients suspected of feigned amnesia should be given an opportunity to explain apparent inconsistencies in their presentation. In this regard, the implausibility of patients' explanations (such as "my mind suddenly became crystal-clear") or marked improvements in subsequent test performance may be indicative of malingered amnesia.

Table 5.3. Threshold Model for Malingered Amnesia

Consider malingered amnesia if any of the following are present:
A. Criminal charges pending
B. Loss of general knowledge or skill
C. Impairment of immediate memory (e.g., digit span)
D. Poor free recall with normal serial position curve
E. Forced-choice recognition memory worse than chance
F. Low confidence ratings to potential memory aids (e.g., more time, cues)
G. For patients with known or suspected neurological disorders:
   1. Inconsistent pattern of deficits (requires expertise in disease-specific and lesion-specific memory impairments)
   2. Loss of personal identity (e.g., name, address)
H. For patients without neurological disorders:
   1. Severe deficits in new learning
   2. Low scores on MMPI Scales 1, 2, and 3 (if intoxicated during amnesic episode)

Conclusions

The detection of malingered amnesia is a particularly difficult assessment task. In clinical situations, the investigator is hampered by both the diverse forms of real amnesia as well as by the absence of any external criteria for malingering (other than confession). Reliance on simulation studies, on the other hand, neglects the motivational and personality factors that may be at work in the actual malingerer. The forensic expert must be prepared to combine data from the subject's clinical history, presentation and pattern of cognitive deficits with available research literature on both real and simulated amnesia in making the determination of malingering. Just how these various factors should be combined in individual cases is highly dependent on the clinical presentation and available psychological measures.

6

Malingering of Posttraumatic Disorders

PHILLIP J. RESNICK

Psychiatric disorders that occur after trauma include posttraumatic stress disorders (PTSD), depressive disorders, anxiety disorders, conversion disorders, postconcussion syndromes, and occasionally, psychoses. This chapter will focus primarily on malingered PTSD, but it will also cover concussion, conversion disorders, and the *compensation neurosis* controversy. Special emphasis will be given to malingered PTSD in the Vietnam veteran.

The concept of traumatic neuroses first arose from the belief that an accidental concussion to the spine caused abnormalities of the sympathetic nervous system (Clevenger, 1889). The disorder was seized upon by dishonest litigants seeking compensation after accidents (Hamilton, 1906). Prior to this concept, personal injury cases were based on obvious injuries, such as loss of a limb or an eye, shown by unmistakable objective evidence (Trimble, 1981).

Posttraumatic disorders have been given many labels since 1889 (see Table 6.1). Diagnostically, PTSD was classified as gross stress reaction in DSM-I (American Psychiatric Association, 1952) and was subsumed within the diagnostic category of "adjustment reaction to adult life" in DSM-II (American Psychiatric Association, 1968). The introduction of PTSD as an official diagnosis in DSM-III (American Psychiatric Association, 1980) caused a sharp increase in clinicians' sensitivity to this disorder, and heightened concern about potential malingering. The diagnostic criteria for PTSD in DSM-III-R (American Psychiatric Association, 1987) are listed in Table 6.2.

Definitions

Malingering is listed in DSM-III-R (American Psychiatric Association, 1987) as a condition not attributable to a mental disorder. It is defined as the intentional production of false or grossly exaggerated physical or psycho-

Phillip J. Resnick, Division of Forensic Psychiatry, Case Western Reserve University, Cleveland, Ohio.

Table 6.1. Names Used to Describe PTSD

Accident neurosis	Postaccident anxiety syndrome
Accident victim syndrome	Post-accident syndrome
Aftermath neurosis	Posttraumatic syndrome
American disease	Profit neurosis
Attitudinal pathosis	Railway spine
Compensation hysteria	Rape trauma syndrome
Compensation neurosis	Secondary gain neurosis
Compensationitis	Traumatic hysteria
Fright neurosis	Traumatic neurasthenia
Greek disease	Traumatic neurosis
Greenback neurosis	Triggered neurosis
Justice neurosis	Unconscious malingering
Litigation neurosis	Vertebral neurosis
Mediterranean back	Wharfie's back
Mediterranean disease	Whiplash neurosis
Neurotic neurosis	

Note. Adapted from Mendelson (1984).

logical symptoms motivated by external incentives, such as financial compensation. In contrast, *factitious disorders* involve the intentional production of symptoms in order to assume a patient role. Both disorders require a deceitful state of mind.

Several other terms are useful in the description of malingering phenomena. *Pure malingering* is the feigning of disease when it does not exist at all in a particular patient. *Partial malingering* is the conscious exaggeration of existing symptoms or the fraudulent allegation that prior genuine symptoms are still present. In addition, the term, *false imputation* refers to the ascribing of actual symptoms to a cause consciously recognized to have no relationship to the symptoms. For example, authentic psychiatric symptoms due to clearly defined stresses at home may be falsely attributed to a traumatic event at work in order to gain compensation. In addition to conscious deception, some individuals mistakenly believe that there is a relationship between an accident and their psychological or physical disability. These patients may fail to realize that consecutive events do not necessarily have a causal relationship (Collie, 1917). Such genuine misperceptions should be differentiated from conscious attempts at deception.

Reluctance to Diagnose Malingering

The authenticity of mental illness, which is identified largely on the basis of observed behavior and subjective history, can be challenged less readily than the authenticity of physical illness, which is often verified on the basis of

Table 6.2. DSM-III-R Criteria for PTSD

A. The person has experienced an event that is outside the range of usual human experience and that would be markedly distressing to almost anyone, including any of the following:
   1. Serious threat to one's life or physical integrity
   2. Serious threat or harm to one's children, spouse, or other close relatives and friends
   3. Sudden destruction of one's home or community
   4. Seeing another person who has recently been, or is being, seriously injured or killed as the result of an accident or physical violence.
B. The traumatic event is persistently reexperienced in at least one of the following ways:
   1. Recurrent and intrusive distressing recollections of the event (in young children, repetitive play in which themes or aspects of the trauma are expressed)
   2. Recurrent distressing dreams of the event
   3. Sudden acting or feeling as if the traumatic event were recurring (includes a sense of reliving the experience, illusions, hallucinations, and dissociative [flashback] episodes, even those that occur upon awakening or when intoxicated)
   4. Intense psychological distress at exposure to events that symbolize or resemble an aspect of the traumatic event, including anniversaries of the trauma.
C. Persistent avoidance of stimuli associated with the trauma or numbing of general responsiveness (not present before the trauma), as indicated by at least three of the following:
   1. Efforts to avoid thoughts or feelings associated with the trauma
   2. Efforts to avoid activities or situations that arouse recollections of the trauma
   3. Inability to recall an important aspect of the trauma (psychogenic amnesia)
   4. Markedly diminished interest in significant activities (in young children, loss of recently acquired developmental skills such as toilet training or language skills)
   5. Feelings of detachment or estrangement from others
   6. Restricted range of affect, e.g., unable to have loving feelings
   7. Sense of foreshortened future, e.g., child does not expect to have a career, marriage or children, or a long life.
D. Persistent symptoms of increased arousal (not present before the trauma), as indicated by at least two of the following:
   1. Difficulty falling or staying asleep
   2. Irritability or outbursts of anger
   3. Difficulty concentrating
   4. Hypervigilance
   5. Exaggerated startle response
   6. Physiological reactivity upon exposure to events that symbolize or resemble an aspect of the traumatic event (e.g., a woman who was raped in an elevator breaks out in a sweat when entering any elevator)
E. Duration of the disturbance (symptoms in B, C, and D) of at least 1 month.

---

physical and biological evidence of disease. Indeed, the nonpsychiatric physician is more prone than the psychiatrist to identify malingering. Mental health professionals have a low index of suspicion for malingering, given the wide range of conditions that must be considered before making the diagnosis (Pollack, 1982). For example, 11 psychiatric reports failed to mention the possibility of malingering in a man who was "mute" for 2 years after a head injury. However, a skeptical neurologist observed the man speaking normally during a train trip after an office visit (Miller & Cartlidge, 1972).

Concern over legal liability is a major reason for clinicians' hesitancy to label someone a malingerer, even though court testimony about malingering is protected by immunity (Restatement, Torts Sec. 589, 1938). However, most authors conservatively suggest that the clinician should only state that there is no objective evidence to support the patient's subjective complaints (e.g., Davidson, 1952). The possibility of provoking a physical assault by calling a person a malingerer is another source of concern (Hofling, 1965). For instance, one Australian man committed suicide after killing two orthopedic surgeons and wounding a third who had diagnosed him as malingering a back injury (Parker, 1979). An autopsy demonstrated no back injury, thereby proving the doctors "dead right."

Hurst (1940) suggested that there are only two situations in which a diagnosis of malingering can be confirmed with certainty: (1) when malingerers are caught in the act when they think they are unobserved and (2) when malingerers actually confess. Unless the clinician has very strong evidence, it is usually best to state that a firm conclusion is not possible. Although an incorrect diagnosis of a mental disease reflects only upon the clinician, a misdiagnosis of malingering may do a grave injustice to the patient.

Incidence

The incidence of malingered psychological symptoms after injury is unknown. Estimates vary from 1% (Keiser, 1968) to over 50% (Henderson, 1986; Miller & Cartlidge, 1972) depending on whether the source works for insurance companies or plaintiffs' attorneys. The incidence of malingering varies with the nation's economy; for example, it increases when layoffs are imminent (Downing, 1942). Pure malingering is considered rare in posttraumatic cases, but exaggeration of symptoms is quite common (Jones & Llewellyn, 1917; Trimble, 1981). Some malingered claims of psychic damages originate after claims for physical injury are unsuccessful (Henderson, 1986, personal communication).

The incidence of diagnosed malingering varies with the astuteness and skepticism of the clinician. Braverman (1978) found only seven "true" malingerers out of 2,500 industrially injured persons; each malingerer immediately terminated his or her case when confronted with the clinician's suspicion of malingering. A U.S. General Accounting Office follow-up study on persons considered 100% disabled was more alarming. Approximately 40% of those studied showed *no* disability whatsoever 1 year after their disability determinations (Maloney, Glasser, & Ward 1980).

Motivation and Legal Context

North American society has become so litigious that the hypothetical response of an injured worker who has just regained consciousness after a brick has fallen on his head is not "Where am I?" but "Whose brick was it?" (Trimble, 1981). When litigants claim personal injury, especially psychological symptoms after an accident, the public often suspects that they are malingering. Opinions expressed in the media contribute to this skepticism. For example, Berman (1987) wrote, "In most civil liability cases before the bar, you can count on more chicanery, lying, and misrepresentation than a household with a cheating husband, a spendthrift wife, and a teenage delinquent. Another co-conspirator is the malingerer, with his lawyer-fostered dreams of living high on the hog ever after. Tort was its name, but now fraud is its game" (p. 10A). There are few personal injury cases that reach the courts where no allegation of malingering is expressed or at least implied (Lipman, 1962).

Public hostility toward the suspected malingerer is understandable, especially in view of the fact that the malingerer's undeserved financial gain is necessarily associated with another's undeserved loss (Braverman, 1978). Suspicions of malingering help to explain why damages awarded for post-traumatic psychological symptoms are substantially less than those for physical injury, in spite of the fact that limitations on the patient's life may be actually greater (Trimble, 1981).

The primary motivation to malinger PTSD is financial gain. Once an individual becomes a litigant in a personal injury suit or files a worker's compensation claim, the efforts of attorneys for both the plaintiff and defendant may alter the patient's attitudes and the course of the illness. The plaintiff's lawyer may over dramatize the client's impairment to the point of being "a salesman of pain, sorrow, agony, and suffering" (Averbach, 1963, p. 195). In contrast, defense attorneys often assume an attitude of disbelief and imply that the individual is not suffering from *any* genuine psychiatric symptoms. Such litigants may understandably become angry based on the belief that they are going to be cheated (Enelow, 1971).

It is the rare individual who is not influenced to some degree by the possibility that an injury may lead to financial gain (Keiser, 1968). Schafer (1986) believes that having a compensable injury promotes a "little larceny" in most litigants. Financial compensation has different meanings to different people. To one claimant, money may represent security. To another, it means revenge against a hated employer or the person responsible for the accident. To a third, money may serve as a symbol of love. In addition to financial compensation, sympathy and social support may be consciously sought by malingerers (Keiser, 1968).

In cases in which exaggeration or partial malingering is combined with real injury, compensation should be made relative to the extent of the actual injury (Keiser, 1968). Legally, malingering constitutes fraud; if it can be proved, the claimant is not entitled to any payment for the alleged condition. To actually convict an individual of perjury, however, the jury must be convinced beyond a reasonable doubt of intentional faking. Such convictions are rare; it is far more common for civil juries simply to make no award in cases in which they believe that the plaintiff is malingering.

Psychiatric Symptoms Following Trauma

Psychoses are infrequently malingered after personal injury. Although fraudulent plaintiffs are willing to go to a great deal of trouble to get substantial awards, they are rarely willing to be committed to psychiatric hospitals (Davidson, 1952). They are likely to malinger PTSD, and less often depression. In cases of PTSD that follow accidents, the clinical picture may be complicated by physical symptoms, pain, and the sequelae of concussion.

Concussion

Approximately 400,000 closed head injuries occur each year in the United States (Moulton, 1987). PTSD is commonly seen after vehicular accidents that cause head injury and concussion. *Postconcussive syndrome* is manifested by headaches, increased anxiety, emotional lability, concentration deficits, and memory problems (Lishman, 1978). Even without loss of consciousness, head injuries may cause symptoms that can be easily confused with PTSD (Trimble, 1981).

Epidemiological studies indicate that a considerable number of minor head trauma patients report memory impairment, difficulty concentrating, a low threshold for fatigue, and abnormal levels of irritability (Wrightston & Gronwall, 1980). Barth et al., (1983) found that neuropsychological assessment three months after minor head injury (i.e., unconsciousness for less than 20 minutes) showed reduced cognitive efficiency in patients who were not involved in litigation. Mild dysphoria, general psychological discomfort, and problems returning to previous employment were associated with this cognitive dysfunction. In assessing cognitive changes, Wechsler intelligence scores are not particularly sensitive to subtle changes in information processing (Rutherford, Merrett, & McDonald, 1977; Wrightston & Gronwall, 1980). Neuropsychological assessment, with its focus on attention–concentration skills, visuomotor functioning, memory abilities, and emotional status is more useful in the differential diagnosis of head injury and PTSD.

Trimble (1981) observed that available techniques are not sufficient to detect the subtle organic changes that may result from head injury. For example, brain injury due to axonal shearing may not be evident on CT [computerized tomography] scans (Moulton, 1987). In addition, the regions of the brain primarily affected by closed head injuries are the midbrain, temporal and frontal cortex, and areas close to the limbic system. Lesions in these sites may lead to changes in behavior, mood, and feeling without significant cognitive disability.

Kelly (1975) suggested that posttraumatic syndrome is originally the result of minor cerebral damage. From this perspective, impairment is perpetuated mainly by the negative attitudes of the medical profession, which are evidenced by: (1) failure to explain the cause of the symptoms in the first place, (2) denial of the symptoms' existence or the unsympathetic declaration that they are related to the question of compensation, (3) refusing to give proper treatment, and (4) declaring that the symptoms will not disappear until the case is settled.

Conversion Disorder

Patients may have persistent pain or loss of physical functioning after an injury that cannot be explained by organic pathology. The differential diagnosis includes malingering, conversion disorder, and psychogenic pain disorder. The distinction between conversion disorder and malingering can be extremely difficult (see Chapter 2). In both conditions, clinicians are confronted with similar discrepancies between laboratory findings and self-report, between objective signs and subjective symptoms. Tests for malingering that are valid with reference to organic diseases are invalid in conversion disorders (Lipman, 1962; Smith, 1967). The differential diagnosis is further complicated by the fact that individuals with conversion disorders may also malinger.

Both malingerers and patients with conversion disorder may avoid unpleasant activity (e.g., disliked work) and seek support (e.g., financial) from the environment. The critical element that distinguishes conversion disorder from malingering is that conversion symptoms are not under voluntary control. Patients with conversion disorders deceive themselves as well as others; malingerers consciously deceive others, but not themselves (see Table 6.3). Disability due to conversion disorder may serve a wide range of psychological needs. It may legitimize latent dependent needs, allow punitive retaliation against an employer or a spouse, provide escape from an intolerable situation, accomplish temporary resolution of preexist-

Table 6.3. Malingering and Conversion Disorder

Diagnosis	Symptoms for Gain	Awareness of Purpose
Malingering	Yes	Yes
Conversion disorder	Yes	No

Note. Adapted from Trimble (1981).

ing life conflicts, allay anxiety and insecurity, or indulge a masochistic need to experience pain (Martin, 1970).

In contrast to the malingerer, the person with conversion disorder is ill; if the illness can be shown to be caused by a particular injury, it is compensable (Cole, 1970). The clinician's ability to distinguish conversion disorder from malingering depends on his or her ability to measure consciousness, an extremely difficult task. With respect to consciousness, Rosanoff (1920) wrote, "It is strange that so futile a consideration, one so obviously belonging to the domain of metaphysics and not science, as the question of a degree of consciousness of a mental process should . . . be chosen as a criterion of clinical diagnosis!" (p. 310).

Jonas and Pope (1985) suggested that there may be a gender bias in the present diagnostic scheme. Clinicians tend to diagnose somatization disorder and conversion disorder primarily in women—as if clinicians believe that women are the preferred victims of unconscious conflicts and lack voluntary control. In contrast, men are more often assigned a diagnosis of malingering, implying that men tend to be consciously aware of their motivations and in command of their actions.

The following clinical characteristics may assist in the differential diagnosis between malingering and conversion disorder (see Table 6.4).

1. The malingerer often presents as sullen, ill-at-ease, suspicious, uncooperative, resentful (Huddleston, 1932), aloof, secretive, and unfriendly (Engel, 1970). Patients with conversion disorder are more likely to be cooperative (Trimble, 1981) and described as appealing, clinging, and dependent (Engel, 1970).

2. The malingerer may try to avoid examination, unless it is required as a condition for receiving some financial benefit (Engel, 1970; Soniat, 1960). The patient with conversion disorder welcomes examinations (Hofling, 1965; Rosanoff, 1920). Whereas the malingerer may decline to cooperate with recommended diagnostic or therapeutic procedures, patients with conversion disorder are typically eager for an organic explanation for their symptoms (Trimble, 1981) and are anxious to be cured (Rosanoff, 1920; Hofling, 1965).

Table 6.4. Differential Diagnosis for Posttraumatic Malingering and Conversion Disorder

Malingering	Conversion Disorder
Uncooperative, suspicious, aloof	Cooperative, appealing, dependent
Avoids examinations	Welcomes examinations
Refuses employment with partial disability	Accepts employment with partial disability
Describes accident in full detail	Describes accident with gaps and inaccuracies

3. The malingerer is likely to give every detail of the accident and its sequelae; the patient with conversion disorder is more likely to give an account that contains gaps, inaccuracies (Huddleston, 1932) and vague generalized complaints (Chaney, Cohn, Williams, & Vincent, 1984).

The Compensation Neurosis Controversy

The term *compensation neurosis* was introduced by Rigler (1879), in reference to the increase in reported disability following railway accidents after compensation laws were introduced in Germany in 1871 (Trimble, 1981). Kennedy (1946, p. 19) described compensation neurosis as a "state of mind, born out of fear, kept alive by avarice, stimulated by lawyers, and cured by a verdict." In a less emotional vein, Rickarby (1979, p. 333) defined compensation neurosis as "that behavior complex associated specifically with the prospect of recompense and is in contradistinction to traumatic neurosis and psychiatric illness . . . precipitated by the stress of illness, accident, or injury." Patients who are perceived to have disability that is out of proportion to the tissue damage after injury are often labeled as exhibiting "compensation neurosis" (Modlin, 1960).

Miller (1961b) contributed to the controversy about compensation neurosis with his paper on "accident neurosis" following head injury. Clinical features of this syndrome included the subjects' unshakeable conviction in their unfitness for work, an inverse relationship between the degree of disability and the severity of the injury, and absolute failure to respond to therapy until the compensation issue was settled. Miller reported that nearly all the patients (48 out of 50) recovered completely without treatment within two years after the claim was settled. Miller (1961b) has often been quoted in both the literature and the courtroom as evidence that patients are likely to improve with cessation of litigation. Many authors have subsequently disputed this claim (Kelly, 1975; Kelly & Smith, 1981; Trimble, 1981; Mendelson, 1982; Mendelson, 1984; Modlin, 1960; Weighill, 1983). One reason for the lack of agreement between Miller and subsequent authors regarding the effect of compensation on posttraumatic disorders is that Miller employed a rather broadly encompassing definition of malingering. Indeed, Miller (1961b, p. 993) suggested that the distinction between conscious and unconscious motives is of little consequence, "Their only purpose is to make the observer believe that the disability is greater than it really is."

Many studies failed to support Miller's (1961b) original findings. For instance, psychological reactions associated with physical illness in Spain, where there is no provision for compensation, differ very little from those associated with compensable accidents in Australia (Parker, 1977). Thompson (1965) found that only 15% of 190 patients with "posttraumatic psychoneurosis" whose claims had been finalized reported that their symptoms were "better" after litigation had concluded. Similarly, Kelly and Smith (1981) found that few patients with posttraumatic syndrome who had not returned to work by the settlement date went on to return after settlement.

Thompson (1965) reported that financial settlement had a negligible benefit on the course of the illness in 500 patients with posttraumatic psychoneurosis. Mendelson (1981) conducted psychiatric evaluations on 101 patients who were referred after auto or industrial accidents. Sixty-seven percent of the patients failed to return to work nearly 16 months after their compensation claim had ended. In a study with important implications, Kelly (1975) found that when treatment was applied early and efficiently in posttraumatic syndromes, compensation and noncompensation cases did not differ in recovery time. Peck, Fordyce, and Black (1978) found that neither litigation nor representation by attorneys had a significant effect on the pain behavior of persons with worker's compensation claims.

Some attorneys and clinicians use the term "compensation neurosis" as a pejorative epithet. Although "neurotic" is often used as a disparaging term, the further designation of "compensation" is doubly demeaning (Modlin, 1960). Moreover, the diagnosis of "compensation neurosis" is invalid because it is not supported by any of the criteria customarily applied to the validation of disease entities (Mendelson, 1985). The literature does not support the view that such patients invariably become symptom free and resume work within months of the resolution of their claims. On the contrary, up to 75% of those injured in compensable accidents may fail to return to gainful employment 2 years after legal settlement (Mendelson, 1982).

Prognosis after Traumatic Injury

Continued incapacity despite apparent medical recovery after an injury may be due to several factors other than malingering. Physical injury and pain often produce a regression, characterized by a breakdown of the more mature coping mechanisms. Injured patients may become totally dependent on their families, physicians, and attorneys, even though they were formerly quite autonomous. Injury that causes incapacity is a stress upon one's psychological integrity, a challenge to one's self-concept as a mature person, and a fundamental threat to one's sense of personal worth. One reaction to such stress is to abandon ambition in favor of more infantile, dependent activities (Miller & Fellner, 1968). Depression can also delay recovery because patients may lack motivation and interest in what happens to them.

Factors associated with a poor prognosis after injury include older age, low back injury, and loss of libido (Mendelson, 1982). Miller (1961b) has suggested malingered psychiatric symptoms after head injury are more frequent in middle-aged men who have not been happy in their jobs. Indeed, employees in their 50s performing heavy or extremely boring work may need little inducement to accept disability payments (Trimble, 1981). Among severe accident victims, Bulman and Wortman (1977) found that blaming another was a predictor of poor coping, whereas self-blame was a predictor of good coping. Inability to return to work by the time of settlement indicates a bad prognosis (Kelly & Smith, 1981).

Clinical Assessment of Malingered PTSD

The diagnosis of malingered PTSD requires a meticulously detailed history of symptoms, treatment efforts, and careful corroboration of information. While taking the history, the clinician must be careful not to communicate any bias or give any clues about how PTSD manifests itself. If the clinician begins the evaluation in a challenging manner, it may cause patients to think that they must exaggerate symptoms in order to be believed.

The diagnosis of PTSD is based almost entirely on the patient's self-report of subjective symptoms. The accessibility of specific DSM-III-R criteria permit the resourceful malingerer to report the "right" symptoms. The assertion that individuals dream or think about a traumatic event should be verified by others who have heard them talk about it in situations that are not related to the litigation. In addition, the clinician must obtain a detailed history of living patterns preceding the stressor. For example, symptoms such as difficulty concentrating or insomnia may have been present before the traumatic event. Baseline activity in a typical week before the trauma took place should be compared with reported impairment at the time of the evaluation. The clinician must carefully examine the reasonableness of the relationship between the symptoms and the stressor, the time elapsed beween the stressor and symptom development, and the relationship between any prior psychiatric symptoms and current impairment.

Third parties should be excluded from the actual evaluation of the patient for two important reasons. First, the presence of relatives precludes using them to verify the accuracy of symptoms. Second, should the clinician wish to gently confront the patient with the possibility of malingering, the absence of a third party will reduce loss of face. A sympathetic understanding about the temptation to exaggerate symptoms of PTSD increases the likelihood that a person will acknowledge it; trying to shame the person is likely to increase anger and denial.

The clinician who suspects malingering may use certain stratagems based on the belief that use of subterfuge in assessing deceit is justified. Insurance companies routinely make surreptitious videotapes of suspected malingerers (Schafer, 1986). When inquiring about the symptoms of PTSD, the clinician may ask about symptoms that are not typically seen in this disorder. For example, inquiry could be made about symptoms such as increased talkativeness, inflated self-esteem, or decreased need for sleep. Within earshot of the patient, mention could also be made of a very atypical symptom, implying that it is usually present; the clinician can then see if the patient complains of this symptom. In particularly difficult assessments, inpatient obervation may be helpful in monitoring alleged symptoms, such as social withdrawal, sleep disturbance, and exaggerated startle reactions.

Psychological Testing

Clayer, Bookless, and Ross (1984) developed an Illness Behavior Questionnaire that could distinguish between individuals told to exaggerate their injury symptoms, neurotics, and normals (See Chapter 10). Chaney *et al.*, (1984) found that the MMPI can be helpful in distinguishing patients with true PTSD from those with functional disorders. The MMPI profiles of patients with PTSD more closely resemble those of patients who have organic disease, with pain caused by organic pathology, than the profiles of patients with psychogenic pain and/or hypochondriasis.

Sodium Amytal Interviews

The term "truth serum" is a misnomer for Sodium Amytal and other drug assisted interviews. Although Amytal is sometimes useful in recovering genuinely repressed memories, it is not reliable in unmasking malingering (see Chapter 14). Both Baro (1950) and Hofling (1965) found that persons simulating traumatic neurosis retained or further exaggerated their malingered symptoms upon receiving Sodium Amytal. One half of the subjects in the Redlich, Ravitz, & Dession (1951) study were able to maintain a lie under the influence of Sodium Amytal. One soldier, hospitalized for loud outbursts, continued shouting during his Sodium Amytal interview. At one point, however, in the middle of his violent shouting, he said in a quiet voice, "Doctor, give me a cigarette"; he then resumed shouting (Kalman, 1977).

Clinical Applications

I propose a threshold model of eight criteria for determining when clinicians should thoroughly investigate the possibility that an individual is malingering psychological symptoms after a traumatic incident (See Table 6.5). The presence of any one of these criteria in the assessment of PTSD is considered sufficient to meet the threshold model.

A person who has always been a responsible and honest member of society is not likely to malinger PTSD (Davidson, 1952). Malingerers are more likely to be marginal members of society with few binding ties or long-

Table 6.5. Threshold Model for the Evaluation of
Malingering in Posttraumatic Disorders

Any one of the following criteria:
1. Poor work record
2. Prior "incapacitating" injuries
3. Discrepant capacity for work and recreation
4. Unvarying, repetitive dreams
5. Antisocial personality traits
6. Overidealized functioning before the trauma
7. Evasiveness
8. Inconsistency in symptom presentation

---

standing financial responsibilities, such as home ownership (Braverman, 1978). The malingerer may have a history of spotty employment, previous incapacitating injuries, and extensive absences from work. Malingerers frequently depict themselves and their prior functioning in exclusively complimentary terms (Layden, 1966).

The malingerer may incongruously assert an inability to work, but retain the capacity for recreation, for example, enjoyment of theater, television, or card games. In contrast, the patient with genuine PTSD is more likely to withdraw from recreational activities as well as work. The malingerer may pursue a legal claim tenaciously, while alleging depression or incapacitation due to symptoms of PTSD (Davidson, 1952).

Malingerers are unlikely to volunteer information about sexual dysfunction (Chaney et al., 1984; Sadoff, 1978), although they are generally eager to emphasize their physical complaints. Malingerers are also unlikely to volunteer information about nightmares unless they have read the diagnostic criteria for PTSD. Genuine nightmares in PTSD show variations on the theme of the traumatic event (Garfield, 1987). For example, a woman who was raped may have dreams in which she feels helpless and is tortured without being raped. The malingerer who does not know the expected variation in dream patterns may claim repetitive dreams that always reenact the traumatic event in exactly the same way.

Malingerers may seem evasive during the interview and be unwilling to make definite statements about returning to work or financial gain. One method of evading questions is to say that an explanation is too complicated or that it would take too long to explain. When such persons are told that there is no limit on time, they may attempt further evasions, suggesting, for example, that the clinician would not be able to understand the situation even if it were explained (East, 1927).

Contradictions between the first and subsequent versions of events were viewed by Schwartz (1946) as evidence of malingering. However,

depending on inconsistencies of memory as proof of malingering is hazardous. Buckhout (1974) found inaccuracies in memories of observed events in
nonmalingerers. In a series of studies, Loftus (1979) established that memory distortion increases over time, although people become more certain
about the accuracy of their memories. In establishing the presence of malingering, the clinician must differentiate between suspicious memory impairment and expected memory distortions (Rogers & Cavanaugh, 1983).

A clinical decision model for establishing the diagnosis of malingered
PTSD is presented in Table 6.6. This model must be viewed as tentative,
based on the current status of empirical research. The clinical decision
model requires the clinician to establish (1) the individual's motivation for
dissimulation, (2) the presence of at least two associated characteristics, and
(3) strong confirmatory evidence of malingering.

Malingered PTSD in the Vietnam Veteran

In 1979, the U.S. government initiated Operation Outreach to handle read-
justment and psychiatric problems for Vietnam veterans (Lynn & Belza,
1984). Malingering PTSD became much easier after lists of PTSD symptoms were widely distributed by national service organizations (Atkinson,
Henderson, Sparr, & Deale, 1982). In addition, veterans with true PTSD at
Vet Centers and Veteran's Administration (V.A.) hospitals provided other
veterans with opportunities to become aware of these symptoms (Lynn &
Belza).

Estimates of the prevalence of PTSD among Vietnam veterans have
ranged from 20 to 70% (Ashlock, Walker, Starkey, Harmand, & Michel,
1987; Friedmann, 1981; Green, Wilson, & Lindy, 1981). The incidence of
malingered or factitious PTSD in the Reno V.A. Hospital was seven out of

Table 6.6. Clinical Decision Model for Establishing Malingered PTSD

A. Understandable motive to malinger PTSD
B. At least two of the following criteria:
   1. Irregular employment or job dissatisfaction
   2. Prior claims for injuries
   3. Capacity for recreation, but not work
   4. No nightmares or, if nightmares, exact repetitions of the trauma
   5. Antisocial personality traits
   6. Evasiveness or contradictions
   7. Noncooperativeness in the evaluation
C. Confirmation of malingering by one of the following criteria:
   1. Admission of malingering
   2. Psychometric evidence of malingering or strong corroborative evidence of dissimulation

125 patients hospitalized for PTSD in a 5-month period (Lynn & Belza, 1984). This estimate (approximately 6%) may be conservative since only "severe" PTSD cases are hospitalized.

Motives to Malinger Vietnam PTSD

Vietnam veterans may be motivated to malinger PTSD for four primary reasons: (1) to obtain compensation, (2) to be admitted to a V.A. hospital, (3) for glamour, and (4) to reduce punishment for criminal conduct. Obtaining compensation has been the primary motive for veterans to malinger PTSD since the V.A. accepted the delayed type of PTSD as a potentially compensable disorder in 1980 (Bitzer, 1980). When PTSD is malingered for the purpose of gaining hospital admission, it must be distinguished from factitious PTSD. Factitious PTSD allows a veteran to assume the patient role, whereas malingered PTSD may serve other goals, such as providing refuge or documentary support to seek compensation.

Soldiers have regularly fabricated stories about their combat experiences to attain praise, sympathy, or to exaggerate masculine prowess (Pankratz, 1985). Individuals who were not in combat may also need to fabricate military experiences to gain admiration (Lynn & Belza, 1984). Ashlock et al. (1987) suggested that claiming to be a Vietnam veteran in a psychiatric ward may seem like an easy way to gain status by appearing brave and masculine to staff members and other patients.

In the criminal justice system, the diagnosis of PTSD may serve as a basis for an insanity defense, a reduction of charges, or mitigation of penalty. Veterans charged with serious crimes may consequently be highly motivated to malinger PTSD, or to falsely impute a causal link between a crime and genuine PTSD. Three clinical presentations have led to successful insanity defenses. First, a veteran may enter into a dissociative state due to a flashback and resort to survivor skills learned in Vietnam. Second, a veteran with severe survivor guilt may commit acts to have himself killed in order to be reunited with buddies killed in action. Third, a veteran may engage in sensation-seeking behavior, such as drug trafficking, to relive combat excitement (Green, Wilson, & Lindy, 1981). In assessing the validity of the relationship between PTSD and a crime, the clinician should consider whether the crime scene recreates the combat trauma, and whether there was evidence of dissociation or bewilderment at the time of the criminal conduct.

Approaches to Detection

Clinicians evaluating PTSD in Vietnam veterans must exercise special care to maintain their objectivity. Countertransference may occur because of strong feelings for or against the Vietnam war. Recounting of gruesome events in Vietnam, expressions of painful affect, and outbursts of anger can be stressful for both patients and clinicians (Atkinson *et al.*, 1982). Some clinicians feel moved to diagnose PTSD on the basis of fragmentary symptoms because they feel a sense of moral responsibility for the Vietnam veteran as a victim (Atkinson *et al.*; Pankratz, 1985).

The clinical interview is the single most important component in assessing PTSD (Fairbank, McCaffrey, & Keane, 1986). The antipathy many Vietnam veterans feel toward the federal government may interfere with the evaluation process (Atkinson *et al.*, 1982). Some veterans find it very difficult to discuss their traumatic, painful memories with even a sympathetic clinician. Authoritarian clinicians are especially unlikely to gain access to such data. Some veterans try to minimize their difficulty; other veterans exaggerate actual symptoms of PTSD for fear of failing to receive treatment or compensation (Fairbank *et al.*).

The clinician should gather a detailed military history. To receive V.A. compensation, the severity of the stress must be rated as "catastrophic" (Atkinson *et al.*, 1982). Military records and eyewitness accounts are critical because they provide the only independent substantiation of the validity of the trauma and, hence, the disorder (Sparr & Atkinson, 1986). The events most highly correlated with PTSD in Vietnam veterans are participation in atrocities and a high incidence of combat stress (Breslau & Davis, 1987). The relationship between the alleged stressors and the symptoms that are being reexperienced should be carefully elucidated.

Some veterans claiming PTSD underwent no combat or stressful military experience at all. Sparr and Pankratz (1983) reported five alleged Vietnam veterans who presented with symptoms of PTSD; three asserted that they were former prisoners of war. In fact, none had been prisoners of war, four had never been in Vietnam, and two had not been in the military. Lynn and Belza (1984) reported seven veterans who presented with PTSD symptoms to a V.A. hospital despite their never having been in Vietnam or involved in combat. One veteran's fabrications were so convincing that an Outreach Program hired him as a Vet Center counselor.

The veteran's spouse and relatives should be interviewed to validate current PTSD symptoms and assess premilitary behavioral adjustment. It is often difficult to acquire third-party documentation of exposure to combat or other stresses during service in Vietnam. Personnel files are often not revealing. A veteran's unit history files (unit logs) and data from other members of the same unit are better resources. One simple procedure is to see whether the veteran's discharge papers (Form DD 214) indicate overseas service. The discharge papers should also include campaign and service articles (Lynn & Belza, 1984), but the record of awards is not always complete (Early, 1984). Since the veteran's discharge papers may be falsified, it is best to obtain a copy directly from the U.S. Department of Defense (Sparr & Atkinson, 1986). V.A. medical centers have a national Register, which can supply information about prisoners of war through a single phone call. Before concluding that a veteran is lying about Vietnam experiences, the clinician must consider the alternative possibility that all parties to an event may be sworn to secrecy in a guerilla war (Early, 1984).

Graphic stories of battle are not conclusive proof of PTSD. The accounts presented by veterans malingering PTSD can be just as vivid and detailed as those presented by patients with the genuine disorder (Hamilton, 1985). Vet Center consultation with actual combat veterans can help pinpoint lack of knowledge of the geography and culture of Vietnam (Lynn & Belza, 1984). Ashlock et al. (1987) note that some veterans with malingered PTSD were able to pass multiple screening interviews by both Vietnam veterans and staff. Several, however, were discovered by group members within the first two days of the program.

Psychological testing may be helpful in assessing PTSD in veterans. Fairbank, McCaffrey, Keane (1985) compared MMPI scores of Vietnam veterans with PTSD with those of a group of veterans instructed to malinger PTSD. The authors were able to accurately classify over 90% of the subjects. Similarly, Ashlock et al. (1987) noted differences in MMPI scores between veterans malingering PTSD and those who had genuine PTSD. In contrast, Dalton, Pederson, Blom, and Besyner (1986) found that PTSD appears to have a minimal effect on performance on neuropsychological tests.

Blanchard, Kolb, Pallmeyer, and Gerardi (1982) reported that they could discriminate with 95.5% accuracy between veterans suffering from genuine PTSD and a control group by playing an audiotape of combat sounds. They measured veterans' heart rates, systolic blood pressure and muscle tension with a forehead electromyelogram. Measure of the heart rate alone allowed correct classification of 90.9%. Such a procedure would be impractical for the individual clinician, but could be quite helpful to professionals making frequent decisions about veterans' compensation.

Differential Diagnosis

The differential diagnosis of Vietnam PTSD includes malingering, factitious disorder, antisocial personality disorder, and genuine PTSD due to a stressor in civilian life. New life stressors, such as divorce, unemployment, or legal problems may occur after military discharge. The clinician must discern whether a patient's PTSD is the result of the Vietnam experience or a nonmilitary stressor. A coexisting mental disorder, such as psychosis or depression, may further complicate the assessment of PTSD (Atkinson et al., 1982).

The differential diagnosis between antisocial personality disorder and PTSD may be difficult. Although the presence of an antisocial personality disorder does not rule out PTSD, it should increase the clinician's degree of suspicion regarding malingering. Unfortunately, many individuals with PTSD have antisocial symptoms such as an inconsistent work pattern, poor parenting, repeated legal difficulties, inability to maintain an enduring attachment with a sexual partner, episodes of irritability, reckless behavior, failure to honor financial obligations, and a history of impulsive behavior (Walker, 1981). Veterans with PTSD may also show substance abuse, rage, and suspiciousness. Identification of developmental symptoms of antisocial personality disorder (i.e., prior to age of 15) is critical. School records and family interviews are necessary to validate veterans' self-reports.

Clinical Indicators of Malingered Vietnam PTSD

A common chief complaint in veterans with malingered PTSD is fear that they might lose control and harm others (Pankratz, 1985); the expression of this fear is likely to gain them admission to psychiatric hospitals. Malingerers tend to overplay their Vietnam experience. They might say, "I've got PTSD. I've got flashbacks and nightmares. I'm really stressed out" (Merback, 1984). Veterans with true PTSD are more likely to downplay their combat experince—for example, by saying, "Lots of guys had it worse than me."

Melton (1984) suggested several factors that help to differentiate the veteran with genuine PTSD from the malingerer. Whether the veteran attributes blame to himself or others is one good discriminator. On one hand, individuals with true PTSD are likely to feel intense levels of guilt and perceive themselves as the cause of their problems; they seem hesitant to blame their problems on Vietnam. On the other hand, malingerers are more likely to present themselves as victims of circumstance. They will begin the session with statements that imply that their life predicaments are a direct result of Vietnam; they condemn authority and the war. In the first visit, veterans with genuine PTSD are often resistant to openly admitting that their problems may be related to their experience in Vietnam. They are likely to come in because of family members' insistence or the recurrent loss of employment, depression, outbursts of anger, or substance abuse (Melton).

The themes of intrusive recollections and dreams are different in genuine and malingered PTSD. Veterans with PTSD often report themes of helplessness, guilt, or rage. Their dreams generally convey a theme of helplessness with regard to the particular traumatic events that occurred during combat. In malingered PTSD, the themes of instrusive recollections more often display anger toward generalized authority; dreams emphasize themes of grandiosity and power (Melton, 1984). The reported reexperienced "trauma" in malingerers is often not consistent with their self-reports of the original trauma (J. Smith, May 9, 1987; personal communication).

Differences have been observed between veterans with genuine and malingered PTSD in their expression and acknowledgment of feelings. In genuine PTSD, the veteran often denies or has numbed the emotional impact of combat. In malingered PTSD, the veteran will often make efforts to convince the clinician how emotionally traumatizing Vietnam was for him by "acting out" the alleged feelings. The true PTSD veteran generally *downplays* symptoms, whereas the malingerer *overplays* them. For instance, the veteran with genuine PTSD tries not to bring attention to his hyperalertness and suspicious eye movements. In contrast, the PTSD malingerer presents his suspiciousness with a dramatic quality, as if he were trying to draw attention to it. As a further example, the PTSD malingerer may volunteer that he thinks of nothing but Vietnam, and "relishes" telling his combat memories (Melton, 1984).

An important characteristic of PTSD is the avoidance of environmental conditions associated with the trauma. For example, the PTSD veteran may stay home on hot rainy days because of the resemblance to Vietnam weather. Camping may be avoided because the veteran finds himself looking for trip wires in the bush. In addition, crowds may be avoided because combat usually occurred "in a crowd." In malingered PTSD, the veteran is unlikely to report having such postcombat reactions to environmental stimuli (Melton, 1984).

Other characteristics have been noted which differentiate between actual and malingered PTSD in Vietnam veterans. These characteristics, summarized in Table 6.7, include how guilt and anger are experienced. The clinical indicators for malingered Vietnam PTSD are based primarily on case reports and must therefore be considered tentative.

Table 6.7. Clinical Indicators of Malingered Vietnam PTSD

Genuine PTSD	Malingered PTSD
Minimize relationship of symptoms to Vietnam	Emphasize relationship of symptoms to Vietnam
Blame themselves	Blame others
Dream themes of helplessness or guilt	Dream themes of grandiosity or power
Deny emotional impact of combat	"Acts out" alleged feelings
Reluctant to tell combat memories	"Relishes" telling combat memories
Survivor guilt related to specific incidents	Generalized guilt over surviving the war
Avoid environments that resemble Vietnam	Do not avoid environments that resemble Vietnam
Anger at helplessness	Anger at authority

Conclusion

The assessment of malingered psychiatric symptoms after traumatic events is difficult because self-reports of subjective symptoms are difficult to verify. The differential diagnosis between malingering and conversion disorder rests entirely on the clinician's ability to discern what is conscious. The clinician may approach the matter of detecting malingering in PTSD from "the viewpoints of an investigator searching to unearth a crime, a moralist trying to undo a suspected offense against social principle . . . or a contestant locked in game-play with an antagonist" (Braverman, 1978, p. 43). No matter how they perceive their role, clinicians must be thoroughly grounded in the phenomenology of PTSD and be aware of common differences between those with genuine disorders and their malingering counterparts.

7

Children and Deception

KATHLEEN M. QUINN

The Pioneers: Piaget and Kohlberg

Piaget first demonstrated that children and adults do not share a similar understanding of lies and truth. As described in his pioneering book, *The Moral Judgment of the Child* (1948), Piaget questioned approximately 100 children between the ages of 6 to 12 about different aspects of moral reasoning including lying. As formulated by Lewis (1982), Piaget described (see Table 7.1) the development of moral judgment along six major cognitive lines.

According to Piaget the first moral lesson for the child is obedience. The first criterion of what is good is, for a long time, defined by the external will of others, primarily their parents. Piaget believed that children accept and recognize the rules of behavior concerning veracity long before they understand the moral value of truth or the nature of lying. A young child through play, imagination, or spontaneous thinking often modifies or distorts reality. Piaget called these "mistruths without misgivings," "pseudo-lies" (*scheirlüge*), and untrue statements without the intention to deceive. However, Piaget also noted that children nevertheless accept the rule of truthfulness and consider it right that they be punished for these "lies" (Piaget, 1968).

Piaget (1968) postulated a theory of how children evaluate lies. At first the young child thinks there is nothing wrong about lying as long as he is addressing peers. Only lies to adults are blameworthy since it is adults who forbid lies. Later, the child feels that the further the lie departs from reality, the worse it is, regardless of his or her intentions. Piaget used the paradigm of having children compare two lies. One example he used was of a boy telling his mother that he had received a good grade at school when he had not been graded at all. This was compared with his telling her that he had been frightened by a dog as big as a cow. Piaget posited that the child under eight would understand that the first lie was intended to obtain an unearned

Kathleen M. Quinn, Psychiatry Department, Case Western Reserve Medical School, Cleveland, Ohio.

Table 7.1. Piaget's Model of Moral Judgment and Deception in Children

1. *Intentionality*: Young children judge an act by its physical consequences, whereas older children judge an act by intent.
2. *Relativism in judgment*: Young children view acts as either totally right or totally wrong. They assume the adult is always right. However, older children can appreciate possible diversity in view of right or wrong.
3. *Independence of sanctions*: The young child equates an act that is bad with punishment. An older child believes that an act is bad due to its violation of a rule or its harm to others, even if it goes unpunished.
4. *Use of reciprocity*: Children under 8 are egocentric and concrete in their consideration of others. This was demonstrated when a group of children was asked, "What does the Golden Rule say to do if a boy hits you?" Most younger children interpreted the Golden Rule in terms of concrete reciprocity by saying, "Hit him back." By ages 11 to 13, however, most children were able to judge in terms of ideal reciprocity by putting themselves in someone else's situation.
5. *Use of punishment*: Young children expect and advocate severe punishment in retribution for misdeeds, whereas older children seek reform of the individual by urging milder punishment.
6. *Naturalistic views of misfortune*: Children of 6 to 7 view accidents that follow misbehavior as punishment willed by God; older children do not make such a connection.

reward, whereas the second was an exaggeration. However, the first fabrication seemed to the child "less bad" since it was both possible and plausible as compared with the second. Piaget believed that early moral values are derived from external respect of adults' rules and are interpreted according to their content rather than their intent. Piaget called this the *preoperational stage* of moral/cognitive development, which occurs from ages 2 to 7.

Piaget described that the next stage of development of moral values occurred between the ages of 7 and 12, the stage of *concrete operations*. He described the transformation of moral feelings from a unilateral respect of the young child for his or her parents or other adults to a social life based on cooperation and mutual respect among children. He offered as proof the fact that young children play according to borrowed or inherited rules from older children or adults, whereas boys over the age of 7 played by a precise set of shared rules. Younger children believed that the "true rules" of a game were those they learned from authority figures and had always been the game's rules. Latency-age children (6–12 years old), however, felt that a true rule is merely an expression of a mutual agreement. New rules could become true rules if adopted by each child. Piaget held that this developmental step caused rules to be truly respected in practice and not just in words. He also saw mutual respect as engendering a whole new series of moral feelings including honesty among players and the principle of fair play. Piaget found that children at the stage of concrete operations believed that deceit among friends was more morally reprehensible than lying to adults. Finally, in the stage of *formal operations* (14 and above) Piaget described that the morality of cooperation continued, but with the addition that special circumstances and exceptions could be considered.

Piaget also found further age differences for the definition and evaluation of various types of untruths. For example, young children were more likely to define swearing, mistakes, guesses, and exaggerations as "lies." They gave harsher ratings than older children to untrue statements that were unintentional compared with those that were deliberate. The younger children also were found to rate punished lies as worse than those that were believed or resulted in neutral consequences.

In summary, Piaget theorized that children from 5 to 7 are moral realists; that is, any moral fault committed verbally qualifies as deceit. Issues of intention are not considered and innocent mistakes or "bad words" are seen as lies. Before age 8, children also judge the lie by the consequences of the deceit. In one pair of stories, a child intentionally gives the wrong directions to a female traveler, but she finds her way nonetheless. In the second story, the child tries to give the right directions, but the traveler becomes lost. According to Piaget, children under the age of 8 will judge the second child as more culpable than the first since the objective outcome was far worse. Piaget argued that children, by about 10 or 11, become sensitive to the issues of intent. At this age, lies are evaluated subjectively in terms of the speaker's goals in contrast to the younger child who is honest out of a sense of respect to adult prohibitions. Preadolescents and adolescents understand that truthfulness is necessary for social exchange and the maintenance of mutual trust.

Kohlberg (1958, 1964, 1981) using content and methods similar to Piaget's, has studied 84 boys for a period of 20 years. From analysis of interviews focusing on hypothetical moral dilemmas, Kohlberg derived six stages that describe the development of moral judgment from childhood to adulthood (see Table 7.2). Kohlberg's first four moral types closely paralleled Piaget's descriptions of moral judgment seen in the preoperational and concrete operations stages. However, Kohlberg differed with Piaget's formulations of the children's reasons for their choices and their way of

Table 7.2. Kohlberg's Model of Developmental Stages of Moral Judgment

Level I. Premorality
    A. *Type 1*: Punishment and obedience orientation (obey rules to avoid punishment)
    B. *Type 2*: Naive hedonism (conform to obtain rewards)
Level II. Morality of conventional role-conformity
    A. *Type 3*: Good boy morality (conform to rules in order to please and gain approval)
    B. *Type 4*: Authority maintaining morality (conform to avoid censure by authorities)
Level III. Morality of self-accepted moral principles
    A. *Type 5*: Morality of social contract (conform out of respect for community welfare)
    B. *Type 6*: Morality of individual principles of conscience (conform on basis of personal ethical principles)

defining the conflict. For example, whereas Piaget started from the concept of early morality being respect for rules and respect derived from the personal valuing of the authorities who uphold and teach these rules, Kohlberg emphasized the child's desire to avoid punishment as the main motivation for obedience. Kohlberg hypothesized that these stages of moral judgment formed an invariant developmental sequence in which the use of a more advanced stage of thought depended on earlier attainment of each preceding stage. He also concluded that the attainment of each more advanced stage involved a restructuring and displacement of previous stages of thought. More recently, Colby (1978) and Kohlberg (1978) have identified two types of reasoning at each stage: Type A, which emphasizes literal interpretation of the rules of society and Type B, which is a more consolidated form of thought based on the intent of the normative standards. Kohlberg's recent work has failed to confirm the existence of a sixth stage of moral development. He presently views stage six as mainly a theoretical construct, not an empirically confirmed entity, which he sees as representing an elaboration of the B (or advanced) substage of Stage 5.

Both Piaget's and Kohlberg's work has been recently criticized as sexually biased. For example, Gilligan (1982) discussed the sex bias of Kohlberg's samples (mainly male). In addition, Gilligan (1982) and Holstein (1976) have argued that women value personal relationships and responsibility more than male concerns with rights. They argue that moral judgments made by women were scored at lower stages of moral development than those made by men due to these differences since Piaget's and Kohlberg's work equated male emphasis on rights and individual values as more desirable.

Modern Research on Moral Development

Numerous modern studies have attempted to test or replicate Piaget's theories. Several studies (e.g., Crowley, 1968; Gutkin, 1972; King, 1971) have employed methodologies similar to Piaget's, in which subjects have been verbally presented with pairs of written stories contrasting good intentions with relatively serious negative consequences and bad intentions with minor or trivial consequences. Empirical findings support Piaget in that children younger than 8 or 9 base their moral judgments on the consequences of actions rather than the intentions which prompted the behaviors. In contrast, studies by Berg-Cross (1975) and by Chandler, Greenspan, and Barenboim (1973) have demonstrated that this finding (i.e., young children base their moral judgments solely on the consequences rather than the intention of moral actions) is a methodological artifact. When moral dilemmas were presented as single stories, as opposed to a story-pair, or when dilemmas were videotaped, children as young as 6 or 7 could routinely respond to the type of intention in the stories as well as the quantity and quality of the damage involved. Employing an improved research design, Keasy (1977) found that the degree to which children weigh intentions in their judgments increases with age, while the degree to which they weigh outcome information decreases.

A recent study of the developmental changes in children's understanding of lying gave results generally supportive of Piaget's original conclusions on developmentally related definitions of lying (Peterson, Peterson, & Seeto, 1983). The study used 200 subjects evenly divided into groups of 5-, 8-, 9-, and 11-year-olds, as well as adults, who were shown videotaped stories depicting deliberate lies and unintentionally untrue stories. One finding contrary to Piaget's theory was that 95% of the 11-year-olds persisted in calling an exaggeration a lie. Other results suggest that the transition from moral realism to a subjective assessment of lies may be more gradual and individual than Piaget's writings suggest, since 75% of 9-year-olds, and 28% of the 11-year-olds in Peterson's sample gave punishment as the only justification for not telling lies and felt that lies were always wrong regardless of motive or circumstance. These findings suggest that cultural and sampling issues as well as methodological differences need to be studied further to more fully understand moral development in children.

Another major area of controversy has been the degree to which moral thinking and social conduct are consistent. Beginning with the classic studies of Hartshorne and May (1928, 1930), research findings regarding the predictability of the relationship between moral judgment and conduct have been weak, indeterminate, or nonsignificant. Gerson and Damon (1978) conducted an ongoing series of experimental studies involving children ages 4 to 10 and demonstrated an interaction between the child's level of reasoning and specific aspects of the social context which have marked influences on the child's conduct. In one of their major studies, the children were required to distribute among a group of four, a reward for making bracelets. These four, of whom the subject could be any of the first three, consisted of a child who made the most and best bracelets; a child who was the biggest boy or girl in the group; a child who simply did a "nice job"; and a younger child who made bracelets poorly and who was not present at the time of the candy distribution. Each of the three experimental subjects (the first three children) was asked to reach a fair decision concerning the distribution of the reward, and subsequently give their reasoning. A series of control interviews was also conducted including a control group in which each child was asked to distribute a pretend reward (cardboard copies of candy) to him or herself and three other imaginary participants after a hypothetical bracelet-making session. The researchers' general hypotheses were that the children's developing sense of justice would predict certain behavioral tendencies. For example, the children for whom fairness was defined by what the self wanted would reward themselves more than more advanced reasoners would; those children at the highest level of reasoning in which a fair solution was based on the particular nature of the situation, would be the most considerate of the younger, absent child. These hypotheses of the behavior of the children at either end of the reasoning scale were generally confirmed. However, there was a strong tendency (72%) for children to reason at a lower level in the real-life situation than in the hypothetical situation. The children who had the real candy bars showed a strong tendency to prefer themselves in the distribution. The researchers hypothesized that a "self-interest factor" had to be considered in understanding a child's moral behavior in a particular situation.

Prediction of a child's conduct requires detailed knowledge of the situation (for example, whether the child had the real candy bars) and the child's personal understanding and definition of the accompanying moral concepts (such as notions of "equality," "merit," and "need"). The child's objectives (getting as many candy bars for oneself as possible) were the critical motivators in the child's conduct. These findings suggest that the individual child does not respond to an "objective" social context but to his or her unique interpretation of that situation. Many of the subjects reverted to lower level reasoning because such reasoning allowed them to justify their self-serving goals. Finally, in the Gerson and Damon study (1978), another nonmoral objective appeared to be influential, that is, the maintenance of peer relations. It was observed that in the later group discussions of how to distribute the candy, the longer a child was with his peers, the more likely he or she was to agree to an equal distribution.

The relevance of this research is that knowledge of a child's hypothetical moral reasoning can only be taken as an indicator of the child's general capacity for moral understanding, which may or may not be used in any particular real-life situation. Other issues to be considered are whether a child (1) is in a developmental transition from one stage to another, (2) is behaving below his or her abilities in pursuit of a nonmoral goal, or (3) is acting reflexively without moral deliberation.

Detection of Lying in Children

One common reason why children fail at deception is *detection apprehension*, that is, the fear of being caught. A child may feel considerable detection apprehension due to his or her beliefs about parents' (i.e., the targets') skill at identifying lies. Parents often convince their children that they are masterful detectors of deceit. For example, in Terrence Rattigan's play, *The Winslow Boy* (1973), a father says to his teenage son, who has been discharged from naval training school after being accused of stealing a postal money order: "If you did it, you must tell me. I shan't be angry with you, Ronnie [the son],—provided you tell me the truth. But if you tell me a lie, I shall know it, because a lie between you and me can't be hidden. . . . Did you steal this postal order?" (p. 29). In the play the boy denies the misdeed and is believed. However, this strategy only works when both parent and child trust each other. A father who is known to be suspicious even in the face of truth will arouse fear in an innocent child. This arousal of anxiety creates a crucial problem in detecting deception; it is nearly impossible to distinguish an innocent child's fear of being disbelieved from a guilty child's detection apprehension (Ekman, 1986).

Parents often realize that the severity of their punishments is a factor that influences whether children confess or lie about their wrongdoings. If a parent makes clear before questioning that the punishment for lying will be worse than the punishment for the crime, there is a better chance of discouraging lying about transgressions (Ekman, 1986).

Another factor in detection of lying in minors is *deception guilt*, that is, the feeling of guilt about the act of lying. A child may experience deception guilt as extremely uncomfortable. Seeking relief from deception guilt may motivate a confession despite the likelihood of punishment. Indeed, the punishment may be needed in order to alleviate the feelings of guilt (Ekman, 1986).

Deception guilt will be the greatest when lying is not "authorized," that is, when there is no well-defined social norm that legitimizes deceiving the target. Examples of authorized lying for adults include spying, diplomacy, and career criminals. A liar must share social values with the victim to feel deception guilt. People will feel less guilty about lying to those they think are wrong-doers (Ekman, 1986). An adolescent who still feels attached and cares for his or her parents and their shared values may feel some shame and guilt over concealing his or her use of illicit drugs. In contrast, a disaffected child whose parents abuse alcohol may feel little guilt over such a deception. Parents' disapproval will bring forth only anger and contempt over their perceived hypocrisy.

Children's Ability to Detect Deception

In order to detect deception, children must learn that people's observable statements and expressions do not always correspond to their inner beliefs. During the elementary school years children become increasingly aware of these discrepancies (Sarni, 1979). Skilled deception detectors must also come to understand the defining features of a lie, that is, it is a message which the sender knows to be false and with which the sender deliberately plans to mislead. If these characteristics are not fully appreciated, lies are continued to be confused with unintentional mistakes, jokes, sarcasm, exaggerations, or stories of make-believe. Recent research (Wimmer, Gruber, & Perner, 1985) indicated that children first develop a moral judgment of what actions should be rewarded or punished before they develop the ability to accurately label whether or not an action is a lie. Young children's moral realism causes them to label many statements as lies.

Children, as well as adults, must learn to use both verbal and nonverbal skills to assess the veracity and intent of statements. Discrepancies between different components of a message, however, are not always immediately apparent to children. They also appear to use different strategies than adults to understand inconsistencies between verbal and nonverbal elements of communication. For example, when facial and vocal cues are discrepant, preadolescents tend to place greater emphasis on facial cues, which may be less revealing than vocal cues, which adolescents and adults weigh more heavily (DePaulo, Stone, & Lassiter, 1985).

Younger children are most likely to use a literal interpretive strategy when confronted with conflicting data in a message (Ackerman, 1981). Their difficulty in integrating inconsistent clues may be due to their limited information-processing abilities. It may be too difficult for such children to assess several items of information simultaneously. Therefore they use the simple strategy of interpreting utterances literally. This strategy is most likely to occur when the speaker is an adult whom children view as knowledgeable and credible. However, their skepticism about the credibility of adults' statements increases as children mature. Children are able to detect discrepancies between a speaker's statements and other information when the speaker is a child (Ackerman, 1983).

Several studies have examined children's ability to detect deception solely on the basis of the verbal or nonverbal cues within the speaker's statements. In a study by DePaulo, Jordan, Irvine, and Laser (1982), children were asked to watch a videotape on which an adult described someone they liked and someone they disliked, as well as giving statements pretending to like a disliked person and to dislike a liked person. The subjects were at five different grade levels (6, 8, 10, 12, and college). At every grade level subjects tended to believe the emotion that was overtly expressed even when the speaker was lying. However, subjects at every age level did perceive the false expressions of liking as less positive than the sincere expressions of liking, and the feigned expressions of disliking as less negative than the honest expressions of disliking. The three oldest groups viewed the speakers as having more "mixed-feelings" when they were lying than when they were telling the truth. However, only the 12th graders and college students perceived the dishonest messages as more deceptive than the honest messages. There were also systematic changes, varying with age, in the kinds of messages that subjects perceived as deceptive. Younger subjects perceived the adults as more deceptive when they expressed negative affect than when they were positive. This trend tended to reverse with age. DePaulo and her associates noted this tendency of the younger subjects to perceive expressions of negative affect as deceptive was similar to Piaget's observation that

6-year-olds often view naughty words as lies. The authors hypothesized that age differences may be due to the preadolescents' increasingly cynical view of the world. Thus for the older subject if the overt message is kind, they are more likely to see it as a lie than if it is negative.

Morency and Krauss (1982), using children as the "senders," asked first and fifth graders to watch a series of pleasant and unpleasant slides, and to convey a false impression while viewing half of them. Videotapes were made of the children's facial expressions and rated by other first and fifth graders. None of the children could detect the deception of the fifth graders, and the first graders' deception was discernible only when they were watching the pleasant stimuli.

In summary, no empirical evidence was found that young children can detect deception on the basis of verbal or nonverbal cues alone, except occasionally, when trying to detect the deception of other very young children. Since the accuracy achieved by adults at this task is only slightly better than chance (DePaulo et al., 1985), it is not surprising to find that children have great difficulty as well. These findings help to understand one aspect of children's vulnerability to victimization. A young child approached by an adult will have great difficulty assessing the adult's veracity. Only the adolescent, thanks to increasing social and interpersonal knowledge, is even minimally equipped to recognize deception in others. The increasing cognitive abilities of adolescents, with their efforts to try to infer others' feelings, to explain the qualities they see in others, and to reconcile inconsistencies in others' behaviors, facilitate their lie-detection skills.

Learning to Lie

The research in the area of children's learning to lie has focused on the use of nonverbal cues, usually facial cues. These studies show developmental improvements in deceptive abilities throughout the childhood years. For example, in the above-cited study of Morency and Krauss (1982), first graders fooled their peers only when viewing the unpleasant slides. The fifth graders, however, were able to deceive their peers on both types of trials. When these tapes were shown to the senders' parents, the parents were able to detect first graders' deception on both the pleasant and unpleasant slides. The parents were also able to detect the fifth graders' deception when they viewed the pleasant slides. There is evidence, though, that fourth and fifth graders can successfully deceive adults when the adults are strangers (Allen & Atkinson, 1978).

Feldman and White (1980) examined children's ability to control facial expressions and body movements while lying. They hypothesized that as age increased, children's deception would be increasingly revealed by body movements rather than facial expression. Children ranging in age from 5 to

12 years sampled good- and bad-tasting drinks and tried to convince observers for half the trials that the good drink tasted bad or vice-versa. The study, employing undergraduate observers, found that facial expressions of older girls became less revealing, while their body communication became more transparent. In contrast, boys' facial deceptiveness became more obvious with age, while their body movements became better disguised.

Braginsky's (1970) research is one of the few studies of children's verbally based strategies to deceive. In this study, the experimenter gave children a taste of a cracker soaked in a quinine solution. She then offered each child a nickel for each cracker they could convince a peer to eat. The most successful children were those who used many different manipulative behaviors including omissive lies, commissive lies, bribery, two-sided arguments, and blaming the experimenter. The successful children also were rated by judges as sounding more innocent, honest, and calm than the less successful subjects. Gender differences were observed among successful children. The girls often told omissive lies to succeed at the task, whereas boys frequently told commissive lies.

A developmental progression of strategies used by children at various ages and their attempts to deceive has been noted. (DePaulo et al., 1985). Three strategies appear particularly important. The first strategy is best described as no strategy at all. These children demonstrated readily apparent "leaks" of their true emotions. A second strategy involved a naturalistic display of simulated affect. The third strategy was exaggeration or "hamming" of affect. This final strategy tends to be very effective in deceiving others (DePaulo & Rosenthal, 1979). Developmentally, first graders "leak," seventh graders use a naturalistic reproduction strategy, and college students are hams (Feldman, Jenkins, & Popoola, 1979).

In summary, current studies indicate that first graders cannot successfully tell a lie. By fourth and fifth grade, children become more proficient telling lies. These children can fool their peers, adult strangers, and at times, their parents. Between ages 5 and 12, children generally become more adept at hiding their deception verbally. Children are less successful at deceiving when their true feeling is positive than when it is negative. A recent study (Shennum & Bugental, 1982) showed that children between 6 and 12 readily reveal their deception by their voices although there is some evidence that children of this age become increasingly proficient at using their faces to deceive other people.

Clinical Issues

A question often arises in clinical practice: "Is this child lying?" In reviewing the research literature it is apparent that children often deceive to avoid punishment or gain material or social rewards (DePaulo et al., 1982;

Schadler & Ayers-NachamKim, 1983). Lies in children become clinically significant due to their frequency or the importance of their consequences.

The most common clinical presentation of a child who is a persistent liar is the conduct-disordered individual. Stouthamer-Loeber (1986), in reviewing the literature on chronic lying and conduct disorders, found that nearly two-thirds of conduct-disordered children had lying as part of their presenting problem. These children and adolescents present with a repetitive and persistent pattern of conduct in which the basic rights of others or major age-appropriate societal rules are violated (American Psychiatric Association, 1980). Lying is a primary symptom of this disorder but may also be used secondarily to conceal antisocial acts, such as truancy or stealing, or to gain rewards from peers or adults.

An apparently rare form of conscious deception in children and adolescents is malingering of a physical or psychiatric disorder. Malingering is the voluntary production and presentation of false or grossly exaggerated physical or psychological symptoms in pursuit of a recognizable goal (American Psychiatric Association, 1980). Greenfield (1987) recently described an example of feigned psychosis in a 14-year-old girl. Her clinical presentation through three psychiatric hospitalizations was consistent with schizophrenia, including increased withdrawal, deteriorating functioning, auditory hallucinations, confusions, and becoming mute. She disclosed her deception only when she was confronted with an impending placement of her infant daughter in a foster home. At that time her behavior underwent a dramatic change. She became verbal, well organized, and animated. She went on to describe that she had observed an older cousin in a psychotic episode several months earlier. She had also gone on to observe other patients' behavior in her own subsequent hospitalizations. She stated that she feigned the symptoms each time the conditions in her already chaotic household worsened. Her first hospitalization was prompted by her mother's new boyfriend approaching her sexually. Her third hospitalization was prompted by her advancing pregnancy in order to seek the best care for her delivery and to enlist the hospital in arranging to live with the family of her baby's father. Subsequent psychological testing revealed no evidence of a formal thought disorder and a low normal full-scale IQ. She was discharged on no medications with her baby to her boyfriend's parents' home. On two-year follow-up the patient and her child were doing well and she had had no further psychiatric hospitalizations. This case report demonstrates some of the necessary ingredients of successful malingering in this or any age group: (1) the individual is facing a living condition or stress that she finds intolerable; (2) the individual is aware of alternatives to his present dilemma, such as a hospital; and (3) the individual has gained knowledge of the expected signs and symptoms of a well-recognized psychiatric or medical disorder.

A false allegation of sexual abuse may be pursued to seek similar goals, such as alternate placements outside the home. Goodwin, Sahd, and Rada

(1978) describe adolescents who readily acknowledged that they lied about being sexually abused in order to leave conflicted but nonabusive settings. Clinically, older latency-age children and adolescents are most likely to malinger. Malingering requires considerable skill in role-playing, impression-management, and deception; these skills are simply not available to younger children.

Certain psychosocial stressors, such as divorce or abuse and neglect, may promote lying in children. A recent study of latency-age children in divorcing families (Johnston, Campbell, & Mayes, 1985), for example, described a subset of these children actively struggling for acceptance within these families by trying to report what either parent wanted to hear. This strategy included lying as well as informing on other children or an absent parent. Early latency-age children were often detected but the older children became quite astute at deception and manipulating the situation to meet their own needs. These authors foresaw two possible outcomes for these children. For some children, this was the beginning of an early onset of antisocial tendencies. In other cases, children who maintained principal moral reasoning and empathic concern for their parents were viewed as mediators or negotiators.

Similar pressures exist for children in abusive families. The child may lie by omission or commission in order to please the abusive parent. A high premium exists for successful lying in such families since detection may result in further abuse. Another well-described example of lying in abusive families is the suppression phase (Sgroi, 1982) of sexual abuse. During this phase the child victim retracts his or her previous disclosure of sexual abuse. The child, often confronted by overwhelming emotional pressure and loyalty conflict, chooses to lie to keep his or her family intact.

Family attitudes and actions concerning lying and manipulative behaviors appear to form an important model for children's subsequent behaviors. For example, Kraut and Price (1976) demonstrated that the degree of Machiavellianism of fathers and mothers related positively to their children's success in deceiving others but not to seeing through others' attempts at deception. A child's manipulative behaviors and beliefs appeared to be learned separately. A clinical example of the modeling of deception occurs in Munchausen by proxy. By school age some of these children begin to actively participate in the deception concerning their factitious illness (Meadow, 1984b).

Clinical Assessment of Children's Deception

The clinical assessment of children's lying should include data pertaining to each of the following evaluation questions.

1. Does the child have the developmental capacity to deceive? The very young child's statements may be untruths generated by their immature cognitive abilities with no intention to deceive. As a general guideline, children under the age of 6 have been shown to be unable to lie successfully.

2. Does the child or adolescent have a history of persistent lying? If yes, is it possible that this admission is also a lie? This is often a complex area in the assessment of deception since even severely conduct-disordered youth may be telling the truth concerning the clinical or legal issue under investigation.

3. Does the child have a psychiatric disorder which would alter reality testing or cause severe distortion, fantasy, or use of defenses such as massive denial or dissociation? A seriously emotionally disturbed child may make statements which are not lies but rather a product of a mental disorder. Such distortions may include the psychotic adolescent who makes an allegation of sexual abuse against a nurse, despite the presence of witnesses who can attest that no abuse was observed on the occasion in question, or the borderline child who sexualizes interactions. Clinicians should be well informed concerning developmental norms of cognition and the individual child's history, including sexual history, in order to fully investigate complaints.

4. Is there a psychosocial stressor which may promote lying? A careful evaluation should elicit the effect of divorce, or other aspects of family life, on the child. Equally important is the assessment of how the child is coping with psychosocial stressors and what pressures are experienced, either to dramatize the situation or minimize the family conflict.

5. Has the child's deception guilt decreased? Has the child's deception apprehension increased? The clinician should seek to understand the child's beliefs about his or her own statements and whether these beliefs cause the child to have increased or decreased secondary guilt or anxiety which confound the clinical assessment.

6. Is the child pursuing a nonmoral objective? For example, is the child seeking to remain with one parent by bringing an allegation against the other? The clinician should attempt to understand the goal being pursued by the child and how the child believes his or her statements aid in pursuit of the goal.

7. Is an adult lying for the child or distorting the child's communication? Examples may include the conscious deception or overinterpretation by parents in custody and visitation battles or the rare phenomenon of Munchausen syndrome by proxy (see Chapter 2), in which there is a parental falsification of medical illness in children.

8. Is the child's presentation of a psychiatric or medical disorder consistent with a well-recognized illness or syndrome? A clinician should consider malingering, factitious illness, atypical symptomatology, conversion disorder, as well as the somatoform disorders, as differential diagnoses.

9. Does this or previous mental health assessments contain interviewing errors resulting in incorrect assessment of the nature of the child's

communication. For example, highly coercive and leading questioning by an interviewer may lead to the premature conclusion that sexual abuse has occurred.

Clinicians conducting medicolegal assessments of children should anticipate that the possibility of a child's lying will be raised. The evaluation, by addressing systematically the above issues, will be best able to address this issue. As in all cases of deception, clinicians should be prepared to provide detailed and convincing examples of a child's lying and his or her motivation for doing so.

Decision Models for Assessment of Children's Deception

Little has been written concerning conceptual models for assessing the possibility of deception in children, except in the area of sexual abuse. DeYoung (1986) recently developed a model for judging the truthfulness of sexual-abuse allegations, and Green (1986) and Benedek and Schetky (1984, 1987a, 1987b) have described characteristics of false allegations of child sexual abuse. Attempts to detect deception in the area of sexual-abuse complaints has been highly controversial due to the large number of all abuse cases (both physical and sexual) that cannot be either proved or disproved but remain unsubstantiated by investigators. In addition, previously abused children who suffer from unresolved posttraumatic stress disorders (Jones & McGraw, 1987) or children who have observed others being victimized (Lyons, 1987) may present statements consistent with the natural history of abuse, possibly containing explicit details. Only the absence of these validating criteria can now be considered clinical evidence for a fictitious complaint.

A successful conceptual model for judging deception in a child's complaints should be logical and systematic. The model should ask the clinician to assess all aspects of the complaint, the child's psychology and development, family and environmental factors, and the interaction among these issues. The threshold model poses the clinical question of when deception should be investigated (see Table 7.3). Criteria for suspecting deception in children differ in family versus nonfamilial settings. In families with open conflict, such as divorce or separation, a child's loyalty to one parent, or his or her emotional alienation from another parent, may lead to a false allegation against a parent. In these families, one adult or one faction of the family may be the major proponent of a complaint or denial of a complaint which the child may then profess. In families without overt conflict, the major indicator of deception is the inconsistency between the child's physical or emotional presentations and the family's explanations. Other factors raising the index of suspicion of deception include the presence of a severe conduct disorder, referrals for forensic purposes (most notably, custody and visitation contests and civil injury suits), pursuit of other identifiable goals

Table 7.3. Threshold Model for Deception in Children

A. Suspected deception with open family conflict. Use any of the following criteria:
   1. The individual bringing complaint is adult
   2. The child is overly compliant with parents
   3. The child is inappropriately alienated from either parent
   4. The child idealizes either parent
   5. The family presents with "united front" concerning either an allegation or denial
B. Suspected deception but with no family conflict. Use either of the following criteria:
   1. Physical evidence of abuse with denial or inconsistent explanation
   2. Significant change in child's behavior consistent with abuse, with denial of conflict by family
C. Suspected deception in nonfamilial situation. Use either of the following criteria:
   1. Presentation of physical or emotional complaints inconsistent with objective evidence
   2. Presentation of physical or emotional complaints inconsistent with well-recognized illness or syndrome
D. Other specified circumstances. Use any of the following criteria:
   1. Presence of severe conduct disorder
   2. Medicolegal context of presentation
   3. Psychological need to pursue sick role
   4. Pursuit of identifiable external goal through complaint

such as changes in placement or revenge and the psychological need to pursue a sick role seen in factitious disorders.

The clinical decision model frames an investigation around the second major clinical question: When should clinicians conclude that a child is engaging in deception? The clinician can only be certain if the child confesses convincingly to the deceit or is otherwise discovered in the intentional production of false statements or symptoms. Table 7.4 is a proposed model for assisting the clinician in forming an opinion concerning the absence or presence of deception. The clinician using this model should clearly describe

Table 7.4. Clinical Decision Model for Assessing Deception in Children

A. Inconsistency of self-report as evidenced by one of the following:
   1. Markedly inconsistent self-reports with respect to complaint
   2. Self-report markedly inconsistent with verifiable reports
   3. Self-report could not possibly be true
B. Response to direct inquiry which is indicative of dishonesty as noted in one of the following:
   1. Admission of deception
   2. Maintenance of an implausible or highly unlikely explanation in face of contradictory evidence
C. Presence of any of the following:
   1. Self-report the result of mental disorder
   2. Child acting under explicit orders to lie
   3. Child's motivation understandable in light of his or her goals
D. Absence of the following:
   1. Statements by the child consistent with the natural history of the condition
   2. Statement by the child containing explicit details in age-appropriate language.

the statements and/or behavioral observations which support his or her conclusions concerning deception, as well as any possible alternative explanations.

This clinical decision model takes into account three important facets of deception among children. First, are there incongruities in clinical presentation? Second, when confronted with those incongruities, does the child admit to deception or offer an implausible explanation? Third, can the child's motivation for deception be clearly understood? These three criteria address the essence of deception: intentional dishonesties in the service of a recognizable goal.

Conclusion

The assessment of deception among children requires a thorough understanding of cognitive and moral development. Both classic and recent studies highlight the complexity of childhood development and the absence of any simple age-norms for the ability to lie or detect deception. This chapter has sought to offer useful guidelines from the available literature and to provide a stimulus for further research.

Specific dissimulative styles of malingering, defensiveness, and irrelevant responding have not been thoroughly investigated with respect to the assessment of children. With older children and particularly adolescents, some normative data exist on the use of adult measures (i.e., adolescent norms of the MMPI). Examination of normative research (see Chapter 8) strongly suggests that adult-based indicators of dissimulation *should not* be used. Clinicians, when suspecting malingering or defensiveness in children, will need to rely on extensive clinical interviews and corroborative sources. For the detection of deception, threshold and clinical decision models are presented with specific criteria for children.

PART TWO

PSYCHOMETRIC APPROACHES

8

Assessment of Malingering and Defensiveness by Objective Personality Inventories

ROGER L. GREENE

This chapter will review the use of objective personality inventories to assess whether malingering or defensiveness may have been involved in a patient's responses. The primary focus of this chapter will be the Minnesota Multiphasic Personality Inventory (MMPI) (Dahlstrom, Welsh, & Dahlstrom, 1972), since the MMPI is the most widely used and researched objective measure of psychopathology. It shall be assumed that the reader is familiar with the clinical interpretation of the MMPI; interpretive information on the MMPI can be found in Duckworth and Anderson (1986), Graham (1987), Greene (1980), and Lachar (1974). Several other objective personality inventories will also be discussed: the California Psychological Inventory (CPI) (Megargee, 1972), the M Test (Beaber, Marston, Michelli, & Mills, 1985), the Millon Clinical Multiaxial Inventory (MCMI) (Millon, 1983, 1984), and the Sixteen Personality Factor Questionnaire (16 PF) (Karson & O'Dell, 1976). These latter inventories will include, where appropriate, references cited to any interpretive data that are needed.

In the development of the MMPI, Meehl and Hathaway (1946) were convinced of the necessity of assessing two dichotomous categories of test-taking attitudes: plus-getting ("faking-bad") and defensiveness ("faking-good"). These two categories will be called malingering and defensiveness, respectively, throughout this chapter. To assess these two categories of test-taking attitudes, Meehl and Hathaway considered three possible approaches. First, they could give the patient an opportunity to distort the responses in a specific way and observe the inconsistency of the patient's responses to items phrased either identically or in the negative rather than the affirmative. A large number of inconsistent responses would suggest that the patient was either incapable or unwilling to respond consistently. Although Meehl and Hathaway rejected this solution, the MMPI group

Roger L. Greene, Department of Psychology, Texas Tech University, Lubbock, Texas.

booklet form included 16 identically repeated items (Test–Retest [TR] index) (Dahlstrom *et al.*, 1972), and Greene (1978) developed the Carelessness (CLS) Scale that can be used to detect inconsistent responding.

Second, Meehl and Hathaway (1946) considered providing an opportunity for the patient to answer favorably when a favorable response would almost certainly be untrue. This solution would involve developing a list of extremely desirable but very rare human qualities. If a patient endorsed a large number of these items, it is highly probable that the responses would be dishonest. The L (Lie) scale was developed specifically for this purpose. Items for the L scale, based on the work of Hartshorne and May (1928), reflect behaviors that although socially desirable are all rarely true of a given individual. A large number of responses in the deviant direction on the L scale indicates defensiveness.

The F scale was developed according to a variant of this second approach for assessing test-taking attitudes. Items for the F scale were selected primarily because they were answered with a relatively low frequency by a majority of the original normative group. In other words, if a patient endorsed a large number of the F scale items, that person would be responding in a manner that was atypical of most people in the normative group. In addition, the items include a variety of content areas so that any specific set of experiences or interests of a particular individual would be unlikely to influence that person to answer many of the items in the deviant direction.

Third, Meehl and Hathaway (1946) considered using an empirical procedure to identify items that elicit different responses from persons taking the test in an appropriate fashion and those who have been instructed to malinger. Gough's Dissimulation Scale (Gough, 1954, 1957), which was based on this procedure, will be described below. Meehl and Hathaway adopted a variant of this third approach in developing a third validity scale, the K scale. This scale was developed to differentiate abnormal persons who were hospitalized and yet obtained normal profiles, from normal individuals who, for some reason, obtained abnormal profiles. Meehl and Hathaway also empirically determined the proportions of K that, when added to a clinical scale, would maximize the discrimination between the criterion group and the normative group. Since Meehl and Hathaway determined the optimal weights of K to be added to each clinical scale in a psychiatric inpatient population, they warned that with maladjusted normal populations and other clinical populations, other weights of K might serve to maximize the identification of pathological individuals. This issue of the optimal weights to be added to each clinical scale in different populations has received little attention (cf. Greene, 1980; Wooten, 1984).

Assessing the validity of a specific administration of the MMPI or any other objective personality inventory is a process that involves multiple steps, which need to be carried out in a sequential manner. An overview of these steps is provided in Figure 8.1. The clinician will see the various meanings of the concept of validity that are raised at each of these steps and their different effects on overall profile validity as explained below. In explaining each of these steps, the primary focus shall be on research with the MMPI. However, each of these sections will conclude with an overview of how this particular step is evaluated by other objective personality inventories.

Item Omissions

The first step in assessing the validity of any administration of the MMPI is to evaluate the number of items omitted (see Figure 8.1). Item omissions in some senses is a misnomer since in addition to items that the patient does not endorse, the category includes (1) items that the patient endorses both true and false, and (2) items the patient manages to endorse on some area of the answer sheet other than that indicated for a true or false response. Patients occasionally will make comments about the items on the answer

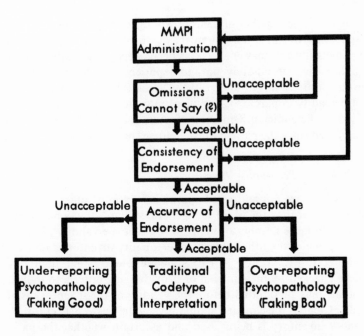

Figure 8.1. Steps in assessing MMPI validity. See text for descriptions of scales/indexes to be used at each stage and their cutting score.

sheet, which the clinician will miss unless it is checked carefully. Consequently, it is important for the clinician to check the answer sheet meticulously and tabulate the number of item "omissions." Tables 8.1 and 8.2 present the number of items omitted by gender in normal individuals and psychiatric patients, respectively.

As can be seen in Table 8.1 five or fewer items were omitted in 76–98% of these normal individuals, and more than 30 items were omitted by less than 1% except for Greene's (1986) sample of adult males. There is a consistent trend for men to omit slightly more items than women in all samples except Colligan, Osborne, Swenson, and Offord (1983). The modal number of items omitted in these normal individuals was zero, and the average number of omitted items was less than four.

The psychiatric samples reported in Table 8.2 omitted slightly more items than the normal individuals. Five or fewer items were omitted in 58–62% of these patients, and more than 30 items were omitted by 5–6%. There do not appear to be any gender or age (adult versus adolescent) differences in the number of items omitted in these psychiatric samples. The finding that psychiatric patients omit more items than normal individuals highlights the importance of assessing items omissions in clinical populations.

Clinical Applications to the MMPI

Omission of a large number of items on an objective personality inventory is an infrequent problem in most clinical assessments since it is readily obvious to the clinician, if the answer sheet has been checked carefully. Occasionally a very defensive or possibly paranoid patient will be encountered who refuses to endorse a large number of the items. These personality characteristics are readily apparent in a clinical interview and consequently easily identified by the clinician. Omission of items is not an issue when malingering is involved since the patient must endorse the items in order to malinger.

Other Objective Personality Inventories

Item omissions are not addressed specifically in most objective personality inventories other than the MMPI. A general statement may be made that an omission of a large number of items may affect the validity of any profile. However, none of the other objective personality inventories reviewed here (CPI, M Test, MCMI, or 16 PF) stated explicitly that item omissions should be checked by the clinician or provided any criteria to indicate how many items may be omitted before the validity of the inventory is affected adversely. Clearly, the clinician should review the answer sheet for whatever personality inventory is being used and ascertain whether the patient has omitted a large number of items. In most instances simply asking the patient to review these items and provide his or her best response is sufficient to

Table 8.1. Frequency of Omitted Items in Normal Samples by Gender

Number of omitted items	Colligan et al. (1983) Adults (%)		Lavin (1984) Adults (%)		Greene (1986) Adults (%)		Greene (1986) College students (%)	
	Male (%) (N = 646)	Female (%) (N = 762)	Male (%) (N = 1031)	Female (%) (N = 146)	Male (%) (N = 163)	Female (%) (N = 238)	Male (%) (N = 208)	Female (%) (N = 224)
0	46.0	45.0	65.7	75.3	55.2	56.3	77.9	77.7
1–5	35.3	36.1	24.4	17.8	20.9	29.4	17.8	20.1
Cumulative %	81.3	81.1	90.1	93.1	76.1	85.7	95.7	97.8
6–10	5.0	4.9	4.1	2.1	11.6	5.9	1.4	1.8
Cumulative %	86.3	86.0	94.2	95.2	87.7	91.6	97.1	99.6
11–30	10.2	10.2	4.8	4.1	4.9	8.4	2.4	0.4
Cumulative %	96.5	96.2	99.0	99.3	92.6	100.0	99.5	100.0
30+	3.5	3.8	1.0	0.7	7.4	0.0	0.5	0.0
M	4.9	5.1	2.5	1.5	3.7	2.5	1.1	0.5
SD	11.1	11.4	9.7	4.8	3.6	4.4	5.6	1.5

Note. Lavin (1984) administered only the first 399 items of Form R to job applicants in the nuclear power industry.

Table 8.2. Frequency of Omitted Items in Psychiatric Patients by Gender

| | Psychiatric patients (Hedlund & Won Cho, 1979) | | | |
| | Adults (%) | | Adolescents (%) | |
Number of omitted items	Male (%) ($N = 8{,}646$)	Female (%) ($N = 3{,}743$)	Male (%) ($N = 693$)	Female (%) ($N = 290$)
0	29.8	28.4	28.0	27.9
1–5	32.3	30.4	31.0	30.8
Cumulative %	*62.1*	*58.8*	*59.0*	*58.7*
6–10	16.8	17.2	21.1	21.7
Cumulative %	*78.9*	*76.0*	*80.1*	*80.4*
11–30	14.7	17.4	14.6	13.1
Cumulative %	*93.6*	*93.4*	*94.7*	*93.5*
31+	6.4	6.6	5.3	6.5
M	8.7	9.3	7.7	8.4
SD	18.1	19.2	13.1	15.1

eliminate this potential problem. Research is needed to address how many items can be omitted on these various personality inventories before their validity is compromised seriously.

Consistency of Item Endorsement

The next step in assessing the validity of the patient's responses, after item omissions have been checked and found to be in the acceptable range, is to assess the consistency of item endorsement (see Figure 8.1). Consistency of item endorsement verifies that the patient has endorsed the items in a reliable manner. This procedure is necessary to ensure that the patient has endorsed the items consistently before any assessment of their accuracy is made. To highlight these differences, *consistency* of item endorsement may be conceptualized as being independent of or irrelevant to item content, whereas *accuracy* of item endorsement is dependent on or relevant to item content. Thus, measures of the consistency of item endorsement assess whether the individual has provided a reliable pattern of responding to the items throughout the inventory regardless of their content, whereas measures of the accuracy of item endorsement assess whether the individual has attempted to distort his or her responses to the items in some specific manner.

Random Sorts

One method of trying to simulate inconsistent patterns of item endorsement has utilized groups of random-sort MMPIs (trues and falses are assigned randomly to each item). Even a cursory inspection of these profiles (see Graham, 1987, p. 29; Greene, 1980, p. 60) will arouse the clinician's suspicions of a random sort, and several validity indices will confirm quickly the high probability of such a response pattern. In general, the larger the number of items on the validity scale/index being used, the better it will detect a random sort. Since the F scale consists of 64 infrequently endorsed items, random sorts should "endorse" around 32 items, which is a T score of 112. Thus, the F scale tends to be one of the most reliable indicators of a random sort (Dahlstrom et al., 1972; Rogers, Dolmetsch, & Cavanaugh, 1983). Random sorts also can be identified rather easily by the TR index (see Table 8.4; Dahlstrom et al., 1972) and the Carelessness Scale (see Table 8.6; Greene, 1978), which will be described below.

A second method of simulating inconsistent responses involves generating groups of profiles based on patterns of item endorsements such as TFTF, TTFTTF, FFTFFT, and so on. These profiles are identified almost as easily as random sorts, and again the larger the number of items on the validity scale/index, the better these profiles are detected (Dahlstrom et al., 1972; Nichols, Greene, & Schmolck, 1988).

Inconsistent Patterns of Endorsement

Patients may endorse the items inconsistently by a variety of methods. Rather than focusing on how patients generate inconsistent responses, the focus here will be on how to assess consistency of item endorsement. Two scales for assessing the consistency of item endorsement on the MMPI are the TR index (Buechley & Ball, 1952; Dahlstrom et al., 1972; Greene, 1979) and the CLS (Greene, 1978). The TR index is the total number of the 16 repeated items that the patient has endorsed inconsistently. The frequency by gender with which normal and psychiatric samples endorsed the items inconsistently on the TR index are provided in Tables 8.3 and 8.4, respectively. Normal samples were very consistent in their endorsement of the TR items, with 95% of these individuals making four or fewer inconsistent responses. Men made slightly more inconsistent responses than women. Gravitz and Gerton (1976) reported similar levels of inconsistent responses in their sample of 2,000 normal individuals undergoing preemployment screening; however, they found that women made slightly more inconsistent responses than men. Psychiatric samples also were very consistent, with 85% of the patients making four or fewer inconsistent responses. Adult and adolescent psychiatric patients scored in a very similar manner on the TR index, which is somewhat unexpected since adolescents generally are seen as being less compliant. The presence of psychopathology did not preclude these patients from being able to endorse the items on the TR index in a consistent manner.

The CLS (Greene, 1978) consists of 12 pairs of empirically selected items that were judged to be psychologically opposite in content. The

Table 8.3. Frequency of Inconsistent Responses on the Test–Retest Index for Normal Samples by Gender

Number of inconsistent responses	Colligan et al. (1983) Adults (%)		Greene (1986) Adults (%)		Greene (1986) College students (%)	
	Male (%) (N = 646)	Female (%) (N = 762)	Male (%) (N = 163)	Female (%) (N = 238)	Male (%) (N = 208)	Female (%) (N = 224)
0	32.2	40.3	27.6	42.9	25.5	36.6
1	29.7	29.5	41.7	36.6	32.2	33.0
2	19.4	14.1	16.0	8.8	20.2	17.9
3	9.7	7.6	3.1	7.6	14.4	6.7
4	4.2	3.9	6.1	2.9	4.3	4.0
Cumulative % (0–4)	95.2	95.4	94.5	98.8	96.6	98.2
Cumulative % (5+)	4.8	4.6	5.5	1.2	3.4	1.8
5	1.1	1.7	3.1	0.8	1.9	1.3
6	1.7	0.9	0.0	0.4	0.5	0.5
7	0.6	0.4	0.0	0.0	0.5	0.0
8+	1.4	1.6	2.4	0.0	0.5	0.0
M	1.48	1.28	1.47	0.95	1.53	1.14
SD	1.76	1.72	1.84	1.15	1.43	1.22

Table 8.4. Frequency of Inconsistent Responses on the Test–Retest Index for Psychiatric Patients by Gender and for Stimulus Avoidance Patterns

Number of inconsistent responses	Psychiatric patients (Hedlund & Won Cho, 1979) Adults (%)		Adults (%)		Stimulus avoidance patterns	
	Male (%) (N = 8,646)	Female (%) (N = 3,743)	Male (%) (N = 693)	Female (%) (N = 290)	Random (%) (N = 100)	Stimulus avoidance (%) (N = 436)
0	18.9	15.0	17.7	22.1	0.0	0.0
1	23.9	21.9	21.9	26.2	0.0	0.0
2	19.7	20.1	18.0	19.0	0.0	1.4
3	13.6	15.6	16.5	11.0	0.0	0.9
4	9.0	9.9	8.7	8.3	1.0	6.2
Cumulative % (0–4)	*85.1*	*82.5*	*82.6*	*86.6*	*1.0*	*8.5*
Cumulative % (5+)	*14.9*	*17.5*	*17.2*	*13.4*	*99.0*	*91.5*
5	6.0	6.9	4.9	4.1	3.0	17.0
6	3.3	4.3	4.2	3.4	6.0	13.8
7	2.4	2.7	3.3	2.8	12.0	17.9
8+	3.2	3.6	4.8	3.1	78.0	42.9
M	2.40	2.67	2.79	2.64	8.06	7.24
SD	1.74	1.77	1.85	1.78	2.00	2.20

Note. Stimulus avoidance patterns were defined as sequences of responses such as TFTF, TTFTTF, FFTFFT, and so on. See Nichols, Greene, and Schmolk (1988) for a complete description.

frequency by gender with which normal and psychiatric patients endorsed the CLS items inconsistently are provided in Tables 8.5 and 8.6, respectively. Normal samples were very consistent in their endorsement of the CLS items, with 97% of these individuals making four or fewer inconsistent responses. There do not appear to be any gender differences in the endorsement of the CLS items. Psychiatric samples also were very consistent, with 85% of the patients making four or fewer inconsistent responses. Adult and adolescent psychiatric patients scored in a very similar manner on the CLS. The CLS appears to perform in a very similar manner to the TR index in assessing the consistency of item endorsement.

One of the advantages of the TR index and the CLS compared with the F scale in the assessment of the consistency of item endorsement is that they are not affected by the presence of psychopathology as the F scale is. Elevations on the F scale can represent either an inconsistent pattern of item endorsement *or* the patient's acknowledgment of the presence of psychopathology *or* the patient's malingering of psychopathology (see Accuracy of Item Endorsement below). In contrast, the TR index and the CLS are relatively unaffected by the type and severity of psychopathology, so they can provide an independent estimate of the consistency of item endorsement. The TR index and the CLS will detect some profiles with inconsistent responses that would be considered valid by traditional validity indicators such as the F scale; they can also demonstrate that the patient has been endorsing the items consistently despite elevated scores on the F scale (Evans & Dinning, 1983; Maloney, Duvall, & Friesen, 1980). These findings indicate that the TR index, the CLS, and the traditional validity indicators are *not* measuring identical processes in test-taking attitudes (Fekken & Holden, 1987).

Although the TR index and the CLS are useful in identifying inconsistent patterns of item endorsement, the clinician should keep in mind that an acceptable score indicates only that the patient has endorsed the items consistently and not necessarily accurately, since the patient can consistently malinger or be defensive. Moreover, since the TR index assesses only the consistency of the patient's responses, it will not detect "all true" or "all false" response sets, which are consistent, but nonveridical, test-taking sets. The TR index will easily detect "random" response sets that would yield a score of approximately 8 (see Table 8.4; Rogers et al., 1983; Rogers, Harris, & Thatcher, 1983). The more subtle nature of the CLS—based on items that are not simply repeated but are psychologically opposite—should enable the clinician to detect a pattern of inconsistent item endorsement in sophisticated patients who might recognize the existence of identical repeated items and consequently go undetected by the TR index. The CLS also is useful in detecting "all true" and "all false" response sets since either response set would result in a total score of seven deviant responses (see Table 3-11 in Greene, 1980). In addition to detecting patients who are *unwilling* to answer

Table 8.5. Frequency of Inconsistent Responses on the Carelessness Scale for Normal Samples by Gender

Number of inconsistent responses	Colligan et al. (1983) Adults (%)		Greene (1986) Adults (%)		Greene (1986) College students (%)	
	Male (%) (N = 646)	Female (%) (N = 762)	Male (%) (N = 163)	Female (%) (N = 238)	Male (%) (N = 208)	Female (%) (N = 224)
0	27.4	31.9	40.5	43.3	26.4	35.3
1	35.8	31.5	25.2	30.7	30.8	31.7
2	19.6	22.8	18.2	19.3	24.5	20.1
3	11.6	8.4	9.2	4.6	9.6	9.8
4	3.6	4.0	4.4	1.3	6.3	2.2
Cumulative % (0–4)	98.0	98.6	97.5	99.2	97.6	99.1
Cumulative % (5+)	2.0	1.4	2.5	0.8	2.4	0.9
5	1.2	0.6	2.5	0.8	1.4	0.9
6	0.6	0.8	0.0	0.0	1.0	0.0
7	0.2	0.0	0.0	0.0	0.0	0.0
8+	0.0	0.0	0.0	0.0	0.0	0.0
M	1.35	1.26	1.19	0.92	1.47	1.15
SD	1.24	1.21	1.31	1.03	1.31	1.13

Table 8.6. Frequency of Inconsistent Responses on the Carelessness Scale for Psychiatric Patients by Gender and for Stimulus Avoidance Patterns

Number of inconsistent responses	Psychiatric patients (Hedlund & Won Cho, 1979)				Stimulus avoidance patterns	
	Adults (%)		Adolescents (%)			
	Male (%) (N = 8,646)	Female (%) (N = 3,743)	Male (%) (N = 693)	Female (%) (N = 290)	Random (%) (N = 100)	Stimulus avoidance (%) (N = 436)
0	12.6	8.8	9.7	10.0	0.0	0.0
1	22.1	19.7	16.9	19.0	0.0	0.5
2	23.5	22.8	21.9	24.1	0.0	1.8
3	17.8	19.0	20.6	16.9	2.0	5.5
4	11.8	14.9	12.7	14.1	4.0	10.6
Cumulative % (0-4)	87.8	85.2	81.8	84.1	6.0	18.4
Cumulative % (5+)	12.2	14.8	18.2	15.9	94.0	81.6
5	6.4	8.0	9.1	9.0	16.0	13.1
6	3.4	3.9	5.2	3.8	16.0	28.9
7	1.7	1.8	2.9	2.8	28.0	19.0
8+	0.7	1.1	1.0	0.3	34.0	20.4
M	2.40	2.67	2.79	2.64	5.90	6.08
SD	1.74	1.77	1.85	1.78	1.71	1.71

Note. Stimulus avoidance profiles were defined as sequences of responses such as TFTF, TTFTTF, FFTFFT, and so on. See Nichols, Greene, and Schmolk (1988) for a complete description.

the MMPI appropriately, the CLS also seems to detect patients who are psychologically confused and *unable* to answer the MMPI appropriately. In such a case, an interview with the patient usually enables the clinician to recognize the patient's mental confusion.

Bond (1986) and Fekken and Holden (1987) have noted that carelessness is *not* the primary cause of inconsistent responding to the CLS items in normal students. It may be more appropriate to call the CLS an inconsistency scale which does not imply any motivation by the patient for his or her inconsistent responses.

Clinical Application to the MMPI

Specific cutting scores (TR > 5, CLS > 5, or TR + CLS > 9) may be used to assess consistency of item endorsement on the MMPI. Table 8.19 also provides the other information that is needed to implement the process for assessing the validity of an objective personality inventory outlined in Figure 8.1. The importance of assessing consistency of item endorsement *before* trying to assess accuracy of item endorsement cannot be overstressed. Otherwise, inconsistent patterns of item endorsement may be labeled inappropriately as malingering (Rogers *et al.*, 1983).

A variety of reasons exist to explain why a patient may endorse the items inconsistently on any objective personality inventory. These potential reasons are summarized in Table 8.7 as well as how each of them may be resolved.

Table 8.7. Potential Causes of and Solutions for Inconsistent Item Endorsement

Cause	Solution
1. Patient has not been told why the MMPI is being administered	1. Explain why the MMPI is being administered and how the data are to be used
2. Inadequate reading ability or comprehension; inadequate educational opportunity	2. Present the MMPI orally by tape administration (see Chapter 2, Greene, 1980)
3. Limited intellectual ability	3. Present the MMPI orally by tape administration (see Chapter 2, Greene, 1980). Dahlstrom, Welsh, and Dahlstrom (1972) reported that tape administrations are effective with IQs as low as 65.
4. Too confused psychiatrically or neuropsychologically	4. Readminister the MMPI once the patient is less confused
5. Still toxic from substance abuse	5. Readminister the MMPI once the patient is detoxified
6. Noncompliant or uncooperative	6. Be sure patient understands the importance of the MMPI for treatment/intervention and readminister the MMPI. If the patient is still noncompliant that issue becomes the focus of treatment

Other Objective Personality Inventories

Consistency of item endorsement is generally assessed by a single scale on most other objective personality inventories. These scales are usually similar to the F scale on the MMPI in that they are composed of items with low frequency of endorsements.

The Infrequency scale of the CPI was developed by selecting items which were endorsed by no more than 5% of the normative samples. Since high scores on the CPI were designed to measure positive traits, the deviant response was reversed for each item and the scale was renamed as the Communality scale. T scores of 30 or lower on the Communality scale usually are seen in random responses, and may be seen in malingering (Megargee, 1972).

The Validity index on the MCMI (Millon, 1983) is designed to identify random or confused responding. The Validity index consists of four non-bizarre items which were endorsed by less than .01% of the patients among clinical populations. An Index score of 2 or more renders the profile invalid, and if the report is being interpreted by the automated interpretive system it is terminated. A score of 1 is labeled unreliable, and the clinician is advised to be cautious.

The Random scale on the 16 PF is made up of 31 items with a cutting score of 5 or greater, used to identify random responses (Karson & O'Dell, 1976, pp. 153–154). This scale only can be scored on Form A of the 16 PF. Scoring the Random scale is somewhat complicated since 23 items are scored if endorsed and 8 items if they are not endorsed.

All of these objective personality inventories provide some means of assessing consistency of item endorsement and at least preliminary data on these scales. All of them, except for the 16 PF, provide for routine scoring of these scales by the clinician. More research is needed with each of these inventories to determine how well these scales assess consistency of item endorsement in various clinical settings with different patient samples.

Accuracy of Item Endorsement

The next step in the process of assessing the validity of an objective personality inventory, after item omissions and consistency of item endorsement have been checked, is to verify the accuracy of item endorsement (see Figure 8.1). Accuracy of item endorsement verifies whether the patient has adopted a response set to either malinger or be defensive. Since the patient's inventory data only reveal that the items have been endorsed inaccurately, it is necessary to determine the patient's motivation for inaccurate item endorsement from a clinical interview and a review of the patient's reasons for taking the personality inventory.

Several assumptions and related issues about malingering and defensiveness must be made explicit before the scales and indexes for assessing accuracy of item endorsement are discussed. First, it will be assumed that malingering and defensiveness represent a unitary continuum, which is characterized by the malingering at one end and defensiveness at the other (see Figure 8.2). Consequently, accurate patterns of item endorsement gradually will shade into malingering or defensiveness as one moves up or down this continuum; no exact point exists at which the patient's performance suddenly reflects either malingering or defensiveness. Instead, a probability statement can be made that this patient's performance has a particular likelihood of reflecting either malingering or defensiveness. Second, it will be assumed that patients, who are endorsing the items inaccurately, will malinger or be defensive in general rather than trying to simulate a specific mental disorder or a set of symptoms. It is very difficult for patients to take an objective personality inventory convincingly as if they have a specific mental disorder (this has been documented frequently; see Gough Dissimulation Scale—Revised, cited in the next paragraph). Third, the presence of malingering or defensiveness *cannot* be taken as evidence that the patient does or does not have actual psychopathology, since a patient who actually has some specific mental disorder can also malinger or be defensive about the presence of psychopathology. The scales and indexes to assess accuracy of item endorsement *cannot* determine whether the patient actually has psychopathology, only whether the patient has provided an accurate self-description.

In assessing the accuracy of item endorsement, it is more efficient to discuss procedures for assessing malingering first and then defensiveness since the same scales and indexes do not always work for both response sets. Malingering can be assessed by the Wiener and Harmon (Wiener, 1948) Obvious and Subtle scales, the Gough Dissimulation Scale (Ds) (Gough,

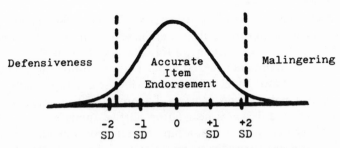

Figure 8.2. Assessing accuracy of item endorsement. It is *not* necessary to use the same percentile for the cutting score to identify malingering and defensiveness. The hypothetical cutting scores illustrated in this figure have been set deliberately at different percentiles.

1954, 1957), Critical Items (cf. Lachar & Wrobel, 1979), the F scale, and the F-K Dissimulation Index. Defensiveness can be assessed by the Wiener and Harmon (Wiener, 1948) Obvious and Subtle scales, the Positive Malingering Scale (Cofer, Chance, & Judson, 1949), Critical Items (cf. Lachar & Wrobel, 1979), the L scale, and the K scale. The reader should realize that it is *not* necessary to score all of these methods for assessing malingering or defensiveness for every patient. Several methods will be illustrated within each response set, and the reader will need to decide which method is most appropriate for his or her specific treatment setting and patients. Each of these response sets will be examined in turn.

Malingering

Wiener and Harmon Obvious and Subtle Scales

Examining endorsements to subtle versus obvious items has shown some promise in detecting malingering and defensiveness. In the early research in this area, Wiener and Harmon (Wiener, 1948) performed a rational inspection of MMPI items identifying obvious items as those that were easy to detect as indicating emotional disturbance, and subtle items as those that were relatively difficult to detect as reflecting emotional disturbance. This procedure resulted in the identification of 110 subtle and 146 obvious items. Although Wiener and Harmon had intended to develop subtle and obvious subscales for each clinical scale, it was possible to do so for only five scales: Scales 2 (D), 3 (Hy), 4 (Pd), 6 (Pa), and 9 (Ma). Thus, the total score on each of these five scales can be divided into a subtle score and an obvious score, which could be evaluated for their respective contributions to the total score. The other clinical scales were composed primarily of obvious items, so it was not possible to develop subtle and obvious subscales. These clinical scales include the scales that require the most K-correction (Scales 1 (Hs), 7 (Pt), and 8 (Sc).

Research on the Wiener and Harmon (Wiener, 1948) subtle and obvious items has demonstrated their usefulness in identifying both malingering and defensiveness (Anthony, 1971; Harvey & Sipprelle, 1976). The available research does not suggest explicit criteria for defining a malingering response set based on the subtle and obvious scales. It probably is safe to assume that a patient who achieves T scores of 70 or more on all five obvious scales and T scores near 50 on all five subtle scales is trying to overreport. The converse relationship between scores on the obvious and subtle scales should arouse the suspicion of a defensive response set. Since it will be assumed that malingering and defensiveness are a general process, one method for creating a criterion to assess these response sets would be to sum the differences between the obvious and the subtle scales. (This procedure is illustrated in Table 8.8). The T scores for each of the obvious and subtle scales has been calculated, their difference determined on each clinical scale, and these differences summed into a single overall measure. It is important that the raw scores on the obvious and subtle scales be converted to T scores *before* computing this difference score since the obvious and subtle scales do not have the same number of items. For example, the Scale 2 (D) obvious scale consists of 40 items, whereas the subtle scale has only 20 items. Employing this method, a patient with a difference score of +207 strongly suggests malingering. In contrast, a patient with a difference score of −99 strongly suggests defensiveness.

Three issues must be addressed before the use of this difference score is explored. First, there are other obvious and subtle scales which could be used to assess accuracy of item endorsement (cf. Greene, 1980, pp. 60–64). The Wiener and Harmon (Wiener, 1948) Obvious and Subtle scales were selected because they have the longest history of usage in the MMPI field. Indeed, the high degree of item overlap among the various obvious and subtle scales and their high correlations suggest that any of these obvious and subtle scales would work equally well (Dubinsky, Gamble, & Rogers, 1985). However, Ward (1986) has noted that the definition of item subtlety varies in different sets of obvious and subtle scales. This issue needs to be considered in future research. Second, the question of whether large differences on the individual clinical scales have any significance has not been explored.

Table 8.8. Assessing Accuracy of Item Endorsement by the Difference between Obvious and Subtle Scales

Scale	Patient 1		Patient 2	
	T score	Difference	T score	Difference
2 (D)				
Obvious	98		50	
Subtle	28	+70	74	−24
3 (Hy)				
Obvious	95		41	
Subtle	45	+50	64	−23
4 (Pd)				
Obvious	98		45	
Subtle	55	+43	66	−21
6 (Pa)				
Obvious	83		48	
Subtle	52	+31	67	−19
9 (Ma)				
Obvious	82		37	
Subtle	69	+13	49	−12
Sum of Difference Scores		+207		−99

Note. Wiener and Harmon's (Wiener, 1948) Obvious and Subtle scales were used in these examples.

For example, it is not clear whether a difference of +30 points on Scale 2 (D) has the same meaning as +30 points on Scale 9 (Ma). Third and finally, it must be explicit that these obvious and subtle scales are *not* being used to predict specific external criteria, since it is reasonably well established that obvious scales are better predictors of most criteria than subtle scales (Jackson, 1971). Instead the difference between the obvious and subtle scales is being used as an index of the accuracy of item endorsement.

Tables 8.9 and 8.10 present the distribution of this difference score on the Wiener and Harmon (Wiener, 1948) Obvious and Subtle scales by gender for normal and psychiatric samples, respectively. The mean difference score in normal samples is in the range of 0 to −30, whereas in psychiatric samples it is in the range of 50 to 60. Psychiatric samples score slightly higher on this index than do normal ones, which is to be expected since they should be acknowledging the presence of some form of psycho-

Table 8.9. Distribution of Difference Scores between Obvious and Subtle Scales for Normal Samples by Gender

	Greene (1986)			
	Adults (%)		College students (%)	
Difference score	Male (%) ($N = 163$)	Female (%) ($N = 238$)	Male (%) ($N = 208$)	Female (%) ($N = 224$)
276–300	0.0	0.0	0.0	0.0
251–275	0.0	0.0	0.0	0.0
226–250	0.0	0.0	0.0	0.0
201–225	0.0	0.0	0.5	0.0
176–200	0.0	0.0	0.9	0.0
151–175	0.0	0.0	1.0	0.9
126–150	0.6	1.3	3.9	1.3
101–125	2.5	1.6	3.8	3.6
76–100	6.1	2.6	7.2	4.0
51–75	8.6	3.3	12.0	9.4
26–50	10.4	8.8	12.0	12.5
1–25	10.5	6.8	16.9	17.0
− 24–0	12.8	17.6	17.8	13.8
− 49−−25	14.8	16.0	12.5	18.8
− 74−−50	22.0	18.2	7.2	11.6
− 99−−75	6.8	14.7	2.9	3.5
−124−−100	4.9	8.8	1.4	3.6
−149−−125	0.0	0.4	0.0	0.0
M	11.9	−30.5	19.1	0.2
SD	59.1	56.4	61.7	56.8

Table 8.10. Distribution of Difference Scores between Obvious and Subtle Scales for Psychiatric Samples by Gender

| | Psychiatric patients (Hedlund & Won Cho, 1979) | | | |
| | Adults (%) | | Adolescents (%) | |
Difference score	Male (%) ($N = 8,646$)	Female (%) ($N = 3,743$)	Male (%) ($N = 693$)	Female (%) ($N = 290$)
276–300	0.3	0.1	0.1	0.0
251–275	0.7	0.2	0.9	0.0
226–250	1.7	1.0	1.5	1.0
201–225	2.8	1.9	2.7	2.4
176–200	3.9	3.4	4.3	4.2
151–175	5.3	5.2	4.8	6.9
126–150	6.9	7.0	6.9	7.9
101–125	8.9	9.1	10.1	13.8
76–100	10.2	11.4	10.3	8.3
51–75	10.9	10.9	8.6	9.6
26–50	10.8	11.6	11.1	10.0
1–25	9.7	10.7	12.6	4.2
− 24–0	8.8	9.2	11.1	10.0
− 49−−25	7.8	7.1	7.2	8.9
− 74−−50	5.7	5.7	3.9	6.2
− 99−−75	3.4	3.6	2.3	3.2
−124−−100	1.8	1.3	1.5	2.7
−149−−125	0.4	0.6	0.1	0.7
M	56.5	51.8	58.4	55.5
SD	85.1	79.7	81.8	85.7

pathology that will increase their score on the obvious scales. The psychiatric samples also are more variable on this index with their standard deviations about 50% larger than the normal samples. The distributions appear to be relatively normal in all of the various samples. There appear to be few gender or age (adolescent versus adult) differences in any of the samples.

Based on the data presented in Table 8.10, the clinician can decide what percentage of patients should be labeled as malingering. Clearly difference scores in the range of 250–300 are strongly suggestive of malingering. However, the clinician must decide what is the lower limit for classifying a patient's responses as reflecting malingering. For example, if difference scores of 200 or higher are deemed to be suggestive of malingering, 5.5% of the male patients (0.3% + 0.7 + 1.7 + 2.8) and 3.2% of the female patients (0.1% + 0.2 + 1.0 + 1.9) exceed this criterion. When a patient's responses have been identified as reflecting malingering, the standard profile is no longer interpretable since it reflects an invalid response set. The clinician should describe the patient's style of malingering, determine the potential causes for this response set, and assess the implications for treatment/ intervention; the clinician should *not* attempt to interpret the codetype or any of the individual scales.

A difference score above whatever cutting score is used to identify malingering must be used as presumptive rather than definitive evidence of this response set. It is always necessary to verify that the patient is malingering rather than actually experiencing severe psychopathology. When the difference score exceeds 200, it should be readily apparent by an interview whether the patient is malingering, since if the patient's responses were accurate, pervasive and severe psychopathology should be present. Occasionally in an inpatient setting, difference scores above 200 will be seen in a nonmalingering patient. In an outpatient setting, it is extremely unlikely for difference scores in this range to reflect actual psychopathology since the patient should be so overwhelmed that he or she would be unable to function.

Gough Dissimulation Scale—Revised

The Gough Dissimulation (Ds) Scale (Gough, 1954) consists of 74 items, later revised to 40 items (Ds-r) (Gough, 1957), which significantly differentiated a group of neurotic patients from groups of college students and professional psychologists instructed to simulate the responses of neurotic patients on the MMPI. The items pertain not to neuroticism but to the prevailing stereotypes about neuroticism. The psychologists and students scored three to four times higher than neurotic patients on the Ds scale. The professional psychologists were only slightly better at simulating neurosis than the students, and both groups were easily identified by the Ds scale.

A study by Mehlman and Rand (1960) offers general support for Gough's findings that persons attempting to simulate psychopathology on the MMPI can be identified readily by their responses to the inventory items. They presented 45 MMPI items to clinical psychologists, graduate students in psychology, and undergraduates and asked them to indicate the clinical scale on which each item was found. There were no differences between the groups in their ability to indicate the scale on which the item appeared, and all groups could accurately identify only about four or five items. These results are not surprising because MMPI scales were formed empirically, not rationally. Since these persons could not guess which scales contained various items, the implication is that they also would be unable to distort their responses to simulate accurately a specific form of psychopathology and achieve an elevated score on the appropriate scale.

In investigating the Ds scale, Anthony (1971) reported that it had an optimum hit rate of 86% in identifying male patients with nonpsychotic diagnoses referred for psychological testing who were instructed to exaggerate their presenting symptoms. The Ds scale had a higher hit rate in identifying these patients who were malingering psychopathology than did either the raw score on the F scale or the F-K index, although the differences in hit rate were not statistically significant. Thus, the Ds scale appears to deserve serious attention in its usefulness in identifying malingering.

Tables 8.11 and 8.12 summarize the range of scores that are seen on Ds-r by gender for normal individuals and psychiatric patients, respectively. In about 10% of the normal individuals, T scores of 70 or higher occur. The same is true for 30% of the adult psychiatric patients, and 40% of the adolescent psychiatric patients. If a T score of 90 or higher on the Ds-r scale were used to indicate malingering, 6–9% of the psychiatric patients would be classified as endorsing the items inaccurately with little difference between the adult and adolescent patients, whereas none of the normal adults and 0.5% of the college students would be so classified.

Lachar and Wrobel Critical Items

Despite the inherent difficulties in understanding responses to individual MMPI items (difficulties that provided the orginal impetus for the empirical selection of items on the MMPI), clinicians have been unwilling to ignore the information that might be contained in those responses. The original set of "critical" items, which were thought to require careful scrutiny if answered in the deviant direction, was rationally or intuitively selected by

Table 8.11. Distribution of T Scores for Gough Dissimulation Scale–Revised (Ds-r) in Normal Samples by Gender

| T score range | Colligan et al. (1983)[a] | | Greene (1986) | | | |
| | Adults (%) | | Adults (%) | | College students (%) | |
	Male (%) ($N = 646$)	Female (%) ($N = 762$)	Male (%) ($N = 163$)	Female (%) ($N = 238$)	Male (%) ($N = 208$)	Female (%) ($N = 224$)
90+	0.3	0.3	0.0	0.0	0.5	0.4
80–89	1.0	0.6	0.0	0.4	5.8	0.8
70–79	3.6	4.8	9.2	6.6	9.6	8.4
60–69	16.4	15.8	11.0	18.5	18.2	23.7
50–59	35.1	30.4	32.5	21.3	30.8	28.2
40–49	39.3	42.4	43.6	45.7	34.6	33.9
0–39	4.3	5.7	3.7	7.1	0.5	4.5
M	51.5	51.6	52.8	52.2	56.7	55.0
SD	9.7	9.8	10.3	10.2	11.4	10.4

[a]Colligan, Osborne, Swenson, & Offord (1983) scored the original Gough Dissimulation Scale.

Table 8.12. Distribution of T Scores for the Gough Dissimulation Scale–Revised (Ds-r) in Psychiatric Samples by Gender

| | Psychiatric patients (Hedlund & Won Cho, 1979) | | | |
| | Adults (%) | | Adolescents (%) | |
T score range	Male (%) (N = 8,646)	Female (%) (N = 3,743)	Male (%) (N = 693)	Female (%) (N = 290)
110+	0.2	0.1	0.2	0.0
100–109	2.1	1.6	3.5	0.6
90–99	5.0	4.7	5.8	5.8
80–89	7.7	8.4	11.6	12.1
70–79	15.8	16.9	18.0	24.5
60–69	17.9	22.6	20.2	22.1
50–59	22.7	20.5	24.7	16.9
40–49	26.1	21.9	15.3	16.2
0–39	2.4	3.7	0.7	1.7
M	61.8	62.4	65.9	65.8
SD	16.3	15.4	16.1	14.8

Grayson (1951). Grayson's early work on critical items has since been followed by the development of other sets of critical items (see pp. 170–178 in Greene, 1980). Since these critical items have obvious, or face-valid, content, they provide another means of assessing the accuracy of item endorsement. The Lachar and Wrobel (1979) critical items will be used to illustrate this procedure, although any critical item set could be used to assess accuracy of item endorsement. Regardless of the set of critical items that are used, the rationale for assessing accuracy of item endorsement will remain the same.

Lachar and Wrobel (1979) developed their critical items to be face-valid (obvious) descriptors of psychological concerns. They first identified 14 categories of symptoms that summarized problems that (1) motivate people to seek psychological treatment and (2) help the clinician make diagnostic decisions. Then 14 clinical psychologists read each MMPI item and nominated items that would be face-valid indicators of psychopathology in one of these 14 categories. These items were empirically validated by contrasting the item-response frequencies for normal and psychiatric samples matched for sex and race. Lachar and Wrobel were able to validate 130 of the 177 items nominated. After eliminating 19 items that duplicated content, they arrived at a final list of 111 (20.2%) critical items out of a possible 550 items.

The total number of Lachar and Wrobel critical items that are endorsed by the patient can become another index of the accuracy of item endorsement. A patient who is trying to malinger would be expected to endorse a large number of these items, whereas a patient who is trying to be defensive would be expected to endorse few of them. Tables 8.13 and 8.14 summarize by gender the total number of Lachar and Wrobel critical items that are endorsed by normal individuals and psychiatric patients, respectively. The normal individuals endorse a range from 18 to 26 (16–23%) of these items, the psychiatric patients endorse 36 to 40 (32–36%). There do not appear to be any gender or age (adolescent versus adult) differences in the endorsement of these critical items. As would be expected, psychiatric patients endorse more of these items and are more variable in endorsing them, with standard deviations almost twice as large as those for normal individuals. The fact that normal individuals endorse 16–23% of these items may suggest that at least some of these items are not as "critical" as originally thought. It is also interesting to note that almost 20% of these psychiatric patients endorse fewer total critical items than the average normal individual. Again, it should go without saying that such measures of malingering and defensiveness do *not* indicate whether the person has psychopathology, only that the person does not endorse the items accurately.

Table 8.13. Distribution of Total Number of Lachar and Wrobel (1979) Critical Items Endorsed in Normal Samples by Gender

| | Colligan *et al.* (1983) | | Greene (1986) | | | |
| | Adults (%) | | Adults (%) | | College students (%) | |
Total critical items[a]	Male (%) ($N = 646$)	Female (%) ($N = 762$)	Male (%) ($N = 163$)	Female (%) ($N = 238$)	Male (%) ($N = 208$)	Female (%) ($N = 224$)
91+	0.0	0.0	0.0	0.0	0.0	0.0
81–90	0.0	0.0	0.0	0.0	0.0	0.0
71–80	0.0	0.0	0.0	0.0	0.5	0.4
61–70	0.3	0.2	0.0	0.0	0.9	0.0
51–60	0.6	0.4	2.5	2.1	6.8	2.3
41–50	1.7	2.4	6.1	1.3	8.6	5.8
31–40	6.5	6.7	8.0	13.4	17.8	17.4
21–30	21.2	18.0	20.8	18.5	22.1	26.8
11–20	40.7	40.5	33.8	40.8	35.1	37.0
0–10	29.0	31.8	28.8	23.9	8.2	10.3
M	16.9	16.5	19.4	18.6	26.4	23.4
SD	9.9	10.1	12.5	10.9	14.1	11.9

[a]These are the total number of critical items endorsed, *not* T scores.

Table 8.14. Distribution of Total Number of Lachar and Wrobel (1979) Critical Items Endorsed in Psychiatric Samples by Gender

| | Psychiatric patients (Hedlund & Won Cho, 1979) | | | |
| | Adults (%) | | Adolescents (%) | |
Total critical items[a]	Male (%) (N = 8,646)	Female (%) (N = 3,743)	Male (%) (N = 693)	Female (%) (N = 290)
91+	0.3	0.3	0.7	0.0
81–90	1.8	1.4	2.6	1.7
71–80	3.9	3.2	4.8	4.2
61–70	6.9	7.3	6.6	11.7
51–60	10.7	12.7	13.0	13.8
41–50	14.3	18.0	16.2	19.3
31–40	18.6	18.7	16.7	15.2
21–30	20.3	19.3	21.7	14.4
11–20	17.3	14.1	13.9	16.9
0–10	5.9	5.0	3.8	2.8
M	36.5	38.0	39.2	40.5
SD	19.3	18.3	19.5	19.3

[a]These are the total number of critical items endorsed, *not* T scores.

F Scale

The F scale is the traditional index of malingering on the MMPI, since its items were selected to detect unusual or atypical ways of endorsing (Dahlstrom *et al.*, 1972). Elevations on the F scale can occur for several reasons: (1) inconsistent patterns of item endorsement, (2) the presence of actual psychopathology, and (3) malingering. Consequently, it is very difficult to ascertain the reason(s) for an elevation on the F scale without considering the other indicators of the consistency and accuracy of item endorsement. For example, it probably is safe to conclude that a raw score greater than 26 (T score > 100) on the F scale does not reflect actual psychopathology, but it could reflect either an inconsistent pattern of item endorsement or malingering. Since different clinical decisions will be made depending on the reason, it is important for the clinician to use the other validity indicators described in this chapter to make this discrimination. Thus, the best use of the F scale is in conjunction with other validity indicators.

F-K Index: Gough Dissimulation Index

Another validity indicator, the F-K index (Gough Dissimulation Index), has been developed by combining two of the three traditional validity scales.

The reader is cautioned *not* to confuse the F-K index (Gough Dissimulation Index) with the Gough Dissimulation Scale—Revised (Ds-r), which was described above. The Ds-r is a set of empirically derived items designed to assess malingering, whereas the F-K index utilizes the relationship between the standard validity scales of F and K to assess malingering. Gough (1947, 1950) suggested that the F-K index—the *raw* score of the F scale minus the *raw* score of the K scale—would be useful in screening MMPI profiles for accuracy of item endorsement. If the F-K index was greater than +9, the profile was designated as malingering. If the F-K index was less than 0, the profile was classified as being defensive. Intermediate scores on the F-K index (0–9) indicated accurate item endorsement, that is, valid profiles. Gough (1950) reported that the F-K index readily detected malingering; in one sample it accurately classified 97% of the authentic profiles and 75% of the malingering ones.

Most studies of the F-K index in identifying malingering on the MMPI have utilized normal persons who were instructed to feign psychopathology. Numerous investigators working with student subjects (Cofer *et al.*, 1949; Exner, McDowell, Pabst, Stackman, & Kirk, 1963; Hunt, 1948) have confirmed the ability of the F-K index to identify students who are instructed to malinger; some of these investigators (Exner *et al.*, 1963; Hunt, 1948), however, also noted that the F scale alone identified malingering even more efficiently than the F-K index.

Anthony (1971) found the F-K index to have limited success working with patients referred for psychological evaluation. He instructed 40 male nonpsychotic patients to exaggerate their presenting psychopathology when they took the MMPI a second time. Using the cut-off points on this index suggested by Gough (1947), Anthony reported that fewer than half (16) of the 40 exaggerated profiles were identified by the F-K index. Almost one-half (17) of the exaggerated profiles had a raw score on the F scale of less than 15, which would directly account for the limited success of the F-K index in identifying the exaggerated profiles since the raw score on the F scale is close to 9, even before the raw score on the K scale is subtracted. Anthony found that, even when using different cutting scores on the F-K index, he could only correctly classify 75% of the profiles. Thus, the F-K index seems to be more limited in its usefulness with patients who are exaggerating their psychopathology than with normal individuals. Thus, in clinical settings, the F-K index may, at best, screen a few malingering patients.

Tables 8.15 and 8.16 summarize the distribution of scores for the F-K index (Gough Dissimulation Index) by gender in normal individuals and psychiatric patients, respectively. The normal individuals achieve mean scores of nearly −10 on this index, whereas the psychiatric patients achieve mean scores near 0. If F-K scores greater than +10 are said to be malingering, almost 25% of the adolescent psychiatric patients and 16% of the adult

Table 8.15. Distribution of Difference Scores on the F-K Index (Gough Dissimulation Index) in Normal Samples by Gender

	Colligan et al. (1983)[a]		Greene (1986)			
	Adults (%)		Adults (%)		College students (%)	
Difference score	Male (%) (N = 305)	Female (%) (N = 335)	Male (%) (N = 163)	Female (%) (N = 238)	Male (%) (N = 208)	Female (%) (N = 224)
16+	0.3	0.0	0.0	0.0	0.0	0.0
11–15	1.0	0.0	0.0	0.4	4.3	1.3
6–10	1.7	0.9	5.5	1.7	3.9	2.3
1–5	3.2	3.3	1.2	2.9	13.4	7.6
−4–0	11.5	9.8	10.5	13.1	18.8	18.7
−9−−5	25.6	23.3	33.7	26.0	25.0	31.7
−14−−10	33.7	31.7	12.9	23.5	23.1	27.2
−19−−15	17.8	22.9	32.5	29.9	10.5	8.5
−−20	5.2	8.1	3.7	2.5	1.0	2.7
M	−9.8	−11.2	−10.0	−10.3	−5.6	−7.2
SD	6.6	6.2	7.0	6.1	7.6	6.5

[a]Colligan, Osborne, Swenson, & Offord (1983).

psychiatric patients would be so classified. Since the F scale also may reflect the presence of actual psychopathology, it would be expected that this index would have a high false-positive rate (patients who are said to be malingering who are actually experiencing significant psychopathology). A cutting score much higher than +9 would be needed on the F-K index to decrease the number of false positives; it is not clear whether a more appropriate cutting score can be identified for this index since the F scale also is elevated by actual psychopathology.

Clinical Applications to the MMPI

Five different indices to assess malingering have been described. The reader will need to select the scale/index that is most appropriate for his or her specific patients and treatment setting. It is *not* necessary to use several of these scales/indexes simultaneously since they are correlated highly and consequently are very redundant. For example, the correlations among the Wiener and Harmon (Wiener, 1948) Obvious and Subtle scales, the Ds-r scale (Gough Dissimulation Scale—Revised) (Gough, 1957), and the Lachar and Wrobel (1979) critical items range between .88 and .92 in Hedlund and Won Cho's (1979) psychiatric samples, whereas the correlations between the scale and the F-K index (Gough Dissimulation Index) (Gough, 1947) and these three scales/indexes range from .70 to .86 in these same samples.

Table 8.16. Distribution of Difference Scores for the F-K Index (Gough Dissimulation Index) in Psychiatric Samples by Gender

| | Psychiatric patients (Hedlund & Won Cho, 1979) | | | |
| | Adults (%) | | Adolescents (%) | |
Difference score	Male (%) ($N = 8,646$)	Female (%) ($N = 3,743$)	Male (%) ($N = 693$)	Female (%) ($N = 290$)
36+	0.5	0.3	1.0	0.0
31–35	0.9	0.7	1.3	0.3
26–30	1.6	1.2	2.3	1.1
21–25	2.4	2.4	5.5	4.1
16–20	4.3	4.3	5.8	6.6
11–15	6.3	6.3	7.3	12.4
6–10	8.8	10.0	11.4	11.0
1–5	13.4	12.9	14.5	15.9
−4–0	17.8	18.6	14.5	13.4
−9–−5	18.2	18.6	17.1	14.2
−14–−10	14.5	15.1	12.5	12.0
−19–−15	8.3	7.1	4.8	7.3
−20	3.0	2.5	2.0	1.7
M	−1.3	−1.3	1.8	1.1
SD	11.8	11.3	12.7	11.5

A point worthy of reemphasis is that once a profile has been defined as reflecting malingering, it *cannot* be interpreted as a valid profile. The patient's specific reasons for malingering should be ascertained by a clinical interview, and the profile can be described as reflecting such a process; however, neither the MMPI codetype (the highest clinical scale or the high-point pair) nor the individual scales can be interpreted. The reader also should note that in Figure 8.1 once an MMPI is said to be characterized by malingering, the interpretive process stops. The patient could have the MMPI readministered, although such a procedure may not result in a valid profile. Once a patient is motivated for whatever reason to malinger, it may be difficult for him or her to endorse the items accurately in subsequent administrations. It is not known whether malingering would persist across treatment settings for a particular patient, although Audubon and Kirwin (1982) found at least some situational influences on response style.

Although the codetype from a malingering profile *cannot* be interpreted, several empirical correlates of such profiles have been identified in a manner similar to Marks, Seeman, and Haller's (1974) description of a K+ profile. Both Greene (1988) and Hale, Zimostrad, Duckworth, and Nicholas (1986) found that patients who malingered were very likely to terminate treatment within the first few sessions; frequently they did not return after the initial session. This finding that these patients terminate treatment quickly is almost exactly the opposite of what might be anticipated, since these patients are sometimes described as "pleading for help" and would be expected to remain in treatment longer than most patients. Additional research is needed to determine whether there are other empirical correlates of malingering.

Other Objective Personality Inventories

Most objective personality inventories provide some means of assessing malingering. The same scale may be used to assess both malingering and defensiveness (e.g., MCMI: Millon, 1984) or separate scales may be employed (e.g., the CPI: Megargee, 1972; 16 PF: Karson & O'Dell, 1976). When the same scale is used to assess both malingering and defensiveness, it will be described in this section; when a separate scale is used to assess defensiveness it will be described in the next section of this chapter.

The CPI uses the Well-Being scale to assess malingering. The Well-Being scale is virtually identical with the Gough Dissimulation Scale—Revised (Ds-r), which was described above. The deviant response for the items was reversed so that low scores now reflect malingering and high scores reflect well-being. Little research exists on the validity of the Well-Being scale as an index of malingering (Megargee, 1972).

The M Test (Beaber *et al.*, 1985) has been developed to identify malingering of schizophrenic symptoms. The M Test consists of three types of items: 8 confusion items; 10 items that are true indicators of schizophrenia; and 15 items that are *not* true indicators of schizophrenia. These latter 15 items tapped nonexistent entities, atypical hallucinations, excessively severe symptoms, and atypical delusions. None of these 33 items was endorsed by normal college students over 10% of the time. They found that the M Test had 82.6% classification accuracy in distinguishing between schizophrenic patients and students who malingered schizophrenia. Since the M Test is new, there has not been additional research on it.

The MCMI contains scales which are used to correct for malingering or defensiveness. The weight factor is designed to correct for these response sets by lowering or raising all personality pathology and symptom disorder scales (Scales A through PP) if malingering or defensiveness, respectively, are identified. "The Weight Factor is calculated by the degree of positive or negative deviation from the mid-range of the composite raw score total of the eight basic personality scales" (Millon, 1983, p. 14). Total raw scores above 165 are indicative of malingering, whereas total raw scores below 94 are indicative of defensiveness and render the profiles invalid. There are no published studies which actually have validated these cutting scores. Within these cutting scores, the weight factor is used to adjust the indicated scales for the degree of malingering or defensiveness. An adjustment score also is used to correct individual scales based on which personality pattern scale is highest. If either the Avoidant (Scale 2) or Passive-Aggressive (Scale 8) personality pattern scale is the highest among these eight scales, the adjustment score lowers the score on six scales: S, Schizotypal; C, Borderline; P, Paranoid; A, Anxiety; H, Somatoform; and D, Dysthymia. Conversely, if the Compulsive (Scale 7) or Histrionic (Scale 4) is the highest personality pattern scale, the adjustment score raises the score on these same six scales.

The 16 PF uses the Faking-Bad scale to assess malingering. This scale is only available on Form A of the 16 PF. The Faking-Bad scale is composed of 15 items which were endorsed by subjects who were instructed to give as bad an impression as possible. A cutting score of 6 is used to identify malingering.

Again it is apparent that all of these objective personality inventories provide some means of assessing malingering. These scales are scored routinely on the CPI and MCMI, which should encourage the clinician to be aware of them, and malingering can be assessed on Form A of the 16 PF by the use of additional scales. Limited research exists of the validities of these scales and more importantly on the usefulness of the specific cutting scores that have been suggested.

Defensiveness

Wiener and Harmon Obvious and Subtle Scales

The use of the Wiener and Harmon (Wiener, 1948) Obvious and Subtle scales to assess malingering was described above. These scales also can be used to assess defensiveness. The procedure for calculating the differences between the T scores for the obvious and subtle scales and summing these difference scores to create an index of malingering and defensiveness was outlined in Table 8.8. In the situation where the patient is trying to be defensive, the T scores on the subtle scales will be larger than those on the obvious scales, and as a consequence the difference scores on this index will be negative, reflecting that the patient has endorsed more subtle than obvious items.

Tables 8.9 and 8.10 presented the distribution of this difference score on the Wiener and Harmon (Wiener, 1948) Obvious and Subtle scales by gender for normal and psychiatric samples, respectively. Based on the data presented in Table 8.10, the clinician can decide what percentage of patients should be labeled as being defensive. Clearly, difference scores in the range of −75 to −150 are strongly suggestive of defensiveness. If difference scores of −75 or lower are deemed to be suggestive of defensiveness, 5.6% of the adult male patients (3.4% + 1.8 + 0.4) and 5.5% of the adult female patients

(3.6% + 1.3 + 0.6) exceed this criterion. Similarly, 3.9% of the adolescent male patients and 6.6% of the adolescent female patients exceed this same criterion, which suggests that age per se has little effect on whether a patient will be defensive.

The clinician may decide that a different criterion should be used to identify defensiveness in a particular clinical setting. Unless there is some reason to believe that "normal" individuals may be evaluated in this specific clinical setting, patients with "normal" profiles should be relatively unusual since they would be expected to have some form of psychological problem requiring assessment or treatment. The fact that a sizable proportion of patients achieve negative numbers on this index (see Table 8.10) suggests that defensiveness is not very unusual. Since normal adults' mean scores on this index are about −25 (see Table 8.9), a clinician could decide that any patient, who scores less than −25, is being defensive. By this criterion, 19.1% of the adult male patients and 18.3% of the adult female patients are classified as being defensive. The reader should not conclude that this high percentage of psychiatric patients who are being defensive (almost 20%) necessarily reflects some inherent flaw in this index; instead it simply reflects the large number of patients who are evaluated in a clinical setting and yet are defensive. As the other indexes and scales to assess defensiveness are described below, the reader will see that a similar percentage of patients are identified.

Positive Malingering Scale

The Positive Malingering Scale (Mp) (Cofer *et al.*, 1949) was developed to identify defensiveness. Cofer and his associates asked groups of college students to endorse the MMPI items like an emotionally disturbed person (malingering) or so as to make the best possible impression (defensiveness). They then identified 34 items that were insensitive to malingering and yet susceptible to defensiveness ("positive malingering"). They found that a cutting score of 20 or higher correctly identified 96% of the accurate MMPIs and 86% of the defensive MMPIs. A cutting score of 20 is equivalent to a T score of 69 in men and 73 in women in the original Minnesota normative group. They also noted that scores on the Mp scale tended to be correlated positively to scores on the Wiener (1948) subtle scales.

Tables 8.17 and 8.18 summarize the range of scores that were found on the Mp scale by gender in normal individuals and psychiatric patients, respectively. T scores of 70 or higher were found in 6–7% of the normal individuals and 2–4% of the psychiatric patients. If a T score of 60 or higher was used to identify defensiveness, 17–27% of the psychiatric patients would be classified as endorsing the items inaccurately. The reader should recall how a similar percentage of patients were classified as being defensive by the difference between the Wiener and Harmon (Wiener, 1948) Obvious and Subtle scales.

Table 8.17. Distribution of T Scores for the Positive Malingering (MP) Scale in Normal Samples by Gender

T score range	Colligan et al. (1983)[a]		Greene (1986)			
	Adults (%)		Adults (%)		College students (%)	
	Male (%) (N = 305)	Female (%) (N = 335)	Male (%) (N = 163)	Female (%) (N = 238)	Male (%) (N = 208)	Female (%) (N = 224)
80+	0.0	0.3	0.0	0.0	0.0	0.4
70–79	4.6	5.7	1.8	2.5	4.3	1.8
60–69	15.5	21.8	12.9	9.7	12.5	7.6
50–59	36.6	23.5	46.6	24.4	33.7	32.6
40–49	34.4	37.0	31.3	41.6	38.0	37.1
30–39	8.2	10.2	7.4	17.2	11.0	16.9
0–29	0.7	1.5	0.0	4.6	0.5	3.6
M	52.2	51.5	51.7	46.8	50.6	47.6
SD	9.9	10.7	8.3	10.8	9.5	10.1

[a]Colligan, Osborne, Swenson, & Offord (1983).

Lachar and Wrobel Critical Items

The total number of the Lachar and Wrobel (1979) critical items that are endorsed can be used as another index of the accuracy of item endorsement. A patient who is trying to be defensive would be expected to endorse few of these items since their item content is obvious (face valid) and reflective of psychopathology. Tables 8.13 and 8.14 summarized the total number of critical items by gender that were endorsed by normal individuals and psychiatric patients, respectively. Almost 20% of the psychiatric patients endorsed fewer total critical items than the normal individuals who endorsed an average of 18–26 (16–23%) of these items. That is, nearly 20% of these psychiatric patients endorsed fewer total critical items than normal individuals despite their presence in a clinical setting. Again the reader should note the similar percentage of patients who are identified as being defensive by this index.

L Scale

The Lie (L) scale consists of 15 items that were selected to identify persons who are deliberately trying to be defensive. Although denial and defensiveness are characteristic of most high scorers on the L scale (cf. Graham, 1987; Greene, 1980), patients with any degree of psychological sophistication will not be detected. Thus, low scores on the L scale can occur in defensive individuals, which limits the usefulness of this scale for detecting defensiveness.

Table 8.18. Distribution of T Scores for the Positive Malingering (Mp) Scale in Psychiatric Samples by Gender

| T score range | Psychiatric patients (Hedlund & Won Cho, 1979) | | | |
| | Adults (%) | | Adolescents (%) | |
	Male (%) ($N = 8,646$)	Female (%) ($N = 3,743$)	Male (%) ($N = 693$)	Female (%) ($N = 290$)
80–89	0.6	1.4	0.3	1.0
70–79	4.4	6.4	5.9	5.9
60–69	16.8	15.2	21.8	9.7
50–59	31.7	30.0	38.5	33.1
40–49	31.8	31.5	27.6	37.2
30–39	13.6	12.9	5.8	11.7
0–29	1.1	2.6	0.1	1.4
M	51.3	51.2	54.3	50.4
SD	11.1	12.1	9.8	11.0

K Scale

The K scale is a traditional index of defensiveness on the MMPI, with high scores (T scores > 69) in psychiatric patients indicating defensiveness and the unwillingness to acknowledge any type of psychological distress. These patients typically lack insight into their own functioning, which makes prognosis for any type of psychological intervention very poor. The actual behaviors about which the patient is being defensive probably will not be discernible from the clinical scales since they are likely to be within the normal range.

F-K Index: Gough Dissimulation Index

Gough's initial reservations about the efficiency of the F-K index in detecting defensiveness have been corroborated by numerous investigators. Most studies (Cofer *et al.*, 1949; Exner *et al.*, 1963; Hunt, 1948) have found extensive overlap in the distributions of the F-K index in students who took the MMPI normally and then retook the MMPI being defensive. Consequently, it has been difficult to find any specific score on the F-K index that reliably distinguishes normal student profiles from their defensive profiles. Another problem with the F-K index in identifying defensiveness is that anyone who is acknowledging the capability to handle his or her own problems, who is well adjusted (high raw score on K), and who is not experiencing stress or conflict simultaneously (low raw score on F) will most likely be defined as being defensive rather than normal by this index. Thus, normal persons taking the MMPI often will be inappropriately classified as being defensive.

Several studies have examined the ability of the F-K index to detect defensiveness in clinical populations. Hunt (1948) reported that a score lower than −11 on the F-K index correctly classified 62% of his prison sample who were instructed to be defensive. Grayson and Olinger (1957) and Johnson, Klingler, and Williams (1977), however, found that their psychiatric patients instructed to be defensive could not be detected by the F-K index. Thus, the F-K index appears to be even more limited in detecting defensiveness among psychiatric patients than in identifying malingering in such patients; in either case its utility is questionable.

Part of the reason the F-K index may be ineffective in detecting defensiveness in psychiatric patients may be a function of their inability to be defensive. For example, Grayson and Olinger (1957) discovered that rather than producing a normal or a defensive profile under defensiveness instructions, their patients merely changed the degree of severity or the nature of their behavior disorder. Similarly, Lawton and Kleban (1965) found that their prison sample could not produce a normal profile when instructed to take the MMPI as a person not in trouble with the law. Although their prisoners were able to lower significantly seven of the clinical scales, they could not alter their high-point scales. Grayson and Olinger (1957) did find that those patients in their sample who were able to simulate a normal profile with defensiveness instructions were more likely to receive an early discharge from the hospital. Thus, additional research is needed to investigate whether a normal profile produced by a patient given instructions to take the MMPI in a defensive manner reflects an ability to manipulate the system or is a favorable prognostic sign.

If scores of −10 or lower on the F-K index are used as a criterion of defensiveness, nearly 25% of Hedlund and Won Cho's (1979) adult psychiatric patients and 20% of the adolescent psychiatric patients would be so classified (see Table 8.16). Again, there is a sizable percentage of psychiatric patients who are evaluated in a clinical setting that are being defensive. Since normal individuals routinely achieve negative scores on this index (see Table 8.15), the F-K index will *not* distinguish between normal individuals who should score in this range and psychiatric patients who are being defensive. However, if it is known that this patient should be reporting psychopathology because of his or her presence in a treatment setting, the F-K index can alert the clinician to the possibility of defensiveness.

Clinical Applications to the MMPI

Six different means of assessing defensiveness have been described above. The reader should select the scale/index that is most appropriate for his or her specific patients and treatment setting. The selection of one of these scales/indexes of defensiveness is more difficult than for malingering, since they appear to be measuring slightly different aspects of defensiveness as indicated by their relatively low intercorrelations. For example, the correlations between the Wiener and Harmon (Wiener, 1948) Obvious and Subtle scales and the Lachar and Wrobel (1979) critical items and the Mp scale (Cofer et al., 1949) in Hedlund and Won Cho's (1979) psychiatric samples range between −.30 and −.36. The correlations between the Mp scale and the F-K index (Gough, 1947) also are very low, ranging between −.18 and −.26 in these same samples of patients. Research is needed that examines which of these scales/indexes of defensiveness is most appropriate in a particular clinical setting and that validates these scales/indexes with independent measures of defensiveness.

When a patient's responses have been identified as being endorsed inaccurately because of defensiveness, the standard profile is no longer interpretable since it reflects an invalid response set. The clinician will have little reason to try to interpret such a profile, however, since defensiveness usually results in no clinical scales being elevated to a T score of 70 or higher, and frequently no clinical scales are at or above a T score of 60. The clinician should describe the patient's style of defensiveness, determine the potential causes for this response set, and assess the implications for treatment/intervention.

Once clinicians realize that defensiveness is encountered frequently in a clinical setting, the empirical correlates of such a response set can be studied. It could be expected that patients who are defensive see their problems as less troubling to themselves and, hence, are less motivated to change. Their problems also may be more chronic in nature and consequently they may be more difficult to treat if they remain in treatment. Duckworth and Barley (in press) have provided a summary of the correlates of patients who produce such MMPI profiles.

Other Objective Personality Inventories

Most objective personality inventories also provide some means of assessing defensiveness. If the same scale is used to assess both malingering and defensiveness (e.g., MCMI: Millon, 1984), it was described above. This section will describe the use of specific scales to assess defensiveness on other objective personality inventories.

The CPI uses the Good Impression scale to assess defensiveness. It consists of 40 items which identified high school students who were instructed to endorse the items as if they were applying for an important job or trying to make an especially favorable impression. T scores at or above 60 are thought to raise the issue that the patient may be defensive.

The Motivational Distortion scale of the 16 PF is used to assess defensiveness. It is composed of 15 items which distinguished subjects instructed to endorse the items so as to provide the most favorable picture of them-selves. A cutting score of 6 or higher is used to identify defensiveness.

These other objective personality inventories also contain scales which are designed to assess defensiveness. Limited research exists on these scales to validate their usefulness and the appropriateness of the cutting scores that are suggested.

Conclusion

Table 8.19 summarizes the scales/indexes that can be used to assess consistency and accuracy of item endorsement on the MMPI and the possible cutting scores that might be used in a psychiatric setting. The clinician will need to decide which scale/index of malingering and defensiveness is the most appropriate for his or her clinical setting, and whether raising or

Table 8.19. Cutting Scores for Assessing MMPI Validity

	Acceptable	Marginal	Unacceptable
A. Item Omissions			
1. Cannot Say (?)	0–10	11–30	31+
B. Consistency of Item Endorsement			
1. Test–Retest (TR) index	0–4	5	6+
2. Carelessness (CLS) scale	0–4	5	6+
3. Sum of TR + CLS	0–8	9	10+
C. Accuracy of Item Endorsement			
1. Malingering			
a. Difference score on Wiener and Harmon Obvious and Subtle scales	−7–110	111–190	191+
b. Ds-r scale	<70	70–89	90+
c. Total Lachar and Wrobel critical items endorsed	<51	51–70	71+
d. F scale	<15	15–28	29+
2. Defensiveness			
a. Difference score on Wiener and Harmon Obvious and Subtle scales	+110–−7	−8–−79	<−79
b. Mp scale	<59	59–70	71+
c. Total Lachar and Wrobel critical items endorsed	>22	11–22	<11
d. K scale	<60	60–69	70+

Note. These cutting scores are set so that approximately the 75th percentile separates the acceptable and marginal categories, and approximately the 95th percentile separates the marginal and unacceptable categories in *psychiatric patients*. Clinicians may consider adjusting these cutting scores based on the specific base rates in their patients and the relative cost of identifying a certain percentage of patients' MMPIs as unacceptable. In other settings where the MMPI is administered, such as *personnel selection*, appropriate cutting scores will need to be derived.

It is *not* intended for the clinician to score all of these scales/indexes to assess malingering or defensiveness. The clinician should select the scale/index which is most appropriate for his or her clinical setting.

lowering these proposed cutting scores would facilitate the identification of malingering or defensiveness. The establishment of the base rates with which malingering and defensiveness are encountered in a specific clinical setting is mandatory in deciding if and how these cutting scores should be adjusted. Clinicians need to examine the frequency with which malingering and defensiveness occur and begin to establish the empirical correlates of these response sets so that better assessments, treatments, and interventions can be made. Finally, clinicians should understand that although this chapter has emphasized the MMPI, the same rationale for assessing consistency and accuracy of item endorsement and the need for extensive validation are applicable to all objective personality inventories.

9

Projective Testing and Dissimulation

LANA STERMAC

The susceptibility of psychological tests to malingering and defensiveness has been poorly researched despite the importance of such tests to psychological assessment. This observation is particularly true for projective techniques, which traditionally have been considered to be less vulnerable to dissimulation. This chapter will examine the susceptibility of projective techniques to malingering and defensiveness and the ability of these measures to detect dissimulation. The major focus will be on the Rorschach Inkblot Technique with discussion also of the Thematic Apperception Test, the Holtzman Inkblot Technique and the Group Personality Projective Test.

The Rorschach Inkblot Technique has enjoyed prominent status among clinicians over many years. Despite persistent criticisms regarding its validity and reliability, it has continued to be used widely in clinical practice (Wade & Baker, 1977). Critics of the Rorschach argue that the many years of research yielding negative results on the instrument have failed to "cool the ardor of the Rorschach supporter" (Knutson, 1972, p. 440). Adherents to the technique, however, claim that there have been many difficulties with the empirical investigation of the Rorschach and state that most of the studies completed on it have been inadequate (McArthur, 1972). Weiner (1977) has argued that some of the negative findings on the validity of the Rorschach may be attributed to an over-reliance upon strictly empirical validation studies which compare treatment samples across measures. He asserted that conceptual validation studies which attempt to examine the underlying rationale of measure differentiation among samples may be more appropriate. Rogers and Cavanaugh (1983) state that, in general, it is not the inadequacy of negative findings but the absence of positive findings that questions the interpretive validity of the Rorschach.

Lana Stermac, Forensic Service, Clarke Institute of Psychiatry; Ontario Institute for Studies in Education; and Department of Psychiatry, University of Toronto, Toronto, Ontario, Canada.

Fakability of the Rorschach

Within the vast literature of over 5,000 studies and reports on the Rorschach, only a handful of these have addressed the "fakability" of the test. In a review of this topic, Rogers (1987) stated that "early work on the Rorschach assumed that it was impossible to malinger because of the ambiguity of the stimuli" (p. 47). This assumption was based on the premise that the Rorschach tapped unconscious and therefore inaccessible personality variables. It was further assumed that subjects would not be able to fake results due to their ignorance of the critical response components.

Several early studies began to investigate the notion of the "unfakability" of the Rorschach by examining the ability of subjects to alter their responses according to experimental instructions. Two of the early experimental studies to address this issue (Fosberg, 1938, 1941) supported the notion of the unfakability of the Rorschach. Fosberg conducted two studies ($N = 2$ and 129 respectively) examining response changes under different instructions. In the second study, subjects were asked to complete the Rorschach under standard instructions and then under instructions to perform their best and their worst. Although Fosberg concluded that the Rorschach withstood all attempts at manipulation, serious methodological and statistical criticisms have been noted (Carp & Shavzin, 1950; Feldman & Graley, 1954).

The first simulation study to cast doubt on the unfakability of the Rorschach was carried out by Carp and Shavzin (1950). They asked 20 male undergraduate psychology students to respond to the Rorschach under two sets of instructions administered three weeks apart. One set was designed to make a "good" impression and the other to make a "bad" impression. The results of the study suggested that it was not possible to predict in which direction a subject would "fake" his or her responses. Carp and Shavzin concluded that some subjects were able to distort their protocols according to an instructional set. They suggested, however, that clinicians would likely be able to fully recognize a "faked" test.

A second study, conducted by Eastan and Feigenbaum (1967), also examined the ability of naive subjects to alter their responses to the Rorschach according to instructions. Six male and six female undergraduate students were asked to respond twice to the Rorschach. The first administration involved standard instructions and the second involved instructions to respond so as to avoid recruitment into the army. Subjects were told that poor scores and a poor performance would allow them to avoid military service. Subjects were encouraged to fake the results but were given no further instruction. The data were examined in terms of total number of responses and proportion of responses in selected categories although the particular scoring system used was not specified. The results of the study suggested that readministration of the Rorschach alone produced some differences in response, but that instructions to fake plus readministration produced greater change in both the number and proportion of category responses. The authors concluded that instructions to fake the Rorschach did influence the scores of naive subjects. These two studies generally support the notion of the Rorschach's vulnerability to response manipulation by patients.

Identification of Rorschach Dissimulation

Researchers have also focused on examining variables related to the identification and detection of malingered responses. These studies have reported mixed results about clinicians' ability to detect malingering. In an early study, Feldman and Graley (1954) investigated the ability of clinicians skilled in the use of the Rorschach to distinguish normal from malingered protocols. Two groups of undergraduate psychology students participated in the study. Group 1 ($N = 30$) took a group-administered test, initially with standard instructions and two weeks later with malingering instructions. Group 2 ($N = 42$) took the test only once with standard instructions. The results of the study revealed that subjects made changes in their protocols as a result of the experimental set. These changes were in the direction of greater maladjustment, although few resembled psychotic protocols. Judges skilled in the use of the Rorschach, however, were able to sort these protocols into normal and faked groups with an accuracy above chance expectation (correct classification ranged from 65% to 83%). The authors concluded that abnormality could be simulated at least to some extent on the Rorschach, although this simulation could be detected by experts.

Exner and Wylie (1975) cast doubt on the ability of even "experienced" graduate students with knowledge of schizophrenic Rorschach protocols to simulate or create a set of malingered responses which cannot be detected. Twelve graduate students were asked to "create" these protocols within a 2-hour limit. Three Rorschach experts served as judges and were blind to the purpose of the study; they reviewed the responses and concluded that only one protocol achieved a critical score on the schizophrenic index and was "schizophrenic." Exner noted that malingerers may be identifiable by their use of good form responses and by their very dramatic verbiage. Unfortunately, the limited description of this study leaves several methodological points unclear. It is unknown, for example, whether clinicians were completely blind as to the subjects or only to the purpose of the study. Since the subjects "created" their own protocols, the generalizability of these findings is questionable. Also, interrater reliability coefficients were not reported.

Exner and Sherman (1977) describe another study as further evidence for the detection of defensiveness on Rorschach protocols. Ten schizophrenic patients were asked to repeat the Rorschach with instructions to improve their performance. Subjects were encouraged in this respect by being told that the staff generally felt that they could perform better on the Rorschach. Again, judges blind to the purpose of the study were able to determine that all ten repeated tests were schizophrenic. It is not clear whether any comparison subjects were used. This study is weak on many methodological grounds, most notably in respect to the expectation that schizophrenics are able to alter their responses in more favourable ways. At best, this study could suggest that psychotic patients did not produce successfully "defensive" Rorschach responses when given vague instructions to "perform better."

A more recent study by Pettigrew, Tuma, Pickering, and Whelton (1983) supported Exner and Wylie's (1975) findings on the simulation of psychosis. However, Pettigrew and his associates differed from standard administration by using a multiple-choice group-administered Rorschach. With this format subjects were asked to view the standard blots and select one of four responses, given in multiple-choice format, which they felt were most representative of what the blots resembled. Subjects in the study included as controls 75 undergraduate students and 55 psychotic patients, who received standard instructions, and 62 undergraduate student malingerers, who were asked to respond as they though a psychotic or insane person would. The response categories included the following four types: (1) good form with bizarre wording, (2) good form with neither bizarre nor elaborate wording, (3) poor form with nonbizarre wording and, (4) poor form without elaboration or bizarre wording. The core percepts were derived from tables of perceptual accuracy as advocated by Exner (1974).

The results of the study revealed that malingerers gave significantly more good form with bizarre wording (Type 1) responses than did normal individual or psychotics. The mean respose frequency was 31.50 ($SD = .41$) for malingerers, 13.31 ($SD = 6.74$) for psychotics, and 14.96 ($SD = 6.01$) for normal individuals. If a cutoff score of 29 or greater was used, 62.9% of malingerers, none of the psychotics, and 1.3% of the normal persons were classified as malingerers. In addition, malingerers chose significantly more good form (Type 2) responses than did psychotics. The authors conclude that, as hypothesized by Exner (1978), attempted simulation of psychosis on the Rorschach is associated with good-form, bizarre-wording responses on the multiple-choice format of the test. Although they suggest that this type of administration may be useful as an index of attempted simulation of psychosis, they do point out the bias in restricting answers to the four category types. Therefore, this study did not directly address the ability of clinicians or others to blindly detect or differentiate malingerers from others.

Seamons, Howell, Carlisle, and Roe (1981) have also reported that malingerers can be detected by a clinical judge. They examined the ability of inmates and forensic patients to alter Rorschach responses according to instructions. Forty-eight subjects (36 schizophrenics) with differing amounts of psychopathology were asked to respond to the Rorschach as (1) normal, well-adjusted individuals and (2) mentally ill, psychotic individuals. All protocols were administered and scored with the Exner (1974) system at the institution where the subject resided. A psychologist experienced with the Rorschach examined the protocols to determine which had been given under which specific instructions and to determine which protocols were psychotic. The judge was able to accurately differentiate between protocols according to instructions to appear normal or to appear mentally ill with 80% accuracy.

The results of the Seamons *et al.* (1981) study indicated that varied instructions affected content-area responses but not ratios, percentages, and deviations. Under the instructions to simulate mental illness, more dramatic responses including blood, mutilation, and hatred were found. Although this study appears to strongly support the unfakability of the Rorschach, several limitations have been noted (Ziskin, 1984). First, use of one judge in differentiating the protocols may raise the question of specific ability or, as noted by Ziskin, the possibility of "cueing." Second, the high percentage of schizophrenics used in the study may have influenced the results and limited generalizability. It has already been noted (Exner & Sherman, 1977) that the ability of schizophrenics to alter Rorschach responses is probably limited.

Another approach to the investigation of malingering on the Rorschach has been to examine the protocols of identified malingerers and to compare them with patient groups. Bash and Alpert (1980) administered the Rorschach to 30 identified malingerers, 30 schizophrenics who reported hallucinations, 30 schizophrenics with no reported hallucinations, and 30 nonpsychotic psychiatric patients. All subjects were inpatients in a prison ward of a hospital. The Rorschach was one of a number of tests administered and was scored according to the Klopfer system by a rater blind to the group designation. A special scoring system for malingering was developed for the Rorschach. This study did not focus individually on the Rorschach, yet its results suggested that, based on group means, Rorschach scores of malingerers could be used to discriminate malingerers from others. Using this special scoring, the overall performance of malingerers was exaggerated as observed on higher point scores. Although this study is important in that independently identified malingerers were used as subjects, it raises several methodological questions. First, the rationale for the selection of the scoring categories and the malingering scoring was not presented. Second, it is unknown what cutoff scores were used and what percentage of malingerers could be accurately classified by them.

Several studies have reported negative results in the ability of clinicians to accurately detect malingerers. Albert, Fox, and Kahn (1980) carried out one of the best controlled and most methodologically sound studies on the ability of seasoned clinicians to detect malingering on the Rorschach. They obtained Rorschach protocols from six psychiatric inpatients (paranoid schizophrenics) and 18 university undergraduates. Student subjects were asked either to complete the Rorschach under standard instructions ($N = 6$) or to fake the Rorschach ($N = 12$) with specific instructions to malinger paranoid schizophrenia. Malingerers were equally divided into informed (i.e., 25-minute tape on schizophrenia) and uninformed groups. Experts ($N = 46$) were fellows of the Society for Personality Assessment with an average 20.6 years of postgraduate experience, who were contacted through the mail and invited to examine four protocols. They were asked to provide (1) a psychiatric diagnosis, (2) their degree of certainty of the diagnosis, (3) their overall ratings of psychopathology, and (4) their judgments about the likelihood of malingering. The results of the study indicated the clinicians were unable to detect malingering either by uniformed or informed malingerers. Although role sophistication did affect ratings of the degree of psychopathology, it did not affect clinicians' ability to identify malingerers.

Mittman (1983) examined the ability of experienced Rorschach clinicians to identify the malingering of schizophrenia among groups of (1) depressed inpatients (2) inpatient schizophrenics, (3) uninformed malingerers, (4) informed malingerers, and (5) normal controls. Controls received standard instructions, and experimental subjects were asked to malinger schizophrenia. Clinicians ($N = 90$) each judged five randomly assigned and formally scored protocols, although it is not clear which scoring system was used. Clinicians were asked to evaluate the protocols and render a diagnosis. Results revealed that judges diagnosed the Rorschach protocols of uninformed malingerers as schizophrenic less frequently than those of either informed malingerers or schizophrenics. No percentages were reported in this study. Mittman concluded that, contrary to Exner's findings, the Rorschach is susceptible to malingering when respondents are well informed about their role.

In summary, clinicians' ability to identify dissimulated protocols remains an issue open to controversy and debate. Several studies have raised important questions on the susceptibility of the Rorschach to malingering and the ineffectiveness of clinicians to detect dissimulated protocols.

Exner (1978) has asserted that malingering on the Rorschach would probably be impossible if protocols were collected and scored according to the standardized procedures of the Exner system. Indeed, none of the negative studies of the Rorschach regarding the detectability of malingering employed the Exner system. As noted in the introduction, however, the absence of negative studies does not demonstrate the validity of any measure. Existing studies with positive results utilizing the Exner system have several important limitations. First, the studies have unduly restricted themselves to malingering of schizophrenia. Second and more importantly, none of the studies have established specific cut-off scores and attempted their cross-validation. Third, all Exner studies rely solely on a simulation design and therefore are limited by the constraints of this methodology as discussed in the introductory chapter.

Clinical Applications

The conflicting and fragmentary nature of Rorschach research on dissimulation constrains the establishment of threshold and clinical decision models. It is possible, however, to synthesize studies with positive findings and develop criteria to alert clinicians to the increased likelihood of a dissimulated protocol. Table 9.1 summarizes the threshold criteria for Rorschach protocols. This table combines Rorschach indicators with other clinical and environmental indicators in providing a clinical threshold for suspecting dissimulation. Given that the majority of studies have established susceptibility of the Rorschach to dissimulation, the threshold criteria are deliberately low.

A clinical decision model for definitely establishing malingering and defensiveness on the Rorschach is not possible, given the paucity of dissimulation research. Perhaps the most defensible approach would be to discard *any* Rorschach protocol where dissimulation is suspected. No research, with the exception of Seamons and his associates (1981), has addressed the interpretability of dissimulated Rorschach protocols. It would therefore appear prudent not to attempt clinical interpretation of a suspected protocol.

Research by Pettigrew and his colleagues (1983) suggested an innovative approach toward establishing malingering on the Rorschach. In cases of

Table 9.1. Threshold Model for Assessing Dissimulation on the Rorschach

---

Any of the following criteria:
A. Malingered Protocols
   1. Rorschach indicators:
      a. Good form with dramatic or bizarre wording
      b. Dramatic content (mutilation, blood, and hatred)
   2. Other indicators:
      a. Other clinical evidence of malingering
      b. Patient is not self-referred and suspected of dissimulation
B. Defensive Protocols
   1. Rorschach indicators:
      (none established)
   2. Other indicators
      a. Other clinical evidence of defensiveness
      b. Patient is not self-referred and suspected of dissimulation

---

suspected malingering, clinicians may wish to readminister the Rorschach, employing Pettigrew's multiple-choice format. Individuals whose Rorschach responses are characterized by Type 1 responses (good form with bizarre wording) might then be designated as malingerers and excluded from further interpretation of their original Rorschach protocol. More specifically, any protocol with 29 or more Type 1 responses should be considered highly suspect.

Dissimulation research only peripherally addresses the issue of defensiveness. Studies by Exner and Sherman (1977) and Seamons and his colleagues (1981) would suggest that schizophrenic patients have considerable difficulty in presenting themselves as nonpsychotic. Clinicians may therefore be less concerned about possible defensiveness in patients with well-documented schizophrenic histories than other patient groups. No data are available on how nonpsychotic patients may deny or minimize their psychological inpairment on the Rorschach. The absence of impairment on the Rorschach should not by itself be taken as evidence of adjustment.

Other Personality Measures

The Thematic Apperception Test (TAT) is another projective test which has been widely used in clinical practice. Although Adcock's (1971) general review of the TAT emphasizes its limitations in clinical practice, Eron (1972) notes that the good concurrent validity of the TAT may justify its continued use in clinical and diagnostic work. As with the Rorschach, the large body of research investigating the TAT has largely ignored the question of its fakability or susceptibility to malingering. The studies which have examined faking have focused largely on the modification of responses to the TAT.

An early study by Kaplan and Eron (1965) investigated the ability of both naive and sophisticated (i.e., graduate students with training in projective testing) subjects to consciously control or fake responses on a number of TAT measures. Seventy-two subjects completed all 20 TAT cards with instructions to respond as typical college students ($N = 36$) or as aggressive, very hostile persons ($N = 36$). Six measures were selected which had good interrater reliabilities ranging from .81 to .89 with concordance rates of 74 to 88%. The results of the study revealed that subjects could consciously modify their affect scores on the TAT. It was also found that sophisticated subjects were able to fake more effectively than naive ones. In a related study, Young (1972) found that subject's responses to the TAT could be altered by indirect clues about the perceived expectations of examiners.

Hamsher and Farina (1967) provided support for the ability of subjects to consciously control their responses to the TAT. In their study, students were asked to respond to six cards of the TAT with instructions to be as open and revealing about themselves or as closed and guarded as possible.

The results of their study again suggested that subjects could exercise control over the degree of openness and self-revelation in their responses.

Two other studies (Holmes 1974; Orpen, 1978) have also reported consistent evidence supporting the conscious control of responses to the TAT. Only one study, however, has addressed the clinicians' ability to detect defensiveness. Holmes conducted two experiments investigating subjects' abilities to fake responses. The first study addressed the general ability of 60 naive undergraduate students to either (1) fake a high level of achievement and motivation in their stories or (2) to respond honestly. Holmes concluded that the results offered strong and consistent evidence that subjects can effectively modify their responses. A second experiment investigated the ability of subjects to conceal overall personality traits as opposed to only achievement and motivation levels. Again, the results indicated that subjects could conceal aspects of their personalities. In both experiments an independent clinician examined randomly selected stories ($N = 60$ and $N = 30$) in an attempt to identify which had been written under defensive instructions, but he was unable to categorize subjects at a rate better than chance.

Only one study has addressed the ability of subjects to modify their responses on the Holtzman Inkblot Technique. Kreiger and Levin (1976) investigated the role of expectation in the Holtzman responses for 23 male schizophrenic inpatients. Subjects were asked to respond twice to the Holtzman: initially, with the expectation that they were being interviewed as a hospital employee, and secondly, with the expectation that they were being interviewed as a psychiatric patient. Each administration involved an abbreviated Holtzman (i.e., 15 of 45 inkblots), which selected for tendency to elicit pathological responses. Seven variables were scored on the Holtzman system (Holtzman, Thorpe, Swartz, & Herron, 1961). The results indicated that mean scores in the normal (hospital employee) condition were significantly lower (i.e., in the direction of less psychopathology) than in the patient condition. The authors concluded that psychotic verbalizations and perceptual distortions on the Holtzman varied as a result of role expectation. Although, as Kreiger and Levin point out, this variability could be accounted for by a number of factors (including its abbreviated format) this study does indicate that Holtzman Inkblot responses are modifiable in the direction of concealing psychopathology.

The fakability of other projective tests has also been demonstrated. Brozovich (1970) evaluated the ability of graduate students to fake scores on the Group Personality Projective Test (GPPT). The GPPT is a 90-item multiple-choice test which uses stick figure drawings. Respondents are asked to view a scene and select one of a set of multiple-choice answers that describes what they believe is taking place. Thirty-eight graduate students were asked to complete the GPPT twice: initially with instructions to malinger (i.e., to appear emotionally disturbed) and one week later to respond defensively (i.e., to appear well adjusted). The study did not specify the mental status of the subjects, and the question of the overall adjustment of the students must be raised. Seven scores related to emotional disturbance were used although the standardization and scoring were not detailed. The results of the study indicated that graduate students were able to fake both good and poor personality patterns. Although this study is weak methodologically, it does appear to indicate that responses on the GPPT can be altered according to experimental instructions.

The few studies completed on dissimulation with the TAT and the Holtzman Inkblot Technique limit their clinical application. Due to the lack of specified content areas in the TAT and mean scores or suggested cutting scores for the Holtzman, these projective techniques may not be useful for detecting dissimulation. As noted earlier, it is strongly advised to discard any TAT or Holtzman tests where dissimulation is suspected.

Conclusion

This chapter has examined the susceptibility of projective techniques to malingering and defensiveness. From the review of studies completed in this area, it is apparent that the issue of deception on projective tests has been inadequately investigated. Many of the studies described have serious methodological limitations, which compromise their results, limit generalizeability, and leave numerous unresolved questions. Adequately described and controlled studies are clearly needed.

Due to the paucity of empirically based studies investigating the susceptibility of projective tests to deception, clinical applications are limited. A clinical decision model for definitely establishing malingering and defensiveness is not possible at this time, although a threshold model for assessing dissimulation on the Rorschach has been proposed. The absence of empirical data prevents the formulation of threshold or decision models for any other projective techniques. Finally, clinicians should be sensitized to the vulnerability of projective measures to dissimulation and not perceive the ambiguity of the stimuli as any safeguard against either malingering or defensiveness.

10

Malingering on Intellectual and Neuropsychological Measures

LOREN PANKRATZ

Neuropsychological functioning is an increasingly important component of clinical assessment. Symptoms can no longer be viewed from a single etiology or explanatory model. Behavior must be illuminated from multiple perspectives to ensure that all malfunctioning systems are identified.

Neuropsychological assessment attempts to measure how cognitive, emotional, and social functioning are influenced by cerebral problems. Accurate assessment is dependent on patient cooperation because neuropsychological techniques mostly measure behaviors that can be consciously modified. That is, because a patient can report wrong information, respond slowly, act uncoordinated, and deny comprehension, his cooperation must be secured in order to evaluate his case satisfactorily. Patients might be tempted to perform at less than optimal levels if they believe a brain dysfunction might excuse their behavioral problems. But the brain influences all behavior beyond clearly delineated intellectual deficits, including intentions, cooperation, attributions, and judgment. The neuropsychologist must avoid attributional errors in both directions.

The first section of this chapter highlights some of the psychosocial disorders that are frequently influenced by brain dysfunction. The troublesome behaviors associated with hysteria, head injury, and neurological disorders have often been analyzed in terms of personality variables or neurotic tendencies. Neuropsychological assessment is now an essential part of any psychological evaluation of these and other disorders. The second section of the chapter focuses on the tests and testing strategies used by neuropsychologists for the assessment of suspected malingering. In the third and final section, the methods of symptom validity testing are described at some length.

Loren Pankratz, Portland V.A. Medical Center, and Departments of Medical Psychology and Psychiatry, Oregon Health Sciences University, Portland, Oregon.

Differential Diagnosis and Malingering

Neuropsychological assessment often plays an important role in making the differential diagnosis of apparent deception and exaggeration. Deceptive acts must be distinguished from deceptive symptoms, that is, symptoms with an organic basis that appear willfully contrived. Most often these issues are not mutually exclusively, which makes careful clinical assessment even more essential.

Hysteria and Conversion Disorders

The condition once called hysteria is an example of a disorder in which psychological factors mimic neurological conditions. Although the formal diagnosis of hysteria has now been split asunder (Hyler & Spitzer, 1978), psychogenic symptoms and conversion disorders have been studied under the rubric of hysteria. The symptoms of specific interest to us involve the sensory or motor spheres. Such symptoms appear to be a nonverbal communication of stress or a pantomime request for help (Ford & Folks, 1985).

The studies of hysteria and conversion symptoms show that a large number of patients thought to have only functional symptoms are subsequently diagnosed with organic disease, especially neurological problems (Guze & Perley, 1963; Merskey & Buhrich, 1975; Slater & Glithero, 1965; Stefansson, Messina, Meyerowitz, 1976; Watson & Buranen, 1979; R. A. Whitlock, 1967). If followed over time, the majority of these patients (about 60%) are shown to develop a wide variety of neurological and degenerative diseases. Examples include the early stages of multiple sclerosis, epilepsy, encephalitis, cerebrovascular disease, and psychiatric disorders.

Personality testing alone may lead to overinterpretation of dynamic factors and social stressors, obscuring neuropathological conditions. The cautious clinician should resist providing psychosocial explanations without careful neuropsychological evaluation. Transitory disturbances of cognitive functions may be particularly elusive, such as those arising from iatrogenic and drug-induced disorders (Hawkins, 1979), caffeinism (Stephenson, 1977), basilar artery migraine (LaWall & Oommen, 1978), or a host of other brain syndromes (C. E. Wells, 1978).

In addition to neuropsychological issues, the clinician must consider organic disorders that have ostensibly been ruled out. All psychiatric patients are at high risk for undetected physical illness both related and unrelated to their presenting symptoms (Browning, Miller, & Tyson, 1974; Hall, Gardner, Stickney, LeCann, & Popkin, 1980; Hall, Popkin, Devaul, Faillance, & Stickney, 1978). The genesis of conversion symptoms is multifactorial, occurring in the presence of medical problems, personality disorders, sexual maladjustment, and brain lesions (Merskey & Trimble, 1979).

Traditionally, clinicians rely on a number of signs to make the diagnosis of a functional disorder. A recent study raised serious doubts about the validity of these traditional positive findings (Gould, Miller, Goldberg, & Benson, 1986). Thirty consecutive patients admitted to a neurology service with acute onset of neurological problems were studied. Most were stroke victims and all had confirmed central nervous system damage. Seven separate signs associated with faking were evaluated in each subject: (1) history suggestive of hypochondriasis, (2) potential secondary gain, (3) *la belle indifference*, (4) nonanatomical or patchy sensory loss, (5) changing boundaries of hypalgesia, (6) sensory loss (pinprick or vibration) splitting the midline, and (7) giveaway weakness.

All 30 patients with acute central nervous system damage showed at least one of the signs associated with psychogenic symptoms. Most had more than one sign, and one patient demonstrated all seven. Seventy percent of the patients showed sensory abnormalities considered characteristic of malingering, like patchy sensory loss. Most patients appeared to deny their own sensory reality to please the physician, easily changing their responses according to suggestion. The affect, the history, and the physical findings can all point to conversion disorder even when neurological findings are unmistakably present. In addition, patients with neurological disorders may lie because of poor judgment (Pankratz, Binder, & Wilcox, 1987) or because they want to ensure a thorough examination (Reich & Gottfried, 1983).

A wide range of traditional sensory–motor conversion symptoms have been noted subsequent to closed head injury (Weinstein & Lyerly, 1966). Onset of symptoms ranged from immediate to eight months. One male patient with a left-hemisensory syndrome claimed a blow on the left side of his head had left him "half a man." A patient with stuttering attributed the problem to having his throat cut (tracheotomy). The reported symptoms were usually symbolic. Furthermore, the language of these patients was often characterized by violence with dramatic accounts of the accident, in contrast to a comparable brain-injured group of patients without conversion symptoms. It was not immediately obvious that these symptoms were caused by neurological problems, yet the temporal relationship was undeniable. Clearly, neuropsychological assessment is necessary for patients with functional symptoms, especially those who have experienced head injury.

Head Injury

Problems of misdiagnosis have commonly occurred in the assessment of patients who sustain head injury. Many of these patients have been labeled neurotic. The term *traumatic neurosis* was coined by Oppenheim in 1886 (Jones & Llewellyn, 1917) and referred to neuron damage of a molecular nature. Unfortunately, early research on head injury usually failed to appreciate the difference between trauma (behavior changes secondary to neuron damage) and neurosis. Symptom complaints were usually viewed as avoidance and therefore evidence of neurosis, hysteria, or malingering.

An influential English neurologist, Henry Miller, popularized the idea of accident or compensation neurosis (see Chapter 2). He based his conclusions on 4,000 patients examined for medical-legal assessment after accidents (Miller, 1961a, 1961b, 1966; Miller, & Cartlidge, 1972). He believed, concurring with many neurologists and psychologists before him, in an inverse relationship between compensation neurosis and the severity of injury and that compensation neurosis was related to social class. Further, he stated that symptoms were resolved only after court settlement; as long as the possibility of compensation remained viable, patients maintained their symptoms. Many clinicians subsequently believed that rehabilitation or intervention was useless until after settlement.

Miller was insightful and some of his clinical observations remain valid today for the detection of fraud. However, from his particular role in the medical-legal system he probably overattended and overreacted to those patients who took advantage of their illness. He focused the attention of clinicians on illness behavior, neurosis, and malingering; the reality of the postconcussive syndrome was obscured. Furthermore, some of his assumptions about head injury are now known to be wrong. For example, skull fractures, rather than indicating more serious brain injury, may actually be associated with less brain damage than when the head is free to move and thus less likely to fracture.

Psychological and legal factors certainly have an influence on recovery from injury, especially head injury. However, strong evidence now exists that many of the behaviors clinicians once called neurotic were the natural sequelae of brain injury. One of the first studies to show the behavioral effects of head injury was conducted at the Boston City Hospital from 1942 to 1944 under the direction of Denny-Brown (Kozol, 1945; 1946).

This study revealed that most "neurotic" symptoms appeared shortly after discharge from the hospital and were most severe 3 to 6 weeks after discharge. Symptoms generally receded at the end of 3 months after injury; however 50% of the patients had some symptoms persist for 6 months and 15% had some symptoms that persisted a year or longer. These purportedly "neurotic" symptoms included anxiety states, fatigue (neurasthenia), nervousness, and hypochondriasis. The tone of the reports clearly revealed the belief that these symptoms were caused by trauma, not created by psychological processes. No correlation was found between the pretraumatic personality and posttraumatic symptoms. For example, neurotics and psychopathic personalities were no more likely to manifest these symptoms than normal persons.

Studies continue to show that even apparently mild head injury can occasionally cause severe complications (Binder, 1986). Symptoms are consistently found in head-injured persons not involved in compensation, and symptoms are not necessarily resolved by settlement (Denker & Perry, 1954; Jacobson, 1969; Kelly, 1975; Merskey & Woodforde,1972; Oddy, Humphrey, & Uttley, 1978; Wrighton & Gronwall, 1981). Similarly, groups of patients with posttraumatic stress who have the possibility of monetary compensation are not different from patients without the possibility of compensation (Burstein, 1986).

Posttraumatic amnesia (see Chapter 5) is difficult to assess, especially for untrained observers, and often the conclusions of specialists disagree. Physicians may not consider ordering neuropsychological assessment in the emergency room or during initial hospitalization, especially in the absence of focal neurological signs. Months later, if symptoms persist, testing will be requested when acute symptoms have subsided. The patient may be angry or depressed by the trauma or by consequent unemployment.

A classic nightmare in assessment is the request to evaluate the effects of a head injury following a motorcycle accident. If the patient has a history of antisocial behavior, the problems of impulsivity, poor judgment, and irritability may be longstanding. Preexisting disorders and suspected dissimulation are difficult to untangle. Distinguishing the contributions of the head injury is difficult for the most experienced neuropsychologist. Although there are expected well-defined syndromes following brain injury, a multitude of unanticipated symptoms may also be found.

Symptoms, Neurological Disorders, and Brain Dysfunction

Studies on the behavioral sequelae of brain injury demonstrate the variety of deficits that occur and how subtly the symptoms can be woven into the personality of the patient (Brooks & Aughton, 1979). Many changes, on first impression, do not seem as neurological as they do behavioral or related to personality; however, brain problems may mimic characterological disorders (Gorenstein, 1982; Horton, 1976). As described above, studies have shown a clear temporal relationship between head injury and conversion symptoms. Similarly, symptoms that mimic traditional psychiatric disorders also appear after brain injury or brain metastatic neoplasia, such as mania (Cohen & Niska, 1980; Jamieson & Wells, 1979; Shukla, Cook, Mukherjee, Godwin, & Miller, 1987) and obsessive–compulsive disorders (Jenike & Brotman, 1984; McKeon, McGuffin, & Robinson, 1984). Patients with frontal lobe damage may appear on psychiatric wards with a full spectrum of incorrect psychiatric diagnoses, since frontal release signs are not necessarily present as a clue from the neurological exam (McAllister & Price, 1987). Even highly specific sexual disorders like pedophila may have onset after brain injury (Mersky & Trimble, 1979; Regestein & Reich, 1978), although these symptoms occur in the context of other serious personality changes.

Many disorders, once thought to be adequately explained in terms of religious deviations or intrapersonal pathology, are now understood with a neurological model. Examples include movement disorders, seizures, syphilis, vitamin deficiencies, and misidentification syndromes.

MOVEMENT DISORDERS

Movement disorders, for example, are easily mistaken for anxiety reactions because symptoms increase with stress, direct testing, and the intrusiveness of observation (Lees, 1980). Dystonias are sometimes simulated in emergency rooms as a ploy to obtain anticholinergic drugs such as benztropine mesylate (i.e., Cogentin) (Rubinstein, 1978; Shipko & Mancini, 1980). In other cases, clinicians are at a loss to explain why individuals would elect to mimic such a restricted role. Nevertheless, dystonic syndromes have been simulated through acting (Batshaw *et al.*, 1985), induced by surreptitious ingestion of drugs (Weddington & Leventhal, 1982), and reported as a conversion symptom (Roth, 1980).

SEIZURES

Perhaps seizures, like no other disorder, illustrate the spectrum of disordered behavior that can be imitated. Epilepsy has been known as the most popular malady of the malingerer (Malingering, 1903). It has been mimicked by beggars (Collie, 1913), pickpockets (MacDonald, 1880), con artists (Nash, 1976), goldbrickers (Gavin, 1843; Riley & Massey, 1980), prisoners of war (Ironside, 1940), fraudulent insurance collectors (Jones & Llewellyn, 1917), Munchausen syndrome patients (Pankratz, 1981), patients with factitious posttraumatic stress disorder (Sparr & Pankratz, 1983), and transient psychiatric patients (Pankratz & Lipkin, 1978).

The onset of seizures has been associated with hysteria (Hafeiz, 1980), drug abuse (O'Rahilly, Turner, & Wass, 1985), dissociative disorders (Volow, 1986), and sexual threat or exploitation (LaBarbera & Dozier, 1980). A wide spectrum of medical problems may cause seizures including brain injury, metabolic disorders, infections, neoplasms, alcoholism, degenerative diseases, and organ system malfunction, usually cardiovascular (Desai, Porter, & Penry, 1982). An extensive but contradictory literature describes an association of temporal lobe epilepsy with aggressiveness (Devinsky & Bear, 1984), with many temporal-lobe patients blaming their disabling problems on seizures.

Even in specialized epilepsy clinics an estimated 10 to 15% of the patients have pseudoseizures (Riley & Roy, 1982). To make matters even more confusing, 30% of patients with documented pseudoseizures also have well-documented real seizures (Luther, McNamara, Carwile, Miller, & Hope, 1982). Children as young as 5 years of age have feigned seizures, and some of these young fabricators also have documented, as well as feigned, seizures (Morgan, Manning, Williams, & Rosenbloom, 1984). Epilepsy is by far the most commonly fabricated disorder reported by parents involved in the Munchausen syndrome by proxy, an outrageous form of child abuse (Meadow, 1982; 1984a).

Patients can effectively simulate seizures in part because of the wide variety of forms they take. A clinical exam cannot successfully identify malingerers (Desai et al., 1982). MacDonald (1880) described patients who feigned epilepsy even when needles were inserted under the fingernails, when burned with fire, or when irritants were put in their eyes. One hundred years later the same problems of diagnosis still exist. Levy and Jankovic (1983) described a patient feigning seizures who completely suppressed optokinetic nystagmus, the visual threat reflex, corneal reflexes, the auditory startle response, and responses to deep pain.

Individual psychological and neuropsychological assessment of the suspected feigning patient must rest on knowledge of these potential roles and the variations of real seizures. One of the most interesting dimensions, particularly for the neuropsychologist, is the interictal behavior syndrome of temporal lobe epilepsy (Bear & Fedio, 1977; Waxman & Gerschwind, 1975). Although some suggest this syndrome merely reflects psychiatric illness (Mungas, 1982), patients with this syndrome show a variety of specific traits that results in interpersonal difficulties with subsequent referrals for assessment and treatment. These problems evolve from an interesting integration of personality traits secondary to brain dysfunction. They include, for example, anger, narrow philosophical interests, and an inability to judge important from unimportant facts in a controversy. Differences exist between right temporal involvement and left temporal involvement, illustrating hemispheric asymmetry in the expression of affect.

MUNCHAUSEN SYNDROME

People caught in apparently deliberate, purposeful acts of deception are sometimes seen to have hidden, but nontrivial, brain problems. My research on Munchausen syndrome patients suggests that perhaps one-third are characterized by nondominant hemisphere or frontal lobe problems (Pankratz, 1981; Pankratz & Lezak, 1987). The subgroup of brain-dysfunctioned Munchausen patients had all the psychodynamic problems commonly described in the Munchausen syndrome (see Chapter 2). They traveled widely to obtain multiple hospitalizations, achieving their goals of medical treatment through clever manipulation of factitious symptoms. All were facile with medical terminology, had good verbal skills, and an impressive fund of information. However, the more obvious verbal skills obscured deficits in conceptual organization, management of complex information, and judgment.

It was not possible to establish a temporal relationship between the onset of Munchausen behavior and the brain dysfunction. Damage may have occurred well after the onset of the Munchausen behavior. The Munchausen style of drug abuse, multiple surgeries, and self-inflicted disorders undoubtedly places the patient at greater risk. Nevertheless, the brain dysfunction seems to contribute to the patients' problems in significant ways.

The diagnosis of Munchausen syndrome is made on the basis of multiple hospitalizations and the unusual role assumed by the patient. The state of health is not at issue (Asher, 1951), and the diagnosis can be superimposed on other psychiatric disorders. Nevertheless, careful evaluation, including neuropsychological assessment, is the first responsibility of the clinician, no matter how obvious the deceptions or how personally distasteful the behavior.

Assessment Strategies

Neuropsychological approaches in the United States evolved mainly from experimental psychology; its techniques have generally relied on statistical methods, cutting scores, and other actuarial approaches. The research on the detection of deception has usually been studied using the "individual difference" approach. In this strategy normal subjects are asked to simulate mental retardation or brain damage on a particular test. Results are then compared to their optimal performances, usually showing that simulators made statistically different responses. Cutting scores are suggested for the optimal classification of patients and malingerers, with the assumption that the simulators scored similar to actual malingerers.

The Individual Test

Many individual tests are available to identify patient deception. Naive simulators will usually not be able to produce the results of actual patients. On the Benton Visual-Retention Tests, for example, both qualitative and quantitative differences were found between patients and simulators (Benton & Spreen, 1961). The mean score of simulators was lower than the mean score of brain-damaged patients. Qualitatively, simulators made more errors of distortion but fewer omissions, perseverations, and size errors than the patients. Similarly, persons simulating mental deficiency on the Benton generally scored lower, but they produced more bizarre responses in their attempt to mimic retardation (Spreen & Benton, 1963).

The manuals of most tests review studies conducted on simulators so that clinicians can become familiar with the style and scores of these subjects. In most cases, simulating subjects and malingerers overact the part of the patient they are attempting to mimic. For example, in a study of the Bender-gestalt a trained clinician correctly identified 89% of the college students who simulated brain damage with a false-positive rate of 5% (Bruhn & Reed, 1975).

This single-test approach has problems both in terms of research methodology and clinical application. Clinicians must consider whether the research suggesting a cutting score included patients similar to the patient being tested. For example, depressed patients may also score like simulators because they do not properly attend to the test-taking situations. This observation leads to questions about how many studies are needed, and how many variables must be tested before measures are employed clinically. Further, a good test for the detection of malingering may not be relevant for measuring the symptoms of the particular patient sent for assessment.

The most bothersome problem is that single tests evaluate only a few circumscribed tasks mediated by the brain. A single test like the Bender-gestalt gives unacceptably high rates of diagnostic error producing too many false-negative errors (Bigler & Ehrfurth, 1981). Such imprecision results in error rates for identifying malingerers and for wrongly classifying honest patients. Statistical probabilities leave the possibility of an error in judgment. Indeed, to never make the diagnosis of malingering would probably be the safest call, particularly in situations where the base rate of deception is low.

Gronwall and Wrightson (1974) described a "paced auditory serial-addition task" that could be used as a measure of recovery from brain injury. This test is an index of the rate at which information presented can be processed. In this test 61 digits are presented by tape at a precisely paced interval. The subject's task is to add each digit to the one immediately preceding it. Thus, if the subject hears 2-8-6-1, he should respond (immediately after hearing the "8") with 10-14-7. Four trials are given, with digits presented at rates of speed ranging from one every 2.4 seconds to one every 1.2 seconds. This test is particularly attractive because the practice effect is negligible after the second administration. Further, scores are not highly related to premorbid intelligence or arithmetic skill.

Deliberate faking and poor motivation are identified easily on the paced auditory serial-addition task. When it is given during the recovery period, scores naturally improve over time. Variations from the typical recovery pattern are easily spotted and can be resolved within the rehabilitation milieu. Deliberate faking and poor motivation are also suggested by deviation from two normal patterns. First, brain-damaged patients make fewer errors and omissions during the first third of a trial. Secondly, there is usually little variation in scores for each trial at a session (Gronwall, 1977).

Although the paced auditory serial-addition task is quite powerful in distinguishing malingerers from patients, it does not tell the complete story about recovery. Gronwall and Wrightson (1981) suggest at least three different effects on memory which may resut from simple closed head injury. The first is a deficit in information-processing ability, which is measured by the serial-addition task. The second effect is a deficit in the ability to place material into long-term memory. The third effect is a deficit in the ability to retrieve material once it has been stored. These final two effects are not measured by the serial-addition task, suggesting again that no single test is sufficient for an adequate evaluation of neuropsychological deficits and feigned impairment.

The Neuropsychological Battery

Halstead (1947) developed a battery of tests to measure "biological intelligence," which was also used to differentiate patients with cerebral lesions from those without lesions. Discriminations were based on cutting scores and an impairment index. Several versions of this test battery were developed to assess the many activities of the brain (Reitan & Davison, 1974).

In contrast to American neuropsychology, Soviet neuropsychology evolved primarily from clinical neurology. Alexander R. Luria (1966) developed his expertise from careful observation of single cases. He was known for his understanding of the brain's functional systems and his insights into brain–behavior relationships. Although Luria never intended the specific use of tests for assessment, he anticipated the operationalism of his techniques. Toward that end, Christensen (1975) published a series of tests based on Luria's clinical methods. The Luria-Nebraska Neuropsychology Battery was a further development of these procedures (Golden, Hammeke, & Purisch, 1979).

Test batteries were a great advancement over individual tests, but their use for identifying the site of damage quickly became overshadowed with the introduction of noninvasive radiological techniques and scanning devices. Nevertheless, the test battery remains ideal for a comprehensive assessment of brain function.

Faking a Test Battery

Heaton, Smith, Lehman, and Vogt (1978) obtained extensive neuropsychological test results and MMPI profiles on 16 head-injured patients and 16 simulators. Group comparisons revealed that simulators showed significant abnormalities, but the pattern of their deficits was different from those produced by genuine head-injured patients. Simulators performed very poorly on motor and sensory tasks but better on cognitive tests sensitive to brain damage.

The neuropsychological test results and MMPI profiles of all subjects were reviewed by ten neuropsychologists. Their ability to assess malingering was not impressive and ranged from chance level to 20% above chance. The degree of confidence in their judgments and level of clinical experience did not affect accuracy. However, the neuropsychologists lacked clinical information on the patients, such as the details of the injuries (or what injury was simulated), findings of neurological clinical laboratory tests, the course of recovery, preinjury behavior, and actual responses to individual items. Perhaps this information would have helped them classify subjects at a better rate.

Two discriminant analyses were created from the subjects of the study, one using the neuropsychological variables and the other using the MMPI variables. These formulas were applied to an additional 84-patient sample. Of the 42 who were strongly believed to be malingerers, 64.3% were classified as malingerers by one or both formulas. Of the 42 who had no evidence or reason to exaggerate, 26.2% were misclassified as malingerers by one or both formulas.

The discriminant analysis improperly identified stroke victims as malingerers, presumably because they had severe sensory-motor deficits similar to the responses of the simulators. The study convincingly demonstrated that blind clinical judgment and cutting scores should not be used alone in clinical settings. One final criticism of the Heaton *et al.* (1978) study deserves to be mentioned. MMPI profiles from the simulator group displayed a greater range and degree of psychological impairment and had elevated scores on the F scale. In contrast, actual malingerers of neuropsychological deficits usually downplay their psychopathology. Therefore, the discriminant analysis score that relied on MMPI profiles may have limited value in actual clinical settings.

The problem of simulation research on malingering can also be seen in a second study on faking test batteries. Goebel (1983) attempted to identify the protocols of brain-injured patients from those of normal individuals (controls) and a group instructed to malinger. Only 2 out of 102 simulators were successful. However, correcting statistically for base-rate problems, Goebel noted that malingerers are more likely to be misclassified as the base rate of malingering decreases. This observation follows the general rule that rare events are more difficult to predict.

Goebel (1983) inadvertently reinforced several common misunderstandings about malingering. Two implicit assumptions are (1) that malingerers are normal people who cheat, and (2) that brighter people are able to cheat better than others. Some posttest interviews by Goebel shed light on these interesting assumptions. Of those instructed to fake, 10% subsequently reported they made no attempt at all. Noncomplying subjects reported that they were too honest to fake or were too motivated to do their best, thus being unable to fulfill the instructions. Incidentally, 20% of the original simulating subjects of the Heaton *et al.* (1978) study were not able to malinger and were eliminated from further consideration in the study.

One successful simulator in Goebel's (1983) study reported that her strategy was to "lie a lot . . . play dumb, try to appear frustrated, keep getting fidgety" (p. 740). This strategy worked, and she did not rely on

intelligence or knowledge about brain-behavior relationships for her success. Ordinary people have difficulty playing the role of a malingerer; good
actors and highly motivated individuals may not.

The author's clinical experience suggests that malingerers and patients
with factitious disorders have no difficulty in the role of deceiver, and some
have had lifelong training (Lilienfeld, VanValkenburg, Larntz, & Akiskal,
1986; Purtell, Robins, & Cohen, 1951). Not only can malingerers produce
reasonable dissimulation in terms of test scores and response styles, they can
also feign sincerity, the emotion judged a measure of honesty (Abel, 1970;
Trivers, 1971).

Similarly, clinicians often fail to appreciate that motivation does not
necessarily arise from intelligence. If one looks at the "Ten Least Wanted
Patients" list (Pankratz & McCarthy, 1986), these particularly difficult
Munchausen patients had little formal education and would not be judged
bright—one had the appearance of a "mental defective." However, each
patient taught several generations of students about diseases that never
existed.

The Individual Approach

Neuropsychological assessment is most valuable in the examination of the
malingering patient when the clinician understands the underlying neurological pathology and the purpose of each test. Information from the
medical history, the radiological findings, the clinical tests, and the behavior
must converge appropriately. Indeed, cutting scores provide little information compared with knowing whether test results are or are not compatible
with the alleged symptoms and disorder.

The individual approach to assessment has been pursued by Muriel
Lezak in her influential work on neuropsychological assessment (Lezak,
1983). Again, the history of the patient is as important as the performance
on tests. The damaged or dysfunctional brain will perform some tasks at a
less-than-optimal level; the assessment is understood best in terms of deficit
testing. The fraudulent patient has difficulty displaying deficits compatible
with the disorder he or she is attempting to feign.

Once the individual testing approach is pursued, some tests that might
be easily malingered may retain good screening value in the clinical setting.
For example, the blind evaluation of Rorschach protocols is easily susceptible to malingering of serious disturbances, even with uninformed subjects
(Albert, Fox, & Kahn, 1980; see also Chapter 9). Nevertheless, it can be
highly informative to observe a specific individual taking the Rorschach.
Benton (1945) suggested the striking feature is the contrast between the
patient's behavior while taking the Rorschach and his or her behavior on the
other tasks. The malingering patient is likely to be characterized by extraor-
dinary meagerness of response, slow reaction times, failure to give common

popular responses, and a general attitude of perplexity and pained compliance.

Brain-damaged patients may also have meager responses, slow reactions, and perplexity on the Rorschach; however, this response style would also be expected on other tasks measuring similar problem-solving ability. The deceptive patient may perform poorly on equivalent tasks, then suddenly have no idea how to perform poorly on the Rorschach. Although the Rorschach is not typically viewed as a neuropsychological test, certain mental skills are required and certain attitudes are expressed during testing. Patients should be consistent and not suddenly seek feedback cues from the clinicians about their performance. Patients with organic problems may have reasons to be tentative about the assessment process, but they should not suddenly become evasive, guarded, and concerned about what their responses will reveal.

The neuropsychologist observes whether failures are inconsistent. Sometimes failures are transparent, like the near misses of the Ganser syndrome. At other times, patients miss simple items on self-administered tests but cannot perform as defectively when asked questions directly (i.e., on Wechsler subtests). Patients complaining of memory loss frequently fail too many items on general information and comprehension subtests, not understanding the difference between short-term and long-term memory.

Similarly, inconsistencies occur between the patient's activities and the test performance. For example, one particular patient traveled several hundred miles by public transportation for an assessment. However, she claimed memory and orientation problems that would preclude her safe arrival (Binder & Pankratz, 1987). As a further example, a mother described severe coordination problems in her daughter. Later the clinician learned that the daughter regularly exercised and groomed her horse without problems. Although many similar stories circulate among professionals, not all are equally convincing. A lack of response to pain when distracted, unobserved, or given placebo, for instance, is an unreliable measure of deception.

The individual testing strategy focuses on the deficit claimed by the patient. A physician may conduct a complete physical exam (a screening battery) on a patient with a bruised elbow, but he or she will carefully attend to the function of the wrist, elbow, and shoulder. Similarly the main energy of the neuropsychologist will be spent administering tests that can help describe the severity and extent of the specific deficit. In this enterprise it is important not only to know the expected scores of persons of similar age and education, but also to understand cerebral function and how tests measure each part.

A patient suspected of feigned neurological deficits claimed that he had no energy or motivation. The Trail-Making Test (Reitan, 1958) was administered for evaluating the possibility of executive function loss secondary to frontal lobe damage. On part B, the patient properly connected the circles, alternating between numbers and letters, until he reached G and then 8. He paused and suggested the next response should be E, which had already been used. He seemed confused. After a considerable delay, he was asked to review the task, which he conceptualized clearly. He was then asked to repeat the alphabet, which he did by following G with E. He did not finish the task, and his timed score was obviously in the defective range. He failed the test but for the wrong reason. He demonstrated no problem with shifting mental sets between numbers and letters but then "failed" because of a Ganzer-like inability to remember the alphabet.

Tests Specifically for Malingerers

Early psychophysiological tests of deception focused on responses to the word association test. One branch of this work evolved into polygraph testing (Larson, 1932). Reaction time to stimuli was part of this early research, and at one time was expected to provide clues about guilt and deception (Goldstein, 1923; Langfeld, 1921; Spencer, 1929). Andre Rey devised a reaction-time test and two memory tests specifically for the identification of malingering; these tests were described by Lezak (1983).

DOT COUNTING

Patients complaining of intellectual impairment or visuoperceptual problems are asked to count dots on 3 × 5-inch cards. Each card has a different number of dots, and the cards are presented so that the task varies in difficulty at an uneven rate. Norms are provided for the times expected for each card. Additionally, another set of cards can be presented that has the dots grouped, making it even easier to count than the ungrouped cards. Again, norms are provided for expected rates.

This test has essentially two features to entangle the uncooperative patient. First, patients will not know how long responses should take for impaired persons, thus they can easily fall outside the expected norms. Secondly, a deceptive patient would not be able to time responses appropriate to the difficulty of the task (number of dots to count) when the cards are given in a scattered order.

MEMORIZATION OF 15 ITEMS

Another test by Rey (Lezak, 1983) was designed to assess the memory of patients suspected of exerting minimal effort. Fifteen different items are presented to remember, but in reality the test is quite simple because items are arranged in easily remembered sets. The patient views the display for 10 seconds, and a 1- or 15-second delay can be imposed before asking for the responses.

Goldberg and Miller (1986) administered this test to 50 psychiatric patients and 16 persons with mental retardation. Without exception, the psychiatric patients were able to remember at least 9 of the 15 items, although they produced some complete row-omission errors. Clinical experience with malingerers shows that they fail to recall items and row configurations, revealing a performance at less than optimum rates. Mentally retarded persons were less capable of remembering nine items, and 37.5% recalled eight or fewer items. Their typical errors were perseverations and reversals—obvious indicators of mental deficiency.

WORD RECOGNITION

A 15-word list is read to the patient, who is then asked to underline all the words from that list embedded in a 30-word list. The number of words properly identified is then compared with the first trial of the Rey Auditory-Verbal Learning Test (AVLT) (Lezak, 1983). Because the first trial of the AVLT is a recall task, the expected performance should not equal or exceed the number of words recognized on the Word Recognition task.

Symptom Validity Testing

In 1961, Brady and Lind described a unique individual assessment for a man with a 2-year history of hysterical blindness. Theodore and Mandelcorn (1973) introduced the two-alternative, forced-choice technique with a similar patient. In 1975 it occurred to me that these techniques could be used to assess the complaint of any sensory deficit, and later, for any memory problem (Pankratz, 1979). Since that time I have worked with many patients with these procedures and have referred to this approach (following the suggestion of Muriel Lezak) as *symptom validity testing*. Because symptom validity testing has not been previously described in depth, this section is designed to provide the clinician some familiarity with the technique.

Symptom validity testing is a technique that can be adapted to the assessment of sensory or memory deficits (Pankratz, 1983; Pankratz, Fausti, & Peed, 1975). The test has been used for suspected complaints of blindness, color blindness, tunnel vision, blurry vision, deafness, anesthesias, and memory loss. In each case the patient claimed an inability to perceive or remember a sensory signal. Unfortunately, no one has yet devised a way to use symptom validity testing to evaluate claims of internal sensory signals, like back pain.

Each test must be constructed precisely for the complaint of the individual and to anticipate the responses of the reluctant patient. The clinician must first identify a reproducible stimulus for which the patient claims a perceptual or memory deficit. The stimulus is then presented over a large number of trials (usually 100) using the two-alternative, forced-choice technique.

Coin flipping provides a familiar model to understand this procedure. For example, a blind person cannot perceive the sensory cues necessary to call heads or tails correctly except at a chance rate. No scoring advantage is achieved by calling heads or tails in any pattern or order. Heads and tails are the only possible responses (two-alternative), and the task requires the subject to make only one response (forced-choice).

Model Variations

The forced-choice paradigm can be varied. A three-alternative design may be used, but it lowers the odds of a correct hit rate to one in three. Experience suggests that the simple, more obvious, two-alternative design is most effective.

Figure 10.1 shows a strategy that describes the coin flip. This model was used in the assessment of a male patient who claimed to have a memory deficit (Pankratz, 1983). He sat at a table in view of two lights (one red and one white) on the ceiling about 10 feet in front of him. His task was to remember which light was flashed after being distracted by a 15-second assignment. The distractor was the Symbol Digit Modalities Test (Smith, 1968). This test requires placing the proper number below each symbol according to a key given at the top of the page. The following instructions were given:

> One of these two lights will be turned on for about 2 seconds. After the light goes off, you will be asked to do this difficult symbol task which will take all your concentration. At the end of 15 seconds, you will be asked to remember

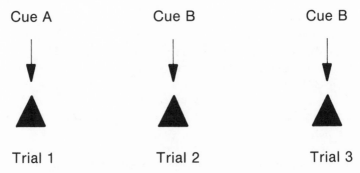

Figure 10.1. Random occurrence of a cue within a set.

which light went on. If you can't remember, please make your best guess. We will continue with many trials, which may cause you some mental strain. Some people have trouble remembering the correct response, but do your best to guess which light was on.

The model presented in Figure 10.2 assumes that a response did or did not occur, for example, a light is or is not switched on for a blind subject to identify, or a subject with a touch anesthesia is or is not touched when told "now." Figure 10.3 shows the signal presented at time "one" or at time "two"; for example, a light flashes on the count of one or on the count of two. Another example would be a touch on the count of one or on the count of two.

The Expected Response

A 50% hit rate is expected from any patient who declares at the outset that he or she cannot perceive the test stimuli in a two-alternative procedure. The untruthful patient is in a dilemma when confronted with repeated trials. If he or she holds to the denial and tries to manage the impression of a disability, then he or she runs the risk of revealing too much. On the other hand, if the deceptive patient properly identifies the cues, he or she openly admits that the deficit is not as severe as first claimed. In most clinical situations deceptive patients "guess" wrong too frequently. In doing this, the final results are often below the probabilities of chance. Even when the final score is within normal limits, the response pattern may be incompatible with the notion that the stimulus did not register at all.

Symptom validity testing provides an opportunity to show more than a low score. It has the potential to demonstrate that the patient performed *below the probabilities of chance*. Scoring below a norm can be explained in many different ways, but scoring below the probabilities of chance cannot

Cue Occurs   No Cue Occurs   Cue Occurs

Trial 1   Trial 2   Trial 3

Figure 10.2. Random occurrence of a cue within a set.

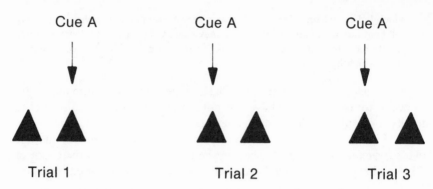

Figure 10.3. Random presentation of the cue within one of the two sets.

be easily dismissed. This finding is strong evidence of malingering, that is, evidence that the patient received the sensory cues and denied the perception (Pankratz *et al.*, 1987).

Patients miss the expected 50% hit rate for several reasons. Deceptive patients naturally seem to answer negatively when asked if they can perceive a stimulus cue. That is, anyone trying to present a disability has an internal feeling that answering correctly half the time is too high. Even if the patient realizes that a 50% rate is expected, it is difficult to keep track of responses (Haughton, Lewsley, Wilson, & Williams, 1979). Small variations from the norm become improbable rapidly, as Table 10.1 shows.

Responses to Assessment

In addition to recording a final score, the clinician observes the patient's response to testing. This provides corroborating information about whether the patient is truthful. Any patient who honestly denies an ability to perceive the test signal has no reason to be anxious during the test.

Patients attempting to exaggerate a disability usually have considerable anxiety that may appear at any stage of the assessment process. Table 10.2 lists when and how patients may expose symptoms of stress. For example, some are anxious immediately and talk excessively to delay assessment. Others argue about the design of the test or insist that they cannot do the task.

Resistance is not a unique feature of symptom validity testing but is expected of malingering patients with any assessment procedure. Nevertheless, symptom validity testing usually elicits more anxiety than other assessment approaches. Most patients are prepared to talk about their symptom or take a personality test. However, repeated presentation of the rejected stimulus is frequently so threatening that deceptive patients seize any opportunity to abort assessment.

Table 10.1. Probabilities Associated with Number of
Correct Responses in 100 Trials

Correct responses	z	p (one-tailed)
50	0.0	.5000
49	0.10	.4602
48	0.30	.3821
47	0.50	.3085
46	0.70	.2420
45	0.90	.1841
44	1.10	.1357
43	1.30	.1151
42	1.50	.0668
41	1.70	.0446
40	1.90	.0287
39	2.10	.0179
38	2.30	.0107
37	2.50	.0062
36	2.70	.0035
35	2.90	.0019

One common response is to violate the rules of the test. Patients do this
by avoiding the delivery of the sensory cue. For example, a patient claiming
blindness might look away from the source of the light signal. Another ploy
to avoid the rules is to respond with a pattern or repeat the same answer
each time. This will, of course, ensure a 50% hit rate. When this happens, the
alert clinician can change from one assessment strategy to another (see
figures) and begin again after requesting compliance with the rules.

Table 10.2. Potential Behavioral Responses of
Deceptive Patients to Symptom Validity Testing

A. Resists assessment
   1. Appears frightened
   2. Talks excessively
   3. Argues about testing
B. Violates rules of testing
   1. Avoids signal cue
   2. Responds with a pattern
   3. Repeats same answer
C. Explains away success
   1. Finds glitch in presentation
   2. Provides implausible explanation
D. Admits cue perception
   1. Becomes exhilarated at success
   2. Accepts plausible explanation

Another strategy of the anxious patient is to respond correctly but explain away the success. Patients do this by finding a glitch in the testing procedure that provides an excuse to abort testing. For example, the sound of one light switch might be different from the sound of another switch. Then the patient might say, "I can't see which light is on, but I can tell by the sound that you turned on this light over here." That test must then be halted, and the patient has defeated the assessment. Therefore, when designing the test, care must be taken to avoid sensory leaks in the presentation. Some patients provide an explanation (or pseudoexplanation) about how they responded properly in spite of their deficit. One patient declared that he could feel the heat from a small light bulb at the distance of three feet.

Compliance and Treatment Strategies

A patient suspected of feigned symptoms is frequently in conflict with his physician about the etiology of his symptom. He senses that the physician believes his symptom is all in his head or caused by emotional distress. Therefore, the patient will become immediately more defensive or defiant if asked about feelings or personal issues. The sensitive clinician can focus the interview on understanding the phenomenology of the patient and the problems it causes in his life (Pankratz & Glaudin, 1980; Pankratz & Kofoed, 1988). This will reduce the conflict and prepare the patient for assessment.

Symptom validity testing can be presented as an opportunity to learn more about any trace perceptions that might still exist. With this face-saving offer, the patient may use the repeated trials for modifying or eliminating the alleged deficit. Labeling a problem in a way that is acceptable to the patient can avoid controversy over etiology and establish an atmosphere of cooperation and expectation.

Clinical Assessment

I have described my preference for the individual assessment approach over test batteries. In particular, the individual approach allows the clinician to focus immediately on specific symptoms, selecting tests that permit evaluations of the deficit from different viewpoints. Symptom validity testing, as another option, is particularly robust because it has the potential for revealing scores outside the range of expected probabilities.

At times, however, symptoms cannot be assessed directly. In these cases, the clinician should administer tests specifically designed for malingering. The assumption is that many deceptive patients will try to convey the impression of a disability regardless of what test is administered. Another option is to begin assessment with any standard psychological test that can screen for malingering and deception, such as the MMPI. Depending on the referral question, the clinician may choose to suspend further testing if the test scores are blatantly invalid.

Discrepancies as Unreliability

Many neuropsychological tests do not have norms that can be confidently applied to the spectrum of patients assessed. The clinician must judge whether available norms are appropriate to the individual on factors such as age, education, and sex. Even more daunting to the application of normative data are the problems associated with complications within patients, such as the effects of medications, practice effects of repeated test administration, and coexisting medical and psychiatric disturbances.

Experienced neuropsychologists make allowances for patients with multiple problems, sometimes by altering the way a test is administered. Similarly, the procedures for establishing the normative data may not be followed exactly by neuropsychologists confronted by a difficult case. In this regard, clinicians not familiar with the traditions of neuropsychological assessment may not be acquainted with these clinical decisions. For example, time limits on the Block Design subtest of the WAIS are sometimes ignored, and paper and pencil may be provided to assist the patient in solving Arithmetic subtest problems. In other cases, tests are given under "demand" or "limit-testing" conditions. For example, memory tests may be given on a delayed recall, although normative data is given for immediate recall. The patient must be individually assessed, not merely compared with normative responses, to make certain that apparent dissimulation is not an artifact of testing.

Threshold Model

The threshold criteria for *suspecting* dissimulation should be set fairly low. That is, many different diagnostic clues suggest the possibility of deception and should trigger a thorough evaluation. Table 10.3 presents a threshold model with criteria which suggest malingered neuropsychological presentation.

Unusual or unexpected findings do not necessarily represent dissimulation. Once any threshold criterion has been met and the assessment complete, the clinician must evaluate the meaning of the findings. First, the appearance of dissimulation may result from the unreliability of the tests. Secondly, if dissimulation is present, a diagnosis other than malingering may be present.

Table 10.3. Threshold Model of Malingered Neuropsychological Impairment

Any one of the following criteria:
1. Near misses to simple questions.
2. Gross discrepancies from expected norms
3. Inconsistency between present diagnosis and neuropsychological findings
4. Inconsistency between reported and observed symptoms
5. Resistance, avoidance, or bizarre responses on standard tests
6. Marked discrepancies on test findings that measure similar cognitive ability
7. Failure on any specific measure of neuropsychological faking

Clinical Decision Model

A major goal of this book is the establishment of clinical decision models based on explicit criteria for determining dissimulation. With reference to intellectual and neuropsychological impairment, the formidable array of clinical presentation and possible etiologies (e.g., organic, functional, dissimulated, and mixed) do not allow the establishment of reliable and explicit rules for assessing malingering.

Clinicians who are not experienced neuropsychologists should employ measures specifically designed for malingerers and should use symptom validity testing, which does not necessarily require an understanding of brain–behavior relationships. Without extensive training in neuropsychology, clinicians should limit their conclusions to the more general assessment of unreliability and avoid more specific determinations of malingered neuropsychological deficits.

The following guidelines for assessing malingering provide a general format for the evaluation of suspected neuropsychological deficits. This section is included primarily for neuropsychologists, in lieu of a clinical decision model.

Guidelines for Assessing Malingering

The clinician must distinguish malingering from neuropsychological impairment, neurological disease, psychiatric disorder, and degrees of poor motivation. Such assessment includes the following issues:

1. Are the medical findings insufficient to explain the test scores?
2. Are the scores consistent with a psychiatric disorder?
3. Are the patient's test findings congruent with the patient's complaint and clinical examination?
4. Is there other clinical or historical evidence to suggest a diagnosis of malingering?

The first step in assessing questionable neuropsychological deficits is to evaluate whether the performance could be understood in terms of the medical conditions. In addition to the spectrum of neurological disorders, many medical conditions and their treatments may cause reduced cognitive functioning. In some cases, the neuropsychologist may have limited expertise for knowing all the possible complications. Therefore, the referring physician and other medical sources must be consulted.

Atypical symptoms create varying degrees of suspicion. Some symptoms are possible but unlikely, and others are anatomically impossible. Sometimes patients display impossible symptoms, however, when they believe the symptom *should* be present or when they believe the symptom will ensure a more thorough evaluation. Additionally, patients may respond positively to suggestions of the examining physician in an attempt to be as cooperative as possible. Not all such patients can be properly labeled as malingerers. At times the *style* of the patient prompts the referral process more than the symptom presentation itself. It is important not to confuse the distasteful patient with the deceptive patient.

A second step in assessment of suspected neuropsychological deficits is to examine the possibility of a psychiatric disorder. In this case, the clinician must be sensitive to the style and content of the questionable findings. Most patients with psychiatric and psychosocial disorders have associated physical symptoms, many of which can modify the results of neuropsychological testing. For example, patients with personality disorders may dramatize symptoms without any specific intent to malinger. Delusional patients may have problems with abstract judgment, reflected in their testing. In addition, depressed and obsessive patients may score poorly on tests of concentration and attention, each for different reasons. As a final example, elderly depressed patients sometimes appear demented but are more properly diagnosed with pseudodementia. The interaction of psychiatric disorder and neuropsychological functioning is a complex topic which is now receiving increased attention.

The third step in assessment is to evaluate discrepancies and incongruities in the clinical presentation, especially where they appear to contradict the test findings. Discrepancies can be inaccurately attributed to the patient when different practitioners are involved in selectively collecting background data and on certain testing procedures vulnerable to evaluator bias. It is essential to use reliable clinical data, based preferably on direct clinical observation. When discrepancies do exist, the patient should be asked to help clarify the discrepant information.

The fourth and final step in assessment is to review the patient's history for evidence of serious deceptions and to consider prior history in the context of the current presentation. This step reminds the clinician that not all deceptions can be identified through the interviews and the testing process. Sometimes patients hide past deceptions, self-injury, factitious disorders, and previous assessment. Therefore, the clinician must take responsibility to gather previous records and verify enough personal history to be confident in the diagnosis. In the final analysis, the clinician must incorporate an extensive data base with these guidelines in making the determination of malingering.

Conclusion

The neuropsychologist assesses the integrity of brain function in an attempt to understand unusual symptoms or behavior patterns. It is important to maintain objectivity throughout these assessments. Referral sources frequently have drawn their own conclusions and can be highly invested in their own perspectives. To counter this, clear descriptions of patient behavior, history, and brain function will make a contribution to the unbiased understanding of the patient.

Some persons suspected of deception will be struggling with compliance, or experiencing depression secondary to chronic illness or the effects of prolonged social isolation. Others will be outrageous in their implausible presentations and obviously motivated by financial compensation. However, it is possible that any of these patients will also have poor self-control and defective judgment secondary to brain dysfunction. The clinician must be careful not to prejudge patients on the basis of their initial presentation or past reputation. Careful investigation includes the assessment of brain function, psychological disorders, and potential for treatment.

PART THREE

SPECIALIZED METHODS

11

Drug-Assisted Interviews to Detect Malingering and Deception

RICHARD ROGERS
ROBERT M. WETTSTEIN

The use of barbiturate-facilitated interviews as an avenue to truth has had a long and colorful history. Beginning in the 1930s, case studies began to appear which advocated the use of Sodium Amytal (amobarbital) in the treatment of highly agitated patients and the elicitation of suppressed and repressed material (Bohn, 1932; Horsley, 1936; Lindemann, 1932). Since that time, drug-assisted interviews have been employed for such diverse purposes as abreactions in dissociative or posttraumatic mental disorders, diagnosis of organic and functional psychoses, treatment of war neuroses and conversion reactions, investigation of amnesia, and examination of possible deception (Kwentus, 1981; Naples & Hackett, 1978; Perry & Jacobs, 1982). This chapter will briefly review empirical studies of drug-assisted interviews and relate their findings to the clinical literature on drug interviews and deceptions.

Empirical research has examined the use of barbiturates and other psychoactive substances in facilitating diagnostic inquiry. It is important to emphasize that these studies have made no attempt to systematically investigate the therapeutic value of drug-assisted interviews or their efficacy in the assessment of deception. Hain and his associates from the University of Virginia (Hain, Smith, & Stevenson, 1966) conducted the first controlled studies of amobarbital comparing its results to hydroxydione (an anaesthetic), methamphetamine, and a saline placebo. A sample of 49 nonpsychotic psychiatric patients, previously known to the investigators, were administered one of the above four substances in a double-blind procedure. Based on a 60-minute drug-assisted interview, patients did not differ in their

Richard Rogers, Metropolitan Toronto Forensic Service (METFORS), Clarke Institute of Psychiatry, and University of Toronto, Toronto, Ontario, Canada.

Robert M. Wettstein, Department of Psychiatry, and Law and Psychiatry Program, University of Pittsburgh, Pittsburgh, Pennsylvania.

rate or amount of speech, desuppresion or derepression across drug conditions. Patients with hydroxydione had more difficulty with ease and clarity of speech, less anxiety, and decreased ability to attend in comparison with the other conditions. Patients with methamphetamine experienced the most anxiety and the highest degree of attentiveness. Patients in the amobarbital condition tended to fall in the intermediate range on these variables. Results of a 24-hour postinterview survey suggested that more changes in perception resulted from the methamphetamine than other conditions, although such changes appear relatively balanced between positive and negative effects. The investigators further acknowledged that the use of conservative dosages of medications may have minimized drug effects across conditions. Despite further analysis of these results (Smith, Hain, & Stevenson, 1970; Stevenson, Buckman, Smith, & Hain, 1974), the usefulness of these techniques in eliciting suppressed or repressed materials failed to be demonstrated.

Dysken and his associates (Dysken, Kooser, Haraszti, & Davis, 1979) conducted a double-blind study in which 20 nonmedicated, newly admitted inpatients were administered amobarbital and placebo interviews in a counter-balanced, within-subjects design. A statistically nonsignificant trend was observed for the drug condition in eliciting additional information. The authors conclude that amobarbital interviews were no more effective than placebo interviews in eliciting symptoms of schizophrenia and depression. Interestingly, they note its diagnostic usefulness with a catatonic schizophrenic patient who responded specifically to the amobarbital interview.

Dysken, Chang, Casper, and Davis (1979) conducted a comprehensive review of case studies and empirical research from 1930–1974. The reviewers found that most of the reported literature was uncontrolled, nonrandom case studies involving a wide range of dosages and samples. The review found, however, without exception that drug-assisted interviews had some value in diagnosis and treatment of psychiatric patients. Because of the lack of experimental rigor, Dysken and his colleagues recommend that the use of barbiturates be limited to (1) mobilizing catatonic patients, (2) the diagnosis of intellectual impairment, and (3) lessening negative affect associated with trauma. In contrast, Marcos, Goldberg, Feazell, and Wilner (1977), in an uncontrolled study of 31 uncommunicative and negativistic inpatients, yielded highly positive results in establishing rapport and eliciting symptomatology. Such marked discrepancies between positive outcomes of uncontrolled studies and the relatively negative results of the few experimental studies has yet to be adequately explained. One likely explanation is that the uncontrolled studies, although lacking in methodological rigor, are addressing more relevant cases. In psychiatric patients not manifesting substantial suppression and repression, it is unlikely that any technique might elicit much new information.

Drug-Assisted Interviews and Dissimulation

Research on the effectiveness of drug-assisted interviews in the assessment of malingering has been limited to a handful of case studies. The emphasis of the following discussion will therefore be primarily on the clinical literature as it relates more generally to dissimulation. Issues which must be considered under the rubric of dissimulation and drug-assisted interviews are (1) fakability of sedation, (2) suggestibility under sedation, (3) degree of control over self-report, and (4) emergence of new symptoms.

No research has been undertaken to examine the fakability of sedation in drug-assisted interviews. Since dosages of amobarbital are clinically titrated to ensure a deep state of relaxation, it is conceivable that a patient may attempt to look more sedated that he or she actually is. Much reliance is placed on the clinician to observe the pharmacological effects of amobarbital carefully. As noted by MacDonald (1976) and Herman (1985), patients may show an initial euphoria and talkativeness, yet with heavier dosages manifest a thickening and slurring of speech, skipping numbers in counting backwards from 100, and nystagmus. Given the specificity of these physiological signs, it is unlikely that a patient could successfully feign these symptoms. It is possible that the use of such shorter-acting barbiturates as amobarbital may allow the clinician to more closely control the degree of sedation and thereby minimize the likelihood of feigned sedation. Physiological studies are not available on changes in pulse, respiration, or cerebral-cortical electical activity associated with drug-assisted interviews; such research would provide a more objective basis for ruling out the possibility of simulated sedation.

A concern raised by the literature on hypnosis is whether patients in drug-assisted interviews are hypersuggestible. Research by Orne (1979), for example, suggests that hypnotized subjects may respond to the demand characteristics of the hypnotic situation and be encouraged to have more memories, whether accurate or not. A further concern is that patients' distortions under amobarbital might become pseudomemories, indistinguishable from other memories. Empirical studies are silent on both the issues of hypersuggestibility and pseudomemories. On a clinical basis, clinicians must attempt to avoid at all costs implicit or explicit messages that either the patient (1) is not telling the whole story, or (2) is deliberately distorting his or her self-report. Such demand characteristics may unduly influence the patient to either embellish or change his or her recall. Further, based on the analogue with clinical hypnosis (Putnam, 1979; Zelig & Beidleman, 1981), clinicians should assiduously avoid leading questions. Given the possible vulnerability for pseudomemories, clinicians should ask open-ended, nondirective questions to the maximum extent feasible when conducting drug-assisted interviews (Herman, 1985; MacDonald, 1976; Rogers, 1986a).

The most critical dimension of drug-assisted interviews is the degree of control patients have over their self-report. The primary mechanism of such interviews is the disinhibitory function of the barbiturate on a patient's attempt to withhold or distort his or her self-report. Despite early and unsupported claims of amobarbital as a "truth serum," it is generally accepted that the degree of control exerted by an individual is highly variable (Rogers, 1986a). Early case studies have noted that patients may deliberately misrepresent events or information during a drug-assisted interview (Lambert & Rees, 1944; Ripley & Wolf, 1947). Adatto (1949), in interviews with 50 forensic patients, found three subjects who had fabricated new accounts of their behavior while under drug-assisted interviews. This finding would seem to suggest that at least some patients may not only maintain prior fabrications, but create *de novo* deceptions during their drug-assisted interviews. Pertinent to the above discussion of hypersuggestibility and pseudomemories, these three patients had (1) engaged in dissimulation prior to the drug-assisted interview and (2) admitted to fabricating the stories during follow-up interviews.

Redlich, Ravitz, and Dession (1951) conducted a study of nine normal subjects who were asked by the first examiner to reveal one or several shame- or guilt-producing incidents in their lives. Subjects were then instructed to create a "cover story" which would be maintained throughout a drug-assisted interview with an independent clinician. Two subjects provided rather trivial guilt-producing incidents (i.e., lying about age and stealing two library books while a teenager) and were able to maintain the deception without difficulty. Of the remaining seven who admitted to substantial guilt-producing behavior, two made complete admissions and two partial admissions during the amobarbital interviews. Although limited in sample size, these findings suggest considerable variability in patients' degree of control over self-reporting.

No research is available on what types of patients under which circumstances will attempt to maintain dissimulation during drug-assisted interviews. Empirical study is necessary to establish whether the content of a dissimulating patient is identifiable in its presentation from that of nondissimulating patients. For example, is the presentation of a dissimulating patient unduly rigid and rote in comparison to others? As a related issue, research is needed on paralinguistic and nonverbal cues of dissimulating patients when struggling to keep their stories consistent.

A final consideration is the emergence of new or different symptoms during drug-assisted interviews. Research would suggest that most psychiatric patients do not significantly alter their clinical presentation during drug-assisted interviews (Dysken, Chang, Casper, & Davis, 1979; Dysken, Kooser, Haraszti, & Davis, 1979; Kwentus, 1981). Research by Woodruff (1966) on schizophrenics, depressed patients, and control groups, found that schizophrenic patients occasionally disclosed previously unreported delusions and hallucinations but not affective symptoms during drug-assisted interviews. Depressed patients and control groups manifested no differences in symptoms. Further, patients suspected of organic brain syndrome may demonstrate previously absent disorientation, confabulation, and denial of illness (Weinstein, Kahn, Sugarman, & Linn, 1953; Weinstein, Kahn, Sugarman, & Malitz, 1954). The clinician must therefore be alert that changes, as noted above, may be found in nondissimulating psychiatric patients. Indiscriminant changes in symptomatology, including the emergence of contradictory symptoms, greatly increase the likelihood of dissimulation.

Dissimulation of Neurological and Somatic Disorders

Malingering of a variety of neurological symptoms, syndromes, and diseases is encountered in a variety of clinical, industrial, and legal settings, with an undetermined prevalance. This dissimulation has included malingered pain, anesthesia, hyperesthesia, dizziness, visual changes, blindness, deafness, gait disorder, tremor, contracture, stuttering, dysarthria, aphasia, mutism, seizures, amnesia, fugue states, delirium, dementia, and coma (Gorman, 1984; Miller & Cartlidge, 1974; Plum & Posner, 1980; Shoichet, 1978; Stevens, 1986). Such symptoms may be maintained for long periods of time, often prompting invasive diagnostic procedures, or elaborate physical therapies. In clinical reports, amobarbital interviews have been reported as useful in the differential determination of conversion reactions versus malingering or organic disease. Amobarbital prompts a usually transient remission of functional disorders in general, and conversion reactions in particular (e.g., aphonia, amnesia, confusion, gait impairment, paralysis, dystonia), but an exacerbation or precipitation of neurological dysfunction (e.g., disorientation, pathological reflexes, paresis); an exception is cases of intoxication-induced cognitive impairment or ictal psychosis in which improvement occurs (Perry & Jacobs, 1982; Plum & Posner, 1980; Ward, Rowlett, & Burke, 1978; Weinstein et al., 1953). The malingerer of organic symptoms may refuse the amobarbital interview, and his or her symptoms will usually fail to respond to its use (Lambert & Rees, 1944; Stevens, 1986). Furthermore, patients with organic pain continued to experience their pain and physical complaints while under amobarbital; those with functional pain syndromes improved during amobarbital, and those who malingered either guarded against the relaxation produced by amobarbital, or became agitated, histrionic, and later hostile when confronted with the diagnosis (Shoichet, 1978)

     Several clinical studies have questioned the usefulness of amobarbital in the detection of malingered neurological impairment. Dysken, Steinberg, and Davis (1979) demonstrated that amobarbital did not interfere with the ability of normal volunteers to simulate catatonic stupor. With respect to malingered amnesia, a subject may variously maintain the amnesia, present pseudomemories (fantasies) to the interviewer, or respond to the drug with an accurate report of his or her past behavior (Gerson & Victoroff, 1948). As yet, however, there is no controlled research to support the clinical experience in this area.

For the identification of neurological malingering, clinicians must have sufficient consultations to provide comprehensive physical and neurological examinations of the suspected patient in order to detect signs and symptoms of any diagnosable organic disorder. Differential diagnoses may require extensive neuropsychological testing (see Chapter 10) or specialized neurological testing including skull x-rays, lumbar puncture, electroencephalogram, CT (computerized tomography) scans, nuclear magnetic reasonance scans, and auditory and visually evoked potentials to exclude organic neuropathology. As in the case of functional psychiatric disorders, the amobarbital interview is generally considered an adjunctive, rather than definitive, procedure in assessing suspected neurological malingering.

Use of Drug-Assisted Interviews in the Identification of Dissimulation

Practical considerations in the use of drug-assisted interviews involve threshold and clinical decision models. These two models attempt to capture essential issues of *when* drug-assisted interviews should be conducted (threshold model) and *how* dissimulation is determined (decision model). The following sections will briefly delineate these two models.

Threshold Model

The paucity of validity studies on the usefulness of drug-assisted interviews would argue for its selective use and conservative interpretation. From this perspective, the authors recommend its use only in circumstances where other better validated methods are unsuccessful and the diagnostic issue is considered essential. Based on this reasoning, Table 11.1 provides a summary of diagnostic issues for which drug-assisted interviews may be considered.

Drug-assisted interviews might best be conceptualized as a challenge test (Rogers, 1987) which may, in certain cases, assist in establishing of dissimulation. The term "challenge test" is applied, since its finding may assist in *ruling in* but not *ruling out* dissimulation. Given the limited studies reported above, the absence of any observable dissimulation is not necessarily indicative of honesty and self-disclosure. Therefore, drug-assisted interviews may be selectively employed to assess dissimulation, but have no utility in determining truthfulness.

Table 11.1. Threshold Model for the Use of Drug-Assisted Interviews in the Assessment of Dissimulation

Clinical Presentation	Criteria
Elective mutism	Any current presentation
Suspected amnesia	Inconsistent with psychogenic or organic amnesia
Circumscribed episode of a major mental illness	Only when corroborative data is absent and retrospective assessment is essential
Denial of suspected psychosis	Rare situations where inpatient observation and corroborative interviews are inconclusive
Improbable self-report	Only when self-report is critical to a dispositional or forensic issue
Unexplained neurological symptoms such as seizures, stuttering, and aphasia	Only when neuropsychological and neurological procedures are inconclusive and other clinical data is suggestive of dissimulation

Clinical Decision Model

The clinical literature (e.g., Herman, 1985; MacDonald, 1976) has focused primarily on the role of drug-assisted interviews in the determination of malingering. Drug-assisted interviews appear, however, to have a greater application in the establishment of deception and defensiveness regarding functional psychiatric syndromes than in the determination of malingering. As previously noted, subjects can withhold information or deceive during amobarbital interviews (Adatto, 1949; Gerson & Victoroff, 1948; Lambert & Rees, 1944; Ripley & Wolf, 1947). The criteria for establishing dissimulation in drug-assisted interviews have not been clearly articulated. Discussions in the clinical literature often center on marked inconsistencies in self-report as the sole indicator of dissimulation (e.g., Rogers, 1986a). Such an approach is unnecessarily limited since other indicators may be potentially more useful (see Table 11.2).

Clinicians should be observant of inconsistencies in self-report in the drug-assisted interview itself and as the interview data compare with prior clinical presentations. In addition, nonverbal attempts to withhold information, such as clenching jaws or refusing to respond, may provide useful evidence of patients' attempts to withhold and possibly distort their self-report. In contrast, indicators of autonomic arousal, paralinguistic cues, and inconsistencies in affect, although representing avenues of future research, are inappropriate for clinical assessment since they lack any validation in this context. In particular, inconsistencies in affect are likely to be the result of the drug interview itself (see, for example, Smith *et al.,* 1970) and have no bearing on determining the interviewee's veracity.

Table 11.2. Indicators of Deception in Drug-Assisted Interviews

Indicators	Comments
Spontaneous admission of dishonesty	Not reported in clinical literature; would require careful follow-up
Inconsistencies in self-report and in prior clinical presentation or within drug interview itself	Most common indicator in clinical literature, particularly in prior clinical presentation; not valid with leading questions
Nonverbal indicators of witholding information	Potentially useful though not discussed in clinical literature; examples would be clenching jaws or selective mutism
Autonomic arousal	Analogous to polygraphy; not studied in experimental or clinical literature
Paralinguistic cues	Social psychological studies are not generalizable to drug interviews
Inconsistencies in affect	Unlikely to be useful, given affective changes with drug interviews
Admission of dishonesty in follow-up interview is either spontaneous or comes when confronted with inconsistencies	Potentially most useful; negated by leading questions or confrontation in drug interviews

Admissions of dishonesty, either given spontaneously during the drug-assisted interview or in a subsequent follow-up interview are potentially the most useful in establishing dissimulation. If different or contradictory material is elicited during the drug-assisted interview, the clinician should always employ a follow-up inquiry. During the subsequent interview, the clinician should offer the patient an opportunity to clarify these apparent discrepancies. Admissions of dissimulation with exploration of the patient's motivation in a follow-up interview are invaluable in establishing dissimulation.

The use of drug-assisted interviews as the sole measure for establishing malingering or defensiveness is discouraged. For specific styles of dissimulation (i.e., malingering and defensiveness) drug-assisted interviews are best conceptualized as an adjunct measure, providing clinical support in those

Table 11.3. Clinical Decision Model for Establishing Dissimulation in Drug-Assisted Interviews

Description	Criteria
Unreliable	Markedly inconsistent self-report *or* nonverbal indicators of witholding
Probable dissimulation	*All of the following:* Markedly inconsistent self-report Admission of dishonesty in follow-up interview Motivation for deception is understandable in light of patient's goals

cases where such investigations are necessary. As noted above, findings from drug-assisted interviews must be interpreted conservatively, given the limited validation research. Table 11.3 provides a model for establishing the unreliability or probable dissimulation of a particular patient. It should be observed, with regard to the latter category, that an admission of dissimulation and an understanding of the motivation for such dissimulation are necessary for making this determination.

Nonbarbiturate Interviews

This chapter is mainly devoted to the discussion of barbiturate interviews and their potential role in the assessment of dissimulation. Investigators have also examined the use of amphetamines and subclinical dosages of an anesthetic (e.g., hydroxydione) in the evaluation of dissimulation. In addition, an argument could be made for the use of placebo drug interviews (see, for example, Dysken, Kooser, Haraszti, & Davis, 1979) as a potential method of eliciting new information. These alternatives to barbiturate interviews will only be briefly discussed, since there is essentially no research on their usefulness in assessing dissimulation.

Amphetamines, either alone or in combination with barbiturates, have been used to facilitate recall and derepression in treatment cases (Kwentus, 1981). Their effect in comparison to phenobarbital, hydroxydione, and a placebo have been described (Smith *et al.*, 1970). Use of methamphetamine produced the most anxiety, greatest ease of speech, and highest degree of attention in comparison with the other conditions (Hain *et al.*, 1966).

Hydroxydione has also been investigated in drug-assisted interviews. In research reported by Hain and associates (1966), 500 mg. of hydroxydione resulted in more incoherent and inconsistent speech, less anxiety, and less attentiveness than the amobarbital, amphetamine, and placebo conditions. Hydroxydione has been employed in one case study to assist with a highly defensive patient who had denied a suicide attempt (Peck, 1960). According to Kwentus (1981), hydroxydione is not currently available.

Ethical and Forensic Considerations

The process of obtaining informed consent[1] for drug-assisted interviews in problematic when the purpose of such interviews is the detection of malingering and deception. Fully informed consent, whether oral or written,

---

1. Obtaining the patient's consent to the interview itself may be a problem in a diagnostic setting such as a psychiatric or medical emergency room when the patient presents with an apparently altered mental status such as delirium (Fogel, Mills, & Landen, 1986).

would require that the subject be informed that the examination is being conducted for the sole purpose of assessing malingering and deception, as well as the likely consequences of such an evaluation. Additional consent disclosures include the nature of the procedure, its physiological risks, its alternatives, and the right of the subject to terminate it at any time (Fabian & Billick, 1986). Some examiners, however, might conclude that such extensive disclosures would interfere with the accuracy of the interview data, and decide to withhold them, arguably without ethical justification, on the basis of the "therapeutic privilege" as an exception to informed consent.

Several legal evidentiary problems are presented by the use of drug-assisted interviews in forensic assessments (Annotation, 1986). The interview results are usually admissible at trial when the interviewer testifies that all or part of his or her conclusions are based on the test. Inculpatory or exculpatory statements made during the drug-assisted interview, as in any forensic interview, however, are generally not admissible at trial to prove the truth of an issue; drug-assisted interviews will not be admissible as "truth serum" (Adelman & Howard, 1984).

Conclusion

As a general rule, drug effects on human subjects are determined by the interaction among a variety of specific and nonspecific factors. These factors include the setting, personality of the patient, expectancies of the patient and physician, the type and quality of the relationship between the patient and physician, preparation of the drug, its route and schedule of administration, as well as the pharmacological properties of the drug (Buckalew & Coffield, 1982). This multiplicity of factors is even more critical to keep in mind in the context of drug-assisted interviews used to detect malingering and deception, undoubtedly a complex interpersonal and investigational procedure. Here, an injected substance is used purportedly to reveal memory, affect, or cognition not ostensibly available to the subject or others, or to assess authenticity of the patient's presentation.

Despite the paucity of research data concerning the use and misuse of drug-assisted interviews to detect dissimulation, clinicians continue to find such interviews, particularly using short-acting barbiturates such as amobarbital, useful in the diagnosis and treatment of mental disorders. For functional psychiatric disorders, clinical reports indicate that drug-assisted interviews are more useful in detecting defensiveness rather than malingering. Amobarbital interviews may also prove to be useful in detecting malingering of neurological syndromes, although controlled research is not available. In both cases, however, drug-assisted interviews should only be employed as adjunctive procedures, conducted after other evaluations and investigations have proved to be inconclusive.

12

Assessing Deception: Polygraph Techniques

WILLIAM G. IACONO
CHRISTOPHER J. PATRICK

Use of the polygraph in lie detection has been widespread for close to 70 years and continues to inspire fresh controversy. To many, the psychophysiological assessment of deception has great appeal. They believe that polygraph testing provides a straightforward, efficient means of verifying the truth and wonder why anyone would challenge techniques that pose such obvious benefits to legal proceedings, criminal investigations, and personnel evaluation and screening. In contrast, critics condemn polygraph testing as an invasion of privacy and an infringement of civil liberties; they argue that the procedures are too prone to error to justify their widespread use.

It has been estimated that between one and four million Americans are subjected to lie detector tests each year (Lykken, 1981). In 1982, the U.S. federal government alone administered approximately 23,000 polygraph examinations, an annual increase of 325% since 1973 (Office of Technology Assessment, 1983). The many different applications of polygraph tests include (1) the examination of suspects, complainants, and witnesses in police investigations; (2) employer screening of prospective and current employees; (3) insurance claim investigations; (4) defense counsel checks on the veracity of their clients; (5) identification of prison inmates who have violated institutional rules; (6) paternity and child custody cases; (7) substantiation of claims made in civil suits; and (8) the resolution of family disputes. Given the pervasive use of polygraph testing and its profound impact on those who are confronted by lie detector tests, it is surprising how little is known about the practice of polygraphy outside of the polygraph profession. In part to remedy this situation, the present chapter provides a basic overview of the field of polygraphy, including instrumentation, professional training, types

William G. Iacono, Department of Psychology, University of Minnesota, Minneapolis, Minnesota.

Christopher J. Patrick, Department of Clinical and Health Psychology, University of Florida, Gainesville, Florida.

of tests, and future directions. Its primary thrust, however, is on the underlying rationale and validity of specific polygraph procedures. Each of the major techniques is described with a concomitant review of the pertinent research literature to determine how accurately these techniques classify deceptive and truthful individuals. In addition, factors that may influence their accuracy, such as the use of drugs and physical countermeasures, are considered. Finally, clinical applications of these techniques are discussed.

Overview

Instrumentation

Polygraph operators conduct their examinations with a multichannel electronic recording instrument that is often manufactured to fit inside a small suitcase or attache case. Physiological responses to the test questions are monitored by measuring respiration, cardiovascular activity, and skin resistance. Expandable pneumatic tubes, positioned around the upper thorax and abdomen, reflect the changes in chest circumference that accompany inspiration and expiration. A partially inflated blood pressure cuff attached to the upper or lower arm records relative changes in blood pressure and provides an index of pulse. Another channel is used to detect alterations in palmar sweating from a pair of electrodes attached to the fingers of one hand. Although significant advances in psychophysiological knowledge and technique have been made in the last 4 decades, these have had little impact on the field of polygraphy, with many examiners using instruments and recording procedures that differ little from those employed in the 1950s.

Common misconceptions about the polygraph are that the machine is capable of detecting lies or that guilty people produce a characteristic lie response (Lykken, 1981). On the contrary, all the equipment can do is record the changes in autonomic arousal that are elicited by the questions. Polygraphers assume that these changes reflect the nervous system's response to the act of deception, although there is no way to distinguish a response associated with deception from that associated with any other human emotion. For example, inquiries about possible misconduct could elicit any of a variety of emotions, including embarrassment, anger, fear, or guilt, but the pattern of physiological response could not be used to uniquely identify one of these feelings or to differentiate any of them from the act of lying.

The Polygraph Examiner

A polygraph examination is a complex form of interrogation. It demands sophisticated clinical interviewing skills, requires knowledge of psychophysiological measurement, and has many of the properties of a psychological test. Despite this, very few polygraph examiners are trained as psychologists. The vast majority are graduates of polygraph training schools which are administered and staffed primarily by professional polygraphers. Attempts to establish minimal standards for the practice of polygraphy have led to the accreditation, by the American Polygraph Association, of about 30 U.S. polygraphy schools and one in Canada. In addition, 31 states require their examiners to be licensed.

Those training programs approved by the American Polygraph Association boast the strictest entrance requirements and have a curriculum that spans a minimum of 7 weeks. The amount of time devoted to topics in psychology and physiology varies widely at these institutions, and can amount to as little as 10 hours of in-class instruction.

Types of Polygraph Tests

Polygraph tests are typically used in two contexts: specific incident investigations and screening situations. Specific-incident investigations deal with a discrete issue, which may be a criminal act or some other form of transgression (e.g. adultery or leakage of corporate secrets). In this case, a specific act has been committed, and the polygraph test issue is, "Did you do it?" or "Do you know who did it?" In the screening situation, the polygraph examiner is concerned with the subject's honesty in a broader context. Test questions are generally of the form "Have you ever. . . ?", or "During the period in question, did you. . . ?" An example of a screening situation is the preemployment polygraph test, where the examiner wishes to find out whether the subject has a history of nonproductive behavior (e.g., alcoholism, frequent job loss, criminal activity) which would make him or her a poor employment risk.

Different polygraph procedures are employed for these two testing purposes. Although certain experimental approaches such as the Guilty Knowledge Test (GKT) are potentially relevant, their discussion will be presented later. This section will concentrate on the three most widely used field procedures: the Control Question Test and the Peak of Tension Test for specific incidents, and the Relevant/Irrelevant (or Relevant/Relevant) test for screening.

Control Question Test

The Control Question Test (CQT) was introduced by police examiner John Reid in 1947 and since then has become the technique of choice among polygraphers who conduct specific-incident investigations. During the last 4 decades, the technique has undergone considerable revision in terms of question format, administration, and scoring. However, these modifications have been neither systematic nor universally adopted, so that at present the CQT has a number of variants (cf. Raskin, 1986b; and Reid & Inbau, 1977).

The typical CQT consists of approximately ten questions. Included among these are questions designed to put the subject at ease and to assess his or her preoccupation with extraneous matters. These general questions do not figure into the scoring of the test. Two other types of questions are used to evaluate the subject's truthfulness: relevant and control questions. Relevant questions address directly the matter under investigation (e.g., "Did you shoot Fisbee on the night of September 22?"), whereas the control questions consist of accusations about past behaviors similar to the main issue of the test (e.g., "Before the age of 27, did you ever deliberately hurt someone?"). The control questions are developed by the examiner through discussions with the subject during a pretest interview. An attempt is made to establish control questions that the subject will deny, but with some misgivings, either because he or she knows it is a lie or is unsure of its truthfulness. According to CQT theory (Raskin, 1982; Reid & Inbau, 1977), the innocent subject should react more strongly to the control questions because their content concerns him or her more directly; the guilty subject, on the other hand, should display larger reactions to the relevant questions. A decision regarding the subject's truthfulness is arrived at by comparing the physiological responses to the two types of questions.

The typical control question test consists of a lengthy (1–2 hour) pretest interview followed by a test phase in which the subject's responses to the test questions are monitored on the polygraph. At least three "charts" (i.e., three separate presentations of the questions) are administered in the test phase, with the positions of the relevant and control questions varied from chart to chart to minimize habituation. In the most current practice, each relevant question is always paired with a control item in the question sequence. This procedure, known as the "zone of comparison" format (Backster, 1962), provides for a semiobjective analysis of the charts. A score from +1 to +3 is assigned to a question pair if the response to the control question is larger, with the magnitude of the score reflecting the size of the difference. Similarly, a score from −1 to −3 is assigned if the relevant question elicited a larger response. Separate scores are derived for each physiological channel, and the sum of the scores over charts, channels, and question pairs provides the basis for a decision. A total score of −6 or lower results in a deceptive verdict, a total score of +6 or higher results in a truthful verdict, and scores between −5 and +5 are ruled inconclusive or indefinite. Although advantageous from the standpoint of objectivity and reliability, this numerical scoring system has not been universally adopted. Many polygraphers continue to use a global, impressionistic decision-making strategy which incorporates case facts and subject behaviors as well as the chart data.

Authorities in the field (e.g., Raskin, 1982, 1986b; Reid & Inbau, 1977) agree that the suceess of the CQT is largely dependent on what transpires during the pretest interview. Besides providing the examiner with an opportunity to become familiar with the subject and to explain the test procedure, the pretest interview is used to focus the subject's "psychological set" (Barland & Raskin, 1973) on the appropriate set of questions (i.e., control questions for innocent and relevant questions for guilty subjects). Two types of strategies are used. The first is to convince the subject that the polygraph can successfully detect lies. The examiner projects an air of confidence and authority, and advises the subject that research has shown the technique to be nearly infallible. A demonstration or stimulation ("stim") test, in which the examiner records the subject's response to a "known lie," is used to reinforce this claim. For example, the examiner might have the subject select a card from a stacked deck; he then convinces the examinee that the polygraph detected which card was chosen (see Reid & Inbau, 1977).

A second tactic for establishing the correct psychological set is to continually emphasize the importance of complete truthfulness to the outcome of the test. The subject is told to answer each and every test question truthfully and with complete confidence. The examiner is careful not to distinguish between the control and relevant items in terms of their bearing on the outcome. In reviewing the control questions, the examiner will query complete denials, but at the same time subtly discourage the subject from admitting too much. A suspect is thus left with the impression that it is important to be truthful, but that too many admissions of offensive behavior will elicit concern from the polygrapher and create doubts about the suspect's integrity. In this way, according to CQT theory, the innocent will focus their concern on the control questions, because they are unsure about the truthfulness of their answers and because they believe these responses will affect the test results.

Peak of Tension Test

The Peak of Tension Test (POTT) was developed by Leonard Keeler, a pioneer in the field of lie detection (Bartol, 1983). This procedure is used when information about a crime is available that only the real culprit would know. A series of questions (usually seven) is constructed, each concerning the critical detail. An example of a POTT is presented in Table 12.1. In this case, a sexual assault was commited by an unknown male wielding a red-handled knife. During this test, the man was instructed to answer "no" to each question so that if he was guilty, he would lie to the critical question. The phrase "peak of tension" refers to the expected escalation in psychological tension and physiological arousal that occurs in anticipation of lying to the critical item. In most cases, the correct alternative would be positioned

Table 12.1. An Actual Example of a Peak-of-Tension Test Developed to Identify the Perpetrator of a Violent Sexual Assault

1. Regarding the sexual assault on that girl, do you know for sure if the color of the handle of the assailant's knife was brown?
2. Do you know for sure if it was blue?
3. Do you know for sure if it was yellow?
4. Do you know for sure if it was red?
5. Do you know for sure if it was black?
6. Do you know for sure if it was green?
7. Do you know for sure if it was white?

near the middle of the sequence to allow for a clear build-up of tension to that point, followed by relaxation.

A variant of this procedure is sometimes used in cases where the critical information is not known to the police, for example, the location of a body in a suspected homicide. In this case, the suspect might be questioned regarding the possible locations where the body might be found. A consistent peak on one of the alternatives would provide investigators with a lead. This test procedure is commonly known as the searching POTT.

The Employee Screening Test

Screening tests, in contrast to specific-incident investigations, contain relevant questions such as "Have you ever been fired from a place of employment?" or "During the past year, have you stolen anything of value from your employer?" The general nature of such relevant questions makes it difficult or impossible to establish effective controls; therefore, polygraph examiners typically use a modified relevant/irrelevant (R/I) test for purposes of pre- and postemployment screening. As the name implies, the R/I test includes just two types of questions: Relevant questions, dealing with matters of interest (e.g., theft, alcohol, and drug use) and irrelevant questions, such as "Is today Thursday?" or "Were you born in Canada?"

Before the development of the CQT, the R/I test was used routinely in all contexts, including specific investigations. Under the assumption that changes in physiological responding could be attributed solely to the act of lying, more pronounced reactions to the relevant as compared with the irrelevant items were interpreted as evidence of deception. Since the demise of the "specific lie response" notion, polygraphers have adopted an R/I screening procedure that has been termed the relevant/relevant (R/R) technique (Iacono & Patrick, 1987). In the R/R test, irrelevant items appear less frequently and are included to provide a rest period or "return to baseline" rather than a norm for comparison purposes. A judgment about the subject's truthfulness is made by comparing responses to the various relevant questions, each covering a separate issue. If over the course of the test (at last three charts) the subject exhibits particularly strong reactions to one or more of the relevant issues in relation to the rest, the examiner will conclude that the subject has lied or that he or she is particularly sensitive about these issues for some hidden reason. In this case, the subject would be expected to account for these responses and possibly submit to further tests to verify his or her claims.

To a much greater degree than in specific-incident investigations, screening examiners utilize the polygraph primarily as an interrogational tool. In many instances the final outcome, rather than being based on a subjective or quasi-objective analysis of the charts, is based on the admissions made by the subject. For this reason, Lykken (1981) has characterized the screening test as a "bloodless third degree."

Validity

The Control Question Test

THE POTENTIAL FOR ERRORS

As Lykken (1981) has noted, the validity of the CQT is limited by the soundness of the assumptions on which the test is based. For the CQT to be effective, the following assumptions must be met:

1. The examiner must be able to formulate relevant questions that guilty subjects will answer deceptively.
2. The examiner must be able to construct control questions that subjects will answer untruthfully or at least with some doubt as to their truthfulness.
3. An innocent person will be more disturbed by the control questions than by the relevant questions.
4. A guilty person will be more disturbed by the relevant questions.

The first and fourth of these assumptions, which determine primarily how well the test will work with the guilty, are not unreasonable, although there may be circumstances where they do not hold. For example, the polygraph examiner will only be able to formulate adequate relevant questions when the case information is accurate and when the questions deal with fact rather than intent or motive. A male burglar, accused of taking a diamond ring from a house he looted, might not respond to a question regarding its theft if the owner had actually lost the ring before the crime was committed. Accusations that do not deal with objective facts or use vague language may permit guilty individuals to issue denials without feeling that they are lying. For example, the questions "Did you pass the counterfeit money?" and "Did you have sexual intercourse with Jane Fisbee?" are more likely to be answered catagorically than "Did you *know* the money you were passing was counterfeit?" or "Did you *force* Jane Fisbee to have sexual intercourse with you?"

The fourth assumption should hold in most applications of the CQT, although circumstances may occur where guilty suspects respond more strongly to the control than relevant questions, either because of the strong emotions associated with control questions or habituation to relevant questions. For example, control questions may deal with other illegal or embarrassing acts perpetrated by the defendant. Habituation to the issues raised by relevant questions may lessen the psychophysiological response to these items. Many suspects who submit to polygraph tests have been repeatedly confronted with the charges contained in the relevant questions and have repeatedly denied them. The only new issues raised during the CQT are the control questions, the novelty of which may elicit strong responses in some individuals. Habituation to the relevant items is undoubtably made worse when suspects are retested by another examiner because the control questions are more likely than the relevant items to differ across occasions.

Virtually everyone who challenges the accuracy of the CQT can trace his skepticism to the seemingly implausible nature of assumptions 2 and 3, which determine how the test will function with the innocent. It is doubtful that suspects are necessarily lying or concerned when they respond to the control questions. An unusually virtuous individual or a person whose memory is imperfect may offer honest denials to these charges. Moreover, the ambiguous nature of these questions may afford subjects the opportunity to convince themselves that they can answer "no" and be truthful.

The control question is supposed to control for the emotional impact of the relevant question which, unlike its counterpart, takes the form of a serious accusation often associated with dire consequences. To the extent that control questions do not serve their purpose, either because the subject is unconcerned about them or more threatened by the consequences of responding to the relevant question, innocent persons are likely to fail the CQT.

It is important to note that polygraphers have considerable latitude in the formulation of control questions. They must choose items that are neither too trivial nor too threatening to avoid respectively false-positive and false-negative outcomes. To achieve this goal, they must convince the examinee that it is crucial to tell the truth, while discouraging excessive admissions and qualifications that would enable the suspect to issue an honest denial. In addition, the operator must choose control questions so they fit the unique qualities of the person being interrogated and the crime. A polygrapher would be more likely to use as a control question "Have you ever committed a criminal offense that has gone undetected?" than "Have you ever told a lie to keep out of trouble?" when the subject of the polygraph interrogation had a 20-year criminal history, but the second sample question would clearly be more appropriate for an individual without such a record. Toward this end, the more serious the consequences of being classified deceptive, the more serious should be the issues raised in the control questions.

The lack of standardization inherent in the CQT affords considerable leeway in how the test will be structured and conducted. Under these circumstances, it is possible that the polygrapher may inadvertently bias the test to produce a desired outcome, perhaps based on preconceived notions of guilt or innocence. Although the influence of expectancy effects on experimental outcomes has long been recognized by psychologists (Rosenthal, 1966), there are no published reports in the lie detection literature that examine this phenomenon. However, a May 1986 broadcast of the CBS television program "60 Minutes" provocatively illustrated the power of expectancy effects. CBS arranged to have three different polygraph firms each examine four employees regarding the theft of a camera. No camera was actually stolen, and, without the knowledge of the employees, each polygrapher was told that a different worker was suspected by management of having committed the theft. The results were clear. In each instance, the deceptive verdict was assigned to the employee implicated by management.

The preceding paragraphs suggest why the CQT might produce errors, and few would deny that errors occur. The controversy about the CQT concerns how many mistakes are made and whether the test is, as critics suspect, biased against innocent persons. These questions can only be answered with empirical research, which, as will be shown below, can be used to defend quite different conclusions depending on the studies chosen for analysis.

CRITERIA FOR AN ACCEPTABLE VALIDITY STUDY

The conclusions that are drawn about the accuracy of the CQT are determined in part by the research methodology. In view of the impact polygraph test conclusions have on the lives of those subjected to these procedures, the criteria for an acceptable validity study should be no less stringent than those used in the evaluation of psychological and medical diagnostic tests. To assess the validity of a new test for the diagnosis of a mental illness, scientists must compare the test results of experimental and control groups. In so doing, it is important to: (1) employ as experimental-group subjects individuals who were mentally ill rather than college students who were feigning emotional disturbance, (2) ensure that those in the experimental group are in fact mentally ill and that subjects in the control group are normal, and (3) interpret the test results blindly, that is, without knowledge of the diagnostic status of the subjects. These same criteria of using real-life cases instead of simulations, having adequate criteria for establishing ground truth (guilt or innocence), and analyzing polygraph charts without access to case facts and other information about the suspect, must be applied to the evaluation of polygraph tests.

Hence, the laboratory studies published to date, in which naive volunteers simulate criminal behavior by enacting a mock crime, cannot be used to establish the accuracy of polygraph tests. Laboratory crimes place subjects in situations where the motivational and emotional concerns are quite dissimilar from those involved in real-life polygraph examinations. A chief dissimilarity is the fact that there is no reason for experimental subjects to fear detection. Unlike real life, the guilty have little incentive to defeat the test, whereas the innocent are less likely to be bothered by the relevant questions and more likely to be disturbed by the privacy-invading control questions. The results of even well-conducted laboratory studies would be overestimates of CQT accuracy.

If field studies based on actual criminal investigations are used to evaluate the validity of polygraph tests, an important issue concerns how ground truth is determined. Judicial outcomes cannot be used to establish the truth because some people are falsely convicted of crimes and, for practical reasons, some innocent individuals will plead guilty to crimes they did not commit. Also, because legal procedures prevent the admission of certain evidence and hold to the standard "beyond a reasonable doubt," many guilty defendants will escape conviction. Finally, the use of a judicial criterion is unacceptable when the decision is influenced by the results of the polygraph test.

An improvement over the use of judicial verdicts involves the use of a panel of experts in criminal law such as judges, prosecutors, and defense attorneys. The panel can be asked to review all the case facts (with the polygraph data removed), ignore legal technicalities, and render a judgment based on the available evidence.

The most commonly employed method for establishing ground truth has been to rely on confessions to identify the culpable and clear the innocent. Although occasionally confessions are false and those who confess may differ in important ways from those who do not, the major problem with this strategy is that the confessions are often obtained by polygraphers after the subject has failed the test. This procedure introduces bias. Since the polygrapher will only endeavor to obtain a confession when the polygraph test yields a deceptive outcome, guilty individuals who defeat the test will never be asked to confess and consequently, will not be included in a validity study. Moreover, innocent people who fail the test, because they do not confess, will never be included in validity study. Hence, the only cases incorporated in validity studies will be those wherein the assessment of the original examiner was correct, with the verified cases chosen for study biased in favor of demonstrating high accuracy for the technique. Because the confession will always be more dependent on the guilty person failing the polygraph test than on the innocent suspects passing it, this procedure will overestimate accuracy more for the guilty than for the innocent. Under these circumstances, it should be no surprise if for the cases chosen for a validity study, the original examiners are 100% correct (e.g., Horvath, 1977). Proponents of polygraphy point to this datum as evidence that the test is infallible when in fact it is an artifact of how cases are selected.

Because of these kinds of concerns, a number of authorities have challenged various studies that use confessions (Horvath, 1976; Lykken, 1981; Raskin, 1978). They have asserted that when the confession confirms the original polygrapher's conclusion, having other examiners blindly re-score the same charts provides more an index of interscorer reliability than a measure of validity.

Analysis of CQT Field Studies

Only ten published field studies can be employed in assessing the accuracy of the CQT. The characteristics of all but one of these investigations are summarized in Tables 12.2 and 12.3. The one investigation not included

Table 12.2. Classification Accuracy of Published Control Question Test Field Studies

Study	Number of cases		% Correctly classified[a]		
	Innocent	Guilty	Innocent	Guilty	Overall[b]
Professional Polygraphers' Research					
Horvath & Reid (1971)	20	20	91	85	88
Hunter & Ash (1973)[c]	10	10	86	88	87[c]
Slowick & Buckley (1975)	15	15	93	85	89
Wicklander & Hunter (1975)	10	10	95	92	93
Davidson (1979)	11	10	100	90	95
Yankee, Powell & Newland (1986)	25	26	98	100	99
Totals[d], Six Studies	91	91	94	91	93
Social Scientists' Research					
Barland & Raskin (1976)	11	40	45	98	71
Horvath (1977)	28	28	51	77	64
Kleinmuntz & Szucko (1984a)	50	50	63	75	69
Totals[d], Three Studies	89	118	57	83	70

[a]Inconclusive cases were eliminated when computing these figures.
[b]Based on the mean of the accuracies computed for the innocent and guilty cases.
[c]Accuracy figures based on the average of two blind chart analyses performed by each chart evaluator.
[d]Average hit rates were calculated by weighting each study by the number of cases examined.

Table 12.3. Methodological Characteristics of Control Question: Test Field Studies

Study	Criterion for ground truth	Source of cases	Method of case sampling	Method of chart scoring	Used standard procedures?
Horvath & Reid (1971)	Confession	Author's files	Unspecified	Global	Yes
Hunter & Ash (1973)	Unspecified	Author's files	Unspecified	Global	Yes
Slowick & Buckley (1975)	Unspecified	Polygraph firm	Random	Global	Yes
Wicklander & Hunter (1975)	Unspecified	Author's firm	Unspecified	Global	Yes
Davidson (1979)	Confession	Unspecified	Initially random, 30% of charts eliminated	Numerical	No
Yankee, Powell, & Newland (1986)	Confession & judical outcome	Police agency	Consecutive cases, some charts eliminated	Numerical	Yes
Barland & Raskin (1976)	Panel	Referrals to author	Consecutive referrals	Numerical	Yes
Horvath (1977)	Confession	Police agency	Initially random, some charts eliminated	Global	Yes
Kleinmuntz & Szucko (1984a)	Confession	Polygraph firm	Unspecified	Global	No

(Bersh, 1969) did not use blind chart scoring, and, as the author of the study appropriately noted, it was not possible to determine the relative contributions of the polygraph charts, the case facts, and the behavior of the examinee, to the polygrapher's classifications.

The remaining nine studies can be divided into two groups composed of the first six and last three studies listed in the tables. The first group of investigations were all published by professional polygraphers in police and polygraph trade journals. As Table 12.2 indicates, the hit rates for correct classification in all of these studies were 85% or better, with somewhat higher hit rates reported for innocent than for guilty suspects.

Unfortunately, these first six studies lack important methodological details, which constrains the confidence one can place in their findings (see Table 12.3 for an overview). Four studies (Hunter & Ash, 1973; Slowick & Buckley, 1975; Wicklander & Hunter, 1975; Yankee, Powell, & Newland, 1986) did not specify the criteria used to establish ground truth. In one of these studies (Yankee *et al.*, 1986), judicial outcome was used to establish ground truth in an unspecified proportion of the cases (W. J. Yankee, personal communication, April 11, 1986). In addition, four of the seven investigations (Davidson, 1979; Horvath & Reid, 1971; Hunter & Ash, 1973; Wicklander & Hunter, 1975) provided insufficient detail regarding how the polygraph records were chosen. As a result, the representative nature of the charts remains unknown and it is not possible to reproduce the case samples. In the Yankee *et al.* study, polygraph operators, rather than the study investigators, selected the cases. The absence of investigator control over this aspect of the research procedure opens this report to the criticism that the polygraphers may have inflated polygraph accuracy by making available only charts in which the ground truth criterion was strongly corroborated by the polygraph charts. Further, two studies (Davidson, 1979; Horvath & Reid, 1971), excluded 30% or more of the original sample employing arbitrary criteria. On this point, Yankee *et al.* omitted an unspecified number of charts containing "other than the normal polygraphic recordings and notations" (p. 110). Moreover, the procedure used to identify the initial sample of cases was not specified in four of these reports (Horvath & Reid, 1971; Hunter & Ash, 1973; Slowick & Buckley, 1975; Wicklander & Hunter, 1975); polygraph charts reportedly came from suspects tested by the authors or from case files of a polygraph firm.

The remaining three studies presented in Tables 12.2 and 12.3 were conducted by social scientists, three of whom (Barland, Horvath, and Raskin) are also trained polygraphers. As can be seen from Table 12.2, the results of these studies contrast sharply with those obtained in the other investigations. Hit rates are generally lower, and, on average, the blind chart evaluators performed at slightly better than chance level with innocent suspects.

These investigations are also not without shortcomings, many of which are subtle and cannot be ascertained from the original reports. The Barland and Raskin (1976) study has been criticized by the study's authors (Barland, 1982; Barland & Raskin, 1976; Raskin & Podlesny, 1979) because information that was provided to the independent panel was poorly prepared and incomplete. Attention has also been directed toward another component of this investigation which included 16 suspects whose charts were verified by confessions (Raskin, Barland, & Podlesny, 1978). Twenty-five polygraphers blindly rescored these charts and achieved a 90% overall accuracy rate when inconclusive judgments were eliminated. Unfortunately, only four of the suspects were innocent and hit rates were not presented separately for guilty and innocent groups. Thus, this report added little to the accuracy estimates contained in the original Barland and Raskin (1976) study.

Animadversions have also been leveled at the Horvath (1977) report. Chief among them has been the assertion that the innocent group, rather than being composed entirely of criminal suspects as Horvath (1977) claimed, contained 13 victims of crimes that were suspected of falsifying their police reports (Barland, 1982). Such "confirmatory" polygraph tests, because they are conducted with someone involved with the crime, often elicit strong emotional feelings and are believed by many polygraphers to produce excessive false-positive errors. This factor could have contributed to the low accuracy (51%) obtained with the innocent suspects. However, according to F. S. Horvath (personal communication, September 18, 1984), removing the victims from the analysis increased the overall hit rate from 64% to 67% and had little effect on the false-positive rate.

Another limitation of the Horvath (1977) study concerns the replacement of an unspecified number of cases using arbitrary criteria (Horvath, 1974, p. 97). In consultation with a polygraph examiner from the police agency that provided the polygraph data, various charts were eliminated due, for example, to "artifacts" and "effort to 'beat' the polygraph." Although this procedure may have boosted the hit rates for this study, the representative nature of the resulting purified sample remains undetermined.

The low hit rates obtained in both the Horvath (1977) and Kleinmuntz and Szucko (1984a) studies could stem from the fact that the blind evaluators were not trained in numerical scoring. Raskin (1978; Raskin & Podlesny, 1979) has noted that in the absence of the extrapolygraphic data to which they are accustomed, polygraphers using the global scoring approach may be unable to make adequate assessments. At least for the Horvath study, this explanation seems unlikely because the ten blind evaluators obtained an interrater reliability of .89 and diagnosed only 1% of the cases inconclusive, indicating that they were able to make reliable decisions and that they had few misgivings about the quality of the available data.

Various aspects of the Kleinmuntz and Szucko (1984a) investigation may have served to deflate accuracy rates. In a subsequent report presenting information pertinent to this study, Kleinmuntz and Szucko (1984b) revealed that the polygraphers (1) based their decisions on a single chart (decisions are normally based on three), (2) were not allowed to make inconclusive verdicts, (3) were trainees in the final stage of their internships. All of these factors provide for a nonoptimal appraisal of polygraph validity.

None of the studies listed in Tables 12.2 and 12.3 clearly describes how confessions were obtained. Because it is established practice to interrogate those who fail tests, it is likely that almost all of the confessions were obtained by polygraphers who concluded their subjects were deceptive. As mentioned previously, this method of obtaining criterion data is not independent and probably generates overestimates of polygraph accuracy, especially for guilty suspects. A further limitation of these studies is that the credentials and experience of the polygraphers who administered the examinations were not presented. The effectiveness of the CQT would appear to be highly dependent on the clinical skills of the examiner; if poorly trained operators administered the tests, the hit rates of blind evaluators will suffer accordingly.

EXTENDING INVESTIGATION ON THE VALIDITY OF THE CQT

Proponents and opponents of polygraphy carve up the published field studies in predictable ways. Proponents ignore the shortcomings of the seven studies with favorable outcomes and argue that the three studies reporting low hit rates provide unfair tests of polygraph accuracy. Opponents are skeptical of the reports of professional polygraphers that have not undergone the scrutiny of scientific review prior to publication and that are lacking in crucial details. They rely instead on the field investigations conducted by social scientists which have produced results that can be predicted from the weaknesses inherent in the assumptions underlying the CQT. In an effort to shed some light on the heated debate surrounding the validity of the CQT, we conducted a study of CQT validity with the Royal Canadian Mounted Police (RCMP). The study was designed to avoid the pitfalls of previous research. First, all examiners were well-trained professionals (most of them graduates of the same accredited polygraph school, the Canadian Police College), used numerical scoring and state-of-the-art techniques, and had many years of experience as detectives and polygraph operators. Second, the initial sample consisted of every RCMP test administered over a 5-year period in a large metropolitan area; detailed criterion information was collected by systematically reviewing police files on every case. Third, only cases that were verified by confession of the guilty party (including confessions from individuals who were not administered a test) or by a statement from the victim (victims were not tested) that no crime was committed (e.g., an allegedly stolen item was found, after the polygraph tests were administered, to have been misplaced by the owner) were studied. Fourth, all charts were blindly rescored by two RCMP examiners using numerical techniques. As expected, considering how cases were selected, a high degree of accuracy was evident when the original examiner's opinion was compared with the criterion: Excluding inconclusive results, 100% of the guilty and 90% of the innocent subjects were identified correctly. However, when the charts were blindly rescored, much lower accuracy rates were obtained, especially for innocent subjects. The hit rates, with inconclusive cases eliminated, are summarized in Table 12.4. The results are highly concordant with the social scientists' studies listed in Table 12.2 and lend further weight to the argument that the CQT is biased against innocent persons.

These hit-rates compare remarkably well with the findings of an analogue study, which we completed recently (Patrick & Iacono, 1986). Unlike

Table 12.4. Results of Royal Canadian Mounted Police Polygraph Validity Study

		Percent Correctly Classified	
Ground truth	*N*	Deceptive	Truthful
Guilty	49	98	2
Innocent	20	45	55

other analogue studies, the design gave subjects strong motivation to avoid detection. Forty-eight inmate volunteers, half of whom had committed a mock theft, were tested on this issue by experienced professional polygraphers using contemporary field equipment and CQT procedures. The examiners did not know which inmate committed the theft and were unaware of the base rate for guilt. Subjects were advised prior to being tested that consequences for the entire group were dependent on individual performance. If no more than 10 of the 48 volunteers failed the polygraph test, everyone would receive a bonus of $20.00 at the end of the study; if more than 10 were judged to be deceptive, then no one would receive the bonus. Further, an agreement was made that if more than 10 failed and the bonuses were not distributed, the names of those who failed would be circulated so these individuals could be held accountable to the other prisoners. (In actual fact, no names were revealed and bonuses were ultimately awarded without regard to group performance.) Because of the strong peer pressure atmosphere that exists within the prison, the inmates were quite concerned about the outcome of their polygraph tests and the possibility that their performance could lead to their peers being deprived of what, by prison standards, was a substantial sum of money. Under these conditions, blind independent chart evaluations using numerical scoring resulted in correct classification for 20 of 24 guilty subjects and 10 of 24 innocent subjects. Excluding inconclusive results, 87% of the guilty and 56% of the innocent were accurately identified.

The Peak of Tension Test

To our knowledge, no published research exists on the validity of the POTT. However, unlike the more widely used CQT, there are sound reasons for believing that the POTT will work, given that four conditions are met: (1) the person responsible for the crime knows the critical detail; (2) the critical item has not become known to innocent subjects through the media or the police; (3) the POTT questions appear equally plausible and are of approximately equal emotional value; and (4) one and only one of the test items is of significance to the crime (see Barland & Raskin, 1973). Given these conditions, the probability that an innocent subject would produce his or her largest reaction to the critical question on a seven-item POTT (assuming that Question 1 is used as a buffer to absorb the subject's initial response) would be 1 in 6.

If more than one critical detail was known, so that two or more POTTs could be constructed, the probability of a correct test result would be greater. In fact, the rationale underlying the Guilty Knowledge Test (Lykken, 1959, 1960) is essentially a series of POTTs. Although the POTT is a potentially useful technique, which, like the more complex Guilty Knowledge Test provides greater protection for innocent subjects, our experience is that it is used infrequently by field examiners, and then only as an adjunct to the CQT. The reasons for this underutilization appear to be twofold. First, the technique is *not* appropriate in cases where salient, critical details are unavailable or are known to the public at large. Second and more importantly, most field polygraphers consider the POTT to be superfluous because they believe the more widely applicable CQT is nearly infallible.

The Employee Screening Test

No field investigation of the employee screening (R/R) version of the R/I test has been conducted. However, the R/R procedure, although perhaps preferable to the traditional R/I test, suffers from obvious limitations. It is unreasonable to assume that various relevant issues, even if answered truthfully, will have equivalent emotional impact. Furthermore, it is also unreasonable to assume that explanations from a truthful subject will reduce responsiveness to sensitive issues on subsequent tests. The assumption is that if a subject has admitted everything of importance in regard to a particular question, he or she will be able to answer it with a clear conscience and minimal chart reaction. This tenuous logic has yet to be empirically tested.

Sackett and Decker (1979) have suggested other reasons why the polygraph is likely to be less accurate in the screening situation than in criminal investigations. Whereas in criminal tests only a single issue is involved, screening examinations typically cover multiple issues. In this case, unless the polygraph were nearly infallible, the cumulative error rate associated with multiple judgments would result in a large proportion of misclassifications overall; that is, the more material covered, the greater potential for error. A second point is that the amount of time devoted to a single issue in the screening test usually amounts to just a few minutes, as compared with 2 to 3 hours in a criminal test.

Advocates of employment polygraph testing argue that such criticisms are irrelevant because screening decisions tend to be based on examinee admissions rather than the polygraph results per se. With regard to preemployment testing, Horvath (1985) has stated, "Most persons rejected for employment are rejected not because of their untruthfulness (as indicated by the polygraph test) but rather because of their statements demonstrating to their potential employer their basic unsuitability for particular employment—a narcotics user who is rejected from employment in a drug warehouse, an embezzler who is rejected as a bank teller, an operative of a foreign government who is rejected for work involving national security matters, and so forth" (p. 45). According to Horvath, less than one-third of the 30% of applicants who fail screening tests (i.e., less than 10% of all applicants) fail because of a negative polygraph result.

What potential problems occur with screening polygraph tests? Even when admissions are made, the polygraph examiner must still distinguish between minor issues and guilt so serious as either to exclude a job applicant from further consideration or provide grounds for firing an existing employee. Lykken (1981) has argued that in many cases polygraph examiners' reports of "damaging admissions" are overstated and misleading. One reason is that the examiner's mandate is to screen out dishonest people, creating pressure on him or her to fail at least some examinees (Lykken, 1981; Kleinmuntz & Szucko, 1982). From the cynic's point of view, the screening test is a "fishing expedition" (Lykken, 1978); unless the examiner makes a "catch" from time to time he or she could be out of a job.

Another point, relevant to preemployment screening, concerns the distinction between identification and prediction as the goal of polygraph testing (Sackett & Decker, 1979). Unlike specific-incident investigations, where the polygrapher's job is to find out "who did it," the preemployment screening situation requires the examiner to assess whether a person is likely to be a bad employment risk. The implicit assumption is that someone who admits to misconduct in the past is more likely to repeat similar behavior in the future. At present, there is no formal evidence that polygraph screening is an effective answer to internal theft and other forms of employee misconduct (Office of Technology Assessment, 1983), much less a predictive measure in individual cases.

A final issue concerns the relatively small proportion of examinees (about 25%, according to Lykken, 1981) who do not admit to anything during the screening test. According to Lykken, this atypical group may include a substantial number of habitual liars who are not sufficiently moved by guilt to confess. Contrary to its intended purpose, the polygraph test may screen out honest and highly conscientious persons in favor of undersocialized individuals who may easily pass polygraph tests (Lykken, 1984b). Support for this notion comes from a study in which candidates for a police training program completed the California Psychological Inventory (CPI) before submitting to a polygraph test for screening purposes (Thurber, 1981). Analyses revealed that a candidate's passing of the polygraph test could be classified with 97% accuracy using his or her CPI score alone. The best discriminator was found to be the Good Impression subscale, a measure of the tendency to "fake good" or present oneself in a socially desirable fashion. One interpretation of this result is that the candidates who passed the screening test were those best equipped to "talk their way through" the procedure.

Countermeasures

A growing interest has been expressed in what countermeasures might allow suspects to "beat" a polygraph test. Although a wide variety of potential countermeasures exist (see Barland & Raskin, 1973; Raskin, 1986b), recent research has focused on three specific categories: personality, drugs, and physical countermeasures.

A number of authorities (e.g., Barland & Raskin, 1973; Ferguson & Miller, 1974; Floch, 1950; Lykken, 1981) have speculated that psychopathic individuals may routinely defeat polygraph tests. Clinical characteristics of the psychopath include an absence of guilt or remorse, a seeming imperturbability in the face of threat, and an unusual ability to manipulate and deceive (Cleckley, 1976). In addition, laboratory studies have repeatedly demonstrated that psychopaths are physiologically hyporesponsive to aversive or threatening stimuli (Hare, 1978).

Raskin and Hare (1978) tested criminal psychopaths using CQT procedures and found that they were just as easily detected as nonpsychopathic prisoners. These findings were immediately challenged on the grounds that (1) the polygraph charts were not scored blindly, leaving room for extapolygraphic cues to influence judgments of guilt and innocence, and (2) the examinees were motivated by monetary gain and had nothing to lose by failing the test (Lykken, 1978, 1981). The latter is a problem because there is evidence that psychopaths are no less physiologically responsive when competing for rewards (Schmauk, 1970).

Patrick and Iacono (1986) arranged for equal groups of psychopathic and nonpsychopathic prisoners to undergo polygraph tests in a group threat situation. As previously noted, subjects were advised that monetary rewards for the group as a whole were dependent on individual test results, and that if the rewards were lost, the persons responsible would be made known to the group. No individual incentives were offered for passing the test. Assessments of psychopathy were performed using Hare's diagnostic criteria (Hare, 1980) with equal groups of psychopaths and nonpsychopaths assigned randomly to "guilty" and "innocent" conditions in a mock crime paradigm. Based on blind numerical chart analyses and CQT procedures, guilty psychopaths and nonpsychopaths were detected with a high degree of accuracy (87% overall). Similar to the findings of Raskin and Hare (1978), the difference in hit rates for the two groups was nonsignificant.

Another popular notion is that drug or alcohol ingestion prior to a polygraph test might reduce physiological responsiveness sufficiently to allow a deceptive individual to escape detection. In support of this hypothesis, Waid, Orne, Cook, and Orne (1981) found that 73% of guilty subjects who took a polygraph test while under the influence of a tranquilizing drug (meprobamate) produced truthful outcomes. However, these results had questionable external validity because the test used lacked realism and the subjects were poorly motivated. Using an improved methodology, Iacono, Boisvenu, and Fleming (1984) found that diazepam (a widely used tranquilizer) and methylphenidate (a stimulant) were completely ineffective as countermeasure drugs. More recently, Iacono, Cerri, Patrick, and Fleming (1987) replicated this study using both meprobamate and diazepam, as well as propranolol, a commonly prescribed cardiac medication that inhibits sympathetic nervous system activity. None of these drugs reduced detection rates below the level obtained with a placebo; the overall hit rate for guilty subjects was 90%. Therefore, it appears that antianxiety drugs and propranolol cannot be used to defeat a polygraph test (in these studies, the GKT was used).

A related concern is that intoxication during the perpetration of a crime, a common occurrence among offenders, might affect the outcome of a lie detection test. Bradley and Ainsworth (1984) found that mild alcohol intoxication during the commission of a mock crime reduced detectability in a subsequent polygraph examination. One implication of these findings is that other widely used street drugs, such as marijuana, barbiturates, and amphetamines, might have similar effects. Another implication, which remains untested, is that psychological processes which alter memory or sense of responsibility for a crime, such as rationalization, repression, and denial, might influence test outcomes (Floch, 1950; Reid & Inbau, 1977). Psychological distortion is a frequent concern in the testing of sexual offenders, who are renowned for their use of psychological defenses (Langevin & Lang, 1985).

Physical countermeasures are perhaps the most serious threat to the validity of the polygraph with guilty suspects. Honts and his colleagues (Honts, Hodes, & Raskin, 1985; Honts Raskin, & Kircher, 1983) found that as many as 78% of highly motivated subjects were able to "beat" a CQT polygraph test after being trained to augment their responses to the control questions by biting their tongues or pressing their toes on the floor. These physical maneuvers were so subtle that the polygraph examiner was unable to tell when subjects were using them. Although the results of Honts et al. (1983, 1984) and others (Dawson, 1980; Rovner, Raskin & Kircher, 1979) suggest that countermeasures cannot be used effectively without formal training, this fact is less than comforting in view of arguments that countermeasure training is most likely to occur when the stakes are high, for example, when foreign agents are screened for national security employment (Lykken, 1984b). One solution may lie in the use of counter-counter-measures. Honts *et al.* (1983) successfully identified 80% of their counter-measure subjects from a blind analysis of electromyographic (EMG) record-ings obtained during the polygraph test. However, this safeguard is rarely used in actual tests because most field polygraph instruments are not de-signed to record EMG activity.

Base Rates

The confidence placed in the outcome of any particular application of a test depends not only on the test's accuracy, but also on base rates (Brett, Phillips & Beary, 1986; Meehl & Rosen, 1956). The base rate refers to the proportion of the population to be evaluated that possesses the trait of interest, in this case, deception. When the base rate of a characteristic is other than 50%, the level of confidence one can place in the test's conclusion will not be equivalent to the accuracy with which classification is achieved. To determine if a polygraph test is appropriate for a given application, the probable base rate of deception must be considered.

When the base rate of guilt is below 50%, as it may be in preemploy-ment screening or when the police use the polygraph as an investigative tool, a disproportionate number of false-positive errors will be made. Base rates well above 50% might arise when the case against a defendant is strong enough to obtain an indictment. In this situation, if defense lawyers try to enter exculpatory tests into evidence, a disproportionate number of false-negative errors will ensue.

A hypothetical example of how different base rates affect the degree of confidence one can place in polygraph test outcomes is illustrated in Table 12.5. When the base rate of guilt is near zero, almost all of the deceptive polygraph verdicts will arise from the testing of innocent persons, and a high false-positive error rate will result. When the fraction of guilty individuals nears 1.00, most of the errors will consist of guilty suspects being diagnosed truthful, and a large proportion of false-negative errors will result.

The Future of Polygraphic Lie Detection

The polygraph techniques most frequently used in field examinations were developed independent of sound theoretical models and systematic experi-mental investigation. Even the control question test, the most widely re-searched of these techniques, rests on a precarious foundation of deceit: Its success depends on the degree to which subjects can be convinced that one category of questions is more important than the other, and that the polygraph can unerringly detect lies. Considering the longevity of the poly-

Table 12.5. Base Rate for Deception and the Probability of Correct and Incorrect Classification

Deception base rate	Correct decisions		Incorrect decisions	
	True-negative	True-positive	False-negative	False-positive
0	100	0	0	100
5	98	8	2	92
10	97	18	3	82
20	93	33	7	67
30	89	45	11	55
40	83	56	17	44
50	77	66	23	34
60	69	74	31	26
70	59	82	41	18
80	46	89	54	11
90	27	95	73	5
95	15	97	85	3
100	0	100	100	0

Note. For the purposes of this illustration, the accuracy of the polygraph test was that determined by the studies of Barland and Raskin (1976), Horvath (1977), and Kleinmuntz and Szucko (1984a). The hit rates for innocent and guilty persons were taken from the bottom row of Table 12.2 and were, respectively, 57% and 83%.

graph, its continued use appears a certainty. The emphasis of this section will therefore be on future developments of the polygraph.

The Guilty Knowledge Test

A more theoretically sound alternative to the CQT for specific incident investigations is the Guilty Knowledge Test (GKT) (Iacono, 1985; Lykken, 1959, 1960). Like the POTT, the GKT probes for guilty knowledge, that is, details concerning a crime or incident that would be known only to the true culprit. A GKT includes a series of questions about the crime posed in multiple-choice format. Each question concerns one detail of the crime, with multiple-choice alternatives including the correct answer as well as other equally plausible but incorrect choices. The advantage of the GKT over the POTT is obvious—the more questions included in the test, the lower the probability that an innocent subject would fail. With a GKT comprised of ten questions, each having five possible alternatives, the odds are less than one chance in ten million that an innocent person would respond most dramatically to the relevant item in each and every question.

The GKT also provides a statistical safeguard against deliberate efforts to defeat the test. Any response pattern that deviates significantly from random suggests the use of countermeasures to conceal guilt (Lykken,

1960). For example, if a subject deliberately enhanced his or her reaction to one of the irrelevant alternatives on each test question, he or she could still be detected by consistently showing the second largest reaction to the relevant alternative. Similarly, a response pattern in which reactions to relevant items were consistently the smallest would be statistically aberrant and suggestive of distortion.

Consistent with theoretical expectations, labortory studies using simulated crimes have shown the GKT to be highly accurate. These studies are summarized in Table 12.6. Most of these investigations indicate that high accuracy is possible; the median hit rates for guilty and innocent subjects are 90% and 100% respectively. However, a few of the studies report hit rates for guilty subjects that are disappointingly low. Some of these disappointing results may be accounted for by methodological factors. Iacono et al. (1984) showed that tests with too many or too few questions produce more false-negative and false-positive errors, respectively. Hence, the 45% classification accuracy for guilty subjects reported by Forman and McCauley (1986) is probably due to their use of a highly abbreviated three-item GKT (Lykken, 1987). The study by Stern, Breen, Watanabe, and Perry (1981) reported one of the lowest accuracy rates for innocent subjects. In this study, the correct GKT answers were made salient to the innocent subjects by having them read a letter, prior to the test, in which were embedded the words and phrases that were used to compose the correct GKT alternatives. Finally,

Table 12.6. Summary of Laboratory Studies Using the Guilty-Knowledge Test

Study	Number of subjects		% Correctly classified		
	Guilty	Innocent	Guilty	Innocent	Overall[a]
Lykken (1959)	50	48	88	100	94
Davidson (1968)	12	36	92	100	96
Podlesny & Raskin (1978)	10	8	90	100	95
Balloun & Holmes (1979)	18	16	61	88	75
Gieson & Rollison (1980)	20	20	92	100	96
Bradley & Janisse (1981)	96	96	59	89	74
Stern, Breen, Watanabe, & Perry (1981)	23	23	96	89	93
Bradley & Warfield (1984)	8	8	100	100	100
Iacono, Boisvenu, & Fleming (1984)	43	12	91	100	96
Forman & McCauley (1986)	22	16	45	94	70
Iacono, Cerri, Patrick, & Fleming (1987)	43	10	90	90	90

[a]Based on the mean of the accuracies computed for the innocent and guilty subjects.

Iacono *et al.* (1984) noted that a small but significant number of guilty subjects quickly stop responding to GKT alternatives. Although Iacono and associates (Iacono *et al.* 1984, 1987) excluded such individuals from their analyses, no other investigators have done likewise. The inclusion of these rapid habituators would serve to inflate false-negative error rates.

Whether guilty subjects would be detected with greater or lesser frequency in real-life cases is difficult to predict. Although the fear of detection is undoubtably stonger in the field situation, memory for relevant crime details may be poorer than in laboratory studies where subjects are "forced" to attend to the critical details which appear on the GKT.

Statements about the field validity of the GKT cannot be made because the techinque is not used by field polygraphers. Until professional examiners become convinced of the limitations of the CQT, this situation is unlikely to change. Even then, some significant obstacles would have to be overcome before the GKT could be used routinely. First, a concentrated effort would have to be made to gather crime details that could serve as valid GKT items. This effort could be accomplished by having a trained GKT examiner accompany investigators to the crime scene. Although there will always be circumstances in which the GKT would be clearly inappropriate (e.g., a rape case in which the sole issue is consent), these cases are probably less frequent than is commonly assumed. Second, standards would have to be established for the construction of a proper GKT. These standards would include routine pretesting of potential questions with known innocent subjects to elminate biased items. Third, the release of crime-relevant information during the course of an investigation must be carefully controlled. Special policies would have to be established to prevent guilty knowledge from filtering through to the public via the news media. In addition, case investigators would have to be trained to withhold such information from potential suspects during interrogations that preceded the polygraph examinations.

Computerized Lie Detection

A computer scoring program has recently been developed for use with the CQT (Kircher & Raskin, 1982). The program converts the analogue signals from a laboratory polygraph to digital form so that the physiological recordings can be analyzed as they are obtained during the polygraph test. The scoring algorithm compares responses to the relevant and control questions on the test using research-based criteria. The resultant score is entered into a Bayesian statistical model to estimate the probability that the subject was truthful on the test. According to Raskin (1986b), this computerized analysis "is an automatic, objective, and reliable procedure that provides an easily interpretable result on a continuum from 0.0 (extreme deceptive result) to 1.0 (extreme truthful result)" (p. 100).

Although advantageous from the standpoint of reliability, the use of this procedure in field cases is potentially hazardous. In the first place, the accuracy of the decisions is limited by the validity of the CQT, which remains in doubt. Equally important is the fact that the scoring algorithm developed by Raskin and his colleagues (Kircher & Raskin, 1982) is derived exclusively from laboratory data. As discussed earlier, the motivational atmosphere of a real-life polygraph test is likely to be much different from that of an analogue test, making it imprudent to generalize from one context to the other. The effect of the computer in this case is to provide a facade of objectivity and infallibility to a procedure which may be fundamentally flawed. Lykken has described this research as "the 'marriage of two myths,' the computer and the polygraph, that will spawn only new 'mythlets'" (quoted by Joyce, 1984, p. 7).

The useful features of computer technology should be combined with polygraph techniques which are solidly grounded in theory and research. For example, a statistical program would be well-suited to the GKT. An algorithm could be designed to estimate the probability that a particular pattern of responses is associated with truthfulness, or with deliberate distortion.

Cortical Response Measures

A fundamental problem in the physiological detection of deception is that there is no autonomic response pattern that is uniquely associated with lying. Similar responses may result from questions evoking anger, fear, and other emotions. The possibility remains, however, that specific brain responses may be discovered which reflect the cognitive activity associated with lying. Based on previous research showing that the P300 component of the event-related brain potential (ERP) is elicited by rare and task-relevant events, but not by frequent and irrelevant events, Farwell and Donchin (1986) analyzed ERP responses to "guilty knowledge" items and obtained 100% hit rates for "guilty" and "innocent" subjects. Although the testing situation was highly artificial, these data suggest that brain responses can be used to detect crime-relevant knowledge. A more interesting question is whether specific patterns of cortical responses would discriminate between truthful and deceptive subjects in a "Did you do it?" paradigm. Positive findings might suggest this approach as an alternative to the CQT in specific-incident investigations.

Ethical Concerns

Aside from its questionable scientific status, ethical objections to polygraph testing have been raised. Most concerns involve the use of the polygraph in employment settings (Benson & Krois, 1979; Craig, 1984; Lykken, 1974,

1981; Matusewitch, 1981; Office of Technology Assessment, 1983; Orne, Thackery, & Paskewitz, 1972; Sackett & Decker, 1979). The foremost objection is that polygraph subjects are misinformed about the examination. The majority of innocent people who consent to be tested do so with the belief, promulgated by the polygraph industry and its proponents, that the procedure is nearly infallible and that they have little to fear. Indeed, subjects are sometimes given literature asserting the infallibility of the technique and the virtual absence of risk to honest individuals. If still dubious about the procedure, the subject is confronted by the results of the "stim test," which may be contrived or manipulated by the polygrapher to produce the desired effect.

In addition, the subject is not informed about one of the important functions of polygraph tests, that is, eliciting confessions. As noted above, Horvath (1985) commented that the primary value of employee screening techniques was their ability to elicit damaging admissions. In addition, the CQT is also used to obtain confessions. In addition to material divulged when the control questions are reviewed, every person who fails the test is encouraged to own up to his or her wrongdoing during the posttest phase of the interrogation. Seldom are subjects reminded of their rights when confronted with the polygrapher's verdict of a failed test; efforts of skilled interrogators to obtain confessions have been known to extend for several hours beyond the administration of the last chart. As observed by Rogers (1987), it would seem ethically appropriate that polygraphers practice at least at a higher standard of truthfulness than what is only suspected with their clientele.

Clinical Applications

Great caution must be exercised when contemplating the use of polygraph techniques in general; applying them in a clinical setting represents a venture into the unknown. As the foregoing review indicates, there are no validity data on the R/R or POTT techniques; the GKT, although potentially powerful, remains untested in real-life settings; and the CQT may be subject to a substantial false-positive error rate. These techniques have never been systematically evaluated to assess malingering or deception in a clinical population (except several studies of psychopaths, noted above); there is certainly no reason to believe they would work better with mentally disordered individuals than with normal people. Lykken (1974) hypothesized that anxious individuals and those who are autonomically labile might be likely to generate strong physiological reactions to relevant questions on a CQT, thus leading to an increase in false-positive outcomes. This hypothesis has not been empirically tested.

Another reason to be wary of the use of polygraph techniques in clincial settings is that, unlike the other assessment devices, the administration and interpretation of polygraph tests falls outside the realm of expertise of almost all mental health professionals. Because few would be capable of conducting what is, at least by polygraph industry standards, a competent examination, clinicians would have to base their judgments entirely on the work and findings of a polygraph operator. Although one can determine whether or not a given operator meets the standards of the trade, it is not known to what extent such standards ensure a valid test outcome. Except when those who fail a polygraph test confess, polygraph operators seldom receive any feedback about the accuracy of their decisions. As a result, no one, not even the polygrapher, has even a general idea of how much faith to place in the conclusions of a given examination.

Individual differences in polygrapher competence were examined by Kleinmuntz and Szucko (1984a) who studied the classification accuracy of six polygraph examiners at the end of their training course. All were trained at the same polygraph school and apparently had similar levels of experience. False-positive error rates varied between 18 and 50%; false-negative rates spanned 18–36%. Unfortunately, the extent to which such performance variability characterizes the profession is unknown and, at present, there is no way to identify proficient examiners.

A threshold model for the use of polygraphy in the assessment of dissimulation is not proposed. Based on (1) the inherent limitations of polygraph technique, (2) the absence of empirical research on the polygraph with the mentally ill, and (3) the inability to determine the proficiency of professional polygraphers, the referral of psychiatric patients is *not* recommended.

What should a clinician do with CQT polygraph findings that are included as part of the investigative materials in a forensic evaluation? Little is known about how the mentally disordered respond to polygraph tests, so all tests conducted on such individuals should be treated with skepticism. Because of the potentially high false-positive error rate, deceptive conclusions have little probative value and should be given little weight (see Table 12.7). The sole exception to this rule arises when the probable base rate of guilt is high. Returning to the hypothetical example provided in Table 12.5, one can see that confidence in a deceptive verdict is only .56 or less when the base rate for guilt is 40% or less. Because 50% accuracy can be obtained by guessing, under these circumstances the polygraph is functioning at chance level or worse and a deceptive verdict cannot be trusted. As Table 12.5 indicates, as the proportion of guilty individuals in the population increases, substantially greater confidence can be placed in a deceptive verdict.

Truthful verdicts are more likely to improve upon chance prediction, and therefore have potential utility in the overall clinical assessment (see Table 12.7). However, this appraisal comes with a number of caveats. Table 12.5 reveals that when the base rate for deception is high (e.g., over 70%), the truthful polygraph outcome does not improve on chance prediction and

Table 12.7. Clinical Decision Model for Placing Confidence in the Conclusions of a Control Question Polygraph Test

A. Deceptive verdict
 1. Probable base rate of guilt is high
 2. Not mentally ill or retarded
B. Truthful verdict
 1. Probable base rate of guilt is low
 2. No history of substance or alcohol use at time of the offense
 3. No reason to believe physical countermeasures were used
 4. Subject tested under adversarial circumstances, e.g., by the police
 5. Not mentally ill or retarded

may be incorrect more often than correct. Thus the truthful verdict can be trusted only when the base rate of deception is low. In addition, because laboratory studies have shown that alcohol use as well as the application of physical countermeasures may produce false-negative outcomes, little confidence should be placed in truthful verdicts when these factors are believed to be involved. Unfortunately, there is at present no way to know whether effective physical countermeasures were employed and in many cases, the use of alcohol may go undetected.

Finally, it is important that the subject be tested under adversarial circumstances (Lykken, 1981; Orne, 1975). Polygraph operators as well as psychologists with expertise in this field have long maintained that the subject's "fear of detection" is crucial to a valid test outcome. When polygraph tests are arranged by defense lawyers, there is little reason to fear detection, because a defense attorney would never divulge that a client failed a polygraph test. In this situation, it is also likely that a defense attorney believes the client to be innocent. To the extent that this belief is communicated to the polygrapher, an expectancy effect is created, and the polygraph examiner may bias the test to produce the desired outcome. For these reasons, truthful polygraph verdicts should be given credence only when the test is administered under adversarial circumstances (e.g., by a police officer) and it is known beforehand that the test results will become public knowledge.

Conclusion

During the sixty years that have elapsed since Harvard psychologist William Marston introduced the forerunner of the modern lie detector test in 1917, it has emerged as possibly the single most frequently used of individually administered psychological tests. Yet despite this long history and abundant use, surprisingly little is known about the psychophysiological detection of deception and this area of applied psychology remains largely devoid of psychological theory.

Of the polygraph procedures commonly employed, the CQT has received the most attention in the research literature. However, as the foregoing review of the published field studies indicates, the investigations that directly address the validity of the CQT suffer various, and often serious, methodological shortcomings. Studies conducted by professional polygraphers describe a highly accurate procedure. Studies conducted by social scientists indicate, as a critical analysis of CQT theory would lead one to conclude, that the test is strongly biased against the innocent. As a result, no consensus has emerged on the validity of the CQT. As long as this state of affairs persists, the best defense one can offer for the continued use of the CQT is that its accuracy is indeterminate. The same conclusion applies to the employee screening test. There are no data at all bearing on the field accuracy of this procedure. There is an obvious need for more scientific research on these procedures. For such research to influence the practice of polygraphy, it must be sensitive to the needs and constraints of field examiners as well as be experimentally sound.

Other polygraphic techniques, such as the POTT and its more sophisticated extension, the GKT, hold promise because they are based on sound psychological principles. Unfortunately, they have not captured the interest of polygraphers. It is statistically improbable that an innocent person would fail a competently constructed and administered GKT. Because the GKT has not been used in real-life criminal investigations, the extent to which false-negative outcomes may pose a problem for this procedure is unclear. Hence, there is great need for a field study with the GKT. Until such an investigation is carried out, it is too early to routinely use the GKT to assess deception.

13

Hypnosis and Dissimulation

ROBERT D. MILLER
LAWRENCE J. STAVA

Hypnosis evokes in public and even some professional circles the concept of direct access to forgotten memories and withheld thoughts of psychological or forensic significance. This chapter addresses the reciprocal relationship between the memory-enhancing functions of hypnosis and dissimulation from several perspectives. After a general introduction to the study of hypnosis, its clinical applications are discussed, including its ability to assist in memory recall and methods to evaluate the nature of the hypnotic state itself. In the final section of the chapter, the relevance of hypnosis of legal issues is examined.

Overview

The Nature of Hypnosis

Considerable controversy continues within the scientific community as to the nature of hypnosis (Frankel, 1976). From a historical perspective, Mesmer (1779/1948) conceived of hypnosis or "animal magnetism" as a process by which the unequal distribution of magnetic fluids in the human body could be rectified, thus curing disease. His contemporary De Puysegur (1784/1843) compared hypnotism to somnambulism, and emphasized the power of the hypnotist in the hypnotic process. Braid (1843) was one of the first investigators to recognize the importance of the subject's hypnotic characteristics in trance induction. Charcot (1886) and Janet (1907) interpreted hypnosis as similar to the clinical state of hysteria, although Charcot was concerned with neurophysiological aspects, whereas Janet was more interested in the dissociative phenomena associated with both states. Bern-

Robert D. Miller, Forensic Center, Mendota Mental Health Institute, Madison, Wisconsin; Department of Psychiatry, and Law School, University of Wisconsin–Madison; and Department of Psychiatry, Medical College of Wisconsin, Milwaukee, Wisconsin.

Lawrence J. Stava, Forensic Center, Mendota Mental Health Institute, Madison, Wisconsin.

heim (1884/1964) focused on the subjects and conceptualized hypnosis as a state of heightened suggestibility.

More recently, Sarbin and Coe (1972) approached hypnosis from a social psychology viewpoint, and defined it in terms of role playing by the subject. Barber and associates (Barber, Spanos & Chaves, 1974) were critical of the concept of a specific hypnotic *state*, and analyzed hypnosis in terms of the imagination and expectations of the subject. Psychoanalytical writers (Gill & Brenman, 1959; Schilder & Kanders, 1927/1956) use the concepts of transference and regression to explain hypnosis. From this perspective, hypnosis is described as involving an archaic transference in which passive-dependent–dependent longings and magical expectations are directed toward the hypnotist.

White (1941) explained hypnosis as an intertwined process of goal-directed striving in the context of an altered state of consciousness. Employing a process model, Shor (1959, 1962) developed the altered state argument further in connection with his theory that trance represented a fading of the generalized reality orientation. He also incorporated the role-playing concept of Sarbin and Coe (1972) and the archaic transference of the psychoanalysts (Gill & Brenman, 1959; Schilder & Kanders, 1927/1956).

Hilgard (1973) in his neodissociation theory posited a number of control systems arranged in a hierarchical order with a dominant system, which is usually identified by the person as the *self*. Hilgard (1977) reviewed empirical evidence for multiple mechanisms which control thoughts and behavior, and postulated that a nondominant system may exert its control independent of the dominant system. He hypothesized that this process occurs in hypnosis, where the nondominant system is dissociated from the dominant system. Although he built on the work of Janet (1907), Hilgard postulated that trance is a mechanism requiring considerable energy and focus to maintain, in contrast to Janet's view that trance represents a failure of cortical integration.

Our view is that hypnosis represents a very complex phenomenon which is not adequately explained by any single existing theory. However, we see most promise in the three-factor theory of Shor (1959, 1962) and Hilgard's (1973, 1977) neo-dissociation approach. Other theories that do not conceptualize hypnosis as involving an altered state of consciousness do not provide adequate explanations for much of the behavior characterized as hypnotic. The concept of an altered state also seems particularly relevant for the clinical practitioner who often finds such explanatory concepts essential for understanding certain types of psychopathology, such as multiple personality.

Measurement of Hypnosis: Hypnotic Susceptibility Scales

Considerable controversy remains on how to define and measure operationally the hypnotic state. One major effort has been to use sophisticated psychological measurement techniques in the development of scales to measure hypnotic susceptibility. Early efforts to measure susceptibility by Barry, MacKinnon and Murray (1931), Davis and Husband (1931), Friedlander and Sarbin (1938), and White (1930) were largely descriptive and unstandardized. These early attempts have been superseded by methodologically sophisticated scales such as the Stanford Hypnotic Susceptibility Scale, Forms A and B (Weitzenhoffer & Hilgard, 1959), which standardized the original Friedlander and Sarbin scale. Employing the Stanford scales, subjects are given a standardized hypnotic induction and subsequently asked to perform various motor tasks (e.g., eye closure, arm rigidity, and eye catalepsy), which are rated by the investigator. Standardization of the Stanford scales includes excellent interrater reliability of .83 to .90 (Hilgard, 1965), and stability of Form A (i.e., test–retest correlations of .60 over a 10-year period; see Morgan, Johnson, & Hilgard, 1974). The Stanford scales also correlated with subjects' self-reports of pain reduction through hypnotic suggestion at .50 (Hilgard, 1967) and at .78 with clinical estimates of hypnotic responsiveness (Hilgard, 1979).

Form C of the Stanford scale was developed to measure cognitive distortions associated with hypnosis (Weitzenhoffer & Hilgard, 1962). Whereas Forms A and B primarily measured subjects' response to hypnotic suggestions involving motor functions, Form C utilized suggestions to experience positive and negative hallucinations. Interrater reliability is similar to that for Forms A and B, and it is highly correlated with Form A ($r = .70$; Hilgard, 1979). Given this correlation, both the motor and cognitive tests appear to measure the same underlying phenomenon. Since the Stanford Forms A–C do not discriminate well among subjects with high hypnotic susceptibility, the Stanford Profile Scales I and II were developed. They utilize more difficult hypnotic tasks, such as analgesia and deafness (Weitzenhoffer & Hilgard, 1963).

Shor and Orne (1962) developed the Harvard Hypnotic Susceptibility Scale as an adaptation of Form A of the Stanford scales for group administration using self-ratings. Concurrent validity has been assessed by measuring the correlation between the Harvard scale and Form C of the Stanford scale with correlations ranging from .53 to .83 (Bongartz, 1985; Coe, 1964; Evans & Schmeidler, 1966; Sheehan & McConkey, 1979).

Barber and his co-workers developed two scales to assess subjects' ability to become imaginatively involved with hypnotic suggestions based on his cognitive–behavioral model of hypnosis (Barber, 1972; Barber & Wilson, 1977; Spanos & Barber, 1974). The Barber Suggestibility Scale (Barber & Glass, 1962) included eight suggestions representative of those given to hypnotic subjects. Test–retest reliability consistently exceeded .80 (Barber, 1965; Barber & Calverly, 1963; Barber & Calverly, 1964; Barber & Glass, 1962).

Ruch, Morgan, and Hilgard (1974) found correlations of between 0.62 and 0.78 between the Barber Suggestibility Scale and the Stanford Hypnotic Susceptibility Scale, Form A. Barber and Wilson (1977) also developed the Creative Imagination Scale for more direct clinical use. Test–retest reliability was estimated at .82 (Barber & Wilson), and split-half reliability at .89, with a correlation of .60 between the Creative Imagination Scale and the Barber Suggestibility Scale (Kiddoo, 1977). Barber's scales correlate poorly with the Harvard scales (McConkey, Sheehan & White 1979), and have been criticized for ignoring significant components of hypnosis (Hilgard, 1982; Monteiro, MacDonald & Hilgard, 1980).

The Hypnotic Induction Profile (Spiegel & Bridger, 1970) was based primarily on the apparent relationship between the ability of subjects to roll their eyes up on command and hypnotic susceptibility. It is the only widely used test of hypnotic susceptibility which is not significantly correlated with the Stanford scales (Orne et al., 1979).

Extensive research has been conducted on each of these scales. They correlate reliably with clinical observations, and predict responses to other hypnotic experiences moderately well. A limitation to their use in clinical practice for the authentication of trance states is that they have been validated on similar clinical observations with no external criterion of trance validity. In addition, the experimental designs assumed genuine responses on the part of subjects; data are not available on the ability of the scales to detect dissimulation. The scales thus may be useful for threshold estimation of a subject's potential to experience the hypnotic state, but should not be considered as guarantees either of actual susceptibility or of the authenticity of subsequent trance behavior.

The Use of Hypnosis in Clinical Practice

Clinical hypnosis has been used for a variety of reasons in general mental health practice. It has been employed since the days of Janet and Charcot as a device for uncovering unconscious material, and more recently also as an adjunct to behavioral techniques for such purposes as reducing pain, losing weight, and stopping smoking. In such applications, clinicians have usually been concerned more with the results of the procedure than with the validity of the methods. Hypnosis may also be used in circumstances in which the accuracy of the information elicited is important.

When hypnosis is used as a general method for overcoming unconscious resistance, the accuracy of the material produced is usually less significant than the emotional content; screen (i.e., emotionally laden but factually inaccurate) memories are as useful therapeutically as memories of actual events. In contrast, forensic clinicians are generally forced by the prospect of court testimony and cross-examination to be more concerned than are their nonforensic colleagues with the validity of the hypnotic state itself and the material produced under trance. Indeed, the forensic aspects of hypnosis and dissimulation will be discussed in greater detail in a later section of this chapter. Nonforensic clinicians, given the increasing demands to present evidence on the authenticity of trances and trance-derived material, must also become cognizant of hypnosis' vulnerability to dissimulation.

Even within a clinical practice, the validity of the hypnotic state and the reliability of material produced in trance are sometimes significant. Clinicians may be concerned with patients' resistance and utilize hypnosis in an attempt to circumvent defensiveness as part of the treatment process. Further, hypnosis and other purported memory-enhancing techniques such as narcoanalysis are used most frequently in cases of amnesia and related dissociative states. Here, the accuracy of material elicited may be crucial to establishing patients' identities and returning them to their former lives. It therefore becomes important to know how reliable hypnosis is in such cases.

Simulation of Hypnosis

Early clinical literature contains anecdotal case reports of the use of hypnosis to reestablish lost memories in cases of dissociation. These cases are presented at face value, without any systematic attempt to investigate the clinical assumptions that the patient was actually in trance and that the material produced was accurate. More recently, researchers have attempted to address these questions more directly under laboratory conditions.

In one line of investigation researchers have explored the differences between the behavior of subjects who were and others who were not in a state of trance. Erikson (1939) and Rock (1961, cited in Barber, 1962) demonstrated significant differences in subjects' responses to tests of color blindness between hypnotic and nonhypnotic states. In addition, Sears (1932) asked subjects, both in and out of trance, to experience anesthesia in one leg, and then applied painful stimuli to both legs; those in trance flinched when the stimulus was applied to the "anesthetized" leg, whereas those not in trance did not.

Research with hypnotized subjects as their own controls has been criticized by Barber (1962), Pattie (1935), and Sutcliffe (1958) on the basis of (1) the practice effect and (2) wishes of the subjects to please the investigators. Studies using independent control subjects in an attempt to avoid these problems have been reported by Orne (1959, 1972), Sheehan (1971), Sheehan and Tilden (1985), Spanos, Radtke, Bertrand, Addie, and Drummond (1982), and Weitzenhoffer and Sjoberg (1961). These studies employed experimental subjects who had previously been demonstrated to be highly hypnotizable and controls who had been shown not to be hypnotizable, in order to assure that controls were not in trance. Subjects in both studies were exposed to the same hypnotic induction by an investigator, blind to whether or not they were hypnotizable. Again, significant differences between control and experimental groups were demonstrated.

Barber (1962) has criticized these experiments because they did not sufficiently control for the motivational differences between subjects and controls. In addition, Sheehan (1971) pointed out that using nonhypnotizable controls confounded the experiments by comparing subjects and controls with significantly different personality types. To address this concern, Barber compared hypnotized subjects with several groups of nonhypnotized controls, including a group which had been given strong incentives to experience the states to be suggested, but who were not given formal hypnotic inductions. The hypnotized subjects could not be distinguished from high-incentive controls by the standard test measures, although they could be distinguished from low-incentive controls. This final study suggested that subjects who are exposed to situations involving strong demand characteristics, or who have high motivation to experience (or at least to appear to experience) the effects of trance, may be difficult to distinguish from those actually in trance.

The laboratory situations utilized in these research studies are significantly different from clinical situations in which therapists usually have far more knowledge about their patients than researchers do of their subjects. Clinicians have a much greater familiarity with their individual patients, and should be more able to detect attempts to simulate the hypnotic state. Nevertheless, the results of the controlled studies should convince clinicians that it is seldom possible to detect simulation of the hypnotic state itself.

Hypnosis in the Evaluation and Treatment of Memory Loss

A substantial literature exists on hypnosis and memory impairment. Power (1977) contended that genuine amnesia is likely to have a gradual onset, whereas simulated amnesia tends to display an abrupt onset. Bradford and Smith (1979) found that genuine amnesias tend to be patchy, whereas absolute amnesia tends to be simulated. Many authors have suggested that inconsistencies in recall over time tend to indicate simulation (Gorman 1984; Keschner, 1960; Power, 1977; Price & Terhune, 1919; Sadoff, 1974.) Adatto (1949) suggested that patients with genuine amnesia tend to be more upset about their memory loss than simulators. Several authors have suggested that the psychiatric history of the patient and the circumstances of the memory loss, particularly any secondary gain to be derived from that loss, may assist in determining the validity of the claimed amnesia (Bradford & Smith, 1979; Kanzer, 1939; Lennox, 1943; Power, 1977; Sadoff, 1974). For an extended discussion of feigned amnesia and memory loss, the reader is referred to Chapter 5.

Recall without Hypnosis

Before discussing the role of hypnosis in the detection of simulated amnesia, it is first necessary to discuss the research literature dealing with memory recall in general. A large literature exists on the reliability and accuracy of eyewitness reports. Early criticism of the accuracy of such reports came from researchers interested in the mechanisms of memory and its retrieval. Binet (1905) was one of the first to emphasize the suggestibility of witnesses. Bartlett (1932) told short stories to various people and then asked them to repeat the stories at intervals of several years; he found systematic distortions of the memories with time. Whipple (1918) reviewed the psychological literature on eyewitness reports and again demonstrated significant distortions.

There has been a major research effort to examine the influence that a question's form has on a witness' recollections. Investigators have usually presented predetermined scenarios (such as films or staged activities) to subjects and subsequently questioned them about their recollections. Muscio (1916) demonstrated that the form of a question strongly influenced subjects' responses, and that free recall produced less detail but also significantly fewer mistakes than did structured interviews. These findings have subsequently been replicated in many studies (Cady, 1924; Hilgard & Loftus, 1979; Lipton, 1977; Loftus & Palmer 1974; Loftus & Zanni, 1975; Marquis, Marshall, & Oskamp, 1972; Wells, 1978). For example, Lipton demonstrated that subjects who had viewed a film recalled only 21% of 150 possible details but with 91% accuracy in unstructured narrative recall. In structured interviews subjects recalled 75% of the details, but with only 56% accuracy. Loftus and Zanni found that subjects who were asked questions in the form "Did you see *the*. . . ?" as opposed to "Did you see *a*. . . ?" were two to three times more likely to respond positively, regardless of whether the correct answer was "no." Loftus and Palmer found that subjects who were asked questions about filmed automobile accidents using words such as "bumped" or "smashed" estimated the speeds of the vehicles as significantly higher than subjects questioned with words such as "contacted" or "hit." These questions are quite suggestive of expected responses and would be considered leading in legal settings.

Hypnosis and Recall

Some authors, believing that memory is comparable to a videotape recording which cannot be changed but only recalled in greater or lesser detail, have claimed that there is no increase in distortion concomitant with the increased information produced through hypnotically enhanced recall. Arons (1967) asked witnesses to recall information first without hypnosis and then in trance, and reported greater detail with no more distortion after hypnosis. His conclusions have been criticized by Putnam (1979), who pointed out that the greater detail could have resulted from the demonstrated effect of repeated efforts at recall, not from the hypnosis per se.

Reiser (1986) claimed in over 700 police investigative cases that hypnosis enhanced witnesses' recall, and that 80% of the information which could be independently verified proved to be accurate. Schafer and Rubio (1978) also argued that hypnosis does not increase memory distortions. Kroger and Douce (1979), although recognizing the potential distortions inherent in the use of hypnosis, still argued that its value outweighs the problems.

Other authors also believe that witnesses cannot lie while under hypnosis. Bryan (1962) stated that

> it is extremely difficult for a subject to lie while in a deep hypnotic trance. What happens is this: The questions are directed at the subconscious mind rather than the conscious mind, and hence the answers come from the subconscious mind. This is especially true if the questions are rapidly fired one after the other. The patient does not have time to "think" on a conscious level; and because his thinking process is distributed by hypnosis, he can only release information from the subconscious mind. He therefore invariably responds with the correct answer. These conclusions have been verified by Polygraphy and Truth Serum examinations. (p. 245)

Despite these claims, based chiefly on noncontrolled experience in legal contexts, the consensus of research is that hypnosis (1) amplifies all of the distortions found in eyewitness recall discussed above, and (2) that subjects are quite capable of lying while in trance (Ripley & Wolf, 1947). Hilgard and Loftus (1979), Orne (1961), and Stalnaker and Riddle (1932) found that hypnotized subjects recalled events in greater detail than unhypnotized subjects, but that the degree of distortion also inceased. Putnam (1979) failed to find that hypnotized subjects recalled greater detail than those not hypnotized, but did corroborate that hypnotized subjects gave significantly fewer correct and more incorrect responses. He also found that subjects who had been hypnotized were significantly more confident of their answers, even incorrect ones, than were those not hypnotized.

Schafer and Rubio (1978) argued that hypnosis should be useful for enhancing recall of traumatic events by removing witnesses' anxiety, and thus permitting them to recall more fully. Putnam (1979) pointed out that none of the laboratory studies reported attempted to examine this factor, because of the ethical problems involved, and agreed that anxiety reduction might in fact contribute to increased recall in such situations.

The hypnotic simulation studies have clearly demonstrated that subjects are capable of lying while apparently under trance; hypnosis is not a "truth serum." Even without hypnosis, it is clear that it is virtually impossible to avoid suggestion in questioning persons about events which they have forgotten, or for which their memories are unclear. Hypnosis appears, at least in controlled studies, to exaggerate the suggestibility of witnesses, both because of the demand characteristics of the hypnotic situation, and because hypnotizable subjects are more suggestible, even without formal trance induction, than are nonhypnotizable persons. It appears therefore that considerable caution should be exercised in determining the face validity of material produced under hypnosis.

Although patients in clinical practice are less likely to have conscious motives to simulate trance or answers produced under hypnosis than persons evaluated for courts, they are also more likely to have strong reasons to please their therapists. Therefore, the demand characteristics of the hypnotic state are increased. Even a simple encouraging statement that the patient will be able to remember lost material presents a powerful incentive for the patient to remember *something*, regardless of its accuracy.

Clinicians using hypnosis to recover forgotten material or to overcome unconscious resistance should frame their trance inductions and subsequent questions carefully in order to minimize the suggestibility of the situation. Open-ended questions (e.g., "Tell me what you remember") are to be preferred to leading questions (e.g., "Do you remember your father punishing you?") If accuracy is important, efforts should be made to confirm as many of the details produced as possible through independent sources. Clinicians should also be aware of the increased confidence patients have in memories recovered in trance, and not be misled by the strong conviction shown by patients who have been hypnotized.

Clinical Applications

The use of hypnosis to verify the accuracy of patients' responses has limited applicability in clinical practice. Limitations include (1) lack of independent verification that a patient is in fact hypnotized; (2) the ability of certain patients to dissimulate while operationally appearing to satisfy all the criteria for being in trance; and (3) the increased likelihood of inaccurate memories being produced under hypnosis. These limitations are summarized in Table 13.1.

A review of Table 13.1 highlights the difficulties inherent in the employment of clinical hypnosis for the detection of deception. Perhaps the most effective use of hypnosis is in the evaluation of the ambivalent patient who appears to be denying significant psychopathology or trauma. Under these circumstances, the clinician may want to weigh the risks and benefits of employing hypnosis for the elucidation of the patient's dynamics, particu-

Table 13.1. Clinical Application of Hypnosis to the Assessment of Dissimulation

Clinical issues	Research findings
Defensiveness Can hypnosis assist in uncovering denied psychopathology?	Mixed results
Malingering Can hypnosis assist in verifying questioned psychopathology in cases of suspected malingering?	Untested
Deception Can hypnosis assist in the detection of untruthfulness? Can subjects lie under hypnosis?	No Yes
Amnesia Can hypnosis assist in recovery of forgotten memories? Can hypnosis distinguish between actual and feigned amnesia?	Tentatively yes[a] No
Simulated Trances Can clinicians distinguish between actual and simulated hypnotic trances?	No

[a]More information will be recalled, but more inaccuracies will be introduced.

larly since hypnosis itself in highly suggestible patients may in fact create apparent psychopathology if the clinician is not extremely careful to avoid leading questions. Anecdotal case reports yield mixed results on the efficacy of this method (Erickson & Kubie, 1941; Schneck, 1967; Spiegel, Detrick, & Frischholz, 1982). Other applications of hypnosis to the assessment of dissimulation, such as the detection of malingering or of simulated trance states do not appear to be justified by current research data.

A relevant question is whether clinicians should *ever* employ hypnotic techniques in the investigation of dissimulation, given the availability of other methods such as structured interviews and psychometric assessments, whose reliabilities have been more thoroughly demonstrated (see Chapters 8, 10, and 14). Hypnosis may well be most valuable in such situations as part of a coordinated series of assessment procedures, as a "challenge test" through which either the divulging of previously unreported psychopathology or the presentation of highly inconsistent data could be useful in the assessment process. If such phenomena occur, hypnosis may assist in ruling in probable dissimulation. However, if no differences are perceived, the use of hypnosis cannot rule out the possibility, since clinicians can *never* determine the veracity or completeness of patients' self-reports on the basis of hypnosis alone, and artifacts may arise during hypnosis itself which complicate the evaluation.

Clinicians may also wish to consider the use of hypnosis when they are stymied in the evaluation of nonforensic psychiatric patients. Table 13.2 presents a threshold model for the consideration of cases in which hypnosis may be useful. Under these conditions, hypnosis would be used for under-

Table 13.2. Threshold Model for Hypnotic Investigation of Dissimulation

---

Any of the following criteria:

1. Highly anxious nonforensic patients who appear unable or unwilling to discuss psychopathology

2. The assessment of suspected organic amnesia (e.g., blackouts) in nonforensic patients

3. As a "challenge test" to nonforensic patients whose clinical presentation is improbable or preposterous

4. As an attempt to understand the motivation of patients independently assessed as malingering or as suffering from a factitious disorder or a dissociative state

---

standing the motivation underlying the patient's presentation, particularly regarding the denial or minimization of psychopathology, rather than for verification of the patient's honesty concerning the specific content of the reports.

Clinicians must weigh the benefits of potentially increased understanding against the possibility that the patient's actual memories will be distorted even further following hypnosis. The threshold model presented in Table 13.2 specifically excludes the use of hypnosis with patients involved in the civil or criminal courts. As will be discussed later, the use of hypnosis with such patients is particularly controversial, and involves specific motivations to dissimulate which are not usually found in nonforensic patients.

A primary focus of this text is to establish clinical decision-making models with explicit criteria for the determination of dissimulation. Given the inherent difficulties in the use of hypnosis for such determination, it is not possible to construct a definitive model. Clinicians are urged, however, to evaluate carefully any marked contradiction or discrepancies between hypnotic and nonhypnotic interviews. As noted by Orne (1979), much of the assessment in forensic cases, including unstructured and structured interviews, should already be completed prior to the use of hypnosis. The same caveats apply to nonforensic cases. Results from hypnotic interviews should be considered "true" only if they can be independently verified and are psychologically consistent with respect to the particular patient in question. In such circumstances, the use of hypnosis is directed more toward the investigation of a patient's motivation and response style than to the discovery of factual inaccuracies.

Forensic Applications

The most frequent use of hypnosis in the forensic context is in the validation and attempted resolution of apparent memory loss. Two frequent situations occur in which these techniques are called upon: first, to enhance the memories of potential eye-witnesses to legally relevant events, and, second, to overcome claimed amnesia in a defendant in a criminal or civil proceeding. Unlike clinical practice, hypnosis in legal situations is usually performed by consultants brought in explicitly for that purpose.

Hypnosis and Eyewitness Testimony in the Legal Context

Hypnosis has been used for years in an attempt to enhance the memories of witnesses to legally relevant situations such as crimes and events leading to injury or property damage. Until recently, most courts had held that testimony affected by hypnosis was inadmissible because it had not been generally accepted by the scientific community for all the reasons previously presented. (*People v. Ebanks*, 1897; *People v. Harper*, 1969). As hypnosis began to be studied and practiced more scientifically, at least some of its exponents began to argue that it had become sufficiently reliable to serve as the basis for testimony. A number of courts found that hypnosis affects the credibility but not the admissibility of testimony, and thus permitted its introduction (*Clarke v. State*, 1979; *Harding v. State*, 1968; *Key v. State*, 1983; *People v. Boudin*, 1983; *State v. McQueen*, 1978; *United States v. Miller*, 1969).

As the use of hypnosis to enhance or recover memory became more widespread, so did the controversy over its use in the courtroom. In the legal context, where the validity of testimony is in question, the distortions inherent in hypnotically enhanced testimony assumes significant proportion (Diamond, 1980; Orne, 1985). Critics argued that the increased certainty displayed by witnesses who have been hypnotized often makes their testimony completely resistant to cross-examination (Orne, 1979; Diamond, 1980; Worthington, 1979). This apparent certainty, in conjunction with the popular belief that hypnosis is a sort of psychological "truth serum," lends an unwarranted credibility to such witnesses, when in fact their testimony should properly be viewed as *less* credible than that of unhypnotized witnesses (Dilloff, 1977; Spector & Foster, 1977; Wilson, Greene, & Loftus, 1985).

In an affidavit submitted to the U.S. Supreme Court (*Quaglino v. California*, 1978), Orne (1979) recommended five criteria for forensic hypnosis: (1) that only a specially trained psychiatrist or psychologist be employed who is otherwise not involved the case; (2) that only the bare minimum of facts should be presented in writing to the clinician to document the information base; (3) that the subject should be asked for free recall before hypnosis is attempted; (4) that a videotape of the entire session(s) be made; and (5) that no one except the clinician and subject should be in the room during the session(s). These criteria, in part or as a whole, have subsequently found favor with other courts (*People v. Hurd*, 1980; *State v. Hurd*, 1981; *State v. Armstrong*, 1983). However, difficulties in implementing these protections have recently convinced Orne (1985) to call for absolute rejection of such testimony.

At the other end of the spectrum, Dr. Martin Reiser, who established the training seminars in hypnosis for police officers through the Los Angeles Police Department, has completely rejected the contention that hypnosis can distort memories. He has argued in court and in the literature, using anecdotal case reports as well as statements based on over 700 cases, that legally relevant new information was uncovered during hypnosis in 75% of cases and that the information which could be checked against independent sources was found to be accurate in 80% of the cases.

An intermediate position was taken by Spiegel and Spiegel (1984), who recognized the potential for distortion inherent in the use of hypnosis to enhance memory, but argued that it is sufficiently valuable when properly used to warrant its retention. They pointed out that witnesses are seldom tested for hypnotic susceptibility before attempts are made to hypnotize them. If witnesses are in fact not susceptible, then attempts at hypnosis per se should not be expected to introduce any distortions in their recollections. On the other hand, if potential witnesses have high susceptibility, then even routine questioning, without formal trance induction, might be expected to induce significant distortion because of the subjects' suggestibility.

The legal pendulum appears to be swinging away from unrestricted admission of hypnotically enhanced eyewitness testimony. In addition to the courts which have accepted Orne's restrictions, others have held that witnesses who have been hypnotized may not testify concerning anything discussed under hypnosis, although they may testify about matters covered prior to hypnosis (*United States v. Adams*, 1978). Other courts have gone farther and excluded *all* testimony from witnesses who have previously been hypnotized (*Greenfield v. Commonwealth*, 1974; *People v. Shirley*, 1982; *State ex rel. Collins v. Superior Court*, 1982; *State v. Mack*, 1980; *United States v. Andrews*, 1976). However, Reiser (1986) reported that courts or legislatures in Arizona, California, Colorado, Michigan, Nebraska, and New York have recently created exceptions to rules which absolutely bar hypnotically enhanced testimony.

Hypnosis in the Legal Evaluation of Amnesia

Reports in the forensic literature indicate that a significant number of defendants referred for psychiatric evaluation claim to be amnesic regarding the details of their alleged crimes. The reported percentage of criminal defendants who claim amnesia has ranged from 23% (Parwatikar, Holcolmb, & Menninger, 1985), and 31% (Leitch, 1948) to 65% of defendants referred for psychiatric evaluation (Bradford & Smith, 1979). In criminal cases, the issue of the admissibility of hypnotically enhanced testimony is most frequently brought up in the context of competency to stand trial, where it is argued that an amnestic defendant cannot adequately assist his or her attorney. Most courts which have addressed the issue have held that amnesia per se does not bar prosecution (*Bradley v. Preston*, 1968; *Commonwealth ex rel. Cummins v. Price*, 1966; *Davis v. State*, 1978; Note, Amnesia: the forgotten justification for finding an accused incompetent to stand trial (1981); *People v. Thompson*, 1983; *State v. McClendon*, 1948; *United States ex rel. Parson v. Anderson*, 1973; *United States v. Borum*, 1972; *United States v. Stevens*, 1972). One exception is the *Wilson v. United States* (1968) decision by the District of Columbia Circuit Court of Appeals which held that ". . . loss of memory should bar prosecution only when its presence would, in fact, be crucial to the construction and presentation of a defense and hence essential to the fairness and accuracy of the proceedings" (391 F.2d at 462). Other courts have held that treatable amnesia might justify an initial finding of incompetency in order to permit attempts at resolution of the amnesia (*People v. McBroom*, 1968), or a continuance to permit treatment to occur prior to trial (*Cornell v. Sup. Ct.*, 1959). Courts have been reluctant to equate amnesia with incompetency because of the facility with which amnesia can be simulated (Koson & Robey, 1973.)

Because of the popular reputation of hypnosis as a guarantor of truth, defense attorneys have attempted to present the results of hypnotic sessions in which their clients have "recovered" memories which appear to exonerate them. Courts have usually rejected attempts to present the results of hypnotic or Amytal sessions as evidence per se, holding them to be self-serving or hearsay (*People v. McNichol*, 1950; *People v. Ritchie*, 1977; *State v. Papp*, 1979). Hypnosis of defendants to provide information to help construct a defense has, however, been permitted (*People v. Cornell*, 1959; *State ex rel. Sheppard v. Koblentz*, 1962). Prosecutors have also attempted to utilize hypnosis with defendants in order to obtain the "truth" (which in these cases generally means a confession.) There have been cases in which confessions obtained under such circumstances have been held inadmissible (*Leyra v. Denno*, 1954; *People v. Hughes*, 1983.)

Defendants have also claimed that their criminal acts were committed under the influence of hypnosis, and that they should therefore not be held responsible (Note, Hypnotism, suggestibility and the law, 1952). Courts have generally rejected these arguments as well, either refusing to believe that the defendant was in fact hypnotized (*People v. Marsh*, 1959) or holding that hypnosis can not be considered sufficiently powerful to induce an otherwise guiltless person to commit a crime (*People v. Worthington*, 1894).

Hypnosis in Civil Cases

Attorneys in civil cases have also attempted to utilize hypnosis to enhance the memories of witnesses and principals. For example, in *Crockett v. Haithwaite* (1978), the plaintiff was the driver of a car in which her friend was killed. If she had been forced off the road, her insurance would pay for the damages, but would not if the accident were due to her own negligence. Before hypnosis, she had no recollection of any other vehicle. Her attorney recommended psychotherapy for the distress caused by the accident and also suggested hypnosis to help her recover her memories of the accident. Since remembering another vehicle would not only assuage her guilt but also result in recovery of significant damages from the insurance company, the court ruled that her testimony of remembering under hypnosis that a van had forced her off the road was inadmissible.

The Simulation of Hypnosis

Questions concerning the authenticity or power of hypnosis have also arisen in cases in which criminal victims or civil plaintiffs claim to have been victimized as a result of being hypnotized (Note, Hypnotism, suggestibility and the law, 1952). Criminal defenses have also been based on a claim of multiple personality, which is thought to involve autohypnosis (Lasky, 1982). These issues have been discussed by Allison (1984) and Lasky (1982). Some states now bar all testimony from witnesses who have previously been hypnotized. If either the prosecution or the defense wishes to use witnesses who have undergone hypnotic inductions, they must now prove that the witness was *not* in fact hypnotized.

The Bianchi Case

Many of the issues of forensic hypnosis arose in the case of the "Hillside Strangler," which received national attention. The case involved questions of the validity of trance, simulation of amnesia, and simulation of multiple personality. Kenneth Bianchi was ultimately arrested and charged with a series of stranglings in Washington state, and subsequently charged as an accessory in another series which occurred in California. During the pretrial period, Bianchi claimed amnesia for the periods surrounding all the crimes. During evaluation using hypnosis by a series of clinicians, another personality appeared to emerge, which admitted to having committed the crimes. The prosecution brought in Martin Orne, who concluded, after conducting his own attempts at hypnosis, that Bianchi was simulating both the hypnotic state and the multiple personality.

   After independent police investigation had produced strong evidence that suggested Bianchi had been planning his defense for years, Bianchi was ultimately convicted of the murders in Washington (*State v. Bianchi*, 1979). In the subsequent trial for the California murders (*People v. Buono*, 1983) Bianchi's cousin Buono was the principal defendant. The prosecution's case was based substantially on the statements of Bianchi, who had agreed to testify to avoid the death penalty. Because of the California prohibition against testimony by previously hypnotized witnesses, the prosecution had to establish that Bianchi had in fact simulated the hypnotic state in his series of interviews with clinicians in Washington. Dr. Orne's testimony was instrumental in assisting the trial judge in ruling that Bianchi had not been hypnotized, and could therefore testify. The issues involved have been discussed in great detail by the chief expert witnesses (Allison, 1984; Orne Dinges & Orne, 1984; Watkins, 1984.)

Conclusion

Despite the wealth of research which has examined the issues of the simulation of amnesia and of the hypnotic state itself, no definitive tests exist to determine whether or not a person exposed to a hypnotic induction is in fact hypnotized. It is also clear that the validity of material produced under hypnosis is questionable, particularly when obvious motive exists to dissimulate, as in criminal prosecutions.

Clinicians, examining the validity of claimed amnesia, should weigh the various factors which have been associated with validity, such as amnesia which is patchy, gradual in onset, and consistent. When hypnosis in used to recover memories, hypnotic susceptibility should be tested first. If court testimony is to be based on the results of hypnotic interviews, the attorney who requested the evaluation should provide information on the relevant statutes and case law to ensure that all legal requirements are met. If no specific requirements exist, it would be wise to follow Orne's (1979) criteria throughout the evaluation process. These criteria include a specially trained independent consultant who is supplied with a written, preestablished data base, and who obtains the subject's free recall prior to the videotaped hypnotic session(s), which are carried out without the presence of observers.

14

Structured Interviews and Dissimulation

RICHARD ROGERS

Clinical interviews form the central core of current diagnostic and assessment methods. Their role in the assessment of dissimulation is, however, more nebulous since much of the clinical literature on malingering is based on a handful of case studies (see Ziskin, 1981, 1984). Traditional unstructured interviews are often haphazard in their evaluation of malingering and defensiveness with an overreliance on unvalidated or poorly validated indices. The goal of this chapter is to briefly review traditional approaches and to offer as an alternative, standardized methods including the Schedule of Affective Disorders and Schizophrenia (SADS) and a specific experimental measure of malingering, the SIRS. This chapter is organized into three major sections: (1) a brief review of traditional interview methods, (2) the use of the SADS in evaluation of dissimulation, and (3) the development of a SIRS as a structured interview approach to malingering.

Traditional Interview Methods

Clinicians rely heavily on unstructured clinical and diagnostic interviews in their evaluation of psychiatric patients. Such traditional interviews form the basis of history-taking, psychodynamic formulations, and diagnoses of most mental disorders. The greatest asset of clinical interviewing is its versatility and adaptability to diverse patient populations and settings. On scientific grounds, this asset is also its greatest liability. The diversity and individuality of interviews and interviewing styles render impractical the standardization necessary for empirical study. Therefore, the usefulness of traditional interviews in the evaluation of dissimulation is difficult to test empirically.

The sparse research literature on interviews would suggest that motivated patients can both malinger (Rosenhan, 1973) as well as respond defensively (Sherman, Trief, & Strafkin, 1975). What remains unknown is how effective inexperienced and experienced clinicians are at accurately

Richard Rogers, Metropolitan Toronto Forensic Service (METFORS), Clarke Institute of Psychiatry, and University of Toronto, Toronto, Ontario, Canada.

identifying malingering and defensive patients. Although Rogers (1984b) devised a heuristic model, such interview-based clinical observations remain to be empirically validated. Largely because of the heterogeneity of interview styles, traditional approaches remain essentially untestable and of limited clinical applicability in assessing dissimulation.

Rogers (1987) organized interview-based clinical findings for malingering by attitudinal characteristics (i.e., overplayed and dramatic presentation; deliberateness and carefulness) and by clinical indicators (i.e., inconsistent with psychiatric diagnosis, inconsistent with self-report, and overendorsement of obvious symptoms). A summary of clinical findings and representative studies is presented in Table 14.1.

Several comments are necessary regarding the clinical findings summarized in Table 14.1. First, most of the identified variables are based on clinicians' observations with a small sampling of case studies. The discriminability and generalizability of the various indicators is therefore unknown. Second, given the diversity both in malingered presentations and in interview styles, none of the reported variables has explicit criteria. Because of

Table 14.1. Traditional Interviews and Malingering: A Summary of Clinical Findings[a]

A. Overplayed and dramatic presentation
   1. Clownish or fantastic quality (Davidson, 1949)
   2. Theatrical presentation (Ossipov, 1944)
   3. Eagerness to discuss symptoms (Ritson & Forrest, 1970)
   4. Extreme severity (Resnick, 1984)
   5. Indiscriminant endorsement of symptoms (Rogers, 1984b)

B. Deliberateness and carefulness
   1. Repeat questions (Resnick, 1984)
   2. Slower rate of speech (Kasl & Mahl, 1965; Rosenfeld, 1966)
   3. More hesitations (Harrison, Hwalek, Raney, & Fritz, 1978)
   4. Extensive use of qualifiers (Resnick, 1984)
   5. Vague nonspecific responses (Knapp, Hart, & Dennis, 1974)

C. Inconsistent with psychiatric diagnosis
   1. Rapid onset and resolution (Davidson, 1949; Ossipov, 1944; Sadow & Suslick, 1961)
   2. Rarity of symptoms (Resnick, 1984; Rogers, 1986a)
   3. Unusual combinations of symptoms (Rogers, 1987)

D. Consistency of self-report
   1. Contradictory symptoms (Rogers, 1984a, 1986a)
   2. Disparities between reported and observed symptoms (Ossipov, 1944; Wachskress, Berenberg, & Jacobson, 1953)

E. Endorsement of obvious symptoms
   1. More positive than negative symptoms (Rogers, 1986a)
   2. More impaired content than process (Resnick, 1984; Sherman, Tres, & Stafkin, 1975)
   3. More blatant than subtle symptoms (Rogers, 1984b)

Note. Adapted from "The Assessment of Malingering Within a Forensic Context" by R. Rogers, 1987, in D. N. Weisstub (Ed.), *Law and Psychiatry: International Perspectives* (Vol. 3, pp. 216–219) New York: Plenum.

[a]The term *clinical findings* is employed since many of the indicators have little or no empirical basis.

these limitations in unstructured interviews, it is particularly difficult to establish a clinical decision model. Clinicians may wish, however, to employ Table 14.1 as a threshold model and consider cases where two or more variables are present as a sufficient threshold for further investigation.

Clinical cases with numerous and convincing examples of inconsistency with diagnosis and self-report or with a marked overendorsement of obvious symptoms should, of course, be considered as evidence of malingering. In such cases, corroborative data should be sought before a definitive diagnosis of malingering is established. Sources of corroborative data include hospital records, psychometric data, structured interviews, and collateral interviews with others. The notable exception to this reliance on additional clinical data would be in cases where the patient, when confronted with the incongruities in his or her presentation, acknowledges malingering and his or her motivation for this dissimulation.

Few guidelines exist for the clinical assessment of defensiveness employing traditional interview methods. The most striking observation is the disparity between clinical data regarding a patient (i.e., psychiatric history or observations of others) and the patient's presentation. Experimental studies have generally held that even inpatients may modulate their psychopathology and appear to function better, at least for brief periods, than has been characteristic of them in the past (Braginsky & Braginsky, 1967; Fontana, Klein, Lewis, & Levine, 1968; Sherman et al., 1975). The external criterion for these studies was hospital records and extended clinical observations of the patients. Minimization of psychological difficulties may differ both in degree and motivation. For example, patients may wish to appear to be functioning at a higher level to meet an external need (e.g., regain employment or be psychologically fit as a parent) or an internal one (e.g., pride or unwillingness to acknowledge a patient status). Degrees of defensiveness may range from a "glossing over" of minor difficulties to an outright denial of severe psychological impairment. A critical issue in establishing defensiveness is the patient's awareness of his or her response style (Dicken, 1960). A viable alternative is that the patient is simply incorrect in his or her appraisal of psychological distress and impairment. Such misperceptions are sometimes noted in chronically mentally ill individuals who have normalized their psychiatric difficulties.

Defensive patients who deny symptoms are often identified on the basis of the above-mentioned disparity between observed and reported symptoms (studied under "anonymous" and "real-life" conditions; Baker, 1960; Kirchner, 1961). In addition, severe forms of defensiveness are typically characterized by an overly positive presentation and endorsement of "idealistic attributes" (Liberty, Lunneborg, & Atkinson, 1964). More problematic are cases where the patient minimizes but does not deny his or her symptomatology. Such cases, similar to malingering, require careful investigation employing corroborative data. Use of the MMPI (See Chapter 8) is strongly encouraged in any cases where (1) the patient's presentation is consistently more positive than other clinical data, or (2) the patient presents himself or herself in a highly favourable light.

SADS Diagnostic Interview and Dissimulation

The Schedule of Affective Disorders and Schizophrenia or SADS diagnostic interview (Spitzer & Endicott, 1978) was designed as the centerpiece of the NIMH collaborative study on depression. Since a primary clinical issue in this extensive study was the differential diagnosis of affective disorders from other commonly occurring diagnoses, the SADS sought to measure in great detail the intensity, duration, and other manifest characteristics of patients' psychiatric symptomatology (Endicott & Spitzer, 1978). The SADS was constructed for the standardization of diagnostic interviewing in four separate ways: First, it specifies the structure of the interview and the systematic progression of questions regarding possible psychiatric symptoms. Second, the SADS employs standardized clinical inquiries in the form of general nondirectional questions and specific diagnostic probes. Third, the SADS offers a reliable scoring method of quantifying symptom severity and degree of impairment. Fourth, it was designed to be employed with the empirically based RDC or Research Diagnostic Criteria (Spitzer, Endicott, & Robins, 1978).

The SADS was constructed to collect clinical data at discrete periods. For example, Part 1 of the SADS was designed to examine closely the patient's symptoms during the severest part of the last episode and at the present time. In contrast, Part 2 offers a more longitudinal approach to psychiatric disorders with the goal of specifying their onset and the duration of prior episodes.

Nonempirical Approaches to Malingering and Deception

The SADS allows clinicians an in-depth examination of the patient's consistency of self-report. In traditional interviews, it is unclear whether the variability in the patient's self-report is due to (1) changes in the style or emphasis of clinical questions, (2) the idiosyncratic reporting of clinical information, or (3) changes in the patient's self-report. Because of the standardization of SADS, clinicians are able to control other sources of variability and therefore isolate variability in the patient's self-report. Clinicians may test the consistency of the patient's self-report by comparing unstructured interview data to the SADS, by repeat inquiries on critical SADS symptoms, and by comparing self-report on the SADS with corroborative SADS interviews. With respect to this final alternative, Rogers and Cunnien (1986) recommend in cases of suspected dissimulation that relevant portions of the SADS be used in corroborative interviews to offer direct comparisons between the patient's self-report and others' observations.

The SADS requires more skill and sophistication for patients attempting to malinger than traditional interview methods. Although not an impenetrable shield against fabrication, malingering patients must convincingly present detailed self-reports organized into discrete episodes with plausible description of its onset, distinguishing and prominent symptoms, and duration and severity. As noted by Rogers (Rogers, 1986a; Rogers & Cavanaugh, 1981), such dissimulation requires considerable sophistication since potential malingerers often become confused regarding the emergence of symptoms across specific time periods. The task for the malingering patient is made more difficult by their need to consistently differentiate potentially irrelevant and contradictory symptoms from those which are plausible in the simulation of a mental disorder. Faced with this formidable task, the author has observed that some patients simply overendorse a wide array of diverse symptomatology.

Defensiveness is more difficult to assess on the SADS than malingering. Patient's ready denial of any mild experiences of distress would, of course, raise the index of suspicion regarding defensiveness. Most patients presenting for a clinical examination (voluntary or otherwise) are experiencing some subjective distress and at least several mild symptoms. The task for the clinician is to assess whether (1) the total denial of symptoms is consistent with other clinical data, (2) whether the presented symptoms are plausible with the patient's current circumstances, and (3) whether the patient's self-report is consistent with clinical observations. A further consideration, of course, is the deliberateness of any apparent denial, since some patients have such a distorted and inflated self-image, as to be unaware of problems obvious to others. Such distortions should be evident, however, on nonclinical topics, in contradistinction to more selected defensiveness. Perhaps the most dramatic example of defensiveness on the SADS occurs occasionally in personal injury cases when patients categorically deny any symptoms or impairment in their premorbid functioning while asserting catastrophic changes following their injuries.

Empirical Approaches

An inherent difficulty in any study of dissimulation is the absence of a verifiable independent criterion for malingering or defensiveness. One possible alternative, at least in the construction of a threshold model, is to examine normative response patterns. Individuals who manifest highly unusual self-reports, whether they maximize or minimize psychological impairment, reflect a strong likelihood of dissimulation. As with all clinical investigations of dissimulation, clinicians must avoid overreliance on any single indicator of the SADS.

The data reported here are based on 104 patients referred for forensic assessments. This sample includes 64 subjects previously reported (Rogers, Thatcher, & Cavanaugh, 1984) and an additional 40 forensic cases obtained from METFORS, a court forensic clinic in Toronto. The subject pool, although relatively small, was considered useful since the evaluations were court-referred and were therefore, at least to some extent, involuntary. The research strategy was to provide normative data on as many clinical indicators as possible from an empirical model of dissimulation (see Rogers, 1984b). For the examination of malingering, the five clinical indicators were employed, comprised of rare symptoms, contradictory symptoms, symptom combinations, symptom severity, and overendorsement of symptoms. For defensiveness, the three clinical indicators included common symptoms, common symptom groupings, and underendorsement of symptoms.

A commonly accepted approach to the assessment of malingering is the examination of rare symptoms; this indicator is based on the extensive research with the MMPI F scale (see, for example, Dahlstrom, Welsh, & Dahlstrom, 1972). *Rare symptoms* are those which infrequently occur in psychiatric populations. Table 14.2 summarizes symptoms reported by less than 5% of the forensic sample. The usefulness of rare symptoms as an indicator of malingering is probably limited to simulated psychosis, since most of the symptoms reflect uncommon psychotic features. It is interesting to note that none of the sample reported more than three rare symptoms.

The presence of contradictory symptoms or symptom combinations suggests an implausible clinical presentation. *Contradictory symptoms* are comprised of seven pairs of symptoms which measure psychological impairment in opposite directions. These symptoms, presented in Table 14.3, focus

Table 14.2. Rare Symptoms in SADS Evaluations

Rare Symptoms		Percentage in Clinical Range
354	Elevated mood (past week)	4.0
356	Less sleep (past week)	2.0
360	Increased activity (past week)	3.1
427	Thought withdrawal	2.0
430	Delusions of guilt	2.0
432	Somatic delusions	5.0
475	Loosening of associations	4.1
476	Incoherence (past week)	2.9
514	Poverty of content of speech	4.2
515	Neologisms	2.0

Note. Numbers in the left column designate SADS coding of questions.

Table 14.3. Contradictory Symptoms in SADS Evaluations

Contradictory Symptoms		Percentage in Clinical Range
234–353	Depressed and elevated mood	4.8
242–361	Worthlessness and grandiosity	1.9
272–314	Insomnia and hypersomnia	5.1
315–357	Decreased and increased energy	1.0
317–320	Decreased and increased appetite	2.9
326–359	Decreased and increased interests	1.0
334–342	Psychomotor retardation and agitation	1.0

Note. Numbers in the left column designate SADS coding of questions.

almost exclusively on affective symptomatology with depressive and manic symptoms. Contradictory symptoms are probably most useful with unsophisticated malingerers who indiscriminantly endorse psychiatric problems. Indeed, 99.1% of the sample endorsed fewer than two contradictory symptoms. Clinicians must be careful to rule out cyclothymic or bipolar disorders which are rapidly cycling in their assessment of dissimulation, since these disorders may manifest apparently contradictory symptoms. Clinical investigation should clarify, however, the specific time periods for affective disorders, thus distinguishing them from malingering.

Symptom combinations, in contrast to contradictory symptoms, are not necessarily incongruous in their clinical presentation. *Symptom combinations* are operationally defined as the following:

1. symptoms commonly reported by psychiatric patients (i.e., the sample reported more than 30% of individual symptoms in the clinical range),
2. designated pairs of these symptoms rarely occur together in the same patient (i.e., less than 10% endorsed both symptoms).

Unlike contradictory symptoms, symptom combinations are based entirely on an actuarial model and thus have greater applicability with more sophisticated patients. Symptom combinations are presented in Table 14.4; most of the sample (95%) had fewer than five symptom combinations.

Overendorsement of symptoms and symptom severity are based on the logic that potential malingerers overplay their part in either reporting too many symptoms or reporting symptoms of unbearable severity. On the average, forensic patients endorsed 24.2 symptoms ($SD = 11.3$) in the clinical range. In establishing the upper range, less than 5% of the sample reported 45 or more symptoms and less than 1% reported 48 or more symptoms. Cutting scores for symptom severity were established at two

Table 14.4. Symptom Combinations in SADS Evaluations

Unusual Pairing of Common Symptoms[a]		Percentage
317–239	Appetite and current worrying	8.3
317–243	Appetite and current feelings of inadequacy	7.4
317–245	Appetite and current discouragement	6.5
317–266	Appetite and current psychic anxiety	6.5
317–331	Appetite and current anger	6.5
317–419	Appetite and current distrustfulness	8.3
334–245	Agitation and current discouragement	8.3
334–266	Agitation and current psychic anxiety	9.3
428–239	Persecutory delusions and current worrying	9.3
428–245	Persecutory delusions and current discouragement	9.3
428–313	Persecutory delusions and current insomnia	7.4
428–331	Persecutory delusions and current anger	9.3

Note. Numbers in the left column designate SADS coding of questions.

[a]Symptom combinations are organized to facilitate rapid checking. If the patient has not endorsed appetite, psychomotor agitation, or persecutory delusions in the clinical range, then no symptom combination will be found.

levels: (1) ratings on individual symptoms of 5 or greater and (2) ratings of 6 or greater. Table 14.5 provides data for these two criteria with appropriate cutting scores for the top 5% and 1% of the sample.

Indicators of defensiveness were also studied employing the same forensic sample. Indicators, based on Rogers' (1984b) review, consisted of nonendorsement of common symptoms and common symptom groupings, and the overall underendorsement of symptoms. Common symptoms were operationally defined as symptoms reported in the clinical range (i.e., three or greater) by at least 50% of the sample and are summarized in Table 14.6. The rationale for selecting common symptoms in examining defensiveness is based on the clinical observation that some symptoms are widespread among both clinical and normal samples. What distinguishes normal individuals from psychiatric patients is not so much the presence of these

Table 14.5. Symptom Severity in SADS Evaluations

Symptom Severity	Frequency of Symptoms	
	Top 5%	Top 1%
Severe symptoms (ratings $\geq$ 5)	16	19
Extreme symptoms (ratings $\geq$ 6)	9	11

Table 14.6. Commonly Reported Symptoms in SADS
Evaluations

Common Symptoms		Percentage in Clinical Range
234	Subjective feelings of depression	55.2
238	Worrying	55.7
244	Discouragement	51.5
265	Subjective feelings of anxiety	50.0
272	Sleep disturbance	51.5
328	Social withdrawal	55.7
330	Subjective feelings of anger	73.1
332	Overt expressions of irritability	55.3
418	Antisocial behavior	55.7
433	Severity of delusions	54.0

Note. Numbers in the left column designate SADS coding of questions.

symptoms (e.g., worrying and concern about physical health), but their
severity. Therefore, the relative absence of frequently endorsed symptoms
may be indicative of defensiveness. The majority of these symptoms are
concerned with patients' experiences of negative affect. Therefore, a patient
who categorically denies any negative feelings should evoke a high degree of
suspicion regarding defensiveness.

A closely related approach to the denial of common symptoms was the
a priori specification regarding constellations or groupings of symptoms
that would be experienced, at least to some degree, by a large majority of
patients. It was hypothesized that the great majority of patients referred for
forensic evaluations would be experiencing at least one symptom characteristic of a dysphoric state and also report at least one somatic complaint. Six
symptoms representative of dysphoric feelings (i.e., subjective feelings of
depression, worrying, feelings of discouragement, subjective feelings of anxiety, feelings of self-reproach, and subjective feelings of anger) were considered. As expected, only 7% of the patients completely denied dysphoric
feelings with the modal response being four of these symptoms in the clinical
range. Similarly, it was hypothesized that evaluated patients would report at
least one somatic symptom from a possible list of seven somatic complaints
(i.e., somatic anxiety, sleep disturbance, hypersomnia, loss of appetite,
increased appetite, excessive concern with physical health, and decreased
need for sleep). The great majority of patients (81.5%) reported at least one
somatic complaint with the modal response being two symptoms in the
clinical range. Normative data for other clinical samples would be particularly useful since different patient groups may exhibit distinct patterns of
symptom endorsement. Nevertheless, the total denial of any dysphoric state

or somatic complaint should raise the clinician's index of suspicion regarding defensiveness.

A final approach to defensiveness is a review of the SADS protocol for underreporting of symptomatology. As noted above, the average endorsement for the forensic sample was 24.2 symptoms. Only 5% endorsed seven or fewer symptoms while only 1% endorsed four or fewer symptoms. This indicator of defensiveness focuses on those individuals who are attempting to deny all symptomatology and concomitant impairment.

Clinical Applications

The previous discussion focuses primarily on the development of a threshold model. Clinicians who observe a pattern of rare symptoms, contradictory symptoms, or symptom combinations should be alerted to the possibility of dissimulation. Similarly, the indiscriminant endorsement of symptoms or the endorsement of a wide array of symptoms of extreme severity should be viewed as indicating a strong possibility of malingering. Based on the available normative data, a threshold model of malingering was constructed (see Table 14.7). In addition to the explicit criteria discussed above, this model includes any marked inconsistencies in self-report. This judgment is based on variability both in the patient's reported symptomatology and disparities between self-reporting and clinical observation.

Establishing a clinical decision model for malingering in SADS evaluations is a much more difficult task, given the absence of studies employing an independent criterion. A tentative model has, however, been proposed which is comprised of stringent criteria and corroborative data. The stringent criteria includes a highly deviant response pattern, which is consistent with an empirically based model of malingering (Rogers, 1984b). In addition, the clinical decision model requires corroboration either through the patient's admission of malingering or other clinical data (i.e., observational or psychometric findings) which strongly support the SADS-based assessment of malingering.

Table 14.7. Threshold Model of Malingering in SADS Evaluations

Any of the following criteria:
1. Rare symptoms ≥ 2
2. Contradictory symptoms ≥ 1
3. Symptom combinations ≥ 1
4. Symptom severity ≥ 8 symptoms scored 5 or greater
5. Overendorsement of symptoms ≥ 30 symptoms in the clinical range
6. Marked inconsistencies between unstructured self-report and the SADS

Table 14.8. Clinical Decision Model for Establishing Malingering in SADS Evaluations

---

The following criteria:

A. A minimum of two clinical indicators:
   1. Rare symptoms $\geq$ 3
   2. Contradictory symptoms $\geq$ 3
   3. Symptom combinations $\geq$ 5
   4. Symptom severity $\geq$ 17 symptoms scored 5 or greater
   5. Overendorsement of symptoms $\geq$ 45 symptoms in the clinical range
B. Malingered presentation is corroborated by either:
   1. Patient's admission of malingering
   2. Clinical evidence of exaggeration and fabrication based on observation and/or psychometric data

---

The clinical decision model presented in Table 14.8 was deliberately designed, in the absence of cross-validation, to be conservative in its evaluation of malingering. In other words, if errors in judgment are made, this model assumes that greater harm may be caused in misclassifying a disturbed patient as a malingerer than in not accurately identifying all malingerers. This assumption is consistent with the book's conservative approach in avoiding overreliance on any single measure to establish dissimulation.

SIRS (Structured Interview of Reported Symptoms)

The SIRS, or Structured Interview of Reported Symptoms (Rogers, 1986b), is based on an earlier review and synthesis of empirical studies in the assessment of malingering and deception (Rogers, 1984b). Informal observations of professional practice suggested that most clinicians were highly idiosyncratic in their assessment of dissimulation and relied heavily on their own subjective impressions. In addition, it has been observed that clinicians tend to employ only a few empirically based strategies in evaluation of malingering. For example, the majority of clinicians tend to use only the endorsement of rare symptoms (i.e., elevations on the F scale) in the determination of "fake-bad" MMPI profiles. In contrast, work by Greene (see Chapter 8) would suggest that item subtlety, stereotypical symptoms of neurosis, and nonselective endorsement of symptoms are more useful than F scale elevations in the determination of malingering. Thus, the current practices, which involve a high degree of subjectivity and overreliance on a select few indicators of malingering, became the stimulus for a more systematic interview-based approach.

An interview-based approach was selected since it permits a high degree of versatility in clinical assessment. Furthermore, studies from social psychology are consistent with clinical experience, (Tesser & Paulhus, 1983;

Tetlock & Manstead, 1985) in suggesting that responses to paper and pencil measures may not be generalizable to face-to-face interview methods (see also Johnson, Klingler, & Williams, 1977). In addition, since most diagnostic questions are resolved on the basis of clinical interviews, the author concluded that a structured interview approach would be the most appropriate technique for the clinical assessment of malingering.

Strategies for the Assessment of Malingering

Rogers (1986b) identified 15 potential strategies for the assessment of malingering. Eight strategies derived from the empirical literature (Rogers, 1984b), and seven additional strategies were intuitively derived. Other possible techniques were not included because they were either difficult to operationalize within an interview format (e.g., sequencing of specific symptoms in the development of a disorder) or hard to standardize with explicit criteria (e.g., vagueness of malingerers' responses).

Empirical indicators included the following:

1. Symptom Subtlety: Patients attempting to malinger exhibit a tendency to endorse more blatant than subtle symptoms. The obvious versus subtle dimension has been noted both in case studies (Resnick, 1984) and psychometric methods (Rogers, 1984b).

2. Severity of Symptoms: Patients attempting to malinger endorse an unlikely number of symptoms with extreme or unbearable severity. As observed in SADS data, even markedly impaired psychiatric patients endorse only a few symptoms of marked severity.

3. Rare Symptoms: Potential malingerers often have difficulty distinguishing symptoms which are infrequent in psychiatric populations from those which are more common. Such individuals often endorse many rare symptoms.

4. Symptom Onset and Resolution: Most psychiatric disorders, in the absence of a well-defined precipitator, evidence a gradual onset and resolution. Case studies (e.g., Ossipov, 1944) suggest that potential malingerers may not be cognizant of the course of mental disorders and report either an unusually sudden onset or resolution, which is implausible, given the nature of the purported disorder.

5. Improbable Failure Rate: Research has indicated that even severely disturbed patients typically can complete simple cognitive tests (Lezak, 1983). A small percentage of malingerers feign pervasive impairment on tasks which it is likely that all but the most impaired individuals would pass.

6. Reported versus Observed Symptoms: Individuals attempting to malinger are often unaware of the incongruities between their actual presentation and reported impairment. This category consists of easily observable interpersonal behavior which may be verified by the clinician.

7. Clinical Observations: Individuals attempting to dissimulate may manifest differences in their paralinguistic behavior, including how they respond and evidence marked changes in their speech patterns (DePaulo, Stone, & Lassiter, 1984). In addition, clinicians may observe important attitudinal variables, such as an eagerness to discuss or an elaboration of symptoms, a theatrical quality to the presentation, or an obvious response set (Rogers, 1987).

8. *Consistency of Symptoms*: Malingerers often have difficulty remembering which symptoms they endorsed and their severity. By repeating a set of clinical inquiries, this strategy provides a measure of the stability of the patient's self-report. This strategy has been employed successfully by several objective personality measures (see Chapter 8).

The seven nonempirical indicators of malingering were established on the basis of logical and clinical experience. These strategies comprise the following:

1. *Selectivity of Symptoms*: Clinical experience has suggested that some malingering individuals are nonselective or indiscriminant in their endorsement of psychiatric problems. This strategy is simply an overall measurement of symptom endorsement over a broad range of symptomatology.

2. *Improbable or Absurd Symptoms*: As an extension of the rare symptom category described above, improbable or absurd symptoms have a fantastic or preposterous quality which make them unlikely, by definition, to be bona fide symptoms. For example, endorsement of the belief "lampshades were invented for punishment" is very unlikely to be an accurate reflection of a mental disorder.

3. *Overly Specified Symptoms*: Individuals attempting to malinger may endorse symptoms with an unrealistic degree of precision. Such symptoms typically involve a quantifiable problem (e.g., sleeping for 5 hours and 32 minutes every night).

4. *Symptom Combinations*: Patients attempting to fabricate a mental disorder are often unaware of which symptoms are likely or unlikely to coexist. With symptom combinations, the patient is asked whether he or she is currently experiencing several symptoms; these symptoms, although commonly experienced individually, rarely are present simultaneously.

5. *Direct Appraisal of Honesty*: Patients are asked to respond to a variety of specific questions regarding the honesty and completeness of their self-reports. It is hypothesized that some dissimulating patients will affirm consistently their complete honesty and total self-disclosure, whereas most honest patients will acknowledge minor deception or lack of forthrightness.

6. *Defensive Symptoms*: Patients are asked to respond to a variety of everyday problems, worries, and situations which have been experienced by most individuals. In contrast to the other methods, this strategy is composed of very common but slightly negative experiences and is included as a measure of defensiveness. This scale was designed to achieve two purposes:

(a) to provide filler items to reduce the transparency of the measure, and (b) to examine a hybrid (i.e., malingering/defensive) response style.

Development of the SIRS

The original item pool of 330 clinical inquiries was generated based on the previously described strategies. The goal was to establish highly structured questions that were representative of the eight empirically and seven intuitive strategies. From this item pool, two 80-question structured interviews were constructed with items equally divided by strategies and with similar symptom content. These preliminary forms were reviewed independently by eight forensic experts (i.e., psychologists and psychiatrists with a mean of 9.6 years of postgraduate forensic experience) who were selected on the basis of their extensive experience in assessment of malingering. Although most scales were judged adequate with respect to representativeness, the chief criticism was with respect to the obviousness of the items and therefore the transparency of the structured interviews.

A concerted effort to balance the blatancy of items with the likelihood of alternative explanations was made by redesigning nearly one-third of the questions. In other words, the more blatant or unrealistic the questions are, the less likely a nonmalingerer would answer affirmatively. On the other hand, more subtle inquiries, although less transparent and thus more difficult for malingerers to identify, are more likely to be endorsed by nonmalingerers. Therefore, the task is to achieve a middle ground with items of sufficient blatancy as to minimize false positives, yet not so transparent that would-be malingerers avoid their endorsement. One method of achieving this middle ground was to divide more obvious questions into two parts: (1) a fairly innocuous trigger question and (2) a more blatant probe that is only given if the trigger question is answered affirmatively. For example, a trigger question, "does your vision become blurry while reading?" might be followed by a probe, "is this caused by the planet Venus?" Patients are only exposed to the more blatant items if they answer the trigger question affirmatively, thus reducing the overall transparency of the measure. In addition, many questions were rewritten more ambiguously with the same goal of reducing the transparency of the questions.

Scoring of the SIRS is based on three gradations of response: (2) definite yes, (1) qualified yes, and (0) not present. The "definite yes" category is reserved for clearly affirmative responses where the patient makes no attempt to qualify or delimit his or her endorsement. In contrast, the category "qualified yes" is employed for those affirmative responses in which the patient does restrict his or her endorsement. Examples of qualified yes responses are "sometimes" or "yes" followed by a qualifying phrase. The final category "not present" is used to record any negative response. The rationale of this scoring system is to differentiate between endorsements made with reservations and those made without them. Given the greater ambiguity of qualified yes responses, the scoring format will allow clinicians to examine separately definite yes responses. The scoring system was constructed with only three gradations to minimize subjectivity in clinicians' ratings and thereby improve reliability. Similar formats have been employed in structured diagnostic interviews, including the Diagnostic Interview Schedule (Robins, Helzer, Croughan, & Ratcliff, 1981), the SADS longitudinal version (Spitzer & Endicott, 1978), and the Structured Clinical Interview for DSM-III (SCID: Spitzer & Williams, 1986).

Preliminary Validity Research

Data have been collected on two small samples of an inpatient forensic assessment unit in Toronto. The first sample ($N = 35$) was administered the SIRS under a counterbalanced simulation design. Although care was taken to exclude patients who were too severely disturbed to participate in the study, a manipulation check revealed that 14.3% of the subjects could not remember the directions and an additional 34.3% remembered but did not follow the directions to malinger. On the basis of this pilot study, alpha coefficients were generated and further refinements were made in the scoring.

The second sample ($N = 24$) was collected to measure the SIRS' interrater reliability by two independent raters. Subjects were selected consecutively and given instructions to respond to the SIRS interview openly and honestly. In addition, a total of nine patients were independently identified on the basis of clinical judgment as presenting with moderate to severe malingering. These patients were administered the SIRS under honest instructions and subsequently compared with the second sample.

Estimates of interrater reliability for individual items were very encouraging. Table 14.9 summarizes the rank-order correlations averaged for each individual scale. Only an improbable failure rate (consisting of two items) and clinical observations (composed of ratings of paralinguistic cues) evidenced difficulties in interrater reliability.

The scales of the SIRS were constructed on the basis of previously described strategies. As a result of this, it is difficult to know whether measures of internal consistency should reflect underlying strategies for the detection of malingering or the manifest content of its items. For example, an individual feigning schizophrenia is not likely to endorse nonpsychotic symptoms appearing on many of the scales. Although moderate alpha coefficients were achieved on the first sample (i.e., Form A had a mean alpha coefficient of .69, and Form B a mean alpha coefficient of .68, when scales of two items or fewer were excluded), these findings did not hold for the second sample. Given these difficulties in establishing the internal consistency of the scales, one reasonable alternative would be the use of expert judges to assign individual items to scales on the basis of their underlying

Table 14.9. Interrater Reliability of the SIRS

Scales	Items	Interrater reliability[a]	
		A	B
1. Selectivity, subtlety, severity	16	.77	.88
2. Rare symptoms	6	.93	.84
3. Improbable or absurd symptoms	10	.93	.53
4. Symptom onset and resolution	2	.91	.89
5. Overly specified symptoms	5	.90	.83
6. Improbable failure rate	2	.13	.88
7. Symptom combinations	6	.63	.92
8. Reported versus observed symptoms	6	.87	.81
9. Direct appraisal of honesty	5	.96	.96
10. Consistency of symptoms	16	.92	.76
11. Clinical observations	8	.50	.14
12. Defensive symptoms	10	.93	.96

[a]Spearman rho correlations.

strategy. This method would minimize the confounding nature of assessing strategy and content in making estimates of internal consistency. A second alternative, based on much larger validation samples, would be a factor analytic study of the SIRS scales. Needless to say, the scales are not empirically derived and must await further research on the degree to which they represent unitary measures.

Differentiating patterns of endorsement were examined for nine malingerers and 24 nonmalingering patients from the second sample. The nine malingerers, classified on the basis of independent clinical judgment, endorsed a higher frequency of qualified and definite yes responses. For the SIRS as a whole, malingerers evidenced an endorsement rate nearly twice that of nonmalingering patients (.29 vs. .15 item/subject ratio). Similar differences were observed for the SIRS scales, as summarized in Table 14.10, with the exception of defensive symptoms and direct appraisal of honesty. Although preliminary in nature, these findings are particularly encouraging with respect to the SIRS criterion-related validity.

Clinical Applications

Diagnostic interviews form the basis for most clinical determinations of malingering and dissimulation. Because of the importance of assessing deception and the absence of any standardized measures beyond the SADS for doing so, clinicians may wish to cautiously apply the SIRS in a threshold model of malingering. Such an application would attest more to the dearth of interview-based approaches to malingering than to the psychometric

Table 14.10. Percentages of Endorsed Symptoms on SIRS Scales for Patients and Malingerers for "Qualified" and "Definite Yes" Endorsements

Scales	Form A			Form B		
	Patients	Malingerers	p	Patients	Malingerers	p
1. Selectivity and severity of symptoms	25.2	44.5	.0001	17.3	40.7	.00001
2. Blatant symptoms	20.0	47.6	.00001	21.9	43.8	.0008
3. Rare symptoms	6.9	34.0	.00001	8.1	30.0	.003
4. Improbable and absurd symptoms	5.1	21.5	.0001	3.6	15.0	.002
5. Onset and resolution of symptoms	14.6	25.9	.04	21.7	33.3	.61
6. Overly specified symptoms	5.9	21.7	.07	3.3	12.5	.15
7. Symptom combinations	2.4	28.9	.00001	6.8	18.8	.05
8. Reported versus observed symptoms	20.3	27.4	.14	22.9	25.0	.61
9. Clinical observations	8.0	10.9	.33	7.1	8.1	.57
10. Consistency of symptoms	11.8	21.1	.01	4.5	14.3	.002
11. Direct appraisal of honesty	20.0	22.2	.59	19.3	27.5	.19
12. Complete SIRS	16.5	30.6	.01	14.1	28.3	.006

Note. Probability values were computed employing Fischer exact tests (two-tailed).

rigor of the SIRS. The chief advantages of employing the SIRS at this early stage of development are (1) its high degree of interrater reliability and (2) its systematic format with standardized clinical questions.

The threshold model for the SIRS, given its experimental nature, should not exclude from consideration any individuals whose clinical presentation is suggestive of dissimulation. Table 14.11 has identified seven strategies with concomitant cutting scores for the consideration of malingering. Excluded from this table are scales with insufficient items (i.e., self-management of symptoms, of symptom onset and resolution) or with modest reliability (i.e., improbable failure rate and clinical observations). In addition, two scales—direct appraisal of honesty and defensive symptoms—were not employed since they were constructed primarily as measures of defensiveness.

Cutting scores for the threshold model reflect a mean level of item endorsement for malingerers averaged across Forms A and B. These cutting scores should only be used as threshold criteria and suggest further clinical investigation of malingering.

Table 14.11. Threshold Model for the Use of the SIRS in the Assessment of Malingering

Strategies	Cutting scores
1. Nonselective endorsement of symptoms	> 6
2. Number of blatant symptoms	≥ 3
3. Number of "unbearable" symptoms	> 3
4. Rare symptoms	> 3
5. Improbable or absurd symptoms	> 3
6. Symptom combinations	≥ 3
7. Consistency of symptoms	> 3

A clinical decision model is proposed for the use of the SIRS as a measure of *unreliability* rather than of malingering. Unreliability, as defined in the Introduction, is a nonspecific term referring to response styles which are not honest or self-disclosing but where more refined conclusions are not possible. By employing the SIRS as a behavioral sample, it is possible to examine marked inconsistencies in patients' presentations. For example, consistency of symptoms allows the clinician to assess the patient's variability in presentation employing 16 repeated items. In addition, the reported versus observed symptoms permit the clinician a direct comparison between self-report and observational information. Therefore, marked inconsistencies on either of these two scales is strongly indicative of unreliability.

The clinician may also wish to take into account the overall level of symptom endorsement as an indicator of unreliability. For example, none of the nonmalingering patients endorsed more than 40 items on either Form A or Form B of the SIRS. Table 14.12 summarizes cutting scores for the clinical determination of unreliability on the SIRS.

Conclusion

This chapter provides two alternatives to traditional clinical interviewing. The SADS is a well-established semistructured diagnostic interview for the systematic assessment of the onset, duration, and severity of psychiatric

Table 14.12. Clinical Decision Model of the Assessment of Unreliability on the SIRS

Any of the following:
1. Four or more inconsistencies on repeated questions
2. Four or more inconsistencies between reported and observed symptoms
3. Total symptom endorsement exceeding 40

symptomatology. Both heuristic and empirical approaches to dissimulation are presented. In contrast to the SADS, the SIRS is a specific measure for the assessment of malingering and is in its early stage of scale development. The SIRS, constructed on an empirically based model of dissimulation (Rogers, 1984b), has obtained encouraging results in preliminary testing of its interrater reliability and criterion-related validity. The SADS and SIRS were discussed here in relation to the achievement of two objectives: (1) stimulating further research on development of structured interview approaches to dissimulation and (2) offering reliable and standardized interview methods as an alternative to the current reliance on idiosyncratic and unvalidated interviewing.

Structured interviews offer a rich opportunity to investigate closely patients' response styles across different clinical situations. Previous research on traditional interview approaches to dissimulation, despite its importance to clinical practice, is stymied by the absence of standardized methods. Structured interviews, at some sacrifice of versatility, provide such standardization. Research has demonstrated the superiority of such structured approaches in assessing diagnostic issues (e.g., Spitzer & Endicott, 1978); it would be reasonable to assume that such advantages might also assist in the evaluation of specific response styles, closely related to diagnosis.

Clinicians have few reliable tools for the face-to-face assessment of dissimulation. The SADS and, to a lesser degree, the SIRS provide reliable measures of patients' self-reports. The value of consistent measurement for the evaluation of malingering and defensiveness should be not underestimated. The threshold and clinical decision models may afford some opportunity to combine reliable measurement with empirical findings in systematic interview-based measures of dissimulation.

15

Defensiveness in Sex Offenders

RON LANGEVIN

Anomalous sexual behavior, seen in child abuse or rape, involves a surprising number of interrelated factors. It is well known that unusual sexual preferences, substance abuse, a history of violence and poor socialization, as well as biological variables such as sex hormones and neuropathology, may contribute in significant ways to the commission of sexual offences (Berlin & Krout, 1986; Langevin, 1983, 1985). Unfortunately, each of these factors is not fully understood, creating uncertainty in examining issues such as treatment potential and criminal responsibility, and in evaluating the response styles, particularly defensiveness, among sexually anomalous men. Moreover, increased social awareness of child sexual abuse has led to statutory requirements, compelling professionals to report any suspected cases of child abuse to legally designated authorities with an increased likelihood of criminal sanctions (Miller, in press). As a result of these reporting requirements, increased defensiveness has been observed among sexually anomalous men and sex offenders in clinical assessments. For example, Hucker, Langevin, Bain and Handy (1987) examined 100 consecutive cases of men accused of sex offences against children. They found that an alarming 54% denied criminal charges, refused to undergo testing, or did not admit they had *any* problems related to children.

The reluctance of men with sexual anomalies to discuss their peculiar sexual practices with evaluating clinicians is common (Langevin & Lang, 1985). Such individuals often enjoy their modes of sexual expression with little motivation to control them. Indeed, sexually anomalous men frequently claim that nothing is wrong with them but blame society for being too restrictive or punitive. They may even contend that children enjoy sex with them and benefit from the experience. These claims only compound assessment and treatment problems for these men.

In this chapter, the main factors of concern in assessing sexual anoma-

Ron Langevin, Clarke Institute of Psychiatry, and University of Toronto, Toronto, Ontario, Canada.

269

lies will be reviewed briefly and then the modes of defensiveness used by sex offenders and patients will be discussed. The terms "patient" and "sex offender" will be used interchangeably, since they are most often synonymous in assessment and treatment programs. Relatively few men volunteer for clinical services when unusual sexual preferences are involved.

Assessment of Anomalous Sexual Behavior

Sexual Preference

The clinician who examines sexual preferences, either via questionnaire and interview or by use of penile plethysmography, is attempting to determine whether the individual under examination shows an unusual sexual preference. It is assumed that if an individual has such an unusual sexual preference, for example, for children, then his likelihood of engaging in sexual acts with children is greater. Indeed, pedophiles, because of their stable sexual preference, are much more likely to be considered culpable of a sexual offence involving children, regardless of their actual guilt. Nevertheless, detection of a sexually anomalous preference does increase the probability that the accused *could* have perpetrated a particular crime.

Pedophilia, as a sexual preference, presents many problems. The male may show greatest erotic arousal to female or male children, or to both. In some cases, it is not the body characteristics of the youth which is arousing, but some preferred activity, for example, exhibitionism, controlling the child (hyperdominance) or even sadism (see Langevin, 1985; Travin, Bluestone, Coleman, Cullen, & Melella, 1986). In approximately 20% of the cases, the subjects are aggressive with the children, although higher incidences have been reported previously (Christie, Marshall, Lanthier, 1978; Langevin, Hucker, Handy, Hook, Purins, & Russon, 1985).

Detection of violent sexual preferences, such as sadism, is especially important because most often when sadists are sexually aroused they will want to rape or injure someone. Sadists are preferentially aroused (1) by controlling, dominating, and humiliating their victims, (2) by the fear and terror expressed by their victims in the rape situation, and (3) by actual physical injury and even the death of their victim. In some cases, dismemberment of the body and even cannibalism occur. Sadists have been studied in very few empirical investigations, and they are believed to represent less than 5% of the sexually aggressive male population (Groth, 1979). It is noteworthy, however, that they represent 45% of cases seen at the author's clinic (Hucker, Langevin, Wortzman, Dicker, & Wright, 1988; Langevin, Bain, Ben-Aron, Coulthard, Day, & Handy, 1985). Whatever the anomalous sexual preference, the male will fantasize and be driven by his unusual urges. Clinically, sexual preference is the single most important factor to evaluate although many patients attempt to conceal their preferences either because of embarrassment or fear of incarceration.

Substance Abuse

Alcohol and drugs can also play an important role in sexual behavior. It often is assumed that alcohol reduces erectile potency, therefore making such acts as rape more difficult or impossible for the intoxicated male. Nevertheless, actual empirical data contradict this expectation (see Langevin, Ben-Aron, Coulthard, Day, Handy, 1985, for review), with many sex offenders drinking at the time of their offence. Impotence and even feminization induced by substance abuse are very rare and, if seen at all, are more likely in older alcoholics who show clear signs of physical impairment and a longer history of excessive drinking. Men who commit sex offences tend to be younger and may show early signs of alcoholism, such as blackouts or memory loss and family disturbance. Although even in these cases, about a quarter show some liver dysfunction, with liver enzymes abnormally elevated (Bain, Langevin, Hucker, Dickey, & Wright, 1987). It is also possible that, in young men, abuse of alcohol increases levels of the sex hormone testosterone, which is believed to be implicated in sexual drive and arousal (see Langevin, Bain, Ben-Aron, Coulthard, & Handy, 1985; Rada, Laws, Kellner, Stivastava, & Peake, 1983).

Sexually anomalous males may deliberately exaggerate their reported substance abuse prior to sexual misconduct, either to excuse their behavior or to seek mitigation in criminal proceedings. Although such deception is widely suspected, it eludes empirical research, given the impracticality of obtaining blood-alcohol levels just prior to or immediately following a criminal act. Corroborative data is particularly helpful in verifying substance abuse at the time of sexual misconduct, involving statements from the victim regarding the patient's apparent intoxication.

Socialization

Approximately 40% of sexually aggressive men are labeled *psychopaths* (Rada, 1978). This term indicates an extensive criminal history and, in some cases, a futility in attempting to change the conscience and social adaptation of these individuals. An associated feature of antisocial personality disorder is persistent lying and other forms of deception (American Psychiatric Association, 1980). As discussed in Chapter 4, the presence of this disorder complicates greatly any diagnosis based primarily on self-report data. There are no empirical studies available to address the level of deception in psychopathic versus nonpsychopathic sexual offenders. However, with the presence of an antisocial personality disorder, clinicians should exercise considerable care in ruling out deception.

Biological Factors

Sexually anomalous individuals may have brain changes which can influence their sexual behavior (see Cummings, 1985 for a review). Langevin,
Bain, Ben-Aron, Coulthard, & Handy (1985) found right temporal horn
dilatation more frequently in sadistic rapists than in nonsadists or criminal
controls. The finding was extended and replicated by Hucker *et al.* (1988).
Pedophiles have shown organic impairment (Hucker *et al.*, 1986; Scott,
Cole, McKay, Golden, & Liggett, 1984), suggesting impairment in the left
temporal and parietal areas.

A few sex offenders may have unusual sex hormone profiles (Langevin,
1988). Langevin, Bain, Ben-Aron, Coulthard, & Handy *et al.* (1985) reported that sadistic rapists had generally normal levels ot testosterone, but
some had elevated luteinizing hormone (LH) and follicle-stimulating hormone (FSH) levels. There is little evidence that pedophiles show an unusual
sex hormone profile, although Gaffney and Berlin (1984) found an unusual
response to the LHRH, (leutinizing hormone releasing hormone) test, but
their results have not been replicated (Bain, Hucker, Dickey, Langevin, &
Wright, 1987).

Biological variables offer justifiable hope for more precise assessment
of sex offenders, particularly because these are less vulnerable than other
measures to dissimulation. Current research, however, has yet to identify
highly consistent markers or indices that can discriminate accurately enough
to assist in identifying sexually aggressive behavior. Thus, although providing useful corroborative data, netiher structural changes in the brain or
endocrinological differences provide any direct assistance with defensive sex
offenders.

From this review, it is evident that sexually anomalous patients and sex
offenders can be both evasive and defensive. Most standardized measures
on sexually anomalous behavior rely on self-report questionnaires (Langevin, 1985), which are readily faked. The susceptibility of such measures is
summarized in Chapter 16. However, unique to the assessment of sexual
anomalies is the use of penile plethysmography, (i.e., the evaluation of
penile tumescence in response to erotic materials).

Penile Plethysmography

Penile plethysmography or phallometry is ideally used in conjunction with
questionnaires and interviews, as well as with police and victim reports.
Unfortunately, phallometric tests have currently assumed a validity and
reliability far out of proportion to their actual scientific development and
their ability to predict sexual preferences or important features of criminal
acts. The use of penile erections to measure sexual behavior patterns has

high face validity, and this has led to two facile assumptions; (1) that responses in the laboratory to erotic materials reflect sexual preferences, and (2) that these responses can predict an individual's guilt for the sexual crime under consideration. However, few studies have attempted to examine phallometric test results as a predictor of future crimes or as an indicator of current guilt.

Description of Phallometric Devices

Two basic instruments are currently used to measure penile tumescence: the volumetric plethysmograph and circumference strain gauges (see Freund 1981; Langevin 1983). In the volumetric device, developed by Freund (1963), the penis is encased in a glass cylinder with an inflatable rubber cuff at the base of the penis to seal the leakage of air from that source. A hole in the top end of the glass cylinder is connected via rubber or plastic tubing to a recording device so that any penile tumescence forces the air inside the cylinder against a recording instrument such as a volume/pressure transducer. This apparatus is extremely sensitive and it can measure .02 cc volume change, a value far below most men's level of awareness.

The circumference strain gauge may be a metal expansion ring or mercury-in-rubber ring that is placed often at the center of the penis, although researchers are not in full agreement on the best location for optimal measurement. The gauge expands as the penis diameter increases in reaction to erotica. These devices are convenient and can be purchased ready to use from a variety of sources (Barlow, Becker, Leitenberg, & Agras, 1970; Laws & Bow, 1976).

Measurement of Arousal

Volumetric changes are recorded typically as either raw or z-transformed scores, so each person has a mean score of 0 and a standard deviation of 1. Circumferential scores are most often reported as a percentage of 'full erection.' Using each case as its own standard allows for control over individual variability in penis size. Unfortunately, it is not unusual for men to have difficulty obtaining full erections in the laboratory setting, so 75% of full erection or some other standard value for circumference at full erection may be used. The 75% criterion is a subjective judgment rendering the obtained value uncertain. Other approaches which divide the raw score by a constant actually do nothing to alter scores. It seems the procedure used for volumetry (i.e., analysis of raw scores or z scores and use of neutral stimuli), would best be applied for circumference measurement as well.

The volume and circumference measures of the penis are not as highly correlated as one might hope. They share approximately 50% common variance (Freund, Langevin, & Barlow, 1974) so that many mild and subtle reactions to erotica may be missed by the circumference measures (Langevin, 1983; Metz & Wagner, 1981). In some instances, volume and circumference changes may be opposite (McConaghy, 1974a). In such cases, the penis may increase in length faster than it does in diameter resulting in an initial decrease before increasing. Farkas *et al.*, (1979) examined the reliability of the mercury-in-rubber strain gauge and reported that basal penile circumference measurement was highly reliable ($r = 0.94$) but somewhat lower for full erection ($r = 0.75$); a feature which creates some difficulty in using the "75% of full erection" measurement. In addition, the erotic stimulus materials used to elicit circumference responses usually must be presented for a longer duration than volumetric measurement. This is a distinct disadvantage in reference to defensive responses (Abel, Barlow, Blanchard, & Mavissakalian, 1975; Freund, 1971). As Freund (1971) pointed out, because it is possible to inhibit penile tumescence by imagery and nonerotic thoughts, clinicians should minimize defensiveness by presenting a stimulus unpredictably, and as briefly as possible to flood the individual's mind while the penile reaction is being measured.

Instruments have also been developed for measuring female sexual arousal. Vaginal probes measure vasoconstriction or temperature changes in the vaginal wall. These devices are plagued by physiological artifacts and technical problems that currently render them useless for clinical practice (Beck, Sakheim, & Barlow, 1983). The available devices for women are only useful for preliminary research and certainly could not be used as evidence in any court proceedings.

Erotic Materials Used in Phallometric Testing

Sexual arousal and, presumably, sexual preferences of the patient are examined using two general modes of presentation. Most commonly, visual materials are presented in the form of slides or movies composed of (1) nude or seminude male or female adults and children, (2) sexual intercourse, or (3) anomalous sexual acts, such as bondage and beatings. Movies generally produce larger erotic reactions than slides do (Freund, Langevin, & Zajac, 1974; McConaghy, 1974b; Sandford, 1974). The second mode of presentation is audio-recorded descriptions of erotic acts. This latter category is necessary because many men with unusual sexual preferences will be most aroused to the body shape of adult females but they also desire unconventional sexual behaviors, such as exposing, peeping, etc. The audio description offers the opportunity for the respondent's imagination and, presumably, typical sexual fantasies to become operative. Thus, descriptions of rape, intercourse with a child, or of exhibitionism may be presented.

Conventional sexual materials such as pictures of the adult nude female or audio descriptions of sexual intercourse are used in each case as a comparison to sexually anomalous stimuli. Larger penile reactions to anomalous rather than to conventional erotica is considered to be an index of a sexually anomalous preference. In addition, some researchers also include sexually neutral stimuli to take into account the reactivity level of the individual. This technique is useful with overexcited men who react to everything rendering the results invalid. More commonly, the men are nonresponders with virtually no arousal to any stimulus materials. Finally, response decrements are observed with continued presentation of mild erotic stimuli (Freund, McKnight, Langevin, & Cibiri, 1972; Kolarsky & Madlafousek, 1977) so it is important to balance the presentation of stimulus materials to compensate for satiation.

Reliability and Validity of Phallometry

Zuckerman (1971), in his comprehensive review of sexual arousal measures, found penile erection to be the most valid indicator of sexual excitement. Nevertheless, because of the high face validity of phallometry, researchers have rarely attempted to ascertain its reliability and prediction of sexual behavior. In addition, measuring erections makes the goals of such assessments evident to patients and sex offenders; thus, its face validity may contribute to its fakability.

Few reported studies examine the reliability of stimulus materials used in the assessment or treatment of sexually anomalous men (Langevin, 1985; McConaghy, 1976; Zuckerman, 1971). For example, Farkas et al. (1979) reported a test–retest reliability of .74. Freund et al. (1972) noted high internal consistency in their set of materials, as applied to homosexual versus heterosexual men.

The discrimination of homosexual and heterosexual noncriminal subjects ranges from a high of 90%; (Freund, 1963, 1967) to 76% (McConaghy, 1967). The latter study likely would have yielded a higher classification rate if intervals between stimuli had been permitted to allow penile volume to return to baseline. A number of studies have demonstrated that sex offenders against children, as a group, react more to sexually explicit pictures or stories involving children than do controls (Freund, 1967; Freund & Langevin, 1976; Marshall, Barbaree & Christophe, 1986). However, the amount of discrimination of individual pedophiles from controls, based on these stimuli, varies. The most likely explanation for this finding is the heterogeneity of sex offenders against children, with some more attracted to the adult body shape but showing a sexual response preference anomaly for hyperdominance.

The validity of stimuli used in phallometric tests also has been assumed more often than tested. It has been commonly accepted that laboratory stimuli are sexually arousing although, as Zuckerman (1971) noted, low-grade stag movies may elicit hilarity or disgust. As an additional factor, patients may experience subjective arousal without erection. A further confounding issue in assessing the validity of sexual stimuli is that some sadists have been impotent or are slow to arouse physiologically. Alternatively, they may be subjectively aroused but penile output may be low (Langevin, Bain, Ben-Aron, Coulthard, Day, & Handy, 1985).

The assumption that the largest penile responses represent the sexual preference of the individual is a controversial point, especially with reference to stimuli depicting rape and consenting intercourse. Abel, Barlow, Blanchard and Guild (1977) found that rapists as a group responded equally to descriptions of rape and consenting intercourse, whereas other sex offenders, used as controls, reacted somewhat less to the rape stimuli. Abel and his colleagues computed a *rape index*, which is the ratio of the penile responses to rape descriptions divided by the responses to descriptions of consenting intercourse. They found that the rape index was significantly correlated with the degree of force used in the crime. This encouraging work was initially replicated by others but more recently it was questioned (see Langevin, Bain, Ben-Aron, Coulthard, Day, & Handy, 1985; Murphy, Krisak, Stalgaitis, & Anderson, 1984; Quinsey, Chaplin, & Upfold, 1984). Analogous pedophilic or age preference indices have also been developed (Abel, Becker, Mittelman, & Cunningham-Rathner, 1986; Freund & Blanchard, 1986).

The Abel *et al.* (1977) original study leaves substantial doubt concerning how accurately an individual, rather than a group, could be identified using the rape index. The index for rapists should exceed 1 since it is expected that rapists will react more to rape cues than to consenting intercourse. Conversely, nonrapist controls should score significantly less than 1. Using this criterion, only 65% of Abel's original rapists are correctly identified. Even a more liberal cutting score of 0.75 led to a modest improvement (i.e., 70%). Murphy *et al.* (1984) found in their study that, if a cutting score of 1 is used, only 35.7% of rapists are correctly identified at the expense of 26.7% of controls who are misidentified as rapists. This false positive rate is unacceptably high. A cutoff of 0.80 identified subjects as rapists or controls only at a chance level (50%). Current research on the rape index suggests that both rapists and controls react more to consenting intercourse than to rape cues and the differences between groups are, at best, weak.

Murphy *et al.* (1984) have the only study to examine defensiveness with rape stimuli. They instructed research subjects to suppress responses to rape cues. Although the effect was not statistically significant, the mean rape index did drop from 0.93 to 0.61 for rapists and from 0.77 to 0.61 for controls. Cutting scores of either 1 or .75 do not appear to be clinically useful with defensive rapists. The assumption that erotic materials with high face validity will predict sexual preference patterns is not substantiated by current research. The same conclusion is true for sexually explicit materials used to examine other sexual anomalies. For example, Freund and his colleagues' recent phallometric test, even with considerable modifications to reduce defensiveness, can produce only a 60% discrimination between men who admit to and those who do not admit to a sexual preference for children (Freund & Blanchard, 1986; Freund, Chan, & Coulthard, 1979). One may conclude that many of those who do not acknowledge this sexual abnormality, however are lying. It has yet to be demonstrated, (even when the cases of those who do admit their abnormality are taken alone), that all the sexual preference patterns have been sampled.

No valid or standardized phallometric tests are available to assess the major types of sexual anomalies: exhibitionism, voyeurism, transvestism, transsexualism, and sadism (see Kolarsky & Madlafousek, 1983). Even standard tests to examine the reactions to body shapes (i.e. child, pubescent, and adult) such as that devised by Freund et al. (1972) are limited in range and validity. Thus, in considering defensiveness in sexually anomalous patients, it is important to realize that the procedures used, in spite of both their high face validity and prominence in clinical practice, are exceptionally limited. Test development procedures used for psychological tests generally have not been applied to phallometry at all. When such validation is undertaken, it will necessarily be based on responses of men who admit to their sexual preferences (Freund, 1971).

Use of Phallometry in Assessing Defensiveness

The previous discussion does not preclude phallometry as a valuable research and clinical instrument. Rather, it indicates that much work has yet to be done to establish the tests as satisfactory scientific measures. However, the procedure has other limitations, which have led authors such as Freund (1971) to conclude that it is only useful with men who admit their sexual abnormality. Nevertheless, research has attempted to determine how men respond defensively to this test.

Most men do not react automatically to erotic materials presented in a laboratory situation. Especially if one is awaiting trial, anxiety is frequently experienced about the whole assessment and most certainly wtih respect to phallometric testing. Defensiveness is most commonly observed in the *nonresponder*. This term refers to the individual who either does not react at all to the erotic materials or whose responses are so small as to be diagnostically uninterpretable.

The individual may be a nonresponder for a variety of reasons. Older men are not as readily aroused as younger men (Solnick & Birren, 1977). A male offender awaiting trial or sentencing may either intentionally attempt to suppress all responses, which appears to be the most effective way to foil this test, or he may experience an emotional state that inhibits his reactivity. Anxiety is common in these cases, and either alone or in combination with depression, may disrupt characteristic arousal. In fewer cases, disgust or disinterest are important factors in inhibiting arousal. Some men with considerable sexual experience have noted that the materials are dull and nonstimulating. In addition, orgasm just prior to testing can reduce responsiveness, although this too is atypical. Other men are uncooperative, not looking at the stimulus materials or being highly distracted.

Phallometric results with nonresponders, whether they admit their abnormality or not, cannot be interpreted with respect to sexual preferences. Most unfortunately, nonresponse to phallometric testing has been used incorrectly in some court proceedings to assume that the individual is not sexually anomalous. As noted previously, only greater arousal to anomalous sexual materials compared with conventional stimuli is indicative of sexual preference. It is very difficult at present to tell if the patient is suppressing deviant arousal, unless one sees movement artifacts or other signs of tampering with the testing procedure. Interestingly, men who are holding back erotic reactions to children are much more readily detected when faking. The typical tracing of the phallometric response is a smooth, slow-rising asymptotic curve. Attempts to suppress responses appear as an overlay of muscle movement artifacts that are readily detected as spikes in the tracing.

Clinicians also encounter the overreactive cases, as noted in Langevin, Bain, Ben-Aron, Coulthard, Day, & Handy's (1985) research on rapists. When men are deprived of sexual outlets for between three weeks and three months while in jail awaiting assessment or trial, both the sexually anomalous and the ordinary offender may be very responsive to stimulus materials. Differences in overall penile output can distort results in making group comparisons. Langevin and his colleagues found, for example, that nonsadistic rapists appear to react more to audio-descriptions of nonsexual assaults than did sadists or controls who were not sex offenders. Mean penile volume changes for the groups were in the ratio of 4:2:1. Nevertheless when the results were analysed and overall variability in responsiveness taken into account, the mean differences were not statistically significant.

Some men actively attempt to distort phallometric results by increasing reactions to the appropriate categories (e.g., consenting sexual intercourse with an adult female), with or without a concomitant attempt to suppress reactions to deviant categories, such as children or rape (Freund, 1971). It is easier, as has been demonstrated in experiments, to reduce one's responsiveness than to generate erections when there is no desire. However, both sex offenders and community volunteers alike are quite capable of faking an anomalous sexual preference or a normal preference as desired (Abel et al., 1975).

Faking Strategies for Plethysmography

Blanchard (1980) instructed eight normal volunteers to fake increased reactions to children and decreased reactions to adult females. Research participants reported that they complied with the latter instructions through the following strategies: "looking at the slide just as a picture," "counting and becoming blank," "ignoring thoughts the photos ordinarily bring to mind" and "avoiding the details of the photo."

Some men actively stimulate themselves during phallometric testing. They may move the apparatus in attempting to masturbate. They may voluntarily move their perineal muscles, pull in their penis by contracting the groin, tensing the stomach and pelvic muscles or by hyperventilating upon presentation of anomalous materials, or move in some other way to distort the measurements (Blanchard, 1980; Quinsey & Bergerson, 1976). Some laboratories are equipped with cameras to watch the eyes of the subject to ensure that they are paying attention to the materials and do not attempt to manipulate the apparatus.

Henson and Rubin (1971) argued that an effective faking strategy was fantasizing erotic events to increase arousal to conventional sex stimuli and producing competing nonerotic fantasies to inhibit penile response to deviant stimuli. They attempted to defeat the strategy by instructing five men either to "do nothing" to inhibit sexual response, or to inhibit response by "any means possible except not looking at the film." These conditions were repeated with instructions that participants had to describe what was going on in the film as it occurred. Contrary to expectations, no differences were found under the "inhibit" conditions, suggesting that the experimenter-generated instructions to limit competing nonerotic fantasies, did not effectively reduce the men's responses.

Quinsey and Chaplin (1987) were more successful in preventing faking with a competing task. Sixteen normal heterosexual men heard descriptions of conventional intercourse, rape, nonsexual violence, and neutral heterosexual interactions under three conditions. In the first, they were told only to attend to the stimuli. In the second, they were asked to fake an interest in rape and violence but not in conventional intercourse. In the third, the participants were required to do a semantic tracking task to identify sex or violence, as it occurred in descriptions, by pressing one of two buttons. Results showed that participants could fake when so instructed, but they could not under the tracking-task condition. Quinsey and Chaplin noted that participant naivete was important in unsuccessful attempts at faking. They expressed grave doubt that paraphilics would have greater difficulty faking than community volunteers. The offenders are highly motivated to fake and are housed in institutions where knowledge about faking strategies is common.

Rosen and his colleagues (Rosen, 1973; Rosen, Shapiro, & Schwartz, 1975) also found that normal volunteers could suppress or increase penile tumescence on instruction. Research participants were given feedback on their effectiveness in altering penile responses with a white light. Contingent feedback and monetary reward were more effective than random feedback in successful faking. The results suggest that offenders who respond defensively in phallometric testing will do it more effectively with feedback. Similarly, Quinsey and Bergerson (1976) instructed five heterosexual community volunteers to respond so as to indicate sexual interest in female children or male children, or to respond normally. A monetary incentive was offered for successful faking, but only two of the five volunteers were able both to increase penile responses to children and to decrease them to adult females.

Offenders, of course, have their own agenda and rewards for appearing sexually normal. They may be awaiting trial or release from custody and treatment, pending phallometric results. If there is no external feedback about arousal level, awareness that their penises are tumescing may serve as important cues for faking. One reason volumetric measurements are more effective than circumferential measurement is that the former can detect changes as small as 0.02 cc volume change, which is below most men's level of awareness and thus makes defensiveness more difficult. Freund, Langevin and Barlow (1974) compared penile volume and circumference changes simultaneously to standard visual erotic stimuli (Freund et al. 1972) in normal volunteers. Both measurement devices discriminated between reactions to the adult females and those to children and men. However, participants were instructed to press a button when they were aware of penile tumescence. When the data were reanalysed after all responses with button presses were removed, the volumetric approach still discriminated adult female stimuli from children and male stimuli but the circumferential method did not. Thus, testing with volumetric measurement can be devised to provide a minimum of physiological feedback cues to men who attempt to fake, which is a decided limitation of circumference measurement.

Freund has carried out the most extensive work on phallometric faking by sex offenders or sexually anomalous men. In his earlier work he seemed quite confident that it was difficult to fake the phallometric results. Freund (1971) noted that 2 of 22 (9%) heterosexual and 1 of 9 (11%) homosexual men successfully distorted phallometric results (see also Freund, 1963, 1967). The homosexual men were asked to imagine they were having sex with a desired male partner when pictures of adult females were shown and to think of something very disagreeable when pictures of adult males were shown. Heterosexual men were given analogous instructions. The men were more successful at faking with readministration of the test. Three of 20 (15%) heterosexuals and 5 of 15 (33%) homosexuals distorted their reactions.

The more recent work of Freund and his colleagues on North American samples is less optimistic. Freund et al. (1979) attempted to examine 152 men accused of pedophilic acts. A total of 47% of those who did not admit to the charge refused phallometric testing or were nonresponders compared with 25% of those who did admit to pedophilia ($\chi^2 = 5.85$, df $= 1$, $p < .02$, when computed by the present author). Marshall *et al.* (1986) also found that, of 21 incest offenders and 40 pedophilic offenders, 34% and 22% respectively were nonresponders. The authors noted that these are substantial percentages, which represent a serious disadvantage of phallometry.

Overall, of the men responding during phallometric testing in the Freund *et al.* (1979) study, diagnoses of sexual preferences were inaccurate in roughly one-third of those who admitted to the charge and two-thirds of those who did not. Freund and Blanchard (1986) noted that negative diagnoses provide less useful information than positive ones (i.e., it is more significant if an individual shows greatest reactivity to children over adults than if the reverse is true or if there is no response). Freund and Blanchard also noted the great difficulty in distinguishing a sexual preference for adolescents based on phallometric testing.

The research on defensiveness among sex offenders assumes that the accused is guilty or has an anomalous sexual preference. Although the incidence of falsely accused men in this group may be expected to be low, some external criterion of sexually anomalous preferences should be used. For example, the assumption that all sexual offences against children are committed by men who have a sexual preference for minors may be misleading. The offender may be sexually intimate with a child out of curiosity or loneliness, or he may be using the child as a surrogate for a more risky and desired person, for example, exhibitionists often expose themselves to children who will not report them when an adult is desired (Freund *et al.* 1972; Hucker & Ben-Aron, 1985). Unfortunately, many of these diverse offenders against children show a similar profile to conventional heterosexual men, either because they are conventional or because they experience a *response preference* anomaly rather than a *stimulus* anomaly, that is, they prefer exhibitionism or sexual domination (response preference) and not necessarily the body characteristics of children (stimulus preference). The age of the individual being assessed must be noted, since sexual arousal patterns in adolescents are unpredictable and often large in reference to a wide range of unusual stimulus catagories. It is also important to examine the features of the victim of the sexual offence in question. Although phallometric tests use age criterion, many minors are in fact physically developed at a young age.

Many practitioners see the phallometric test as a sexual lie detector with evidence of arousal (e.g., children over adults) as the indication of guilt. However, it is rare that the examining phallometrist will present the actual stimulus situation of the reported crime and determine the individual's reactivity to this particular situation versus some other nonspecific situations. In contrast, the polygraphy often focuses on details of the crime in assessing dissimulation (see Chapter 12). A few studies have attempted to compare phallometry to indices used in polygraphy (e.g., galvanic skin responses (GSR) or heart rate) and have failed dismally (Bancroft & Matthews, 1971; Quinsey, Steinman, Bergersen, & Holmes, 1975; Rosen, 1973). Skin conductance responses, or GSR, do not bear any clear relationship to faking, attempting faking, or to erotic reactivity in phallometric testing.

Denial by Sex Offenders

Sex offenders use two main approaches in claiming innocence when faced with criminal charges or in attempting to avoid involvement in treatment. First, they may admit that they engaged in anomalous sexual behavior but only under special circumstances, such as alcohol intoxication. Second, they may deny the charges altogether. They may feel that the circumstances permit denial; that is, the child is uncertain of details or will be a poor witness, preventing a successful prosecution. Defendants who deny may also assume that their credibility and reputation will withstand the test. For example, the elderly offender who has a long and successful social history may feel that his word will be credible in court against a child's (Hucker & Ben-Aron, 1985). Likewise, the rapist may note that his victim was drinking, casting doubt on her credibility.

If the patient completely denies the sexual misbehavior, the total assessment procedure becomes suspect. The clinician can administer tests such as the MMPI and look at validity indices (see Chapter 8), but those who do not admit to sexual abnormality are likely to refuse to participate. They characteristically report little psychopathology on the MMPI and attempt to present an overly positive picture. Such individuals often report a limited and conventional sexual history, but they may not deny substance abuse or other facets of their background that are indicators of being prone to violence, such as their criminal record. It is rare that sexually anomalous men attempt to malinger a mental illness. The great majority present as nonpsychotic and, if they warrant a diagnosis, are labeled personality disordered (Langevin, Paitich, Freeman, Mann, & Handy, 1978).

Sex offenders may also admit guilt with adamant denials of long-term interest in anomalous sexual activity. Such individuals may point to special circumstances (e.g., marital disharmony and employment difficulties) and not to sexual preference in excusing their behavior. As with defensiveness in non–sex offenders, one encounters degrees of admission and nonadmission.

In the cases of sexually aggressive men, approximately 40% are psychopaths who may present as credible or likeable persons in spite of their crime (Rada, 1978). They often minimize the seriousness and frequency of their own sexual behavior, especially its aggressiveness. They may present as models of proper conduct on an inpatient unit and be quite convincing, further raising their credibility as innocent of the crime. It is therefore essential to have a police report or some other official source of information concerning their previous criminal and psychiatric history, as well as information from the victim and the witnesses to the crime, if any, in order to properly evaluate these sexually aggressive men.

An Empirical Study of Defensiveness in Sex Offenders

In preparing this chapter the author carried out a study of defensiveness in 100 sex offenders, 50 of whom were repeated sex offenders against children, and 50 of whom were sexually aggressive against adult women. The pedophiles were awaiting trial and had been charged with sexual assault on a boy or girl 15 years of age or younger with a minimum 6-year age difference between victims and offenders. The sexual aggressives had forced body contact (e.g., rape, oral-genital, or anal intercourse) on a physically mature woman, 16 years of age or older. There were two inclusion criteria: (1) the offender, at least, had to have been *offered* phallometric testing and (2) he had to be *facing* criminal charges.

A number of measures were examined for their potential relationship to defensiveness. Since men who are more sophisticated are presumably better at evading assessment, such things as age, education IQ (Wechsler Adult Intelligence Scale-Revised, WAIS-R), and criminal history (no previous offence, previous sex offence, previous nonsex offence) were examined. Because brain-injured men may be less able to distort test results, a general criterion of clinically significant findings on the Halstead-Reitan or the Luria-Nebraska Neuropsychological Test batteries, or CT (computer tomography) scans was employed. The commonly used MMPI validity scales (L, F, K, and F-K index) were examined as well as the TR index, Carelessness scale, and Weiner and Harmon (1946) Subtle and Obvious scales for 46 subjects whose MMPI's were completed. The newer Millon Clinical Multiaxial Inventory (MCMI) was examined for its Validity index and Sum scales 1–8 in 56 cases. Since some men claimed that substance abuse was responsible for the offence, actual clinical documentation of alcohol and drug abuse, as well as results from the Michigan Alcoholism Screening Test, the Clarke Drug Use Survey (Langevin, Bain, Ben-Aron, Coulthard, Day, & Handy, 1985), and laboratory tests of liver dysfunction were examined. Since violent offenders may minimize their aggressive behavior, history of physical acting out was considered. International Classification of Diseases (ICD-9) diagnoses were also examined for the presence of psychoses since psychotic individuals are noteworthy for the unreliability of their self-report information. Finally, phallometric testing, employing the procedures of Freund and colleagues (Freund, 1963; Freund *et al.*, 1972), was conducted with measurements of penile volume changes to a standard series of 54 movie clips (both males and females aged 5–8, 9–11, 13–15, 18–25, and sexually neutral landscapes). An experimental series of audiodescriptions of hyperdominance and sadism were also examined. In examining defensiveness, the following four issues were addressed: (1) did the patient refuse phallometric tests or fail to show for repeated appointments? (2) did he attempt to manipulate the outcome of testing? (3) was he a nonresponder, that is, was there insufficient penile responsiveness to make a diagnosis? and (4) could a diagnosis of anomalous sexual preference be made? Overall, the two groups, as noted in Table 15.1, were comparable in degree of admission to the offence in question. Less than one-third of the cases admitted both to their offences and their sexually anomalous preferences. Slightly more than a third admitted committing the offences but denied anomalous erotic preferences, and 13% admitted both yet claimed special circumstances such as drunkenness, loneliness, or marital problems, as precipitators of the offences in question. Four men denied committing the offences but did admit to an anomalous sexual preference (i.e., for children or sexual aggression). Fifteen percent denied everything, claiming mistaken identity or being "framed."

The pedophiles and sexual aggressives differed little in type of defensiveness. Sexual aggressives more than pedophiles had a statistically nonsignificant trend to attribute their sexual misconduct to alcohol and drug intoxication (32% vs. 16% respectively $\chi^2 = 3.55$, df $= 1$, $p < .10$). On the other hand pedophiles who were administered the MMPI had higher mean scores than sexual aggressives on the L scale (raw scores of 5.67 and 4.05 respectively; $t = 2.22$, df $= 44$, $p < .05$). Considering the few differences in the two groups, they were combined for examining defensiveness on phallometric testing.

The outcome of phallometric testing is summarized in Table 15.2 for those who admitted their offenses and those who did not. Fourteen percent of the subjects attempted to actively manipulate or fake results. Attempts at

Table 15.1. Degrees of Admission to Offences Among Pedophiles and Sexual Aggressives

Degree of admission	% Pedophiles	% Sexual aggressives	% Total sample
1. Admits all	32	30	31
2. Admits offence, denies anomalous sex preference	36	38	37
3. Admits offence and preference but claims special circumstances	12	14	13
4. Denies offence, admits anomalous sex preference	4	4	4
5. Denies everything	16	14	15

Table 15.2. Phallometric Testing Outcome and Degree of Admission

Degree of admission	% Diagnosis made	% Nonresponder	% Faker	% Refuses testing
1. Admits all ($N = 31$)	64.5	3.2	9.7	12.9
2. Admits offence, denies anomalous sex preference ($N = 37$)	51.4	8.1	13.5	16.2
3. Admits but claims special circumstances ($N = 15$)	13.3	26.7	20.0	13.3
4. Denies offence, admits anomalous sex preference ($N = 4$)	75.0	0.0	0.0	0.0
5. Denies everything ($N = 13$)	53.8	7.7	23.1	7.7
Total ($N = 100$)	51.0[a]	9.0	14.0	13.0

Note. In one case (Group 3), the offender agreed to do phallometric testing but injury to his penis precluded testing. In a second case (Group 5), the offender "could not follow instructions." Results have been computed excluding these two cases.

[a]In 13% of the cases, diagnosis could not be made despite the responsiveness and cooperativeness of the patients.

faking were most frequently made by those who admitted to the offense but claimed special circumstances (20.0%) or denied everything (23.1%). Even those who admitted the offense were not immune to attempts at faking, with 9.7% meeting this criterion.

Subjects who are either nonresponders or refuse testing include an unknown percentage of patients who are attempting to deliberately minimize their sexually anomalous behavior. In comparing nonresponders in this test, the largest percentage was among those who admitted to the offense but claimed special circumstances (26.7%). Interestingly, there is no apparent distinction between those who admit the offense and those who do not in their refusal of phallometric testing. Of those who admitted to both the offense and anomalous sexual preference 12.9% refused plethysmography.

In summary, the phallometric testing indicated that *all* groups were vulnerable to faking (Group D had insufficient numbers of subjects). It can be inferred from the above data that those who admit to the offense but claim special circumstances are probably the most likely to manipulate or suppress their responses. Indeed, only 13.3% of this category could be diagnosed.

MMPI validity indicators were not useful in discriminating between (1) responders who cooperated with testing and had an interpretable arousal pattern and (2) fakers who manipulated their phallometric testing. Although a considerable degree of defensiveness was observed on the MMPI (32.6% satisfied the criterion of $11 < $ F-K $ < -11$), this was not associated with defensiveness on phallometric testing. Likewise, other measures of dissimulation on the MMPI, were unsuccessful at discriminating between responders and fakers.

Analysis of the MCMI data indicated that 92.9% of the protocols were valid. Results suggested that few attempts were made to distort responses on the MCMI; therefore, no comparisons of responders and fakers on the MCMI validity index could be undertaken. No other measure (WAIS-R, brain damage, substance abuse, violence, etc.) discriminated the defensive from the nondefensive cases.

Summary of Test Results

The sex offender differs from other defensive patients in a number of important ways. Most often, he presents a picture of a psychologically normal individual who attempts to minimize any attraction to children, sexual aggression, or other sexually anomalous outlets. He frequently denies the pending legal charges. He may deny a history of anomalous sexual behavior or may attribute the offence to alcohol and drug abuse. In some cases, a partial denial occurs in which the current problems or substance abuse may be invoked as a contributing factor, even though the offender accepts his responsibility for the criminal behavior.

The phallometric test has been overvalued in contemporary clinical assessments of sex offenders. The number of reliable and valid tests that have been established to date are few in number, although this has not stopped their use in court proceedings. Unlike the polygraph, the phallometric test does not attempt to assess the physiological reactivity to deception about the crime. Rather, it examines a more general sexual attraction to conventional and anomalous sexual stimuli.

Clinical Assessment of the Defensive Sex Offender

Table 15.3 outlines the steps in assessing defensiveness and denial in sexually anomalous patients. An initial interview with the patient can be used to determine if he completely admits to the offense, admits to the offence but invokes contributing factors, does not admit to the offense. Complete denial suggests that the assessment procedure will have to rely mainly on phallometric testing. In sequencing the assessment process, it is valuable to administer phallometric testing to those who admit the offense but deny responsibility and to those who do not admit the offense, immediately following the initial interview. These patients should be given the critical material first and with as short presentations as possible, 10–14 seconds, using the volumetric approach. Such brief presentation allows for less opportunity to manipulate the test situation and produces valid results. With these patients, the diagnosis of an anomalous sexual preference can be made in approximately 50% of the cases. Clinicians can then present them with their patterns of deviant

Table 15.3. Clinical Assessment of Defensive Patients Manifesting Sexually Anomalous Behavior

Procedure	Outcome

A. Initial interview to determine if the patient admits to:
  1. Any current criminal charges
  2. An anomalous sexual preference, and
  3. Does the patient plead "special circumstances"
	Total admitters can proceed with paper-and-pencil tests and laboratory tests in any sequence.
	Nonadmitters and partial admitters should undergo phallometry first with the results discussed.

B. Phallometric testing using volumetric device and standardized stimulus materials	Nonresponse, faking or lack of commitment to the assessment should be discussed. Nonadmitters and partial admitters should be confronted with results that indicate an anomalous sexual preference.

C. Investigation of other pertinent clinical factors:
  1. Sexual preference:
    a. Clarke Sex History Questionnaire
    b. Freund Gender Identity Scale
  2. Substance abuse:
    a. Michigan Alcoholism Screening Test
    b. Drug Abuse Screening Test
    c. Blood tests, especially liver enzyme functioning
    d. Other more detailed substance abuse measures as applicable
  3. History of violence:
    a. Clarke Violence Scale
    b. MMPI
  4. Neuropsychological factors:
    a. CT scan of brain
    b. Halstead-Reitan battery
	Results should be scrutinized for dissimulation, social desirability response set and random responding. Validity scales of the MMPI may prove useful in assessing dissimulation in general, but *not* sexual behavior in particular.

D. Other Coroborating sources of information:
  1. police reports
  2. victim statements
  3. previous hospitalization records
  4. parents, other family interviews
  5. behavior in hospital and jail
	Valuable data to support patients' statements or to confront the nonadmitter

arousal. If the patient admits to his sexual preference at this point, subsequent discussion may assist in gaining honest information on self-report measures.

A second approach to dissimulation is to examine validity indicators of the MMPI and MCMI. These indicators, as noted above, may yield general information about defensiveness but do not contribute to the assessment of sexual preference.

Assessing dissimulation in clinical interviews is often limited in scope because of the difficulty in accessing corroborative information from relevant sources (i.e., lawyers, hospitals, doctors, and victims). The wives, girlfriends, and relatives of sexually anomalous patients may provide valuable information about the individual's sexual functioning and/or social adjustment. Thus, inconsistencies between the patient and others often reveal deception, particularly about claims of satisfactory marital and sexual relationships. For example, the patient may claim to have sexual intercourse two to three times per week, but his wife will report that they have sex once a month and that the patient has difficulty obtaining erections.

The victims' reports to police are also extremely helpful in identifying the defensive sex offender. Often the offender (1) minimizes the nature of his acts and (2) leaves out incriminating details, particularly those indicative of violence. One sexually aggressive male feigned surprise over the report that the prostitutes were upset and ran screaming when he released them. He denied any violent behavior until confronted with victims' accounts of how he placed a revolver in their mouths during the sexual assault.

In some instances, subtle sexual behavior may point to an unusual sexual preference in defensive patients. For example, Langevin, Paitich, and Russon (1985) found that about one-fifth of rapists tend to engage in orgasmic cross-dressing. In addition, sadistic rapists tend to show feminine gender identity on Freund's (1977) GI scale (Langevin, Bain, Ben-Aron, Coulthard, Day, & Handy, 1985). These findings are contrary to social expectations of the rapist as an aggressive, "macho" individual with strong masculine identification. The sexually anomalous male may reveal this information without realizing its suggestive nature. In addition, approximately 41% of sadistic sexual rapists show CT scan abnormalities verus 11% of nonsadistic rapists and 13% of non–sex offenders used as controls. Abnormal CT findings are rare in the general population, suggesting a potential sign of sexual pathology that is not fakable.

Finally, therapeutic efforts with sexually anomalous patients will include a continuation of assessment and likelihood of denial of both deviant interest and activity (Langevin & Lang, 1985). Even men who totally admit to their sexual preference and past behavior may be reluctant to discuss their continued interests and sexual outlets. Rationalizations about children benefiting from sexual contact are common distortions encountered in treatment. Some patients will claim that their desires are under control as a way to avoid additional therapy. Thus, a primary goal of therapeutic efforts with sex offenders will be motivating them to change and overcoming their continued defensiveness.

A major goal of each chapter in this text is the generation of threshold and clinical decision models. Given the frequency of defensiveness among individuals with anomalous sexual preferences, no threshold model is pro-

Table 15.4. Clinical Decision Model for Establishing Defensiveness among Sexually Anomalous Patients

Gross minimization or denial of anomalous sexual behavior as observed in any of the following:

A. Well-established history (prior convictions or previous treatment for a paraphilia) of sexually anomalous behavior that the patient denies.

B. Marked contradictions in patient's self-report, including previous admissions to ongoing sexually anomalous behavior.

C. Results of phallometric testing indicating sexual preference for anomalous sexual behavior and *either*:
   1. Subsequent admission of anomalous sexual preference, or
   2. Corroborative data indicating denial or minimization of types of sexual behavior or its impact on victims

posed. Clinicians should therefore, *in every case*, assess the defensiveness of the individual referred for deviant sexual behavior or possible paraphilia. Available research offers no meaningful criteria for differentiating between reliable and dissimulating individuals suspected of deviant sexual behavior.

A clinical decision model for establishing defensiveness in the evaluation of sexually anomalous patients is presented in Table 15.4. Three criteria are presented in this table: (1) clear evidence of sexually anomalous behavior which a patient currently denies, (2) marked contradictions in self-reporting and (3) deviant sexual arousal supported by corroborative data which are inconsistent with patient's presentation. Other potential indicators were not included in the decision model because of the possibility of alternative explanations. Thus, although it is assumed that many who do not admit their offenses are defensive with respect to their sexual behavior, these denials may be the result of innocence or involuntary memory distortions. Similarly, although results of objective personality measures may reliably indicate overall defensiveness with respect to psychological functioning, these indicators have no diagnostic value with respect to specific sexual behavior.

All patients suspected of defensiveness with respect to their sexual behavior should be confronted with the inconsistent findings or phallometric results. Many patients, as noted above, will admit to their anomalous interests and behavior when confronted with this information. Patients who reluctantly admit, however, to present interests in deviant sexual behavior, are not immune to further defensiveness. Indeed, clinicians should remain alert during both initial and subsequent assessments for the possibility of dissimulation. Research on sexual preference suggests that such deviant interests remain stable and are very unlikely to change suddenly. Any individual either in assessment or treatment who claims a sudden transformation in thinking, sexual arousal patterns, or behavior is highly suspect of dissimulation.

Conclusion

This chapter highlights the complexity of etiological factors and antecedent conditions, and the range of anomalous sexual behavior among individuals referred for assessment. Defensiveness is commonly observed with respect to types of sexual behavior, the violence associated with such behavior, and the emotional and physical consequences for the victims. Clinicians must thoroughly investigate the possibility of defensiveness in every case involving sexual anomalies, whether legally referred or not. Phallometric testing remains the only, if imprecise, measure of deviant sexual arousal. Indeed, this procedure might best be viewed as a "challenge test," which can reliably detect at least some dissimulators. However, the absence of deviant arousal cannot be taken as conclusive evidence of either a patient's forthrightness or his lack of dissimulation.

PART FOUR

SUMMARY

16

Current Status of Clinical Methods

RICHARD ROGERS

Clinical assessment of psychiatric patients is hardly a monolithic enterprise. Clinicians range widely in the techniques they employ and the manner in which they synthesize clinically relevant data. The evaluation process is further compounded by the diversity of diagnostic questions posed either on referral or directly by the clinician. In addition, the heterogeneity of diagnostic styles militates against any single systematic approach for determining malingering, defensiveness, or irrelevant responding.

This chapter attempts to integrate threshold and clinical decision models presented throughout earlier chapters for the determination of dissimulation. In addition, it will discuss the clinical relevance of dissimulation in making treatment and nontreatment interventions, and it will consider the relevance of malingering and defensiveness response styles to referral questions. Finally, this chapter will offer a synthesis of clinical methods in determining dissimulation and establishing gradations of specific dissimulative styles. This chapter is organized into four major sections: (1) usefulness of individual diagnostic methods, (2) clinical relevance, (3) confrontation of suspected dissimulators, and (4) synthesis of clinical data.

Usefulness of Individual Diagnostic Methods

Clinical methods must be reviewed individually with respect to their usefulness in the detection of dissimulation. In establishing the usefulness of any particular method, three distinct issues need to be addressed: susceptibility, identification, and interpretability. *Susceptibility* refers to the vulnerability of a particular clinical method to dissimulation. A cursory inspection of Tables 16.1 and 16.2 reveals that all methods are susceptible to malingering and nearly all methods to defensiveness. *Identification* refers to the ability of a particular clinical method, to identify malingering or defensiveness in an individual patient. Two important caveats which must be borne in mind are (1) nonstandardized use of any of these measures invalidates the reported

Richard Rogers, Metropolitan Toronto Forensic Service (METFORS), Clarke Institute of Psychiatry, and University of Toronto, Toronto, Ontario, Canada.

Table 16.1. Usefulness of Clinical Methods in the Assessment of Dissimulation

Methods	Clinical usefulness		
	Susceptibility	Identification	Interpretation
A. Diagnostic interviews			
1. Malingering	Yes	Variable[a]	Partial[b]
2. Defensiveness	Yes	No	No
B. SADS			
1. Malingering	Yes	Yes[c]	Partial[d]
2. Defensiveness	Yes	Yes	Partial[d]
C. Hypnosis			
1. Deception	Yes	No	No
D. Drug-assisted interviews			
1. Deception	Yes	Partial[e]	No
E. Plethysmography			
1. Defensiveness	Yes	Partial[f]	Partial[g]
F. Polygraphy			
1. Deception	Yes	Partial[h]	Variable[i]

[a]Clinician who systematically probes for Malingering may identify more blatant cases
[b]Use of corroborative interviews
[c]Only if specific procedures are employed (Chapter 14)
[d]Use of the multiple SADS approach
[e]Cases identified are probably accurate; a substantial proportion are not identified
[f]Most patients who suppress deviant sexual arousal are identifiable
[g]By inference, it may be possible to identify suppressed arousal
[h]Under GKT; under CQT the cost is false positives
[i]Under CQT and GKT

dissimulation research, and (2) care must be taken to review available studies reported in the individual chapters, since some methods have limited generalizability to specific patient groups. *Interpretability* refers to the clinical usefulness of the results of a specific method after dissimulation has been discovered. The interpretability of a clinical method is predicated on (1) the accurate identification of dissimulators, and (2) correction formula (e.g., K-correction of the MMPI) or alternative sources of clinical data (e.g., multiple SADS [Schedule of Affective Disorders and Schizophrenia]).

The susceptibility, identification, and interpretability of specific clinical methods are summarized in Table 16.1 and 16.2. Nonpsychometric methods are presented in Table 16.1 with (1) interviews addressing both malingering and defensiveness, (2) plethysmography addressing defensiveness, and (3) hypnosis, drug-assisted interviews, and polygraphy addressing unspecified deception. In addition, most nonpsychometric methods are not consistent in their identification of dissimulators. For example, diagnostic interviews, given the heterogeneity of interview methods, are highly dependent on the competency and thoroughness of the clinician. Furthermore, physiologically based methods are, at best, only moderately accurate in the identification of dissimulators. Of these methods, the polygraph raises particular concern, given its likelihood of misidentifying honest individuals as dissimulators.

Psychometric methods (see Table 16.2) vary widely in the breadth and sophistication of their dissimulation research. Nearly all psychological measures are susceptible to dissimulation. The notable exception is defensiveness on intellectual and neuropsychological testing, since patients cannot perform better than their organic impairment will allow. With respect to identification, objective personality measures are generally more effective than other forms of psychological testing. Indeed, the MMPI remains the single best validated psychological measure for assessing malingering, defensiveness, and irrelevant responding. The Millon Clinical Multiaxial Inventory (MCMI) offers the potential for interpretation of both defensive and malingered protocols; the absence of any published empirical justifica-

Table 16.2. Clinical Usefulness of Psychometric Methods in the Assessment of Dissimulation

Psychometric methods	Clinical usefulness		
	Susceptibility	Identification	Interpretation
A. Rorschach			
1. Malingering	Yes	Variable[a]	No
2. Defensiveness	Yes	No[b]	No
B. Other projectives			
1. Malingering and defensiveness	Yes	No	No
C. MMPI			
1. Malingering	Yes	Yes	No
2. Defensiveness	Yes	Yes	Yes[c]
3. Irrelevant responding	Yes	Yes	No
D. CPI			
1. Malingering	Yes	Partial[d]	No
2. Defensiveness	Yes	Yes	No
E. MCMI			
1. Malingering	Yes	Partial[e]	Partial[e]
2. Defensiveness	Yes	Partial[e]	Partial[e]
F. Intelligence			
1. Malingering	Yes	No	No
2. Defensiveness	No	N/A	N/A
G. Neuropsychological Batteries			
1. Malingering	Yes	Variable[f]	Partial[g]
2. Defensiveness	No	N/A	N/A

[a]More positive results with Exner scoring or Pettigrew procedure

[b]Only exception is psychotics who can be readily identified

[c]Limited in applicability to inpatient samples

[d]Wb scale has not been well validated for the CPI

[e]Although cutting scores and weightings are presented for both malingering and defensiveness, no published studies validate these approaches

[f]Use of the Halstead-Reitan with a discriminant function may identify some malingerers

[g]Depending on individual cases, clinicians may be able to estimate actual level of neuropsychological functioning

tion for the proposed weightings would suggest extreme caution and conservatism in employing these correction formulas. For intellectual and neuropsychological testing, the two available studies (Goebel, 1983; Heaton, Smith, Lehman, & Vogt, 1978) suggests that a multivariate approach may be effective in identifying at least some malingerers on the Halstead-Reitan. The use of specifically constructed measures for assessing feigned cognitive deficits (see Chapters 5 and 10) is strongly recommended.

This discussion highlights, if nothing else, that clinicians cannot afford to be complacent during any phase of their psychiatric/psychological evaluations. Indeed, nearly all clinical methods are susceptible to dissimulation, and there is no empirical justification for assuming that forthrightness in one component of an assessment has any necessary bearing on a patient's subsequent response style. Johnson, Klingler, and Williams (1977) in a study of 228 admissions to Veteran's Administration hospitals found almost no relationship between malingering on the MMPI and during diagnostic interviews ($r = .14$). In other words, patients are not necessarily uniform in their presentation across either time or assessment methods. A high level of clinical practice demands that clinicians remain alert to the possibility of dissimulation during each phase of the assessment, otherwise, the inadvertency of the clinician may be mistakenly reflected in his or her evaluation of the patient's response style.

Clinical Relevance

The clinical relevance of dissimulation varies directly with the degree of distortion, the type of dissimulation, and the specific referral question. For example, a paranoid schizophrenic with an extensive history of auditory hallucinations may attempt to malinger command hallucinations. The clinical relevance of such fabrications would depend greatly on the referral question and vary considerably in relevance depending on whether the patient is seeking voluntary hospitalization or attempting an insanity plea. Indeed, the relevance of any type of dissimulation can only be established with reference to a specific referral question.

Empirical data are not available on the presence and severity of dissimulation by referral questions. On a heuristic basis, however, a tentative model can be proposed on the expected likelihood of malingering and defensiveness by the type of assessment being conducted. Table 16.3 provides the expected likelihood of dissimulation in the evaluation of treatment, vocational, school, and forensic issues.

This model, as noted above, has yet to be empirically tested. It is based rather on commonsense analysis of the degree of voluntariness experienced by patients and their desired outcome of such evaluations. It is interesting to note, given the increased scarcity of inpatient beds, that patients may feel

Table 16.3. Potential for Dissimulation by Types of Clinical Evaluation

	Expected likelihood of dissimulation	
Type of assessment	Malingering	Defensiveness
A. Treatment		
1. Voluntary outpatient	Low	Low
2. Voluntary inpatient	Variable[a]	Low
3. Involuntary inpatient	Low	Moderate
B. Vocational		
1. Rehabilitation assessments	Moderate	Low
2. Job placement/performance	Low	Moderate
C. School		
1. Special education placement	Low	Variable
D. Forensic		
1. Child custody	Low	High
2. Personal injury	High	Low
3. Insanity	High	Low
4. Presentence	Variable[b]	Variable[b]

[a]Where inpatient resources are scarce, voluntary patients may feel compelled to malinger in order to qualify for services.

[b]In minor offences, defendants may hope for treatment alternatives to incarceration by appearing mentally ill. In other cases, defendants may worry that the appearance of mental illness will lead to a harsher sentence.

the need to malinger in order to gain access to public psychiatric units, particularly in larger municipalities (see Chapter 3).

Table 16.3 does not take into account irrelevant or random responding. Such individuals are most likely to be identified on the basis of their clinical characteristics. For example, obvious disinterest, a persistent unwillingness to be involved in the evaluation, and low degree of literacy would all raise the index of suspicion that this individual may not be psychologically engaged in the assessment process or be unable to successfully complete written materials.

Dissimulation within the context of psychological/psychiatric assessment is relevant on two levels. On the first level, it may assist the clinician in establishing *what the patient is not.* With respect to many referral questions, particularly in the area of malingering, it is often more important to establish the authenticity of the patient's reported symptomatology than it is to either investigate the patient's motivation for deception or identify a specific dissimulative style. For example, with a personal injury evaluation, clinicians are more interested in assessing the presence or absence of posttraumatic stress disorder (PTSD) than possible motivations for malingering. The second level of relevance is to examine the dissimulation itself and what the specific characteristics and presentation reveal about the individual. Referral questions are divided between the two levels, with perhaps the majority emphasizing the first level of relevance.

As noted above, the relevance of dissimulation ranges widely with the degree of distortion and the referral question. The question underlying this analysis of clinical relevance is "if the dissimulation was true, what difference would it make with respect to intervention or disposition?" A psychotically depressed woman who feigns suicide ideation to ensure her hospitalization in a crowded public facility should be hospitalized irrespective of her malingering. Likewise, a job applicant who minimizes past episodes of anxiety is likely to be considered for the position regardless of past anxiety episodes. In such cases, the dissimulation may have only a minor influence on the clinical opinion and subsequent decision making. Each case of suspected dissimulation must be evaluated thoroughly, since the clinician cannot determine *prior* to his or her assessment what the potential relevance of malingering and defensiveness might be in an individual case. The issue of relevance must be raised following each assessment in assigning importance of the dissimulation to the overall evaluation of the patient.

Treatment Considerations

The majority of clinical assessments address issues of treatment recommendations and likely treatment outcomes. Little research exists on the relationship of specific styles of dissimulation to treatment response. Clinical interpretations based on the MMPI would suggest that a mild to moderate degree of defensiveness may be evidence of ego strength and positive treatment outcome (e.g., Marks, Seeman, & Heller, 1974). Paradoxically, some exaggeration of psychological impairment as measured by the F scale of the MMPI has been commonly labeled as a "cry for help" and a sign of increased motivation. Recent research would question this latter assumption with empirical evidence that F elevations are associated with poor treatment outcome (see Chapter 8). Despite these clinical interpretations, little is known regarding the relationship of malingering, defensiveness, or irrelevant responding to the (1) type of treatment that should be recommended and (2) likelihood of treatment compliance and favourable outcome. Certainly, patients with extreme presentations of dissimulation would appear to be poor treatment candidates. Individuals who are either categorically denying any psychological difficulties or those who unfalteringly malinger problems which do not exist would not appear, on an intuitive basis, to be amenable to treatment. Mild to moderate degrees of malingering and defensiveness present a more complicated picture. Certainly a common ground may exist with less severe dissimulation for treatment of "real" problems while trust and rapport are being established.

A difficult issue to establish is the patient's motivation for dissimulation and the relevance of this motivation for treatment recommendations. A parent in a child custody dispute may have a strong motivation to deny problems prior to the child custody hearing, but manifest strong motivation for treatment, if treatment is a condition of the custody. Similarly, an involuntary patient may be markedly defensive during the civil commitment proceedings, yet show at least some motivation to participate in treatment once the decision to hospitalize has been judicially determined.

Treatment compliance is an important element in the assessment of treatment recommendations for malingering and defensive individuals. By definition, dissimulators must be viewed as being at cross-purposes with their evaluators. Since dissimulation requires the deliberate distortion of self-reports, dissimulators' sincerity and motivation for treatment are brought into question. One possible strategy would be for the individual clinician to attempt to define a dissimulator's objectives and to assess to what extent the proposed treatment would assist the dissimulator in meeting these objectives.

The assessment of treatability is at best an imprecise process, which relies heavily on trial and error (see Rogers & Webster, 1987). No empirical studies have been found which specifically address the treatment response of dissimulators compared with nondissimulating psychiatric patients. Perhaps the most fruitful approach would be to attempt a contractual arrangement with a dissimulating patient for an explicit treatment intervention over a specified time period. In cases where treatment is deemed essential and nonoptional, enforced treatment would be strictly controlled by statutory requirements with a treatment outcome often limited to the reduction of imminent dangerousness. In these latter cases, the focus is more on the appropriate intervention with less attention paid to treatment compliance or outcome.

Nontreatment Considerations

The nontreatment disposition of psychiatric patients may constitute a substantial proportion of cases where dissimulation may be suspected. Lorei (1970) in a survey of V.A. hospitals found that the clinical interpretation of malingering was second only to dangerousness in importance when assessing the potential dischargeability of inpatients. Patients in preparation for discharge may manifest a strong desire to remain in the hospital or to receive a favorable community placement. Further, outpatients may wish to present themselves as sufficiently impaired to warrant certain benefits (e.g., insurance reimbursement and workmen's compensation) but not so impaired as to risk certain privileges (e.g., permanent loss of employment, hospitalization, or termination of parental rights) (Rogers & Cavanaugh, 1983). Vocational, school, and forensic assessments frequently include such nontreatment dispositions. Such cases are likely to be more adversarial in nature than those which involve treatment only.

The risks and potential benefits accrued from psychiatric/psychological assessment are often explicit and legally sanctioned. In nontreatment assessments, the clinician does not often have the luxury of a reassessment since frequently a binding determination must be made. As the potential risks and benefits increase, the likelihood of dissimulation should also increase.

Nontreatment dispositions typically require the clinician to examine a patient using a specific legal or administrative standard. This standard reflects decisions, often made by agencies, schools, or the courts, which may not be perceived by the patient as either beneficial or benevolent. The emphasis of such assessments is therefore less on the patient's deception and more on to what extent the patient meets the particular standard. Within a nontreatment context, the use of corroborative data become increasingly important in making the appropriate recommendations or dispositions since there is frequently no prior or ongoing professional relationship.

Motivational Considerations

A final issue in considering the clinical relevance of dissimulation is to understand its adaptive functions for the dissimulator. Although clinicians frequently view dissimulation as a negative and complicating factor in clinical assessment, this same behavior may be viewed as positive and adaptive by the dissimulator. Goals of dissimulation may include the maintenance of an individual's sense of autonomy, capacity to function, avoidance of painful circumstances, and avoidance or disengagement from a difficult or nonvoluntary process.

Such objectives, from the perspective of the dissimulator, may be viewed as attempts (successful or otherwise) to maintain a sense of worth or competency, and to minimize avoidable pain or coercion. For example, patients who resist involuntary hospitalization or mandatory treatment may be fighting, whether correctly or not, for their own right to self-determination. Individuals who deny disabling psychological disorders may be struggling to maintain their sense of competence either through work or the continued custody of their children. Other dissimulators, who have experienced physical and/or psychological injuries through the negligence of others, may exaggerate their impairment from their own perspective of justice, believing that no financial compensation can ever equal the losses which they have incurred. Finally, dissimulators may be motivated by an understandable desire to avoid painful or coercive circumstances which may be a factor in presentence evaluations or civil commitment.

A clinician's responsibility goes beyond the mere identification of dissimulators and extends to his or her understanding of their motivations for these deliberate distortions. Inquiry into the patients' perceived risks and benefits may be useful in understanding their motivations. In most cases, this motivation probably extends beyond tangible rewards and punishment of the immediate circumstances and is related to an individual's self-image.

Simply stated as an inquiry, "What would the different outcomes of this assessment mean to an individual's self-perception?" For example, the acknowledgment of a severe psychiatric disorder may well be devastating and unacceptable to a particular person's self-image of being strong and capable. Thus, the role motivation plays in dissimulation must be considered for each individual and addressed within a possibly adversarial context and in relationship to a specific referral question.

An informal review of clinical reports suggests that some clinicians attempt to go one step further and make statements regarding an individual's personality on the basis of his or her specific dissimulative style. Reports may describe dissimulating patients as manipulative, self-serving, dishonest, noncooperative and oppositional. Such inferences should never be made on the basis of malingering and defensiveness alone. As a rule, such attempts to link response styles with personality characteristics should be avoided since an underlying premise of such, often pejorative, interpretations is that only "bad" people dissimulate. It is far more appropriate to describe a patient's apparent motivation than to make unsupported inferences regarding character or personality.

Confrontation of Suspected Dissimulation

An important and perhaps essential component in the clinical determination of dissimulation is to offer the patient some feedback regarding his or her presentation. This process might well include a summary of the patient's presentation and the difficulties or problems that the clinician has in accepting the patient's self-report at face value. Feedback on the patient's response style requires sensitivity, tact, and timing from the clinician.

As a general principle, clinicians should be parsimonious in their feedback and confrontation of patients seen for evaluation. The goals of providing feedback may range from (1) informing the patient of the status of the evaluation, (2) asking the patient for assistance in clarifying incongruities, (3) eliciting more complete information, and (4) giving the patient an opportunity to change his or her self-report. Except under unusual circumstances, the purpose of such feedback/confrontation should not be to extract from the patient an "admission of dissimulation." The clinician should attempt to establish his or her conclusions prior to any discussion of dissimulation. Rather, the purpose is to give the patient an opportunity to clarify areas of ambiguity and, more importantly, to offer insight into possible motivation for the dissimulation. An additional goal, which may be occasionally realized, is for the patient to spontaneously provide a more accurate description of his or her psychological impairment. Such revisions of self-reports must, of course, be carefully scrutinized since they may represent simply another attempt at malingering or defensiveness.

Confrontation with and feedback to a defensive patient typically require the use of corroborative data. Naturally, the clinician should attempt to present his or her observations in a straightforward and nonperjorative manner. The following are examples of feedback and confrontation with a defensive patient:

1. "Although you are telling me that everything is going fine, when I hear about . . . (i.e., description of current problems), I am having some trouble understanding this."
2. "I know how much you want me to believe that you have your problems well under control, but when I see you . . . (i.e., clinical observations of the patient) I don't think this is the case."
3. "Life is not all black and white. Whenever someone tells me only the good side, I become interested in what is being left out. . . ."
4. "According to you, you are having no difficulty handling . . . (i.e., describe a specific problem), but according to . . . (i.e., a reliable informant) you are experiencing. . . ."

Malingering patients, unlike their defensive counterparts, are commonly either inconsistent or improbable in their clinical presentation. The clinician therefore has a wider range of probes in discussing dissimulation with malingerers. Representative probes include the following:

1. "Some of the problems you describe are rarely seen in psychiatric patients. I am worried that you might be trying to make things seem worse than they are."
2. "Earlier in the evaluation you told me . . . , now you are telling me . . . I am having trouble putting this together."
3. "Although you have told me about . . . (i.e., description of current problems), when I observed you, you have not appeared. . . ."
4. "I don't want to hurt your feelings, but I just don't think things are quite as bad as you tell me they are."
5. "According to you, you have . . . (i.e., current problems), but according to . . . (i.e., a reliable informant) you are. . . . Can you help me understand this?"

Irrelevant responders are, by definition, disengaged from the assessment process. This disengagement makes feedback or confrontation particularly difficult since the patient is uninvolved and emotionally distant from the clinician. The clinician must weigh the merits of direct confrontation with irrelevant responders, against the possibility that such confrontation may only further alienate the patient. Representative probes are listed below:

1. "I don't think we got off on the right foot. Can we start over again? Tell me in your words what you see as your problems."
2. "I don't think you're listening to what I have to say, and I know that you're not particularly pleased about being here. How can we make sure that this was not a waste of time for you?"
3. "I know you took these . . . (i.e., psychological tests) for me, but I don't think you paid much attention to how you answered them. What about . . . (i.e., specific test items), which you gave different answers to at different times?'"

As discussed above, the purpose of feedback and discussion is to provide a greater understanding of the patient's motivation. Experienced clinicians have found (e.g., C. R. Clark, personal communication, August, 1986), that matter-of-fact confrontation with respect for the patient's personal dignity and efforts at dissimulation often provides an avenue for further understanding of that patient. Not giving the patient an opportunity to address ambiguities and incongruities within the assessment process may well shortchange the evaluation itself.

Synthesis of Clinical Data

The clinician must integrate an array of clinical findings on the issue of dissimulation and discuss these findings in terms of both the referral question and clinical relevance. Such synthesis of dissimulation material requires the examination of the following factors: (1) consistency of psychological measures, (2) the absence of alternative explanations, (3) hybrid styles of dissimulation, and (4) reporting dissimulation. Each of these factors will be discussed individually.

Consistency of Measures

Given the fallibility of individual diagnostic methods in accurately identifying malingering and defensiveness, the degree of consistency among measures is crucial. If a clinician has ample data based on pencil and paper measures, clinical interviews, and corroborative sources regarding a patient's inconsistent or improbable presentation, then the determination of malingering, defensiveness, or irrelevant responding is a relatively straightforward matter. Unpublished data by Rogers and Dickens (1987) would suggest, however, that there may be marked discrepancies between results of psychological testing (e.g., the MMPI) and clinical interviews. They found approximately 9.4% of forensic patients had fake-bad MMPI profiles but only 3.2% of forensic cases were suspected of definite malingering in independent diagnostic interviews. What should the clinician do if the patient appears reliable on the basis of clinical and corroborative data and yet presents a malingered profile on the MMPI? At minimum, such inconsistencies reduce the degree of certainty in the diagnostic conclusions. Such inconsistencies will be discussed further within the examination of hybrid styles of dissimulation. The absence of such consistency, depending on the particular clinical presentation, may argue for the *unreliable* designation. Suffice it to say, that highly consistent results from different sources of clinical investigation are invaluable in making definite conclusions regarding a specific dissimulative style.

Absence of Alternative Explanations

Specific indicators of dissimulation can be ranked on the degree to which they may be open to alternative interpretations. For example, rare symptoms are, by definition, infrequently seen in the clinical population; the presence of several such symptoms, although perhaps indicative of malingering, does not preclude other interpretations. Table 16.4 summarizes, on an intuitive basis, specific clinical indicators of dissimulation by the likelihood of alternative explanations. Needless to say, the severity and dramatic presentation of symptoms is at least as important as the possibility of alternative explanations.

Table 16.4. Clinical Indicators of Dissimulation and the Hypothesized Likelihood of Alternative Explanations

Clinical Indicators	Chapter References
A. Moderate	
1. Severity of symptoms	5, 6, 14
2. Nonselective reporting of symptoms	4, 6, 8, 14
3. Sudden onset or resolution	3, 5, 6, 7, 14
4. Willingness to discuss symptoms	3, 4, 14
5. Overly dramatic presentation	2, 3, 4, 9, 14
6. Rare symptoms	2, 8, 11, 14
7. Overly specified symptoms	14
8. Admission of everyday problems	8, 14, 15
9. Unusual organic symptoms	4, 5, 10, 11
B. Low	
1. Improbable or absurd symptoms	2, 3, 4, 14
2. Obvious vs. subtle symptoms	3, 7, 8, 14
3. Unlikely symptom combinations	5, 10, 14
4. Contradictory symptoms	3, 8, 10, 14
5. Inconsistent clinical presentation	2, 3, 4, 5, 6, 7, 10, 11, 14
6. Random pattern of responses	8, 14
7. Improbable failure rate	5, 10, 12, 14
C. Nil	
1. Symptom validity procedure	10

The clinical indicators included in Table 16.4 are organized into moderate, low, and nil likelihood that such symptoms occur without dissimulation in clinical populations. Those indicators subsumed under the *moderate* category may also be seen occasionally in honest, nondissimulating patients. Indicators included within the *low* category have a very small probability of being observed, except as isolated examples, within clinical populations. The point of this discussion is, however, not simply to weigh the likelihood of alternative explanations but to consider this as one of many factors in the establishment of specific styles of dissimulation. Finally, symptom validity testing, employing a forced-choice technique in examining a purported deficit, is not open to alternative explanations. A patient, falling below conservatively defined probability levels, must have recognized the correct answer in order to achieve such an improbable failure rate.

Hybrid Styles of Dissimulation

An important task in the clinical determination of dissimulation is whether a patient presenting with a mixed response style should be considered as a hybrid style or an ambiguous clinical presentation. The clinician must be careful not to overinterpret contradictory findings, particularly where the indicators are gathered from distinct sources of clinical data. Two conditions under which diagnostic conclusions regarding hybrid styles may be justified are (1) on circumscribed issues and (2) within specified time periods. An example of circumscribed issues would be the assessment of a suspected child molester who appeared open and honest in the description of his day-to-day functioning with the notable exception of any discussion of pedophilia or other paraphilias. Depending on the quality of the clinical data, the clinician might well conclude that the patient has an honest/defensive response style and provide a thorough description of what is meant by this term.

The second condition would relate to specific periods. Again borrowing from forensic assessments, in occasional personal-injury evaluations, the patient is seen as defensive regarding his or her functioning prior to the injury (i.e., no problems at all) and malingering following the injury. Such clinical presentation would be characterized as a defensive/malingering response style requiring careful explanation to the referral source.

The general guideline for addressing such clinical ambiguities is where any substantial doubt exists, yet motivation is unclear, the case should be labeled *unreliable*. Further, when the clinician is convinced that the patient is deliberately distorting his or her self-report if not clearly malingering, defensive, or irrelevant, the clinician may characterize as *dissimulation*. Hybrid response styles should be reserved for cases where the clinical data are internally consistent and are understandable either with respect to circumscribed issues or specific periods.

Reporting Dissimulation

Chapter 1 provides three gradations of malingering and defensiveness: mild, moderate, and severe. In synthesizing the clinical data, the clinician should attempt to describe the patient's malingering or defensiveness in terms of its severity. Such terms should be reserved for assessment cases where the distortions consistently meet these criteria. Table 16.5 presents the three gradations of malingering and defensiveness with sample descriptions for their inclusion in clinical reports.

The clinician must decide, for the purposes of synthesizing clinical data into a relevant report, what observations of the patient's response style should be included. As noted earlier, the clinical relevance of a patient's dissimulative style must be examined with reference to the referral question. With certain referral questions, discussion of the response style may have little direct bearing on the referral question, and therefore the clinician would have the option of reporting or withholding his or her clinical observations. In the majority of cases, however, the patient's dissimulative style is relevant to the referral question, diagnosis, and capacity to form a therapeutic relationship. In such cases, the clinician should describe the patient's response style including its severity. Although clinicians are encouraged to use the terms employed throughout this book, such terms are in no way a substitution for a thorough description of the patient's response style and its relevance to the assessment. The clinician must address the patient's deliberateness, type of distortion, and degree of distortion. In supporting his or her diagnostic conclusions, the clinician should provide specific examples, preferably employing direct quotes from the patient. In summary, the clinical report should include a detailed description of how the patient is responding, and how this response style relates to both diagnostic issues and the referral question.

Conclusion

The strength of clinical assessment in the evaluation of malingering and defensiveness remains chiefly in the use of well-validated individual measures. The synthesis of these measures is, with few exceptions, more an art of clinical judgment than an empirically based process. It may well be, as noted in other diagnostic cases (Sechrest, 1963), that the accuracy of clinical judgment does not improve incrementally with the number of measures employed. However, use of multivariate statistics certainly merit our attention since they optimize accurate classification; the use, for example, of a discriminant function reduces redundant and potentially irrelevant data in the clinical determination of malingering and defensiveness.

Table 16.5. Severity of Dissimulation: A Sampling of Descriptive Statements

---

A. Mild dissimulation (malingering or defensiveness)
   1. Although minor distortions were observed in the patient's presentation, these are expected, given the context of the evaluation.
   2. Although the patient manifested a slight tendency to minimize (or amplify) his or her self-report, no major distortions were observed.
   3. Although some variations were noted in the patient's self-report, these had no (or little) bearing on diagnosis and disposition.

B. Moderate malingering
   1. Clinical findings clearly indicate that the patient was exaggerating (and/or fabricating) his or her psychological impairment. This was observed in . . . (descriptive examples).
   2. The patient has fabricated several important symptoms including . . . (descriptive examples), these symptoms have direct bearing on the patient's diagnosis and disposition.
   3. The patient has evidenced a moderate degree of malingering as observed in . . . (descriptive examples). This attempt to manipulate the evaluation raises some concern about motivation for treatment.
   4. The patient's self-report appears to be exaggerated (and/or fabricated) with . . . (descriptive examples). Difficulty in assessing the patient's motivation leaves unanswered what is his or her intended goal; the unresolved diagnosis is between factitious disorder and malingering.

C. Severe malingering
   1. The patient is attempting to present himself or herself as severely disturbed by fabricating many symptoms including . . . (descriptive examples).
   2. The patient has evidenced severe malingering by presenting . . . (strategies of malingering, e.g., "rare and improbable symptoms, uncorroborated by clinical observation"). Most notable examples of fabrication are . . . (descriptive examples).

D. Moderate defensiveness
   1. Clinical findings clearly indicate that the patient was minimizing (and/or denying) his or her psychological impairment. The defensiveness was observed in . . . (descriptive examples).
   2. The patient has denied several important symptoms including . . . (descriptive examples); these denied symptoms have direct bearing on the patient's diagnosis and disposition.
   3. The patient has evidenced a moderate degree of defensiveness as observed in . . . (descriptive examples). Such defensiveness is fairly common in patients being assessed for treatment.

E. Severe defensiveness
   1. The patient is attempting to present himself or herself as well adjusted by denying many observed symptoms including . . . (descriptive examples).
   2. The patient has evidenced severe defensiveness by presenting . . . (strategies of defensiveness, e.g., "denial of everyday problems, endorsement of overly positive attributes, and denial of psychological impairment despite overwhelming clinical data to the contrary"). Most notable examples are . . . (descriptive examples).
   3. The patient's self-report includes the denial of any psychiatric difficulties, despite convincing evidence of . . . (DSM-III diagnosis). This severe defensiveness raises some concern about motivation for treatment.

A review of clinical methods by the three criteria of susceptibility, identification, and interpretability delineates clearly the strengths and limitations in our current knowledge of dissimulation. Perhaps the weakest link of this decision process is in establishing the intention and motivation of the patient. As noted in Chapter 2, the degree of consciousness and deliberateness can only be clearly understood when presented in a consistent and unambiguous manner. In less obvious cases, the clinician is compelled to describe the suspected dissimulation and discuss openly the alternative diagnoses.

In summary, clinicians are asked to employ the same degree of thoroughness in the assessment of malingering and defensiveness as they would in establishing any other diagnosis. Clinical reports should include not only the diagnostic conclusions regarding the patient's response style, but also a description of the observed dissimulating strategies with specific examples, preferably quotes, from the patient. Unsupported conclusions regarding dissimulation represent substandard practice, given the importance of such assessments to the diagnosis and disposition of psychiatric patients.

17

Researching Dissimulation

RICHARD ROGERS

A bridgeable division exists between clinical practice and applied research in the assessment of dissimulation. The vast majority of published research studies were conducted on normal college samples with the general goal of establishing group differences between those simulating a deceptive response style and those responding under honest instructions. Many important clinical issues are largely neglected. These include (1) differentiating between malingerers and severely disturbed psychiatric patients with atypical presentations, (2) developing correction formulas (e.g., K-correction factor of the MMPI) for different styles of dissimulation, and (3) developing and validating standardized measures for gradations of dissimulation. Clinicians have been left, until recently, with a choice of either clinically relevant but methodologically questionable case studies or questionably relevant but methodologically sound psychometric and social-psychological studies. A primary goal of this chapter is to review the current status of dissimulation research and to offer constructive suggestions for studies which are both clinically relevant and methodologically sound.

An important element in the integration of clinical practice and applied research is offering researchers an opportunity to grapple with the clinical issues facing practitioners. Often the research questions posed by the academic community, although of intrinsic interest, do not adequately address the realities of clinical practice (i.e., they do not always have external validity[1]). Further, there is little need for research to demonstrate, yet again, what measures are susceptible to malingering and defensiveness. As I observed (Rogers, 1984b) in my review of dissimulation studies, there are *no* psychological measures which are not fakeable. Studies should instead be focused on constructive approaches to the assessment of dissimulation under conditions similar to those faced by clinicians. By outlining these

Richard Rogers, Metropolitan Toronto Forensic Service (METFORS), Clarke Institute of Psychiatry, and University of Toronto, Toronto, Ontario, Canada.

1. This statement does not deny the importance of internal validity to clinical research (see Mook, 1983). Rather, it affirms the essential requirement of external validity or generalizability in applying research findings to clinical decisions.

relevant clinical issues, an invitation is extended for more applied research to solidify the foundation of our knowledge for the assessment of malingering and deception.

Elements of Dissimulation Research

Despite the rich diversity of research methodology and objectives in the study of dissimulation, several core elements can be found in most research. Such elements include instructions, incentives, levels of participation, standardization of measures, and debriefing. The emphasis of this section will be on the commonalities among research methods. Dissimilarities will be subsequently addressed in the individual examination of four basic research designs.

Instructions

Research on dissimulation, with the notable exception of case studies, relies heavily on the use of instructions to create distinct experimental conditions. In spite of this importance, instructions, as described in many research articles, are brief and nonspecific. Subjects may be simply asked to appear "mentally ill" or "emotionally upset." How these instructions are interpreted or considered seriously remains an unanswered empirical question. Based on research in progress (Rogers, Gillis, & Dickens, 1987), nearly 50% of forensic inpatients studied could not remember the instructions or did not follow them in a simple simulation design for the assessment of malingering. This finding speaks to the necessity of pretesting experimental instructions to test their clarity and effect on the subjects. It is speculated that explaining to subjects the importance of their compliance may increase the level of their actual involvement in the study. Dissimulation, perhaps more than other clinical topics, is a study of intentional distortions. Minimal or lip-service compliance with the experimental instructions is likely to produce spurious results, with the serious consequence that the experimenter may not be aware of the invalidity of his or her conclusions.

Instructions for dissimulation research must also take into account that subjects present a *believable* disorder or condition. Therefore, instructions to appear "as mentally ill as you can" may lead to skewed results, since subjects may make no attempt to appear credible. This potential difficulty may be addressed either directly through instructions to create a believable disorder, or indirectly through the creation of a scenario (see, for example, Grow, McVaugh, & Eno, 1980; Rice, Arnold, & Tate, 1983) where subjects realize the importance of not over-dramatizing their impairment (e.g., the experimental goal is to be hospitalized but not appear so disorganized as to require long-term treatment or ECT).

Incentives

Most research on dissimulation offers little or no incentive for successful deception. College students, for example, are typically offered course credit simply for participation in faculty research. No differential rewards exist, however, for the level of performance or the successfulness of the dissimulation. Subjects under these conditions probably bear little resemblance to dissimulators found in clinical practice (see Rogers, 1987).

Research studies should strive to create experimental conditions analogous to those found in psychiatric settings (Garfield, 1978). For example, college students could be given adequate preparation time to attempt to appear as moderately impaired schizophrenics with credit given to those who successfully complete preestablished criteria. In addition, investigators could also take advantage of naturally occurring experiments. For example, there is likely to be an increased incidence of malingering in personal-injury and workmen compensation cases, which offer large financial incentives to those who are successful (Gallucci, 1984). Conversely, job applicant evaluations and child custody assessments are likely to provide intrinsic incentives for the denial or minimization of psychological impairment (for example, see Baker, 1967; Kirchner, 1961).

Most naturally occurring experiments are a combination of tangible and social rewards. For example, rewards for a dissimulator in a personal-injury case may include both a financial settlement as well as social rewards (i.e., on one hand, gaining emotional support for having a bona fide disorder, while, on the other hand, avoiding the disapprobation of being labeled a "faker"). Research studies with normal populations might attempt to approximate these clinical conditions by offering social as well as financial rewards. For example, with subjects' prior approval, a list of "bungling dissimulators" might be published in the university newspaper (see Patrick & Iacono, 1986 and Chapter 12). An alternative would be to ask dissimulating subjects to present themselves to actual clinical settings where the likelihood of being found out would carry greater negative social consequences. Both alternatives have serious ethical concerns which must necessarily be addressed prior to implementing these designs.

A final consideration is what effect the amount of the incentive has on the subjects' performance. In cases where the rewards are great (e.g., personal-injury, child custody, and insanity cases), it is unlikely that experimenters can ever approximate the magnitude of these incentives in their research. Despite this limitation, it is quite possible that nominal rewards including negative reinforcement may offer sufficient motivation for sincere attempts at dissimulation. Conversely, research which depends entirely on goodwill of the subjects as the sole motivation for effective dissimulation, are very limited in their generalizability to clinical practice (see Fisher & Silverstein, 1969, as a probable example of noncompliance with simulation instructions).

Level of Participation

Current research on dissimulation is often limited in its clinical usefulness by the low levels of subjects' participation found in these studies. One reason is the severe constraints on the time availability of subjects, since the majority of studies employ university students, who are typically limited in their participation to an hour or less. In addition, subjects are rarely given any preparation time or opportunities to plan their strategy of deception. In an effort to preserve experimental rigor, the depth and duration of any interaction is strictly controlled. Similarly, clinicians and lay judges in dissimulation studies are often cast into the roles of passive observers. Indeed, such research methodology does not allow the study of either interactions or of clinicians' own decision processes in evaluating the malingering or defensiveness of a particular patient (Rogers, 1987).

Any research study, through its standardized procedures and operationalized criteria, will place some limits on the participation of both subjects and evaluators. Research designs could be devised, however, which would allow for much higher levels of participation without compromising the methodology. One alternative, mentioned briefly above, is to institute pseudonaturalistic studies, where subjects present themselves in actual diagnostic settings. Although this design is not without methodological problems (Spitzer, 1974) and ethical concerns, certainly the research by Rosenhan (1973) attested to the usefulness of this technique in assessing clinicians' ability to identify malingerers. A second alternative would be the use of highly trained confederates who could offer relatively standardized presentations while being assessed by the clinicians being studied. In this design, the confederates would be thoroughly prepared regarding their personal and psychiatric history and current psychological problems; this approach would allow the participating clinicians to employ an array of clinical skills in the assessment of dissimulation. A variation of this second alternative would be the use of videotaped assessments conducted by experienced clinicians and representing a range of diagnostic styles and dissimulating patients (Resnick, 1987). These videotapes would then be shown to samples of clinicians (1) to test their overall ability to identify dissimulators and (2) to determine which diagnostic style is most effective at making such an assessment.

Standardization of Measures

Dissimulation research is often limited by the availability and customary use of standardized measures. Even when such measures exist, as with projective techniques, there is often considerable variation in their application (see, for example, Wade & Baker, 1977). In other areas, as clinical interviews, drug-assisted interviews, and polygraphy, there has been little research on systematically measuring the patients' and malingerers' responses to these techniques. In addition, a new challenge would be to develop standardized measures focused specifically at styles and gradations of dissimulation. At present, with few notable exceptions (e.g., the M test: Beaber, Marston, Michelli, & Mills, 1985), clinically employed measures were not constructed for the assessment of dissimulation or have focused primarily on unspecified deception (e.g., polygraphy).

Debriefing

Debriefing is rarely employed in dissimulation research. This element of research serves two important purposes: (1) as a manipulation check to measure subjects' understanding and compliance with instructions and (2) as a method to study various strategies of dissimulation. Comprehension and compliance with instructions, as noted above, is highly variable and should be assessed in all dissimulation research (Rogers, 1986b). In addition, clinicians often assume or infer the types of dissimulative strategies employed by subjects. A valuable goal of debriefing would be to ask subjects to describe their various strategies and to assess the frequency of specific strategies and their effectiveness against clinicians. Such data are particularly useful in the further development of standardized measures for the assessment of dissimulation.

Current Research Models

Dissimulation research can be divided into four broad categories: case study, psychometric, social-psychological, and psychophysiological. Two important factors in reviewing these research models are *clinical relevance* and *experimental rigor* (see Meehl, 1971, for a thoughtful discussion of differences in clinical vs. research-derived "knowledge"). In certain respects, these important factors are inversely related so that it is nearly impossible to achieve high levels of clinical relevance and experimental rigor within the same study (Konecni & Ebbeson, 1979; Rogers, Dolmetsch, Wasyliw, & Cavanaugh, 1982, are interesting examples of research potential to combine applied psychology questions with laboratory methods). Despite this trade-off component of applied research, most research on dissimulation could be improved on one or both of these areas. Thus, an objective of this section is to review current research models and to offer recommendations with respect to both clinical relevance and experimental rigor.

Case Study Approaches

Case study research in psychiatry and clinical psychology has fallen into disfavor over the last several decades. Despite a vigorous debate over the merits of idiographic and nomothetic research models (e.g., Dukes, 1965; Eysenck, 1954; Marceil, 1977), a cursory review of clinical journals would suggest a much greater emphasis on nomothetic research than on single case descriptions. Insistent demands for greater experimental rigor (e.g., Campbell & Stanley, 1966) and the decreasing popularity of psychoanalytical thought are largely responsible for this change. Regardless of its diminished role in clinical research, the real value of case study approaches is in providing a rich panoply of clinical observations unfettered by research protocols (Scriven, 1976). Such detailed clinical observations on a highly relevant topic offer two decided advantages over other research models. First, case studies offer a variety of relevant hypotheses to be tested by more rigorous designs (Cook, Levitou, & Shadish, 1985). Second, case studies represent the only practical design in the study of rare syndromes as, for example, Munchausen syndrome.

Case study approaches to dissimulation should therefore be encouraged in order to further these relevant goals. For example, the diagnosis of Munchausen syndrome was originally stimulated through a series of case studies initiated by Asher (1951), which eventually led to its current diagnostic status (Stern, 1980). A prime example of how a single case study may stimulate further applied research and improvements in clinical practice is observed in the development of the symptom validity testing. Pankratz, Fausti, and Peed (1975) devised this approach to assess the purported loss of hearing in a 27-year-old man. Additional research based on this single case study has led to a highly useful technique in detecting individuals feigning intellectual and neuropsychological deficits (Pankratz, 1979; see also Chapter 10).

Case study approaches to dissimulation have focused almost exclusively on malingering. Early case studies (e.g., Davidson, 1949; Ossipov, 1944) as well as more recent work (Hay, 1983; Ritson & Forrest, 1970; Sadow & Suslick, 1961; Wachskress, Berenberg, & Jacobson, 1953) have a severe methodological limitation in that they lack any independent criterion for establishing dissimulation. In other words, clinicians who evaluate these cases employ their observations of dissimulating patients to make the diagnosis. They subsequently reverse the process in providing detailed observations of the same patients' malingering. This tautological exercise could be easily modified by employing clinical staff blind to the diagnostic issues regarding dissimulation to make standardized observations of the cases. Similarly, the degree of confidence in the diagnosis of malingering or defensiveness could be improved if it were based on two independent evaluations. The two procedures combined would offer some assurance that (1) the dissimulation was reliably established, and (2) the clinical observations were not confounded by interviewer bias.

A second methodological issue involves the sampling of potential dissimulators. Available case studies typically employ psychiatric inpatients suspected of malingering. Although these samples are, by necessity, nonrandom, it is possible that nonmalingering comparison groups could be employed with patients matched for sociodemographic background and psychiatric history. The advantages of such comparison groups would be to assess, on a preliminary basis, whether the suspected dissimulators' presentation differed significantly from psychiatric patients with atypical presentations (e.g., Hay, 1983). In addition, other samples of suspected dissimulators, including outpatients and forensic patients, could also be studied to increase the subject pool and improve generalizability. These and other methodological issues are summarized in Table 17.1.

Two additional methodological issues are worthy of comment. First, case studies could be improved by further standardizing the assessment procedures. In addition to reporting psychological test results, such studies might also include structured diagnostic interviews and standardized psychiatric histories, such as the Schedule of Affective Disorders and Schizophrenia (SADS) and the Structured Clinical Interview for DSM-III (SCID). Such data, along with additional corroborative information, would allow for a more systematic investigation of the suspected dissimulation. The second methodological issue would be the study of those who admit to sexual deviance (see Chapter 15). Examining the case studies, many individuals suspected of malingering will acknowledge their dissimulation when confronted with the incongruity of their clinical presentation. These cases, particularly from a case study approach, provide a valuable resource for understanding dissimulators' motivation and strategies. Awareness of these

Table 17.1. Case Study Approaches to Dissimulation

Methodological issues	Research practices	
	Current	Proposed
1. Sampling	Nonrandom psychiatric in-patients suspected of malingering	In addition, outpatients and forensic patients
2. Comparison groups	Not employed	Matched comparison groups should be employed
3. Independent criterion	Rarely employed	Evaluators blind to the suspected response style
4. Standardized measures	Psychological testing	In addition, structured interviews and histories
5. Corroborative data	Variable	Independent observations of individuals not involved in the assessment
6. Study of admitters	Clinical presentation	In addition, study their strategies for dissimulation

motivations and strategies is useful both in increasing our understanding of such individuals and in the development of sophisticated detection methods.

Psychometric Research

Psychometric research on dissimulation has a distinct advantage over other designs in its use of standardized psychological measures. This degree of standardization allows for a ready comparison of individuals under different experimental conditions. Because of this convenience, the majority of dissimulation studies employ a simulation design with nonpsychiatric subjects (Rogers, 1987). Unfortunately, the clinical relevance of the bulk of these studies is limited since the sampling procedures, experimental instructions, and incentives for dissimulation do not correspond with clinical practice in mental health settings. Recommendations will be made in the following paragraphs on how clinical relevance could be improved without appreciably eroding experimental rigor.

Psychometric studies have proven the most effective within the domain of dissimulation research for establishing reliable clinical indicators. Particularly with respect to the MMPI, studies have convincingly demonstrated reliable clinical indicators for malingering, defensiveness, and irrelevant responding. This point should not be overlooked: The most effective discriminators of specific dissimulative styles have been the MMPI and similar objective personality measures. This general conclusion would suggest the potential value of applying similar clinical indicators, as those found in objective personality measures to other forms of clinical practice. For example, diagnostic interviewing might well be enhanced through the systematic inclusion of diagnostic questions based on psychometric findings, as in the case with the SIRS.

A review of psychometric approaches to dissimulation in Chapters 8, 9, and 10 underscores the diversity of this research and the range of clinical usefulness of these approaches. Chapter 9 on projective techniques has demonstrated convincingly (1) the fakability of such techniques and (2) the relative absence of any *systematic* method for the accurate identification of dissimulation. In addition, the large majority of these studies address malingering with little or no examination of defensiveness or irrelevant responding. Intellectual and neuropsychological testing, although not vulnerable to defensiveness, can easily be faked. With respect to neuropsychological assessment, available research suggests that single cutting scores may be of limited clinical usefulness in identifying dissimulators. In contrast, studies employing multivariate statistics appear effective at identifying distinctive patterns of responses associated with dissimulation. Further, research on objective personality measures, beyond studies of the MMPI and California Psychological Inventory (CPI), often devote little attention to specific styles of dissimulation. A thorough review of psychological measures by Rogers

Table 17.2. Psychometric Approaches to Dissimulation

Methodological issues	Research practices	
	Current	Proposed
1. Sampling	Random, usually nonpsychiatric subjects	In addition, psychiatric subjects and those suspected of dissimulation
2. Control groups	Usually normal individuals	In addition, psychiatric groups
3. Decision rules	Cutting scores for the MMPI, rare for other measures	Discriminant functions and/or cutting scores for all measures
4. Subjects' compliance	Rarely have follow-up	Collect data on subjects' compliance
5. Simulation instructions	Often general and vague	Make specific, emphasize a "believable" response style
6. Subjects' motivation	Usually no incentives to succeed	Incentives for successful dissimulation
7. Stability of dissimulation	Not assessed	Assess across time intervals and situations

(1984b) clarified the need for additional research on most psychometric measures.

Methodological improvements in psychometric research focus primarily on improving its clinical relevance. Current sampling techniques involve random samples of usually nonpsychiatric subjects in both experimental and control groups. This design could be augmented by the inclusion of psychiatric patients and those suspected of dissimulation. This modification would allow dissimulation research to address two important considerations: (1) How effectively can psychiatric subjects dissimulate? and (2) can dissimulators be differentiated from both normal individuals and psychiatric subjects? These and additional methodological issues are summarized in Table 17.2.

The majority of psychometric studies put forth little effort to approximate conditions experienced by potential dissimulators in clinical settings.[2] First and foremost, subjects asked to dissimulate should be given some incentive (financial or otherwise) for successful deception. As commonly occurs in studies of college samples, incentives are only given for participation (i.e., course credit) but with no rewards for effective dissimulation. This procedure is diametrically opposite to dissimulators in clinical practice whose behavior is usually motivated *only* by a real or perceived gain. Further, simulation instructions should be precise with an emphasis on a

2. This is not true, however, of other applied settings, such as educational placement (e.g., Baker, 1967) or employment selection (e.g., Kirchner, 1961).

believable response style. Studies (e.g., Hoffman, 1968; Posey & Hess, 1984) often provide only vague instructions with no consideration of its credibility. Finally, researchers must study subjects' compliance with instructions as a manipulation check (e.g., Gudjonsson, 1981). Particularly with psychiatric populations, no assumptions can be made regarding subjects' compliance with dissimulation instructions.

Other modifications would include testing the stability of measures with respect to dissimulation. For example, it is unclear how much variability should be expected with repeat administrations of psychometric measures. Clinicians may assume rightly or wrongly that variations in responses are indicative of dissimulation. For example, Moses, Golden, Wilkening, McKay, and Ariel (1983) recommended repeat administrations of the Luria–Nebraska in the assessment of malingering; without test–retest reliability estimates on nonmalingering subjects, clinicians are severely hampered in their interpretation of inconsistent results. As in the case of the MMPI, indicators of dissimulation must be standardized (i.e., use of cutting scores), with the probability of correct classification known. Development of discriminant functions and other multivariate techniques will be necessary for most effective discriminations (see, for example, Goebel, 1983).

A vital issue in the psychometric assessment of dissimulation is the development of correction formulas. McKinley, Hathaway, and Meehl (1948) developed for the MMPI, a "K-correction" formula to approximate the degree of impairment, taking into account the patient's degree of defensiveness. Extensive research with the MMPI is also needed to study, under simulation instructions, an "F-correction" to correct for psychiatric patients attempting to malinger. Such an approach would represent a substantial improvement over current practice, which can only conclude that the profile is invalid. A point worthy of reemphasis is that psychometric measures are, without exception, susceptible to faking. Additional studies have demonstrated that many measures have developed clinical indicators for the reliable identification of dissimulation (Rogers, 1984b, for a review). The unanswered question remains, "how impaired are dissimulators?" The development of correction formulas for both defensiveness and malingering is the only logical alternative for assessing patients in spite of their dissimulation.

Social-Psychological Studies

Social-psychological research on deception is a prime example of solid experimental rigor which too frequently has little clinical relevance. Unlike other dissimulation research, the majority of social-psychological studies follow accepted experimental designs with respect to sampling, procedures, and statistical analysis. Its most obvious shortcoming, from the perspective of assessing dissimulation, is in not asking clinically relevant research questions. For example, practitioners in clinical practice are interested in defining specific styles of dissimulation among clinical samples. In contrast, current social-psychological studies have addressed the ability of nonprofessionals, who in the role of passive observers, attempt to identify global deception and dishonesty (e.g., Littlepage & Pineault, 1978; Maier & Thurber, 1968; Miller et al., 1981).

The clinical relevance of social-psychological research could be greatly improved without affecting its experimental rigor. The current practice of using only normal subjects could be augmented with both psychiatric patients and individuals trained in dissimulation. This modification would allow researchers to address more closely the applicability of research findings to clinical settings. Similarly, studies would be enhanced by the use of mental health professionals as evaluators in order to address what effect, if any, professional training has on the detection of dissimulation. These and other methodological issues are summarized in Table 17.3.

An important modification in social-psychological research would be the study of specific forms of dissimulation, namely, malingering and defensiveness. Unspecified deception has, at best, only limited relevance to the clinical assessment of psychiatric patients. This methodology could, however, be applied in investigating clinically relevant constructs of malingering and defensiveness. Research designs could be further improved by attempting to study gradations of dissimulation on verbal and nonverbal variables. In addition, social-psychological methodology, when applied to clinical practice, should have as its goal the development of explicit decision rules which may be consistently applied in classifying dissimulative response styles.

Table 17.3. Social-Psychological Studies of Deception

Methodological issues	Research practices	
	Current	Proposed
1. Sampling—confederates	Normal subjects	In addition, psychiatric patients
2. Sampling—observers	Random; nonprofessionals	In addition, mental health professionals
3. Comparison groups	Normal subjects	In addition, psychiatric patients and subjects trained in dissimulation
4. Criterion studied	Unspecified deception	Specific styles of dissimulation
5. Decision rules	Not employed	Cutting scores for classifying response styles
6. Level of participation	Brief periods; passive observers	Extensive periods; some studies allowing interactions
7. Motivation	Variable for confederates and subjects	Offer incentives for both deception and detection

Other proposed modifications in social-psychological research would focus on the same goal of improving clinical relevance. At present, evaluators are limited to brief periods of passive observation (Rogers, 1984b). In contrast, clinical assessment, is typically based on extensive observation with an opportunity for interactions. Extensive or multiple observation periods would correspond to actual clinical practice. Further, the motivation of confederates and subjects may play a determinative role in whether or not deception is detected. For example, DePaulo and her associates (DePaulo, Lanier, & Davis, 1983; DePaulo, Stone, & Lassiter, 1984) found that subjects' motivation to deceive was an important factor in nonprofessionals' judgments regarding honesty/deception. She concluded that highly-motivated subjects were more successful at concealing their dishonesty and were less likely to be detected than their poorly motivated counterparts. Thus, the degree of motivation must be considered in applying social-psychological studies to the clinical assessment of dissimulation.

Psychophysiological Approaches to Dissimulation

Psychophysiological measures of dissimulation currently include polygraphy, drug-assisted interviews, and plethysmography. Of these three techniques, only plethysmography has achieved a reasonable degree of clinical relevance and experimental rigor. In contrast, Rogers (1987) found that the bulk of research on polygraph techniques and drug-assisted interviews suffers from both questionable experimental design and limited clinical relevance. As a general comment, all three methods generally lack studies of reliability and consistency. For example, research is needed on all three techniques regarding the stability of measures employing a test–retest paradigm. In addition, few studies exist which examine the interrater reliability of these measures and the extent to which clinicians would achieve the same findings using similar procedures. The following paragraphs will examine each method with respect to its current research status.

The most controversial and widely used technique in the psychophysiological study of dissimulation is the polygraph. Opinions regarding the scientific merit of polygraph research are sharply divided into two camps: those who affirm (i.e., the Raskin school; Raskin, Barland, & Podlesny, 1977) and those who strongly criticize (i.e., the Lykken school; Lykken, 1981) its validity. As noted in Chapter 12, the polygraph is not a single standardized measure but three separate major techniques with countless variations in administration. Most current research relies heavily on general physiological arousal, with the overarching hypothesis that greater arousal is associated with deception (Bartol, 1983). Given both the complexity of physiological responses and advances in the computerization of polygraph records (Raskin, 1986a), a great potential exists for the development of more specific hypotheses regarding differentiating patterns of physiological responses. Such research would allow for the development of more sophisticated theoretical constructs for distinguishing deception from other types of stress reactions.

A major weakness of polygraph research is the absence of an independent criterion for establishing deception. Most polygraphy studies rely on the examiner who administers the polygraph to extract a confession, which is then used to validate the efficacy of that procedure (Rogers, 1987). Such nonindependence unnecessarily confounds research findings on polygraph techniques.

The inclusion of drug-assisted interviews under the rubric of psychophysiological measures is debatable. Despite the administration of a barbiturate, most research on drug-assisted interviews makes little attempt to measure physiological responses (e.g., Dysken, Kooser, Haraszti, & Davis, 1979; Hain, Smith, & Stevenson, 1966). Physical symptoms such as nystagmus and decreased respiration, are only observed on a clinical basis for their presence or absence. A viable alternative would be to record systematically changes in respiration, blood pressure, and skin conductance. Such an approach would allow researchers to establish more precisely the degree of sedation experienced by subjects. Drug-assisted research could standardize the degree of sedation as opposed to the current practice of standardizing the dosage at a conservative level. A second advantage would be an attempt to establish psychophysiological differences for individuals attempting to dissimulate during the drug-assisted interview compared with those who do not. Such an approach would represent a hybrid model, combining drug-assisted interviews with polygraphic methods.

Available research on drug-assisted interviews has focused primarily on the use of barbiturates to facilitate catharsis and the expression of repressed memories in treatment cases (Dysken, Chang, Casper, & Davis, 1979). Further studies are essential, both under simulation conditions and with suspected dissimulators, to examine the usefulness of this approach with malingering and defensive individuals. Without such work, the scientific basis of drug-assisted interviews in the identification of dissimulation cannot be established.

Plethysmographic approaches to defensiveness in sex offenders has been extensively researched. Studies have demonstrated that a high proportion of paraphilic patients consciously minimize their aberrant sexual interests and activities (Abel, Rouleau, Cunningham-Rathner, 1986; see Chapter 15). Phallometric procedures have been useful in identifying comparative arousal patterns to a variety of erotic and aggressive stimuli. The relationship of these arousal patterns to subsequent sexual behavior requires, however, further investigation. It is unclear, for example, whether individuals exist in the normal population who have never engaged in deviant sexual behavior, regardless of any anomalous phallometric results or unusual sexual interests they might have. More extensive work on nonreferred populations may be useful in establishing this relationship.

A second area of research interest concerns the extent to which individuals can control or manipulate their sexual arousal patterns. Research has suggested (e.g., Wydra, Marshall, Earls, & Barbaree, 1983) that countermeasures (i.e., attempts to suppress or modify arousal) are effective under stimulus conditions. A further avenue of research would be to test whether individuals could produce sexual responses that are comparatively more aberrant. Such research would be relevant for those occasional cases where individuals may be attempting to malinger a paraphilia which does not exist.

Hybrid research on establishing deviant arousal patterns might include a combination of phallometrics with the administration of a barbiturate or the use of a polygraph. Such approaches might increase the identification of defensive sex offenders either through decreasing the effectiveness of countermeasures or through the use of additional psychological measures.

Psychophysiological studies of dissimulation could be improved through the specific examination of malingering and defensiveness in psychiatric populations. It is unknown, for example, whether overtly psychotic individuals manifest psychophysiological differences based solely on their psychological impairment (see, e.g., Lynch & Bradford, 1980). Additional methodological issues are summarized in Table 17.4 for improving psychophysiological research. The adoption of explicit decision rules for the classi-

Table 17.4. Psychophysiological Approaches to Dissimulation

Methodological issues	Research practices	
	Current	Proposed
1. Sampling	Normal individuals and suspected offenders	In addition, psychiatric samples
2. Comparison groups	Rarely used in polygraphy	Compare groups across specific measures
3. Independent criterion	Use of confessions	Criteria independent of assessors
4. Specific criterion	Usually unspecified deception	Specific styles of dissimulation
5. Decision rules	Variable	Cutting scores for classifying response styles
6. Standardized procedures	Typically in drug-assisted interviews; not in polygraphy	Standardize all phases of the study
7. Stability of dissimulation	Not assessed	Assess across time intervals and situations

fication of dissimulators would be most useful, particularly in polygraph and drug-assisted interviews. As with all dissimulation research, studies of strategies of dissimulation among those who admit to deception will allow for the further refinement of our conceptual understanding and will possibly result in improved techniques for the identification of dissimulators.

Combined Research Models

The vast majority of dissimulation studies have focused on a single response style (i.e., malingering, defensiveness, or unspecified deception) and the use of a single technique (e.g., the MMPI). Comparisons of MMPI and interview-based data argue against the use of any single measure in the detection of dissimulation with correlations for malingering ($r = .15$) and defensiveness ($r = .01$) being unacceptably low (Johnson, Klinger, & Williams, 1977). An alternative to this single-response-style/single-measure approach is the combination of measures in a multivariate study of dissimulators. For example, research on neuropsychological batteries (Goebel, 1983; Heaton, Smith, Lehman, & Vogt, 1978) has found that the addition of the MMPI improves the classification rate of malingering patients. Research could also combine psychometric approaches with social-psychological methods and psychophysiological measures in a comprehensive study of potential dissimulators. Such research would force researchers and clinicians alike to address inconsistencies among measures. For example, one heuristic observation made by clinicians is that a higher proportion of patients appear to be malingering on the MMPI than during clinical interviews. Is such an observation accurate? If so, what are the characteristics of these individuals and what motivates them to give different response styles under different conditions?

A combined research model would allow researchers to assess the comparative efficacy of different methods within a simulation design. Research could demonstrate, for example, the true- and false-positive rates of individual approaches for psychiatric and nonpsychiatric subjects. As noted above, multivariate approaches could be developed for more accurate classification of dissimulators based on their overall response pattern.

A further advantage of the combined models is that it may allow, with corroborative clinical data, for the development of correction formulas. As noted above, current research has focused almost exclusively on (1) demonstrating the fakability of all psychological measures, or (2) developing clinical indicators for establishing dissimulation. Future research must address two additional issues; *gradations of malingering* and *correction formulas*. Current research strategies (Rogers & Cavanaugh, 1983) typically address dissimulation as if it were a dichotomous variable. Results of such studies are of only limited clinical value in establishing the presence or absence of malingering and defensiveness. Further work is needed in differ-

Summary

entiating degrees of dissimulation among clinical samples. By combining clinical methods, a new avenue is opened in examining these gradations. In addition, some dissimulators use what may represent a hybrid response pattern and exhibit a combination of malingering, defensiveness, and honest responding. A multimethod/multiresponse style approach will allow for a more sophisticated examination of these hybrid response styles.

An additional issue, described in the Psychometric Research section, is the development of correction formulas. Certainly, studies on the K correction of the MMPI suggest the potential value of strategies to determine the type and degree of impairment, irrespective of dissimulation. For researchers or clinicians to conclude only that a particular individual is a dissimulator and the results of his or her assessment are invalid is not entirely satisfactory. As clinicians are certainly aware, the presence of malingering, defensiveness, or irrelevant responding does not necessarily rule out a coexisting mental disorder and psychological impairment. Research is essential on the development of correction formulas for both malingering and defensiveness in a wide range of clinical settings.

Fundamental Questions

This chapter, and indeed this book, represents only a beginning in mapping out future directions for dissimulation research. What is immediately apparent from a comprehensive review of the dissimulation literature is a number of unresearched and underresearched topics. Little is know, for example, about who the dissimulators in clinical settings are and what their motivations are. In addition, the influence of situational and interactional variables on the frequency and severity of dissimulation has not been adequately studied. Finally, virtually no studies exist which examine the significance of dissimulation in the assessment of treatability and legal issues. The following sections will outline briefly fundamental questions in the study of dissimulation.

The Study of Dissimulators

Research has not addressed the sociodemographic variables, clinical characteristics, or psychosocial backgrounds of defensive and malingering patients. Sierles (1984) in a study of V.A. patients and medical students found both diagnostic and sociodemographic variables which were associated with malingering. More comprehensive studies are needed, however, which address a range of research questions.

1. What is the prevalence of malingering and defensiveness among those referred to clinical settings?
2. What proportion of dissimulators have coexisting mental disorders?

3. Are there "pure" dissimulators who consistently deceive, regardless of the situation or any expected payoffs?
4. What are dissimulators' reported motivations for their deceptions?
5. Can degrees of intent be established by dissimulators?

Situational and Interactional Factors

Dissimulation within psychiatric settings is not an isolated event but an important element of an interactive process. The role of clinicians, for example, in unintentionally encouraging or discouraging dissimulation remains unknown. In addition, the intensity of an adversarial situation as perceived by the potential dissimulator is likely to have an important influence on his or her presentation. For instance, it is not surprising that Audubon and Kirwin (1982) found that patients evaluated prior to trial tended to exaggerate their symptoms, but the same individuals, during a postacquittal assessment, tended to minimize them.

Research questions which deserve empirical inquiry include the following:

1. What are mental health professionals' attitudes towards dissimulation?
2. Are differences in professionals' attitudes reflected in either (1) the *actual* frequency of dissimulation or (2) the *perceived* frequency of dissimulation?
3. Can environmental variables be identified that significantly influence patients to dissimulate?
4. Do alternatives exist within the clinical setting for dissimulators to achieve their goals without deception?
5. Do clinical settings exist where the majority of those being evaluated engage in some level of dissimulation?

Dissimulation and Treatability

The role of dissimulation in the assessment of patients' treatability has not been empirically examined. In clinical practice, psychologists sometimes interpret mild defensiveness as a sign of ego-strength (i.e., a positive indicator of treatment success), and alternatively that an exaggeration of symptoms may be a "cry for help." Research by Greene (1987) and Hale, Zimostrad, Duckworth, and Nicholas (1986) (discussed in Chapter 8) did not find empirical support for the "plea for help" hypothesis. Research is needed to test under what conditions either of these two hypotheses is true and how the presence of dissimulation affects clinical decision making on treatment recommendations. Several research questions emerge on the relationship of dissimulation to patients' treatment responses.

1. To what extent do dissimulators comply with and follow treatment recommendations?
2. What are the treatment outcomes for dissimulating patients? In other words, do malingering or defensive patients with coexisting mental disorders respond as well as nondissimulators with similar disorders?
3. How do mental health professionals view dissimulators as treatment candidates?

Dissimulation and Legal Issues

Increasing demands have been placed on clinicians, both forensic and nonforensic, to address a broad range of psycholegal issues (Robitscher, 1980). Such evaluations are conducted in a clearly adversarial context, which may heighten the likelihood of dissimulation. Relevant research is needed to address the role of dissimulation within forensic reports and legal outcome. Research questions include the following:

1. In what proportion of forensic cases is the issue of dissimulation determinative of clinicians' psycholegal conclusions?
2, Given the far-reaching consequences of forensic evaluations, are different clinical criteria needed to differentiate dissimulators from others?
3. What influences do descriptions of dissimulation within clinical reports have on the legal disposition?
4. In public policy terms, what errors (false positives or false negatives) is the criminal justice system willing to tolerate with respect to malingering and defensiveness?

Conclusion

Research on dissimulation can be roughly characterized into three phases: (1) early case studies on which much clinical practice is based, (2) sustained interest in psychometric and social-psychological research emphasizing group differences, and (3) recent developments of specialized methods (e.g., the M test and the Structured Interview of Reported Symptons [SIRS]) for assessing systematically individuals suspected of dissimulation. Large gaps, as highlighted by the fundamental questions posed in this chapter, remain in our understanding of dissimulation and its reliable assessment. Indeed, clinicians and researchers alike must actively resist the *woozle effect* (i.e., the frequent citing of the same substandard research until it obtains a reputable "scientific" status; Gelles, 1980) in cases where the professional knowledge base is simply lacking.

Methodology for the study of malingering and defensiveness, although somewhat fragmented by its diverse origins, is well developed and understood. The impetus for more sophisticated research, combining methodologies, must include practitioners in both design and implementation to ensure the direct clinical relevance, worthy of our empirical efforts.

References

Abel, A. (1970). *The confessions of a hoaxer*. New York: Macmillan.

Abel, G. G., Barlow, D. H., Blanchard, E. B., & Guild, D. (1977). The components of rapists' sexual arousal. *Archives of General Psychiatry, 34*, 895–903.

Abel, G. G., Barlow, D. H., Blanchard, E. B., & Mavissakalian, M. (1975). Measurements of sexual arousal in male homosexuals: Effects of instructions and stimulus modality. *Archives of Sexual Behavior, 4*(6), 623–629.

Abel, G. G., Becker, J. V., Mittelman, M. S., & Cunningham-Rathner, J. (1986, February). *The self-reported molestations of non-incarcerated child molesters.* Paper presented at conference on Assessment and Treatment of Sex Offenders, Florida Institute of Mental Health, Tampa, FL.

Abel, G. G., Rouleau, J. L., & Cunningham-Rathner, J. (1986). Sexually aggressive behavior. In W. J. Curran, A. L. McGarry, and S. A. Shah (Eds.), *Forensic psychiatry and psychology* (pp. 289–314). Philadelphia: F. A. Davis.

Abeles, M., & Schilder, P. (1935). Psychogenic loss of personal identity. *Archives of Neurology and Psychiatry, 34*, 587–604.

Ackerman, B. P. (1981). Young children's understanding of a speaker's intentional use of a false utterance. *Developmental Psychology, 17*, 472–480.

Ackerman, B. P. (1983). Speaker bias in children's evaluation of the external consistency of statements. *Journal of Experimental Child Psychology, 35*, 111–127.

Adatto, C. P. (1949). Observations on criminal patients during narcoanalysis. *Archives of Neurology and Psychiatry, 69*, 82–92.

Adcock, B. (1971). Thematic Apperception Test. In O. K. Buros (Ed.), *Mental measurements yearbook*, (6th ed.) (pp. 245–246). Highland Park, NJ: Gryphon Press.

Adelman, R. M., & Howard, A. (1984). Expert testimony on malingering: The admissibility of clinical procedures for the detection of deception. *Behavioral Sciences and the Law, 2*, 5–20.

Aduan, R. P., Fauci, A. S., Dale, D. C., Herzberg, J. H., & Wolff, S. M. (1979). Factitious fever and self-induced infection. *Annals of Internal Medicine, 90*, 230–242.

Albert, S., Fox, H. M., & Kahn, M. W. (1980). Faking psychosis on a Rorschach: Can expert judges detect malingering? *Journal of Personality Assessment, 44*, 115–119.

Alexander, M. P., & Freedman, M. (1984). Amnesia after anterior communicating artery aneurysm rupture. *Neurology, 34*, 752–757.

Allen, V. L., & Atkinson, M. L. (1978). Encoding of nonverbal behavior by high-achieving and low-achieving children. *Journal of Educational Psychology, 70*, 298–305.

Allison, R. B. (1984). Difficulties diagnosing the multiple personality syndrome in a death penalty case. *International Journal of Clinical and Experimental Hypnosis, 32*, 102–117.

Alpert, M., & Silvers, K. N. (1970). Perceptual characteristics distinguishing auditory hallucinations in schizophrenia and acute alcoholic psychoses. *American Journal of Psychiatry, 127*, 298–302.

Altshuler, L. L., Cummings, J. L., & Mills, M. J. (1986). Mutism: Review, differential diagnosis and report of 22 cases. *American Journal of Psychiatry, 143*, 1409–1414.

American Psychiatric Association. (1952). *Diagnostic and statistical manual of mental disorders*. Washington, DC: American Psychiatric Association Press.

American Psychiatric Association. (1968). *Diagnostic and statistical manual of mental disorders* (2nd ed.). Washington, DC: American Psychiatric Association Press.

American Psychiatric Association. (1980). *Diagnostic and statistical manual of mental disorders* (3rd ed.). Washington, DC: Author.

American Psychiatric Association. (1986). *DSM-III-R in development*. (Second draft). Washington, DC: Author.

American Psychiatric Association. (1987). *Diagnostic and statistical manual of mental disorders* (3rd ed., revised). Washington, DC: Author.

Anderson, E. W., Trethowan, W. H., & Kenna, J. C. (1959). An experimental investigation of simulation and pseudo-dementia. *Acta Psychiatrica et Neurologica Scandinavica, 132,* 5–42.

Andreyev, L. (1902). *The dilemma.* In L. Hamalian & V. Von Wiren-Garczynski (Eds.), *Seven Russian Short Novel Masterpieces.* New York: Popular Library.

Annotation (1986). Admissibility of physiological or psychological truth and deception test or its results to support physicians' testimony. *American Law Reports, 41,* 1369–1385.

Anthony, N. (1971). Comparison of patients' standard, exaggerated, and matching MMPI profiles. *Journal of Consulting and Clinical Psychology, 36,* 100–103.

Arons, H. (1967). *Hypnosis in criminal investigation.* Springfield, IL: Charles C. Thomas.

Asher, R. (1951). Munchausen's syndrome. *Lancet, 1,* 339–341.

Asher, R. (1972). *Richard Asher talking sense.* London: University Park Press.

Ashlock, L., Walker, J., Starkey, T. W., Harmand, J., & Michel, D. (1987). Psychometric characteristics of factitious PTSD. *VA Practitioner, 4,* 37–41.

Assad, G., & Shapiro, B. (1986). Hallucinations: Theoretical and clinical overview. *American Journal of Psychiatry, 143,* 1088–1097.

Atkinson, R. M., Henderson, R. G., Sparr, L. F., & Deale, S. (1982). Assessment of Vietnam veterans for post-traumatic stress disorder in Veterans Administration disability claims. *American Journal of Psychiatry, 139,* 1118–1121.

Audubon, J. J., & Kirwin, B. R. (1982). Defensiveness in the criminally insane. *Journal of Personality Assessment, 45,* 304–311.

Averbach, A. (1963). Medical arsenal of a personal injury lawyer. *Cleveland Marshall Law Review, 12,* 195–207.

Backster, C. (1962). Methods of strengthening our polygraph techniques. *Police, 6,* 61–68.

Baddeley, A. D., & Warrington, E. K. (1970). Amnesia and the distinction between long- and short-term memory. *Journal of Verbal Learning and Verbal Behavior, 9,* 176–189.

Bain, J., Hucker, S., Dickey, R., Langevin, R., & Wright, P. (1987). *The LHRH test in pedophilic men.* Unpublished manuscript, University of Toronto, Toronto, Ontario.

Bain, J., Langevin, R., Hucker, S., Dickey, R., & Wright, P. (1987). *Sex hormones in sexually aggressive men.* Unpublished manuscript, University of Toronto, Toronto, Ontario.

Baker, J. N. (1967). Effectiveness of certain MMPI dissimulation scales under "real-life" conditions. *Journal of Counseling Psychology, 14,* 286–292.

Balloun, D. D., & Holmes, D. S. (1979). Effects of repeated examinations on the ability to detect guilt with a polygraphic examination: A laboratory experience with real crime. *Journal of Applied Psychology, 64,* 316–322.

Bancroft, J., & Matthews, A. (1971). Autonomic correlates of penile erection. *Journal of Psychosomatic Research, 15,* 154–167.

Barber, T. X. (1962). Experimental controls and the phenomenon of "hypnosis": A critique of hypnotic research methodology. *Journal of Nervous and Mental Disease, 134,* 493–505.

Barber, T. X. (1965). Measuring "hypnotic-like" suggestibility with and without "hypnotic induction": Psychometric properties, norms, and variables influencing response to the Barber Suggestibility Scale. *Psychological Reports, 16,* 809–844.

Barber, T. X. (1972). Suggested ("hypnotic") behavior: The trance paradigm versus an alternative paradigm. In E. Fromm & R. E. Shor (Eds.), *Hypnosis: Research developments and perspectives* (pp. 115-182). Chicago: Aldine-Atherton.

Barber, T. X., & Calverly, D. S. (1963). "Hypnotic-like" susceptibility in children and adults. *Journal of Abnormal and Social Psychology, 66,* 589-597.

Barber. T. X., & Calverly, D. S. (1964). Empirical evidence for a theory of hypnotic behavior: Effects of pretest instructions on response to primary suggestions. *Psychological Records, 14,* 457-467.

Barber, T. X., & Glass, L. B. (1962). Significant factors in hypnotic behavior. *Journal of Abnormal and Social Psychology, 64,* 222-228.

Barber, T. X., Spanos, N. P., & Chaves, J. F. (1974). *Hypnotism: Imagination and human potentialities.* New York: Pergamon Press.

Barber, T. X., & Wilson, S. C. (1977). Hypnosis, suggestions, and altered states of consciousness: Experimental evaluation of the new cognitive-behavioral theory and the traditional trance-state theory of "hypnosis." *Annals of the New York Academy of Sciences, 296,* 34-47.

Barland, G. H. (1982). On the accuracy of the polygraph: An evaluative review of Lykken's Tremor in the Blood. *Polygraph, 11,* 258-272.

Barland, G. H., & Raskin, D. C. (1973). Detection of deception. In W. F. Prokasy & D. C. Raskin (Eds.), *Electrodermal activity in psychological research* (pp. 418-477). New York: Academic Press.

Barland, G. H., & Raskin, D. C. (1976). *Validity and reliability of polygraph examinations of criminal suspects.* (Report No. 76-1, Contract No. N1-99-0001). Washington, DC: National Institute for Justice, Department of Justice.

Barlow, D. H., Becker, R., Leitenberg, H., & Agras, W. S. (1970). A mechanical strain gauge for recording penile circumference change. *Journal of Applied Behavior Analysis, 3,* 73-76.

Baro, W. Z. (1950). Industrial head and back injuries. *Industrial Medical Surgery, 19,* 69-71.

Barry, H., Jr., MacKinnon, D. W., & Murray, H. A. (1931). Studies in personality: A. Hypnotizability as a personality trait and its typological relations. *Human Biology, 3,* 1-36.

Barth, J. T., Macciocchi, S. N., Giordani, B., Rimel, R., Jane, J. A., & Boll, T. J. (1983). Neuropsychological sequelae of minor head injury. *Neurosurgery, 13,* 529-533.

Bartlett, F. C. (1932). *Remembering: A study in experimental and social psychology.* Cambridge: Cambridge University Press.

Bartol, C. R. (1983). *Psychology and American law.* Belmont, CA: Wadsworth.

Bash, I. Y. (1978). Malingering: A study designed to differentiate schizophrenic offenders and malingerers. *Dissertation Abstracts, 39,* 2973-B.

Bash, I. Y., & Alpert, M. (1980). The determination of malingering. *Annals of New York Academy of Sciences, 347,* 86-99.

Batshaw, M. L., Wachtel, R. C., Deckel, A. W., Whitehouse, P. J., Moses, H., Fochtman, L. J., & Eldridge, R. (1985). Munchausen's syndrome simulating torsion dystonia. *The New England Journal of Medicine, 312,* 1437-1439.

Beaber, R. J., Marston, A., Michelli, J., & Mills, M. J. (1985). A brief test for measuring malingering in schizophrenic individuals. *American Journal of Psychiatry, 142,* 1478-1481.

Bear, D. M., & Fedio, P. (1977). Quantitative analysis of interictal behavior in temporal lobe epilepsy. *Archives of Neurology, 34,* 454-467.

Beck, J. G., Sakheim, D. K., & Barlow, D. H. (1983). Operating characteristics of the vaginal photoplethysmograph: Some implications for its use. *Archives of Sexual Behavior, 12,* 43-58.

Behar, L. (1977). The Preschool Behavior Questionnaire. *Journal of Abnormal Child Psychology, 5,* 265-275.

Bejerot, N. (1972). A theory of addiction as an artificially induced drive. *The American Journal of Psychiatry, 127*(7), 842–846.

Belt, J. A., & Holden, P. B. (1978). Polygraph usage among major U. S. corporations. *Personnel Journal, 57*, 80–86.

Bender, M. B. (1956). Syndrome of isolated episode of confusion with amnesia. *Journal of Hillside Hospital, 5*, 212–215.

Benedek, E., & Schetky, D. (1984, October). *Allegations of sexual abuse in child custody cases.* Paper presented at the Annual Meeting of the American Academy of Psychiatry and the Law, Nassau, Bahamas.

Benedek, E. P., & Schetky, D. H. (1987a). Problems in validating allegations of sexual abuse. Part I: Factors affecting perceptions and recall of events. *Journal of the American Academy of Child and Adolescent Psychiatry, 26*, 912–915.

Benedek, E. P., & Schetky, D. H. (1987b). Problems in validating allegations of sexual abuse. Part II: Clinical evaluation. *Journal of the American Academy of Child and Adolescent Psychiatry, 26*, 916–921.

Benson, P. G., & Krois, P. S. (1979). The polygraph in employment: Some unresolved issues. *Personnel Journal, 58*, 616–621.

Benton, A. L. (1945). Rorschach performances of suspected malingerers. *Journal of Abnormal and Social Psychology, 40*, 94–96.

Benton, A. L., & Spreen, O. (1961). Visual memory test. *Archives of General Psychiatry, 4*, 79–83.

Berg-Cross, L. G. (1975). Intentionality, degree of damage, and moral judgments. *Child Development, 45*, 970–974.

Berlin, F. S., & Krout, E. (1986). Pedophilia: Diagnostic concepts, treatment, and ethical considerations. *American Journal of Forensic Psychiatry, 8*, 13–30.

Berman, E. (1987, March 25). *USA Today*, p. 10A.

Berney, T. P. (1973). A review of simulated illness. *South African Medical Journal, 47*, 1429–1434.

Bernheim, H. M. (1964). *Hypnosis and suggestion in psychotherapy: A treatise on the nature and use of hypnotism.* (C. A. Herter, Trans.). New Hyde Park, NY: University Books. (Original work published 1884)

Bersch, P. J. (1969). A validation study of polygraph examiner judgements. *Journal of Applied Psychology, 53*, 393–403.

Bigler, E. D., & Ehrfurth, J. W. (1981). The continued inappropriate singular use of the Bender visual motor gestalt test. *Professional Psychology, 12*, 562–569.

Binder, L. W. (1986). Persisting symptoms after mild head injury: A review of the postconcussive syndrome. *Journal of Clinical and Experimental Neuropsychology, 8*, 323–346.

Binder, L. M., & Pankratz, L. (1987). Neuropsychological evidence of a factitious memory complaint. *Journal of Clinical and Experimental Neuropsychology, 9*, 167–171.

Bishop, E. R., & Holt, A. R. (1980). Pseudopsychosis: A reexamination of the concept of hysterical psychosis. *Comprehensive Psychiatry, 21*(21), 150–161.

Bitzer, R. (1980). Caught in the middle: Mentally disabled veterans and the Veterans Administration. In C. R. Figley & S. Leventman (Eds.), *Strangers at home: Vietnam veterans since the war* (pp. 305–323). New York: Praeger Publications.

Blanchard, E. B., Kolb, L. C., Pallmeyer, T. P., & Gerardi, R. J. (1982). A psychophysiological study of post-traumatic stress disorder in Vietnam veterans. *Psychiatric Quarterly, 54*, 220–229.

Blanchard, R. (1980, February). *Perineal muscular contractions and the detection of faking on the phallometric test.* Paper presented to Ontario Psychiatric Association, Toronto, ON.

Bleuler, E. (1944). *A textbook of psychiatry.* New York: Macmillan.

Bohn, R. W. (1932). Sodium amytal narcosis as a therapeutic aid in psychiatry. *Psychiatric Quarterly, 6*, 301–309.

Bond, J. A. (1986). Inconsistent responding to repeated MMPI items: Is its major cause really carelessness? *Journal of Personality Assessment, 50,* 50–64.

Bongartz, W. (1985). German norms for the Harvard Group Scale of Hypnotic Susceptibility, Form A. *International Journal of Clinical and Experimental Hypnosis, 33,* 131–138.

Bradford, J. W., & Smith, S. M. (1979). Amnesia and homicide: The Padola case and a study of thirty cases. *Bulletin of the American Academy of Psychiatry and the Law, 7,* 219–231.

Bradley v. Preston, 263 F. Supp. 283 (D.D.C. 1967), *cert. denied,* 390 U.S. 990 (1968).

Bradley, M. T., & Ainsworth, D. (1984). Alcohol and the psychophysiological detection of deception. *Psychophysiology, 21,* 63–71.

Bradley, M. T., & Janisse, M. P. (1981). Accuracy demonstrations, threat, and the detection of deception: Cardiovascular, electrodermal, and pupillary measures. *Psychophysiology, 18,* 307–315.

Bradley, M. T., & Warfield, J. F. (1984). Innocence, information, and the guilty knowledge test in the detection of deception. *Psychophysiology, 21,* 683–689.

Brady, J. P., & Lind, D. L. (1961). Experimental analysis of hysterical blindness. *Archives of General Psychiatry, 4,* 331–339.

Braginsky, B., & Braginsky, D. (1967). Schizophrenic patients in the psychiatric interview: An experimental study of their effectiveness at manipulation. *Journal of Consulting Psychology, 31,* 543–547.

Braginsky, D. D. (1970). Machiavellian and manipulative interpersonal behavior in children. *Journal of Experimental Social Psychology, 6,* 77–99.

Braid, J. (1843). *Neurypnology: The rationale of nervous sleep considered in relation with animal magnetism, illustrated by numerous cases of its successful application in the relief and cure of disease.* London: John Churchill.

Brandenburg, R. O., Gutnik, L. M., Nelson, R. L., Abboud, C. F., Edis, A. J., & Sheps, S. G. (1979). Factitial epinephrine-only secreting pheochromocytoma. *Annals of Internal Medicine, 90*(5), 795–796.

Brandt, J., & Butters, N. (1986). The neuropsychology of Huntington's disease. *Trends in Neurosciences, 9,* 118–120.

Brandt, J., Rubinsky, E., & Lassen, G. (1985). Uncovering malingered amnesia. *Annals of the New York Academy of Sciences, 444,* 502–503.

Braverman, M. (1978). Post-injury malingering is seldom a calculated ploy. *Occupational Health and Safety, 47,* 36–48.

Breslau, N., & Davis, G. C. (1987). Post-traumatic stress disorder: The etiologic specificity of wartime stressors. *American Journal of Psychiatry, 144,* 578–583.

Brett, A. S., Phillips, M., & Beary, J. F. (1986). Predictive power of the polygraph: Can the "lie detector" really detect lies? *Lancet, 1,* 544–547.

Brierley, J. B. (1977). Neuropathology of amnesic states. In C. W. M. Whitty & O. L. Zangwill (Eds.), *Amnesia* (pp. 199–223). London: Butterworths.

Brittain, R. P. (1966). The history of legal medicine: The assizes of Jerusalem. *Medicolegal Journal, 34,* 72–73.

Brooks, D. N., & Aughton, M. E. (1979). Psychological consequences of blunt head injury. *International Rehabilitation Medicine, 1,* 160–165.

Brough, M. D. (1977). Dermatitis artefacta. *The Hand, 9,* 283–286.

Browning, C. H., Miller, S. E., & Tyson, R. (1974). The psychiatric emergency: A high risk medical patient. *Comprehensive Psychiatry, 15,* 153–156.

Brozovich, R. (1970). Fakability of scores on the group personality projective test. *The Journal of Genetic Psychology, 117,* 143–148.

Bruch, H. (1966). Anorexia nervosa and its differential diagnosis. *The Journal of Nervous and Mental Disease, 141*(5), 555–566.

Bruhn, A. R., & Reed, M. R. (1975). Simulation of brain damage on the Bender-gestalt test by college subjects. *Journal of Personality Assessment, 39,* 244–255.

Bryan, W. (1962). *Legal aspects of hypnosis.* Springfield, IL: Charles C. Thomas.

Buckalew, L. W., & Coffield, K. E. (1982). An investigation of drug expectancy as a function of capsule color and size and preparation form. *Journal of Clinical Psychopharmacology, 2,* 245-248.

Buckhout, R. (1974). Eyewitness testimony. *Scientific American, 231,* 23-31.

Buechley, R., & Ball, H. (1952). A new test of "test validity" for the group MMPI. *Journal of Consulting Psychology, 16,* 299-301.

Bulman, R. J., & Wortman, C. B. (1977). Attributions of blame and coping in the real world: Severe accident victims to their lot. *Journal of Personnel and Social Psychology, 33,* 351-363.

Burstein, A. (1986). Can monetary compensation influence the course of a disorder? *American Journal of Psychiatry, 143,* 112.

Bursten, B. (1965). On Munchausen's syndrome. *Archives of General Psychiatry, 13,* 261-268.

Bustamante, J. P., & Ford, C. V. (1977). Ganser's syndrome. *Psychiatric Opinion, 14,* 39-41.

Butters, N. (1984). The clinical aspects of memory disorders: Contributions from experimental studies of amnesia and dementia. *Journal of Clinical Neuropsychology, 6,* 17-36.

Butters, N., & Cermak, L. S. (1980). *Alcoholic Korsakoff's syndrome: An information-processing approach to amnesia.* New York: Academic Press.

Butters, N., Miliotis, P., Albert, M. S., & Sax, D. S. (1984). Memory assessment: Evidence of the heterogeneity of amnesic symptoms. In G. Goldstein (Ed.), *Advances in clinical neuropsychology* (pp. 127-159). New York: Plenum Press.

Cady, H. M. (1924). *Minor studies from the psychological laboratory of Northwestern University.* Unpublished master's thesis. Northwestern University, Evanston, IL.

Caine, E. D. (1981). Pseudodementia. Current concepts and future directions. *Archives of General Psychiatry, 38,* 1359-1364.

Campbell, D. T., & Stanley, J. C. (1966). *Experimental and quasi-experimental designs for research.* Chicago: Rand McNally.

Carp, A. L., & Shavzin, A. R. (1950). The susceptibility to falsification of the Rorschach psychodiagnostic technique. *Journal of Consulting Psychology, 14,* 230-233.

Cavanaugh, J. L., Rogers, R., & Wasyliw, O. E. (1981). Mental illness and antisocial behavior: Treatment approaches. In W. H. Reid (Ed.), *The treatment of antisocial syndromes* (pp. 3-19). New York: Van Nostrand Reinhold.

Cavenar, J. O., Maltbie, A. A., & Austin, L. (1979). Depression simulating organic brain disease. *The American Journal of Psychiatry, 136*(4B), 521-523.

Cermak, L. S. (1976). The encoding capacity of a patient with amnesia due to encephalitis. *Neuropsychologia, 14,* 311-326.

Cermak, L. S. (Ed.) (1982). *Human memory and amnesia.* Hillsdale, NJ: Lawrence Erlbaum Associates.

Chandler, M. J., Greenspan, S., & Barenboim, C. (1973). Judgments of intentionality in response to videotaped and verbally presented moral dilemmas: The medium is the message. *Child Development, 44,* 315-320.

Chaney, H. S., Cohn, C. K., Williams, S. G., & Vincent, K. R. (1984). MMPI results: A comparison of trauma victims, psychogenic pain, and patients with organic disease. *Journal of Clinical Psychology, 40,* 1450-1454.

Charcot, J. M. (1886). *Oeuvres complete* [Complete works]. Paris: Aux Bureau de Progres Medical.

Christensen, A. L. (1975). *Luria's neuropsychological investigation.* New York: Spectrum.

Christie, M., Marshall, W. L., & Lanthier, R. (1978). *A descriptive study of incarcerated rapists and pedophiles.* Unpublished manuscript. Canadian Penitentiary Services, Kingston, ON.

Clark v. State, 379 So.2d 372 (Fla. 1st D.C.A. 1979).

Clayer, J. R., Bookless, C., & Ross, M. W. (1984). Neurosis and conscious symptom exaggeration: Its differentiation by the illness behavior questionnaire. *Journal of Psychosomatic Research, 28,* 237–241.

Cleckley, H. (1976). *The mask of sanity* (5th ed.). St. Louis, MO: Mosby.

Clevenger, S. V. (1889). *Spinal concussion.* London: F. A. Davis.

Cocklin, K. (1980). Amnesia: The forgotten justification for finding an accused incompetent to stand trial. *Washburn Law Journal, 20,* 289–306.

Cocores, J. A., Santa, W. G., & Patel, M. D. (1984). The Ganser syndrome: Evidence suggesting its classification as a dissociative disorder. *International Journal of Psychiatry in Medicine, 14*(1), 47–56.

Coe, W. C. (1964). Further norms on the Harvard Group Scale of Hypnotic Susceptibility, Form A. *International Journal of Clinical and Experimental Hypnosis, 12,* 184–190.

Cofer, C. N., Chance, J., & Judson, A. J. (1949). A study of malingering on the MMPI. *Journal of Psychology, 27,* 491–499.

Cohen, M. R., & Niska, R. W. (1980). Localized right cerebral hemisphere dysfunction and recurrent mania. *American Journal of Psychiatry, 137,* 847–848.

Cohen, N. J. (1984). Preserved learning capacity in amnesia: Evidence for multiple memory systems. In L. Squire and N. Butters (Eds.), *The neuropsychology of memory* (pp. 83–103). New York: Guilford Press.

Colby, A. (1978). Evolution of a moral-developmental theory. In W. Damon (Ed.), *New directions in child development: Moral development* (pp. 89–104). San Francisco: Jossey-Bass.

Cole, E. S. (1970). Psychiatric aspects of compensable injury. *The Medical Journal of Australia, 1,* 93–100.

Collie, J. (1913). *Malingering and feigned sickness.* London: Edward Arnold.

Colligan, R. C., Osborne, D., Swenson, W. M., & Offord, K. P. (1983). *The MMPI: A contemporary normative study.* New York: Praeger.

Collinson, G. D. (1812). *A treatise on the law concerning idiots, lunatics, and other persons non compotes mentis.* London: W. Reed.

Comment. (1967). Capacity to stand trial: The amnesic criminal defendant. *Maryland Law Review, 27,* 182–193.

Commonwealth ex rel. Cummins v. Price, 421 Pa. 396, 218 A.2d 758 (1966).

Cook, T. D., Levitou, L. C., & Shadish, W. R. (1985). Program evaluation. In G. Lindzey and E. Aronson (Eds.), *Handbook of social psychology* (Vol. 1) (pp. 699–777). New York: Random House.

Corkin, S. (1965). Tactually-guided maze learning in man: Effects of unilateral cortical excision and bilateral hippocampal lesions. *Neuropsychologia, 3,* 339–351.

Corkin, S. (1968). Acquisition of motor skill after bilateral hippocampal lesions. *Neuropsychologia, 19,* 337–356.

Corkin, S. (1982). Some relationships between global amnesias and the memory impairments in Alzheimer's disease. In S. Corkin (Ed.), *Alzheimer's disease: A report of progress* (pp. 149–165). New York: Raven Press.

Corkin, S., Cohen, N. J., Sullivan, E. V., Clegg, R. A., Rosen, T. J., & Ackerman, R. H. (1985). Analysis of global memory impairments of different etiologies. *Annals of the New York Academy of Sciences, 444,* 10–40.

Cornell v. Sup. Ct., 52 Cal.2d 99, 338 P.2d 447 (1959).

Craig, J. (1984). The presidential polygraph order and the fourth amendment: Subjecting federal employees to warrantless searches. *Cornell Law Review, 69,* 896–924.

Cramer, B., Gershberg, M. R., & Stern, M. (1971). Munchausen syndrome. Its relationship to malingering, hysteria, and the physician-patient relationship. *Archives of General Psychiatry, 24,* 573–578.

Crockett v. Haithwaite, No. 297/73 (Sup. Ct. B.C. Can. February 10, 1978).

Crosson, B., Hughes, C. W., Roth, D. L., & Monkowski, P. G. (1984). Review of Russell's

(1975) norms for the Logical Memory and Visual Reproductions subtests of the Wechsler Memory Scale. *Journal of Consulting and Clinical Psychology, 52,* 635–641.

Crowley, P. M. (1968). Effect of training upon objectivity of moral judgment in grade school children. *Journal of Personality and Social Psychology, 8,* 228–232.

Cummings, J. L. (1985). *Clinical neuropsychiatry.* Toronto: Grune & Stratton.

Dahlstrom, W. G., Welsh, G. S., & Dahlstrom, L. E. (1972). *An MMPI handbook.* Vol. I.: *Clinical interpretation* (rev. ed.). Minneapolis: University of Minnesota Press.

Dalton, J. E., Pederson, S. L., Blom, B. E., & Besyner, J. K. (1986). Neuropsychological screening for Vietnam veterans with PTSD. *VA Practitioner, 3,* 37–47.

Damasio, A. R., Graff-Radford, N. R., Eslinger, P. J., Damasio, H., & Kassell, N. (1985). Amnesia after basal forebrain lesions. *Archives of Neurology, 42,* 263–271.

Daniel, A. E., & Resnick, P. J. (in press). Mutism, malingering and competency to stand trial. *Bulletin of the American Academy of Psychiatry and the Law.*

Davidson, H. A. (1949). Malingered psychosis. *Bulletin of the Menninger Clinic, 13,* 157–163.

Davidson, H. A. (1952). *Forensic psychiatry* (2nd ed.). New York: The Ronald Press.

Davidson, P. O. (1968). Validity of the guilty knowledge technique: The effects of motivation. *Journal of Applied Psychology, 52,* 62–65.

Davidson, W. A. (1979). Validity and reliability of the cardio activity monitor. *Polygraph, 9,* 104–111.

Davis, L. W., & Husband, R. W. (1931). A study of hypnotic susceptibility in relation to personality traits. *Journal of Abnormal and Social Psychology, 26,* 175–182.

Davis v. State, 354 So.2d 334 (Ala. Crim. App. 1978).

Dawson, M. G. (1980). Physiological detection of deception: Measurement of responses to questions and answers during countermeasure maneuvers. *Psychophysiology, 17,* 8–17.

de la Fuente, J. R., Hanson, N. P., & Duncan, G. M. (1980). A new look at Ganser's syndrome. *Psychiatric Annals, 10*(10), 62–68.

De Puysegur, A. M. (1843). On the discovery of artificial somnambulism. In A. Teste (Ed.), *Practical manual of animal magnetism* (D. Spillan, Trans.). London: H. Bailliere. (Original work published in 1784)

Denker, R. G., & Perry, G. F. (1954). Postconcussion syndrome in compensation and litigation: Analysis of 95 cases with electroencephalographic correlations. *Neurology, 4,* 912–918.

DePaulo, B. M., Jordan, A., Irvine, A., & Laser, P. S. (1982). Age changes in the detection of deception. *Child Development, 53,* 701–709.

DePaulo, B. M., Lanier, K., & Davis, T. (1983). Detecting the deceit of the motivated liar. *Journal of Personality and Social Psychology, 45,* 1096–1103.

DePaulo, B. M., & Rosenthal, R. (1979). Telling lies. *Journal of Personality and Social Psychology, 37,* 1713–1722.

DePaulo, B. M., Stone, J. I., & Lassiter, G. D. (1985). Deceiving and detecting deceit. In B. R. Schlenker (Ed.), *Self and identity: Presentations of self in social life* (pp. 323–370). New York: McGraw-Hill.

Desai, B. T., Porter, R. J., & Penry, J. K. (1982). Psychogenic seizures: A study of 42 attacks in six patients, with intensive monitoring. *Archives of Neurology, 39,* 202–209.

Deutsch, H. (1982). On the pathological lie (pseudologia fantastica). *Journal of the American Academy of Psychoanalysis, 10*(3), 369–386.

Devinsky, O., & Bear, D. (1984). Varieties in aggressive behavior in temporal lobe epilepsy. *American Journal of Psychiatry, 141,* 651–656.

deYoung, M. (1986). A conceptual mode for judging the truthfulness of a young child's allegation of sexual abuse. *American Journal of Orthopsychiatry, 56,* 551–559.

Diamond, B. (1956). The simulation of insanity. *Journal of Social Therapy, 2,* 158–165.

Diamond, B. L. (1980). Inherent problems in the use of pretrial hypnosis on a prospective witness. *California Law Review, 68,* 313–349.

Diamond, B. L. (1986). Isaac Ray corner addendum. *American Academy of Psychiatry and the Law Newsletter, 11*, 26–28.

Diamond, R., & Rozin, P. (1984). Activation of existing memories in the amnesic syndrome. *Journal of Abnormal Psychology, 93*, 98–105.

Dicken, C. F. (1960). Simulated patterns on the California Psychological Inventory. *Journal of Consulting Psychology, 7*, 24–31.

Doren, D. M. (1987). *Understanding and treating the psychopath*. New York: John Wiley & Sons.

Downing, J. (1942). *Science News Letter, 55*, 392.

Dubinsky, S., Gamble, D. J., & Rogers, M. L. (1985). A literature review of subtle-obvious items on the MMPI. *Journal of Personality Assessment, 49*, 62–68.

Duckworth, J. C., & Anderson, W. P. (1986). *MMPI interpretation manual for counsellors and clinicians* (3rd ed.). Muncie, IN: Accelerated Development.

Duckworth, J., & Barley, W. D. (in press). Normal limit profiles. In R. L. Greene (Ed.), *The MMPI: Use in specific populations*. Philadelphia: Grune & Stratton.

Dukes, W. F. (1965). $N = 1$. *Psychological Bulletin, 64*, 74–79.

Dysken, M. W., Chang, S. S., Casper, R. C., & Davis, J. M. (1979). Barbiturate-facilitated interviewing. *Biological Psychiatry, 14*, 421–432.

Dysken, M. W., Kooser, J. A., Haraszti, J. S., & Davis, J. M. (1979). Clinical usefulness of sodium amobarbital interviewing. *Archives of General Psychiatry, 36*, 789–794.

Dysken, M. W., Steinberg, J., & Davis, J. M. (1979). Sodium amobarbital response during simulated catatonia. *Biological Psychiatry, 14*, 995–1000.

Early, E. (1984). On confronting the Vietnam veteran [Letter to the editor]. *American Journal of Psychiatry, 141*, 472–473.

East, N. W. (1927). *An introduction to forensic psychiatry in the criminal courts*. London: Churchill.

Easton, K., & Feigenbaum, K. (1967). An examination of an experimental set to fake the Rorschach test. *Perceptual and Motor Skills, 24*, 871–874.

Eisendrath, S. J. (1984). Factitious illness: A clarification. *Psychosomatics, 25*, 110–117.

Eissler, K. R. (1951). Malingering. In G. B. Wilbur & W. Muensterberger (Eds.), *Psychoanalysis and culture* (pp. 218–253). New York: International University Press.

Ekman, P. (1986). *Telling lies*. New York: Berkley Books.

Endicott, J., & Spitzer, R. L. (1978). A diagnostic interview: The schedule of affective disorders and schizophrenia. *Archives of General Psychiatry, 35*, 837–844.

Enelow, A. J. (1971). Malingering and delayed recovery from injury. In J. J. Leedy (Ed.), *Compensation in psychiatric disability and rehabilitation*. Springfield, IL: Charles C. Thomas.

Engel, G. L. (1970). Conversion symptoms. In C. M. MacBryde & R. S. Blacklow (Eds.), *Signs and symptoms* (5th ed.) (pp. 650–658). Philadelphia: R. S. Lippincott.

Erickson, M. H. (1939). The induction of color blindness by a technique of hypnotic suggestion. *Journal of General Psychology, 20*, 64–69.

Erickson, M. H., & Kubie, L. S. (1941). The successful treatment of a case of acute hysterical depression by a return under hypnosis to a critical phase of childhood. *Psychoanalytic Quarterly, 10*, 583–609.

Eron, L. D. (1972). Thematic Apperception Test. In O. K. Buros (Ed.), *Mental measurements yearbook* (7th ed.). Highland Park, NJ: Gryphon Press.

Evans, F. I., & Schmeidler, D. (1966). Relationships between the Harvard Group Scale of Hypnotic Susceptibility and the Stanford Hypnotic Susceptibility Scale, Form C. *International Journal of Clinical and Experimental Hypnosis, 14*, 333–343.

Evans, R. G., & Dinning, W. D. (1983). Response consistency among high F scale scorers on the MMPI. *Journal of Clinical Psychology, 39*, 246–248.

Exner, J. E. (1974). *The Rorschach: A comprehensive system*. New York: John Wiley & Sons.

Exner, J. E. (1978). *The Rorschach: A comprehensive system. Vol. II: Current research and advanced interpretation.* New York: John Wiley & Sons.

Exner, J. E., McDowell, E., Pabst, J., Stackman, W., & Kirk, L. (1963). On the detection of willful falsifications in the MMPI. *Journal of Consulting Psychology, 27,* 91–94.

Exner, J. E., & Miller, A. S. (1974). *Protocols of newly admitted prison inmates.* Workshops Study No. 200. Unpublished manuscript.

Exner, J. E., & Sherman, J. (1977). *Rorschach performance of schizophrenics asked to improve their protocols.* Workshops Study No. 243. Unpublished manuscript.

Exner, J. E., & Wylie, J. R. (1975). *Attempts at simulation of schizophrenic-like protocols by psychology graduate students.* Unpublished manuscript.

Eysenck, H. J. (1954). The science of personality: Nomothetic! *Psychological Review, 61,* 339–342.

Fabian, C. A., & Billick, S. B. (1986, October). *Ethical and forensic issues in general psychiatry narcoanalysis.* Paper presented at annual convention of the American Academy of Psychiatry and Law, Philadelphia.

Fairbank, J. A., McCaffrey, R. J., & Keane, T. M. (1985). Psychometric detection of fabricated symptoms of post-traumatic stress disorder. *American Journal of Psychiatry, 142,* 501–503.

Fairbank, J. A., McCaffrey, R. J., & Keane, T. M. (1986). On simulating post-traumatic stress disorder [Letters to the Editor—Dr. Fairbank and associates reply]. *American Journal of Psychiatry, 143,* 268–269.

Falloon, I., & Talbot, R. (1981). Persistent auditory hallucinations: Coping mechanisms and implications for management. *Psychological Medicine, 11,* 329–339.

Farkas, G. M., Evans, I. M., Sine, L. F., Eifert, G., Wittlieb, E., & Vogelmann-Sine, S. (1979). Reliability and validity of the mercury-in-rubber strain gauge measure of penile circumference. *Behavior Therapy, 10,* 555–561.

Farwell, L. A., & Donchin, E. (1986). The "brain detector": P300 in the detection of deception. *Psychophysiology, 23,* 434, (Abstract).

Fekken, G. C., & Holden, R. R. (1987). Assessing the person reliability of an individual MMPI protocol. *Journal of Personality Assessment, 51,* 123–132.

Feldman, N. J., & Graley, J. (1954). Effects of experimental set to simulate abnormality on group Rorschach performance. *Journal of Projective Techniques, 18,* 326–334.

Feldman, R. S., Jenkins, L., & Popoola, O. (1979). Detection of deception in adults and children via facial expressions. *Child Development, 50,* 350–355.

Feldman, R. S., & White, J. B. (1980). Detecting deception in children. *Journal of Communication, 30,* 121–139.

Ferguson, L. R., Partyka, L. B., & Lester, B. M. (1974). Patterns of parent perception differentiating clinic from non-clinic children. *Journal of Abnormal Child Psychology, 2,* 169–181.

Ferguson, R. J., & Miller, A. L. (1974). *Polygraph for the defense.* Springfield, IL: Charles C. Thomas.

Fisher, G., & Silverstein, A. B. (1969). Simulation of poor adjustment on a measure of self actualization. *Journal of Clinical Psychology, 25,* 198–199.

Floch, M. (1950). Limitations of the lie detector. *Journal of Criminal Law, Criminology, and Police Science, 40,* 651–653.

Fogel, B. S., Mills, M. J., & Landen, J. E. (1986). Legal aspects of the treatment of delirium. *Hospital and Community Psychiatry, 37,* 154–158.

Folks, D. G., & Freeman, A. M. (1985). Munchausen's syndrome and other factitious illness. *Psychiatric Clinics of North America, 8*(2), 263–278.

Fontana, A. F., Klein, E. B., Lewis, E., & Levine, L. (1968). Presentation of self in mental illness. *Journal of Consulting and Clinical Psychology, 32,* 110–119.

Ford, C. V., & Folks, D. G. (1985). Conversion disorders: An overview. *Psychosomatics, 26,* 371–382.

References 339

Forman, R. F., & McCauley, C. (1986). Validity of the Positive Control Test using the field practice model. *Journal of Applied Psychology, 71*, 691–698.

Fosberg, I. A. (1938). Rorschach reactions under varied instructions. *Rorschach Research Exchange, 3*, 12–30.

Fosberg, I. A. (1941). An experimental study of the reliability of the Rorschach psychodiagnostic technique. *Rorschach Research Exchange, 5*, 72–84.

Frankel, F. H. (1976). *Hypnosis: Trance as a coping mechanism.* New York: Plenum Medical Book Company.

Fras, I. (1978). Factitial disease: An update. *Psychosomatics, 19*(2), 119–122.

Freund, K. (1963). A laboratory method for diagnosing predominance of homo- or heteroerotic interest in the male. *Behavior Research and Therapy, 1*, 85–93.

Freund, K. (1967). Diagnosing homo- or heterosexuality and erotic age-preference by means of a psychophysiological test. *Behavior Research and Therapy, 5*, 209–228.

Freund, K. (1971). A note on the use of the phallometric method of measuring mild sexual arousal in the male. *Behavior Therapy, 2*, 223–228.

Freund, K. (1975). The present state of the phallometric test of erotic preference. *European Journal of Behavioral Analysis and Modification, 1*(1), 27–28.

Freund, K. (1981). Assessment of pedophilia. In M. Cook & L. K. Howell (Eds.), *Adult sexual interest in children* (pp. 139–179). New York: Academic Press.

Freund, K., & Blanchard, R. (1986). *Phallometric diagnosis of pedophilia.* Unpublished manuscript.

Freund, K., Chan, S., & Coulthard, R. (1979). Phallometric diagnosis with "nonadmitters." *Behavior Research and Therapy, 17*, 451–457.

Freund, K., & Langevin, R. (1976). Bisexuality in homosexual pedophilia. *Archives of Sexual Behavior, 5*, 415–423.

Freund, K., Langevin, R., & Barlow, D. (1974). Comparison of two penile measures of erotic arousal. *Behavior Research and Therapy, 12*, 335–359.

Freund, K., Langevin, R., Satterberg, J., & Steiner, B. (1977). Extension of the gender identity scale for males. *Archives of Sexual Behavior, 6*, 507–519.

Freund, K., Langevin, R., & Zajac, Y. (1974). A note on erotic arousal value of moving and stationary human forms. *Behavior Research and Therapy, 12*, 117–119.

Freund, K., McKnight, C. K., Langevin, R., & Cibiri, S. (1972). The female child as a surrogate object. *Archives of Sexual Behavior, 4*, 509–517.

Friedlander, J. W., & Sarbin, T. R. (1938). The depth of hypnosis. *Journal of Abnormal and Social Psychology, 33*, 453–475.

Friedman, M. J. (1981). Post-Vietnam syndrome: Recognition and management. *Psychosomatics, 22*, 931–943.

Gaffney, G. R. L., & Berlin, F. S. (1984). Is there hypothalamic-pituitary-gonadal dysfunction in paedophilia? A pilot study. *British Journal of Psychiatry, 145*, 657–660.

Gallucci, N. T. (1984). Prediction of dissmulation on the MMPI in a clinical field setting. *Journal of Consulting and Clinical Psychology, 52*, 917–918.

Garfield, P. (1987). Nightmares in the sexually abused female teenager. *Psychiatric Journal of the University of Ottawa, 12*, 93–97.

Garfield, S. L. (1978). Research on client variables in psychotherapy. In S. L. Garfield and A. E. Bergin (Eds.), *Handbook of psychotherapy and behavior change: An empirical analysis* (2nd ed.) (pp. 191–232). New York: John Wiley & Sons.

Gavin, H. (1843). *On feigned and factitious diseases, on the means used to stimulate or produce them, and on the best methods of discovering impostors.* London: John Churchill.

Gelles, R. J. (1980). Violence in the family: A review of research in the seventies. *Journal of Marriage and the Family, 42*, 873–885.

Gendreau, T., Irvine, M., & Knight, S. (1973). Evaluating response set styles on the MMPI with prisoners: Faking good adjustment and maladjustment. *Canadian Journal of Behavioral Science, 5*, 183–194.

Gerson, M. J., & Victoroff, V. M. (1948). Experimental investigation into the validity of confessions obtained under sodium Amytal narcosis. *Clinical Psychopathology, 9*, 359–375.

Gerson, R. P., & Damon, W. (1978). Moral understanding and children's conduct. In W. Damon (Ed.), *Moral development* (No. 2). San Francisco: Jossey-Bass.

Gibbens, T. C. N., & Williams, J. E. H. (1977). Medicolegal aspects of amnesia. In C. W. M. Whitty & O. L. Zangwill (Eds.), *Amnesia* (pp. 245–264). London: Butterworths.

Giesen, M., & Rollison, M. A. (1980). Guilty knowledge versus innocent associations: Effects of trait anxiety and stimulus context on skin conductance. *Journal of Research in Personality, 14*, 1–11.

Gill, M. M., & Brenman, M. (1959). *Hypnosis and related states: Psychoanalytic studies in regression.* New York: International Universities Press.

Gilligan, C. (1982). *In a different voice.* Cambridge, MA: Harvard University Press.

Ginton, A., Daie, N., Elaad, E., & Ben-Shakhar, G. (1982). A method for evaluating the use of the polygraph in a real life situation. *Journal of Applied Psychology, 67*, 131–137.

Goebel, R. A. (1983). Detection of faking on the Halstead-Reitan neuropsychological test battery. *Journal of Clinical Psychology, 39*, 731–742.

Goldberg, J. O., & Miller, H. R. (1986). *Performance of psychiatric inpatients and intellectually deficient individuals on a task assessing the validity of memory complaints.* Manuscript submitted for publication.

Golden, C. J., Hammeke, T. A., & Purisch, A. D. (1979). *Manual for the Luria-Nebraska neuropsychological battery.* Lincoln, NE: University of Nebraska Press.

Goldstein, E. R. (1923). Reaction times and the consciousness of deception. *American Journal of Psychology, 34*, 562–581.

Goodwin, D. W., Alderson, P., & Rosenthal, R. (1971). Clinical significance of hallucinations in psychiatric disorders: A study of 116 hallucinatory patients. *Archives of General Psychiatry, 24*, 76–80.

Goodwin, J., Cauthorne, C. G., & Rada, R. T. (1980). Cinderella syndrome: Children who simulate neglect. *The American Journal of Psychiatry, 137*(10), 1223–1225.

Goodwin, J., Sahd, D., & Rada, R. T. (1978). Incest hoax: False accusations, false denials. *Bulletin of the American Academy of Psychiatry and the Law, 6*, 269–276.

Gordon, B., & Marin, O. S. M. (1979). Transient global amnesia: An extensive case report. *Journal of Neurology, Neurosurgery, and Psychiatry, 42*, 572–575.

Gorenstein, E. E. (1982). Frontal lobe functions in psychopaths. *Journal of Abnormal Psychology, 91*, 368–379.

Gorman, C. A., Wahner, H. W., & Tauxe, W. N. (1970). Metabolic malingerers. *The American Journal of Medicine, 48*, 708–714.

Gorman, W. F. (1982). Defining malingering. *Journal of Forensic Sciences, 27*, 401–407.

Gorman, W. F. (1984). Neurological malingering. *Behavioral Sciences and the Law, 2*(1), 67–73.

Gough, H. G. (1947). Simulated patterns on the MMPI. *Journal of Abnormal and Social Psychology, 42*, 215–225.

Gough, H. G. (1950). The *F* minus *K* dissimulation index for the MMPI. *Journal of Consulting Psychology, 14*, 408–413.

Gough, H. G. (1954). Some common misconceptions about neuroticism. *Journal of Consulting Psychology, 18*, 287–292.

Gough, H. G. (1957). *California Psychological Inventory manual.* Palo Alto, CA: Consulting Psychologists Press.

Gould, R., Miller, B. L., Goldberg, M. A., & Benson, D. F. (1986). The validity of hysterical signs and symptoms. *The Journal of Nervous and Mental Diseases, 174*, 593–597.

Graf, P., Squire, L. R., & Mandler, G. (1984). The information that amnesics do not forget. *Journal of Experimental Psychology: Learning, Memory, and Cognition, 10*, 164–178.

Graham, J. R. (1987). *The MMPI: A practical guide* (2nd ed.). New York: Oxford University Press.

Gravitz, M. A., & Gerton, M. I. (1976). An empirical study of internal consistency on the MMPI. *Journal of Consulting Psychology, 32*, 567–568.

Grayson, H. M. (1951). A psychological admissions testing program and manual. Los Angeles: Veterans Administration Center, Neuropsychiatric Hospital.

Grayson, H. M., & Olinger, L. B. (1957). Simulation of "normalcy" by psychiatric patients on the MMPI. *Journal of Consulting Psychology, 21*, 73–77.

Green, A. H. (1986). True and false allegations of sexual abuse in child custody disputes. *Journal of the American Academy of Child Psychiatry, 25*, 449–456.

Green, B. L., Wilson, J. P., & Lindy, J. D. (1981, September). *A conceptual framework for post-traumatic stress syndromes among survivor groups.* Presentation to 33rd Institute on Hospital and Community Psychiatry, San Diego, CA.

Greene, R. L. (1978). An empirically derived MMPI carelessness scale. *Journal of Clinical Psychology, 34*, 407–410.

Greene, R. L. (1979). Response consistency on the MMPI: The TR index. *Journal of Personality Assessment, 43*, 69–71.

Greene, R. L. (1980). *The MMPI: An interpretive manual.* New York: Grune & Stratton.

Greene, R. L. (1986). [MMPI data research tape for normal adults and college students.] Unpublished raw data.

Greene, R. L. (1988). The relative efficacy of *F-K* and the obvious and subtle scales to detect over-reporting of psychopathology on the MMPI. *Journal of Clinical Psychology, 44*, 152–159.

Greenfeld, D. (1987). Feigned psychosis in a 14-year-old girl. *Hospital and Community Psychiatry, 38*, 73–77.

Greenfield v. Commonwealth, 241 Va. 710, 204 S.E.2d 415 (1974).

Gronwall, D. (1977). Paced auditory serial-addition task: A measure of recovery from concussion. *Perceptual and Motor Skills, 44*, 367–373.

Gronwall, D., & Wrightson, P. (1974). Delayed recovery of intellectual function after minor head injury. *Lancet, 2*, 605–609.

Gronwall, D., & Wrightson, P. (1981). Memory and information processing capacity after closed head injury. *Journal of Neurology, Neurosurgery, and Psychiatry, 440*, 889–895.

Groth, A. M. (1979). *Men who rape: The psychology of the offender.* New York: Plenum.

Grow, R., McVaugh, W., & Eno, T. D. (1980). Faking and the MMPI. *Journal of Clinical Psychology, 36*, 910–917.

Gudjonsson, G. H. (1981). *Some psychological determinants of electrodermal responses to deception.* Unpublished doctoral dissertation, University of Surrey, Surrey, England.

Guthkelch, A. N. (1980). Post-traumatic amnesia, post-concussional symptoms and accident neurosis. *European Neurology, 19*, 91–102.

Gutkin, D. C. (1972). The effect of systematic changes on intentionality in children's moral judgments. *Child Development, 43*, 187–195.

Guttmacher, M. S. (1955). *Psychiatry and the law.* New York: Grune and Stratton.

Guttmacher, M. S., & Weihofen, H. (1952). *Psychiatry and the law.* New York: W. W. Norton.

Guze, S. B., & Perley, M. J. (1963). Observations on the natural history of hysteria. *American Journal of Psychiatry, 116*, 960–965.

Hafeiz, H. B. (1980). Hysterical conversion: A prognostic study. *British Journal of Psychiatry, 136*, 548–551.

Hain, J. D., Smith, B. M., & Stevenson, I. (1966). Effectiveness and processes of interviewing with drugs. *Journal of Psychiatric Research, 4*, 95–106.

Hale, G., Zimostrad, S., Duckworth, J., & Nicholas, D. (1986, March). *The abusive personality: MMPI profiles of male batterers.* Paper presented at the 22nd Annual Symposium on Recent Developments in the Use of the MMPI, Clearwater, FL.

Hall, H. V. (1982). Dangerousness predictions and the maligned forensic professional. *Criminal Justice and Behavior, 9*, 3–12.

Hall, R. C. W., Gardner, E. R., Stickney, S. K., LeCann, A. F., & Popkin, M. K. (1980). Physicall illness manifesting as psychiatric disease. II. Analysis of a state hospital inpatient population. *Archives of General Psychiatry, 37*, 989–995.

Hall, R. C. W., Popkin, M. K., Devaul, R. A., Faillace, L. A., & Stickney, S. K. (1978). Physical illness presenting as psychiatric disease. *Archives of General Psychiatry, 35*, 1315–1320.

Halleck, S. L. (1971). *The politics of therapy.* New York: Harper and Row.

Halleck, S. L. (1975). The criminal's problem with psychiatry. In R. C. Allen (Ed.), *Readings in law and psychiatry* (pp. 51–54). Baltimore, MD: John Hopkins University Press.

Halstead, W. C. (1947). *Brain and intelligence.* Chicago: University of Chicago Press.

Hamilton, J. D. (1985). Pseudo post-traumatic stress disorder. *Military Medicine, 150*, 353–356.

Hamilton, J. E. (1906). *Railway and other accidents.* London: Bailliere, Tindall & Co.

Hamsher, J. H., & Farina, A. (1967). "Openness" as a dimension of projective test responses. *Journal of Consulting Psychology, 31*, 525–528.

Harding v. State, 5 Md. App. 230, 246 A.2d 302 (1968); *cert. denied*, 395 U.S. 949 (1968).

Hare, R. D. (1970). *Psychopathy: Theory and research.* New York: Wiley.

Hare, R. D. (1978). Electrodermal and cardiovascular correlates of psychopathy. In R. D. Hare & D. Schalling (Eds.), *Psychopathic behavior: Approaches to research.* Chichester: Wiley.

Hare, R. D. (1980). A research scale for the assessment of psychopathy in criminal populations. *Personality and Individual Differences, 1*, 111–119.

Harris, J. E., & Morris, P. E. (1984). *Everyday memory, actions, and absent-mindedness.* London: Academic Press.

Harrison, A. A., Hwalek, M., Raney, D. F., & Fritz, J. G. (1978). Cues to deception in an interview situation. *Social Psychology, 41*, 156–161.

Hartshorne, H., & May, M. A. (1928). *Studies in deceit.* New York: Macmillan.

Hartshorne, H., & May, M. A. (1928). *Studies in the nature of character* (Vol. 1). New York: Macmillan.

Hartshorne, H., & May, M. A. (1930). *Studies in the nature of character* (Vol. 2). New York: Macmillan.

Harvey, M. A., & Sipprelle, C. N. (1976). Demand characteristic effects on the subtle and obvious subscales of the MMPI. *Journal of Personality Assessment, 40*, 539–544.

Haughton, P. M., Lewsley, A., Wilson, M., & Williams, R. G. (1979). A forced-choice procedure to detect feigned or exaggerated hearing loss. *British Journal of Audiology, 13*, 135–138.

Hawkins, D. W. (1979). Doctor- and drug-induced diseases. In P. Cutler (Ed.), *Problem solving in clinical medicine.* Baltimore: Williams & Wilkins.

Hay, G. G. (1983). Feigned psychosis—A review of the simulation of mental illness. *British Journal of Psychiatry, 143*, 8–10.

Heaton, R. K., Smith, H. H., Lehman, R. A. W., & Vogt, A. T. (1978). Prospects for faking believable deficits on neuropsychological testing. *Journal of Consulting and Clinical Psychology, 46*, 892–900.

Hedlund, J. H., & Won Cho, D. (1979). [MMPI data research tape for Missouri Department of Mental Health patients.] Unpublished raw data.

Hellerstein, D., Frosch, W., & Koenigsberg, H. W. (1987). The clinical significance of command hallucinations. *American Journal of Psychiatry, 144*, 219–225.

Henderson, J. (1986, October). *Psychic trauma claims in civil and administrative law.* Panel presentation at the American Academy of Psychiatry and the Law Meeting, Philadelphia, PA.

Henson, D. E., & Rubin, H. B. (1971). Voluntary control of eroticism. *Journal of Applied Behavior Analysis*, 4(1), 37–44.

Herman, M. (1985). Amytal and the detection of deception. In R. Rosner (Ed.), *Critical issues in American psychiatry and law* (Vol. 2) (pp. 187–194). New York: Plenum.

Herman, D. H. J. (1986). Criminal defenses and pleas in mitigation based on amnesia. *Behavioral Sciences and the Law*, 4, 5–26.

Hilgard, E. R. (1965). *Hypnotic susceptibility.* New York: Harcourt, Brace, Jovanovich.

Hilgard, E. R. (1967). A quantitative study of pain and its reduction through hypnotic suggestions. *Proceedings of the National Academy of Sciences*, 57, 1581–1586.

Hilgard, E. R. (1973). Dissociation revisited. In M. Henle, J. Jaynes & J. J. Sullivan (Eds.), *Historical conceptions of psychology* (pp. 205–219). New York: Springer Publishing Co.

Hilgard, E. R. (1977). *Divided consciousness: Multiple controls in human thought and action.* New York: John Wiley & Sons.

Hilgard, E. R. (1979). The Stanford Hypnotic Susceptibility Scales as related to other measures of hypnotic responsiveness. *International Journal of Clinical and Experimental Hypnosis*, 21, 68–82.

Hilgard, E. R. (1982). Hypnotic susceptibility and implications for measurement. *International Journal of Clinical and Experimental Hypnosis*, 30, 294–403.

Hilgard, E. R., Crawford, H. J., & West, A. (1979). The Stanford Arm Levitation Induction and Test (SHALIT): A six minute hypnotic induction and measurement scale. *International Journal of Clinical and Experimental Hypnosis*, 27, 111–124.

Hilgard, E. R., & Loftus, E. F. (1979). Effective interrogation of the eyewitness. *International Journal of Clinical and Experimental Hypnosis*, 27, 342–357.

Hirst, W. (1982). The amnesic syndrome: Description and explanations. *Psychological Bulletin*, 91, 435–460.

Hoffman, H. (1968). Performance on the Personality Research Form under desirable and undesirable instructions: Personality disorders. *Psychological Reports*, 23, 507–510.

Hofling, C. K. (1965). Some psychologic aspects of malingering. *General Practitioner*, 31, 115–121.

Hollender, M. H., & Hirsch, S. J. (1964). Hysterical psychosis. *The American Journal of Psychiatry*, 120, 1066–1074.

Holmes, D. S. (1974). The conscious control of thematic projection. *Journal of Consulting and Clinical Psychology*, 42, 323–329.

Holstein, C. (1976). Irreversible, stepwise sequence in the development of moral judgment: A longitudinal study of males and females. *Child Development*, 47, 51–61.

Holtzman, W., Thorpe, J. S., Swartz, J. D., & Herron, E. W. (1961). *Inkblot perception and personality.* Austin, TX: University of Texas Press.

Honts, C. R., Hodes, R. L., & Raskin, D. C. (1985). Effects of physical countermeasures of the physiological detection of deception. *Journal of Applied Psychology*, 70, 177–187.

Honts, C. R., Raskin, D. C., & Kircher, J. C. (1983). Detection of deception: Effectiveness of physical countermeasures under high motivation conditions. *Psychophysiology*, 20, 446, (Abstract).

Hopwood, J. S., & Snell, H. K. (1933). Amnesia in relation to crime. *Journal of Mental Science*, 79, 27–41.

Horsley, J. S. (1936). Narcoanalysis. *Journal of Mental Sciences*, 82, 416.

Horton, P. C. (1976). Personality disorder and parietal lobe dysfunction. *American Journal of Psychiatry*, 133, 782–785.

Horvath, F. S. (1974). *The accuracy and reliability of police polygraphic ("lie detector") examiners judgments of truth and deception: The effect of selected variables.* Unpublished doctoral dissertation, Michigan State University, East Lansing, MI.

Horvath, F. S. (1976). Detection of deception: A review of field and laboratory research. *Polygraph*, 5, 107–145.

Horvath, F. S. (1977). The effect of selected variables on interpretation of polygraph records. *Journal of Applied Psychology, 62*, 127-136.

Horvath, F. S. (1985). Job screening. *Society, 22*, 43-46.

Horvath, F. S., & Reid, J. E. (1971). The reliability of polygraph examiner diagnosis of truth and deception. *The Journal of Criminal Law, Criminology, and Police Science, 62*, 276-281.

Hoyer, T. V. (1959). Pseudologia fantastica. *Psychiatric Quarterly, 33*, 203-220.

Hucker, S. J., & Ben-Aron, M. H. (1985). Elderly sex offenders. In R. Langevin (Ed.), *Erotic preference, gender identity and aggression in men* (pp. 211-224). Hillsdale, NJ: Lawrence Erlbaum Associates.

Hucker, S., & Langevin, R. (1987). Cerebral damage in sexually violent men. Unpublished manuscript, University of Toronto, Toronto, Ontario.

Hucker, S., Langevin, R., Bain, J., & Handy, L. (1987). *Provera therapy for sex offenders against children*. Unpublished manuscript, University of Toronto, Toronto, Ontario.

Hucker, S., Langevin, R., Wortzman, G., Bain, J., Handy, L., Chambers, J., & Wright, S. (1986). Neuropsychological impairment in pedophiles. *Canadian Journal of Behavioral Science, 18*, 440-448.

Hucker, S., Langevin, R., Wortzman, G., Dicker, R., & Wright, P. (1988). Cerebral damage and dysfunction in sexually aggressive men. *Annals of Sex Research, 1*, 1.

Huddleston, J. H. (1932). *Accidents, neuroses and compensation*. Baltimore: Williams and Wilkins.

Hunt, H. F. (1948). The effect of deliberate deception on MMPI performance. *Journal of Consulting Psychology, 12*, 396-402.

Hunter, F. L., & Ash, P. (1973). The accuracy and consistency of polygraph examiner's diagnoses. *Journal of Police Science and Administration, 1*, 370-375.

Hurst, A. F. (1940). *Medical diseases of war*. London: Edward Arnold.

Hyler, S. E., & Spitzer, R. S. (1978). Hysteria spilt asunder. *The American Journal of Psychiatry, 135*(12), 1500-1504.

Hyler, S. E., & Sussman, N. (1981). Chronic factitious disorder with physical symptoms (the Munchausen syndrome). *Psychiatric Clinics of North America, 4*(2), 365-377.

Iacono, W. G. (1984, May). Research on the guilty knowledge test. In D. T. Lykken (Chair), *The detection of deception in 1984*. Symposium conducted at the meeting of the American Association of the Advancement of Science, New York.

Iacono, W. G. (1985). Guilty knowledge. *Society, 22*, 52-54.

Iacono, W. G., Boisvenu, G. A., & Fleming, J. A. (1984). The effects of diazepam and methyphenidate on the electrodermal detection of guilty knowledge. *Journal of Applied Psychology, 69*, 289-299.

Iacono, W. G., Cerri, A. M., Patrick, C. J., & Fleming, J. A. E. (1987). *The effects of meprobamate, diazepam, and propranolol on the guilty knowledge test*. Unpublished manuscript.

Iacono, W. G., & Patrick, C. J. (1987). What psychologists should know about lie detection. In I. B. Weiner & A. Hess (Eds.), *Handbook of forensic psychology*. New York: John Wiley & Sons.

Inbau, F. E., & Reid, J. E. (1967). *Criminal interrogation and confessions* (2nd ed.). Baltimore: Williams and Wilkins.

Ingraham, M. R., & Moriarty, D. M. (1967). A contribution to the understanding of Ganser syndrome. *Comprehensive Psychiatry, 8*, 35-44.

Ironside, R. (1940). Feigned epilepsy in wartime. *British Medical Journal, 1*, 703-705.

Jackson, D. N. (1971). The dynamics of structured personality tests: 1971. *Psychological Review, 78*, 229-248.

Jacobson, S. A. (1969). Mechanisms of sequelae of minor craniocervical trauma. In A. E. Walker, W. F. Caveness, and M. Critchley (Eds.), *Late effects of head injury* (pp. 35-45). Springfield, IL: Charles C. Thomas.

Jamieson, R. C., & Wells, C. E. (1979). Manic psychosis in a patient with multiple metastatic brain tumors. *Journal of Clinical Psychiatry, 40*, 280-282.

Jenike, M. A., & Brotman, A. W. (1984). The EEG in obsessive-compulsive disorder. *Journal of Clinical Psychiatry, 45*, 122-124.

Johnson, J. H., Klingler, D. E., & Williams, T. A. (1977). The external criterion study of the MMPI validity indices. *Journal of Clinical Psychology, 33*, 154-156.

Johnson, V. E. (1973). *I'll quit tomorrow.* New York: Harper & Row.

Johnston, J. R., Campbell, L. E. G., & Mayes, S. S. (1985). Latency children in post-separation and divorce disputes. *Journal of the American Academy of Child and Adolescent Psychiatry, 24*, 563-574.

Jonas, J. M., & Pope, H. G. (1985). The dissimulating disorders: A single diagnostic entity? *Comprehensive Psychiatry, 26*(1), 58-62.

Jones, A. B., & Llewellyn, L. J. (1917). *Malingering or the simulation of disease.* Philadelphia: J. Blackiston's Son & Co.

Jones, D. P. H., & McGraw, J. M. (1987). Reliable and factitious accounts of sexual abuse to children. *Journal of Interpersonal Violence, 2*, 27-45.

Jourard, S. M. (1971). *Self-disclosure: An experimental analysis of the transparent self.* New York: Wiley-Interscience.

Joyce, C. (1984). Lie detector. *Psychology Today, 18*, 6-8.

Junginger, J., & Frame, C. L. (1985). Self-report of the frequency and phenomenology of verbal hallucinations. *Journal of Nervous and Mental Diseases, 173*, 149-155.

Kalman, G. (1977). On combat neurosis. *International Journal of Social Psychiatry, 23*, 195-203.

Kanas, N., & Barr, M. A. (1984). Self-control of psychotic productions in schizophrenics [Letter to the editor]. *Archives of General Psychiatry, 41*, 919-920.

Kanzer, M. (1939). Amnesia: A statistical study. *American Journal of Psychiatry, 96*, 711-716.

Kaplan, M. F., & Eron, L. D. (1965). Test sophistication and faking in the TAT situation. *Journal of Projective Techniques and Personality Assessment, 29*, 498-503.

Karson, S., & O'Dell, J. W. (1976). *A guide to the clinical use of the 16 PF.* Champaign, IL: Institute for Personality and Ability Testing.

Kasl, Q. V., & Mahl, G. F. (1965). The relationship of disturbances and hesitations in spontaneous speech to anxiety. *Journal of Personality and Social Psychology, 1*, 425-433.

Keasey, C. B. (1977). Children's developing awareness and usage of intentionality and motives. In C. B. Keasey (Ed.), *Nebraska symposium on motivation* (pp. 219-260). Lincoln: University of Nebraska Press.

Keiser, L. (1968). *The traumatic neurosis.* Philadelphia: J. B. Lippincott.

Kelly, R. (1975). The post-traumatic syndrome: An iatrogenic disease. *Forensic Sciences, 6*, 17-24.

Kelly, R., & Smith, B. N. (1981). Post-traumatic syndrome: Another myth discredited. *Journal of the Royal Society of Medicine, 74*, 275-278.

Kennedy, F. (1946). The mind of the injured worker: Its effect on disability periods. *Comprehensive Medicine, 1*, 19-24.

Keschner, M. (1960). Simulation (malingering) in relation to injuries of the brain and spinal cord and their coverings. In S. Brock (Ed.), *Injuries of the brain and spinal cord and their coverings* (pp. 410-439). New York: Springer Publishing Co.

Key v. State, 480 So.2d 488 (Fla. 1983).

Kiddoo, K. P. (1977 August). *Personality, cognitive style and imagination-related behaviors.* Paper presented at the annual meeting of the American Psychological Association, San Francisco, CA.

Kiersch, T. A. (1962). Amnesia: A clinical study of ninety-eight cases. *American Journal of Psychiatry, 119*, 57-60.

Kihlstrom, J. F., & Evans, F. J. (1979). *Functional disorders of memory.* Hillsdale, NJ: Lawrence Erlbaum Associates.

Kiloh, L. G. (1961). Pseudo-dementia. *Acta Psychiatrica Scandinavica, 37*, 336-351.

King, C. M., & Chalmers, R. J. G. (1984). Another aspect of contrived disease: "dermatitis simulata." *Cutis, 34*, 463–464.

King, M. (1971). The development of some intention concepts in young children. *Child Development, 42*, 1145–1152.

Kircher, J. C., & Raskin, D. C. (1982). Cross-validation of a computerized diagnostic procedure for detection of deception. *Psychophysiology, 19*, 568–569.

Kirchner, W. K. (1961). "Real-life" faking on the Strong Vocational Interest Blank by sales applicants. *Journal of Applied Psychology, 45*, 273–276.

Kleinmuntz, B., & Szucko, J. J. (1984a). A field study of the fallibility of polygraphic lie detection. *Nature, 308*, 449–450.

Kleinmuntz, B., & Szucko, J. J. (1984b). Lie detection in ancient and modern times: A call for contemporary scientific study. *American Psychologist, 39*, 766–776.

Kleinmuntz, B., & Szucko, J. J. (1982). On the fallibility of lie detection. *Law and Society Review, 17*, 85–104.

Kluft, R. P. (1987). The simulation and dissimulation of multiple personality disorder. *American Journal of Clinical Hypnosis, 30*, 104–118.

Knapp, M. L., Hart, R. P., & Dennis, H. S. (1974). An exploration of deception as a communication construct. *Human Communication Research, 1*, 15–29.

Knutson, J. F. (1972). Review of the Rorschach. In O. K. Buros (Ed.), *Mental measurements yearbook* (7th ed.) (pp. 435–440). Highland Park, NJ: Gryphon Press.

Kohlberg, L. (1958). *The development of modes of thinking and choices in years 10 to 16.* Unpublished doctoral dissertation, University of Chicago, Chicago, IL.

Kohlberg, L. (1964). Development of moral character. In M. L. Hoffman and L. W. Hoffman (Eds.), *Review of child development research* (Vol. 1) (pp. 400–404). New York: Russell Sage Foundation.

Kohlberg, L. (1978). Revisions in the theory and practice of moral development. In W. Damon (Ed.), *New directions in child development: Moral development* (pp. 83–88). San Francisco: Jossey-Bass.

Kohlberg, L. (1981). *The philosophy of moral development.* San Francisco: Harper and Row.

Kolarsky, A., & Madlafousek, J. (1977). Variability of stimulus effect in the course of phallometric testing. *Archives of Sexual Behavior, 6*(2), 135–141.

Kolarsky, A., & Madlafousek, J. (1983). The inverse role of preparatory erotic in exhibitionists: Phallometric studies. *Archives of Sexual Behavior, 12*(2), 123–148.

Konecni, V. J., & Ebbeson, E. B. (1979). External validity of research in legal psychology. *Law and Human Behavior, 3*, 39–70.

Koson, D., & Robey, A. (1973). Amnesia and competency to stand trial. *American Journal of Psychiatry, 130*, 588–592.

Kozol, H. L. (1945). Pretraumatic personality and psychiatric sequelae of head injury: Categorical pretraumatic personality status correlated with general psychiatric reaction to head injury based on analysis of two hundred cases. *Archives of Neurology and Psychiatry, 53*, 358–364.

Kozol, H. L. (1946). Pretraumatic personality and psychiatric sequelae of head injury: Correlations of multiple, specific factors in the pretraumatic personality and psychiatric reaction to head injury, based on analysis of one hundred and one cases. *Archives of Neurology and Psychiatry, 56*, 245–275.

Kraut, R. E., & Price, D. J. (1976). Machiavellianism in parents and their children. *Journal of Personality and Social Psychology, 33*, 782–786.

Krieger, M. J., & Levin, S. M. (1976). Schizophrenic behavior as a function of role expectation. *Journal of Clinical Psychology, 32*, 463–467.

Kroger, W., & Douce, R. (1979). Hypnosis in criminal investigation. *International Journal of Clinical and Experimental Hypnosis, 27*, 358–374.

Kwentus, J. A. (1981). Interviewing with intravenous drugs. *Journal of Clinical Psychiatry, 42*, 432–436.

LaBarbera, J. D., & Dozier, J. E. (1980). Hysterical seizures: The role of sexual exploitation. *Psychosomatics, 21*, 897–903.

Lachar, D. (1974). *MMPI: Clinical assessment and automated interpretation.* Los Angeles: Western Psychological Services.

Lachar, D., & Wrobel, T. A. (1979). Validating clinicians' hunches: Construction of a new MMPI critical item set. *Journal of Consulting and Clinical Psychology, 47*, 277–284.

Lambert, C., & Rees, W. L. (1944). Intravenous barbiturates in the treatment of hysteria. *British Medical Journal, 2*, 70–73.

Langevin, R. (1983). *Sexual strands: Understanding and treating sexual anomalies in men.* Hillsdale, NJ: Lawrence Erlbaum Associates.

Langevin, R. (1985). *Erotic preference, gender identity and aggression in men.* Hillsdale, NJ: Lawrence Erlbaum Associates.

Langevin, R. (1988). Biological factors in sexual aggression. *Annals of New York Academy of Science.*

Langevin, R., Bain, J., Ben-Aron, M. H., Coulthard, R., Day, D., Handy, L. (1985). Sexual aggression: Constructing a predictive equation. In R. Langevin (Ed.), *Erotic preference, gender identity, and aggression in men* (pp. 39–76). Hillsdale: NJ: Lawrence Erlbaum Associates.

Langevin, R., Ben-Aron, M., Coulthard, R., Day, D., Hucker, S., Purins, J., Roper, V., Russon, A. L., & Webster, C. (1985). The effect of alcohol on penile erection. In R. Langevin (Ed.), *Erotic preference, gender identity, and aggression in men* (pp. 101–112). Hillsdale, NJ: Lawrence Erlbaum Associates.

Langevin, R., Hucker, S. J., Handy, L., Hook, H. J., Purins, J. E., & Russon, A. E. (1985). Erotic preference and aggression in pedophilia. In R. Langevin (Ed.), *Erotic preference, gender identity, and aggression in men* (pp. 137–160). Hillsdale, NJ: Lawrence Erlbaum Associates.

Langevin, R., & Lang, R. A. (1985). Psychological treatment of pedophiles. *Behavioral Sciences and the Law, 3*, 403–419.

Langevin, R., Paitich, D., Freeman, R., Mann, K., & Handy, L. (1978). Personality characteristics and sexual anomalies in men. *Canadian Journal of Behavioral Science, 10*, 222–228.

Langevin, R., Paitich, D., & Russon, A. E. (1985). Are rapists sexually anomalous, aggressive or both? In R. Langevin (Ed.), *Erotic preference, gender identity and aggression in men* (pp. 17-38). Hillsdale, NJ: Lawrence Erlbaum Associates.

Langfeld, H. S. (1921). Psychophysical symptoms of deception. *Journal of Abnormal Psychology, 15*, 318–328.

Larson, J. A. (1932). *Lying and its detection.* Chicago: University of Chicago Press.

Lasky, R. (1982). *Evaluation of criminal responsibility in multiple personality and the related dissociative disorders.* Springfield, IL: Charles C. Thomas.

LaWall, J. S., & Oommen, K. J. (1978). Basilar artery migraine presenting as conversion hysteria. *Journal of Nervous and Mental Disease, 166*, 809–811.

Laws, D. R., & Bow, R. A. (1976). An improved mechanical strain gauge for recording penile circumference change. *Psychophysiology, 13*(6), 596–599.

Lawton, M. P. (1963). Deliberate faking on the psychopathic deviant scale of the MMPI. *Journal of Clinical Psychology, 19*, 269–271.

Lawton, M. P., & Kleban, M. H. (1965). Prisoners' faking on the MMPI. *Journal of Clinical Psychology, 21*, 269–271.

Lees, F. (1980). Disorders affecting posture and gait. *Practitioner, 224*, 722–733.

Lennox, W. G. (1943). Amnesia, real and feigned. *American Journal of Psychiatry, 99*, 732–743.

Levin, H. S., Benton, A. L., & Grossman, R. G. (1982). *Neurobehavioral consequences of closed head injury.* New York: Oxford University Press.

Levy, R. S., & Jankovic, J. (1983). Placebo-induced conversion reaction: A neurobehavioral and EEG study of hysterical aphasia, seizure, and coma. *Journal of Abnormal Psychology, 92,* 243–249.

Lewinsohn, P. M. (1970). An empirical test of several popular notions about hallucinations in schizophrenic patients. In W. Keup (Ed.), *Origin and mechanisms of hallucinations* (pp. 401–403). New York: Plenum Press.

Lewis, M. (1982). *Clinical aspects of child development* (2nd ed.). Philadelphia: Lea and Febiger.

Leyra v. Denno, 347 U.S. 556 (1954).

Lezak, M. D. (1983). *Neuropsychological assessment.* New York: Oxford University Press.

Liberty, P. G., Jr., Lunneborg, C. E., & Atkinson, G. C. (1964). Perceptual defense, dissimulation, and response styles. *Journal of Consulting Psychology, 28,* 529–537.

Lilienfeld, S. O., VanValkenburg, C., Larntz, K., & Akiskal, H. S. (1986). The relationship of histrionic personality disorder to antisocial personality and somatization disorders. *American Journal of Psychiatry, 143,* 718–722.

Lindemann, E. (1932). Psychological changes in normal and abnormal individuals under the influence of sodium amytal. *American Journal of Psychiatry, 88,* 1083–1091.

Lipman, F. D. (1962). Malingering in personal injury cases. *Temple Law Quarterly, 35,* 141–162.

Lipsitt, D. R. (1986). The factitious patient who sues. *The American Journal of Psychiatry, 143*(11), 1482.

Lipton, J. P. (1977). On the psychology of eyewitness testimony. *Journal of Applied Psychology, 62,* 90–95.

Lishman, W. A. (1978). *Organic psychiatry.* Oxford: Blackwell Scientific Publication.

Littlepage, G., & Pineault, T. (1978). Verbal, facial, and paralinguistic cues to the detection of truth and lying. *Personality and Social Psychology Bulletin, 4,* 461–464.

Loftus, E. F. (1979). *Eyewitness testimony.* Cambridge: Harvard University Press.

Loftus, E. F., & Palmer, J. C. (1974). Reconstruction of automobile destruction: An example of the interaction between language and memory. *Journal of Verbal Learning and Verbal Behavior, 13,* 585–589.

Loftus, E. F., & Zanni, G. (1975). Eyewitness testimony: The influence of wording of a question. *Bulletin of the Psychonomic Society, 5,* 86–88.

Lorei, T. W. (1970). Staff ratings of the consequence of release from or retention in a psychiatric hospital. *Journal of Consulting and Clinical Psychology, 34,* 46–55.

Ludwig, A. O. (1949). Malingering in combat soldiers. *Bulletin of the US Army Medical Department, 9,* 26–32.

Luria, A. R. (1966). *Higher cortical functions.* New York: Basic Books.

Luther, J. S., McNamara, J. O., Carwile, S., Miller, P., & Hope, V. (1982). Pseudoepileptic seizures: Methods and video analysis to aid diagnosis. *Annals of Neurology, 12,* 458–462.

Lykken, D. T. (1959). The GSR in the detection of guilt. *Journal of Applied Psychology, 43,* 385–388.

Lykken, D. T. (1960). The validity of the guilty knowledge technique: The effects of faking. *Journal of Applied Psychology, 44,* 258–262.

Lykken, D. T. (1974). Psychology and the lie detector industry. *American Psychologist, 29,* 725–739.

Lykken, D. T. (1978). The psychopath and the lie detector. *Psychophysiology, 15,* 137–142.

Lykken, D. T. (1981). *A tremor in the blood: Uses and abuses of the lie detector.* London: McGraw-Hill Book Company.

Lykken, D. T. (1984a). Trial by polygraph. *Behavioral Sciences and the Law, 2,* 75–92.

Lykken, D. T. (1984b). Polygraphic interrogation. *Nature, 307*, 681–684.

Lykken, D. T. (1987). *The detection of guilty knowledge: A comment on Forman and McCauley*. Unpublished manuscript.

Lynch, B. E., & Bradford, J. W. (1980). Amnesia: Its detection by psychophysiological measures. *Bulletin of the American Academy of Psychiatry and Law, 8*, 288–297.

Lynn, E. J., & Belza, M. (1984). Factitious post-traumatic stress disorder: The veteran who never got to Vietnam. *Hospital and Community Psychiatry, 35*(7), 697–701.

Lyons, J. A. (1987). Posttraumatic Stress Disorder in children and adolescents: A review of the literature. *Developmental and Behavioral Pediatrics, 8*, 349–356.

MacDonald, C. F. (1880). Feigned epilepsy. *American Journal of Insanity, 37*, 1–22.

MacDonald, J. M. (1976). *Psychiatry and the criminal: A guide to psychiatric examinations for the criminal courts* (3rd ed.). Springfield, IL: Charles C. Thomas.

Maier, N. R. S., & Thurber, J. A. (1968). Accuracy of judgement of deception when an interviewer is watched, heard, and read. *Personnel Psychology, 21*, 23–30.

Malingering. (1903). *Stethoscope, 6*, 33.

Maloney, M. P., Duvall, S. W., & Friesen, J. (1980). Evaluation of response consistency on the MMPI. *Psychological Reports, 46*, 295–298.

Maloney, M. T., Glasser, A., & Ward, M. P. (1980). *Malingering: An overview*. Unpublished manuscript.

Marceil, J. C. (1977). Implicit dimensions of idiography and nomothesis: A reformulation. *American Psychologist, 32*, 1046–1055.

Marcos, L. R., Goldberg, E., Feazell, D., & Wilner, M. (1977). The use of sodium amytal interviews in a short term community-orientated inpatient unit. *Diseases of the Nervous System, 38*, 283–286.

Marks, P. A., Seeman, W., & Haller, D. L. (1974). *The actuarial use of the MMPI with adolescents and adults*. Baltimore: Williams and Wilkins.

Marquis, K. H., Marshall, J., & Oskamp, S. (1972). Testimony validity as a function of question form, atmosphere, and item difficulty. *Journal of Applied Social Psychology, 2*, 167–186.

Marshall, W. L., Barbaree, H. E., & Christophe, D. (1986). Sexual offenders against female children: Sexual preferences for age of victims and type of behavior. *Canadian Journal of Behavioral Science, 18*, 424–439.

Martin, M. J. (1970). Psychiatric aspects of patients with compensation problems. *Psychosomatics, 11*, 81–84.

Martone, M., Butters, N., Payne, M., Becker, J. T., & Sax, D. S. (1984). Dissociations between skill learning and verbal recognition in amnesia and dementia. *Archives of Neurology, 41*, 955–970.

Matusewitch, E. P. (1981). Fear of lying: Polygraphs in employment. *Technology Review, 83*, 10–11.

McAllister, T. W. (1983). Overview: Pseudodementia. *The American Journal of Psychiatry, 140*(5), 528–533.

McAllister, T. W., & Price, T. R. P. (1987). Aspects of the behavior of psychiatric inpatients with frontal lobe damage: Some implications for diagnosis and treatment. *Comprehensive Psychiatry, 28*, 14–21.

McArthur, C. C. (1972). Review of the Rorschach. In O. K. Buros (Ed.), *Mental measurements yearbook* (7th ed.) (pp. 440–443). Highland Park, NJ: Gryphon Press.

McConaghy, N. (1974a). Measurements of change in penile dimensions. *Archives of Sexual Behavior, 3*(4), 381–388.

McConaghy, N. (1974b). Penile volume responses to moving and still pictures of male and female nudes. *Archives of Sexual Behavior, 3*(6), 565–570.

McConaghy, N. (1976). Is a homosexual orientation irreversible? *British Journal of Psychiatry, 129*, 556–563.

McConkey, K. M., Sheehan, P. W., & White, K. D. (1979). Comparison of the Creative Imagination Scale and the Harvard Group Scale of Hypnotic Susceptibility, Form A. *International Journal of Clinical and Experimental Hypnosis, 27,* 267-277.

McKeon, J., McGuffin, P., & Robinson, P. (1984). Obsessive-compulsive neurosis following head injury. *British Journal of Psychiatry, 144,* 190-192.

McKinely, J. C., Hathaway, S. R., & Meehl, P. E. (1948). The MMPI: K scale. *Journal of Consulting Psychology, 12,* 20-31.

Meadow, R. (1977). Munchausen syndrome by proxy. *Lancet, 2,* 343-345.

Meadow, R. (1982). Munchausen syndrome by proxy and pseudoepilepsy [Letter to the editor]. *Archives of Diseases in Childhood, 57,* 811-812.

Meadow, R. (1984a). Factitious illness: The hinterland of child abuse. *Recent Advances in Paediatrics, 7,* 217-232.

Meadow, R. (1984b). Munchausen by proxy and brain damage. *Developmental Medicine and Child Neurology, 26,* 672-674.

Mednick, S., & Christiansen, K. (1977). *Biosocial bases of criminal behavior.* New York: Gardner Press.

Meehl, P. E. (1971). Law and the fireside inductions: Some reflections of a clinical psychologist. *Journal of Social Issues, 27,* 65-99.

Meehl, P. E., & Hathaway, S. R. (1946). The *K* factor as a suppressor variable in the MMPI. *Journal of Applied Psychology, 30,* 525-564.

Meehl, P. E., & Rosen, A. (1955). Antecedent probability and the efficiency of psychometric signs, patterns, or cutting scores. *Psychological Bulletin, 52,* 194-216.

Megargee, E. I. (1972). *The California Psychological Inventory Handbook.* San Francisco: Jossey-Bass.

Mehlman, B., & Rand, M. E. (1960). Face validity of the MMPI. *Journal of General Psychology, 63,* 171-178.

Melton, R. (1984). Differential diagnosis: A common sense guide to psychological assessment. *Vet Center Voice Newsletter, 5,* 1-12.

Mendelson, G. (1981). Persistent work disability following settlement of compensation claims. *Law Institute Journal (Melbourne), 55,* 342-345.

Mendelson, G. (1982). Not "cured by a verdict." *The Medical Journal of Australia, 2,* 132-134.

Mendelson, G. (1984). Follow-up studies of personal injury litigants. *International Journal of Law and Psychiatry, 7,* 179-187.

Mendelson, G. (1985). Compensation neurosis. An invalid diagnosis. *The Medical Journal of Australia, 142,* 561-564.

Menninger, K. A. (1934). Polysurgery and polysurgical addiction. *Psychoanalytic Quarterly, 3,* 173-199.

Menninger, K. A. (1935). Psychology of a certain type of malingering. *Archives of Neurology and Psychiatry, 33,* 507-515.

Merback, K. (1984). The vet center dilemma: Post-traumatic stress disorder and personality disorders. *Vet Center Voice Newsletter, 5,* 6-7.

Mercer, B., Wapner, W., Gardner, H., & Banson, F. (1977). A study of confabulation. *Archives of Neurology, 34,* 429-433.

Merskey, H., & Buhrich, N. A. (1975). Hysteria and organic brain disease. *British Journal of Medical Psychology, 48,* 359-366.

Merskey, H., & Trimble, M. (1979). Personality, sexual adjustment, and brain lesion in patients with conversion symptoms. *American Journal of Psychiatry, 136,* 179-182.

Merskey, H., & Woodforde, J. M. (1972). Psychiatric sequelae of minor head injury. *Brain, 95,* 521-528.

Mesmer, F. A. (1948). *Mesmerism by Doctor Mesmer: Dissertation on the discovery of animal magnetism* (V. R. Myers, Trans.) London: Macdonald. (Original work published in 1779).

Metz, P., & Wagner, G. (1981). Penile circumference and erection. *Urology, 18*(3), 268–270.

Miller, E. (1986). Detecting hysterical sensory symptoms: An elaboration of the forced-choice technique. *British Journal of Clinical Psychology, 25,* 231–232.

Miller, H. (1961a). Accident neurosis. *British Medical Journal, 1,* 919–925.

Miller, H. (1961b). Accident neurosis. *British Medical Journal, 1,* 992–998.

Miller, H. (1966). Mental after-effects of head injury. *Proceedings of the Royal Society of Medicine, 59,* 257–267.

Miller, R. D. (in press). Conflict of interest between therapist–patient confidentiality and the duty to report sexual abuse of children. *Behavioral Sciences and the Law.*

Miller, H., & Cartlidge, N. (1972). Simulation and malingering after injuries to the brain and spinal cord. *Lancet, 1,* 580–586.

Miller, H., & Cartlidge, N. (1974). Simulation and malingering in relation to injuries of the brain and spinal cord. In E. H. Feiring (Ed.), *Brock's injuries of the brain and spinal cord* (5th ed.) (pp. 638–667). New York: Springer Publishing Company.

Miller, M. H., & Fellner, C. (1968). Compensable injuries and accompanying neurosis: The problem of continuing incapacity despite medical recovery. *Wisconsin Law Review, 1968,* 185.

Miller, T. R., Bauchner, J. E., Hocking, J. E., Fontes, N. E., Kaminsky, A. P., & Brendt, D. R. (1981). How well can observers detect deceptive testimony? In B. D. Sales (Ed.), *Perspectives in law and psychology. Volume 2, The trial process* (pp. 145–179). New York: Plenum.

Millon, T. (1983). *Millon Clinical Multiaxial Inventory manual* (3rd ed.). Minneapolis: Interpretive Scoring Systems.

Millon, T. (1984). Interpretative guide to the Millon Clinical Multiaxial Inventory. In P. McReynolds & G. J. Chelune (Eds.), *Advances in psychological assessment* (Vol. 6), pp. 1–40). San Francisco: Jossey-Bass.

Milner, B. (1978). Clues to the cerebral organization of memory. In P. A. Buser & A. Rougeul-Buser (Eds.), *Cerebral correlates of conscious experience* (pp. 139–153). Amsterdam: Elsevier.

Mittman, B. L. (1983). Judges' ability to diagnose schizophrenia on the Rorschach: The effect of malingering. *Dissertation Abstracts International, 44,* 2148-B.

Modlin, H. (1960). *Neurosis and trauma, roundtable presentation.* Washington, DC: American Psychiatric Association.

Modlin, H. (1986). Compensation neurosis. *Bulletin of the American Academy of Psychiatry and the Law, 14,* 263–271.

Monteiro, K. P., MacDonald, H., & Hilgard, E. R. (1980). Imagery, absorption and hypnosis: A factoral study. *Journal of Mental Imagery, 4,* 63–81.

Mook, D. G. (1983). In defense of external invalidity. *American Psychologist, 38,* 379–387.

Moore, G. L., McBurney, L., & Service, F. J. (1973). Self-induced hypoglycemia: A review of psychiatric aspects and report of three cases. *Psychiatry in Medicine, 4*(3), 301–311.

Morency, N. L., & Krauss, R. M. (1982). The nonverbal encoding and decoding of affect in first and fifth graders. In R. S. Feldman (Ed.), *Development of nonverbal behavioral skills* (pp. 181–199). New York: Spring-Verlag.

Morgan, A. H., Johnson, D. L., & Hilgard, E. R. (1974). The stability of hypnotic susceptibility: A longitudinal study. *International Journal of Clinical and Experimental Hypnosis, 22,* 249–257.

Morgan, M. E. I., Manning, D. J., Williams, W. J., & Rosenbloom, L. (1984). Fictitious epilepsy [Letter to the editor]. *Lancet, 2,* 233.

Moscovitch, M. (1982). Multiple dissociations of function in amnesia. In L. S. Cermak (Ed.), *Human memory and amnesia* (pp. 55–79). New York: Plenum.

Moscovitch, M. (1984). The sufficient conditions for demonstrating preserved memory in amnesia: A task analysis. In L. R. Square and N. Butters (Eds.), *The neuropsychology of memory* (pp. 104-114). New York: Guilford Press.

Moses, J. A., Golden, C. J., Wilkening, G. N., McKay, S. E., & Ariel, R. (1983). *Interpretation of the Luria-Nebraska neuropsychological battery* (Vol. II). New York: Grune & Stratton.

Moss, M. B., Albert, M. S., Butters, N., & Payne, M. M. (1986). Differential patterns of memory loss among patients with Alzheimer's disease, Huntington's disease, and alcoholic Korsakoff's syndrome. *Archives of Neurology, 43*, 239-246.

Mott, R. H., Small, I. F., & Andersen, J. M. (1965). Comparative study of hallucinations. *Archives of General Psychiatry, 12*, 595-601.

Moulton, J. (1987, April). *Assessment of head injuries.* Presentation to American Academy of Psychiatry and the Law, Midwest Chapter, Cincinnati, OH.

Mungas, D. (1982). Interictal behavior abnormality in temporal lobe epilepsy. *Archives of General Psychiatry, 39*, 108-111.

Murdock, B. (1962). The serial position effect in free recall. *Journal of Experimental Psychology, 64*, 482-488.

Murphy, W. D., Krisak, J., Stalgaitis, S., & Anderson, K. (1984). The use of penile tumescence measures with incarcerated rapists: Further validity issues. *Archives of Sexual Behavior, 13*(6), 545-554.

Muscio, B. (1916). The influence of the form of a question. *British Journal of Psychology, 8*, 351-389.

Nadelson, T. (1979). The Munchausen spectrum. Borderline character features. *General Hospital Psychiatry, 2*, 11-17.

Naish, J. M. (1979). Problems of deception in medical practice. *Lancet, 2*, 139-142.

Naples, M., & Hackett, T. P. (1978). The amytal interview: History and current uses. *Psychosomatics, 19*, 98-105.

Nash, J. R. (1976). *Hustlers and con men.* New York: M. Evans & Co.

Nichols, D., Greene, R. L., & Schmolck, P. (1988). Criteria for assessing consistency of item endorsement on the MMPI: Rationale, development, and empirical trials. *Journal of Clinical Psychology*, submitted for publication.

Note. (1952). Hypnotism, suggestibility and the law. *Nebraska Law Review, 31*, 575-596.

Note. (1981). Amnesia: The forgotten justification for finding an accused incompetent to stand trial. *Washburn Law Journal, 20*, 289-301.

Note. (1982). The use of hypnosis to refresh memory: Invaluable tool or dangerous device? *Washington University Law Quarterly, 60*, 1059-1085.

Oddy, M., Humphrey, M., & Uttley, D. (1978). Subjective impairment and social recovery after closed head injury. *Journal of Neurology, Neurosurgery, and Psychiatry, 41*, 611-616.

Office of Technology Assessment. (1983). *Scientific validity of polygraph testing: A research review and evaluation* (Report No. OTA-TM-H-15). Washington, DC: Author.

Ogden, T. H. (1979). On projective identification. *International Journal of Psychoanalysis, 60*, 357-373.

O'Rahilly, S. O., Turner, T. H., & Wass, J. A. H. (1985). Factitious epilepsy due to amitriptyline abuse. *Irish Medical Journal, 78*, 116-117.

Orne, M. T. (1959). The nature of hypnosis: Artifact and essence. *Journal of Abnormal and Social Psychology, 58*, 277-299.

Orne, M. T. (1961). The potential uses of hypnosis in interrogation. In A. D. Biderman & H. Zimmer (Eds.), *The manipulation of human behavior* (pp. 169-215). New York: John Wiley & Sons.

Orne, M. T. (1972). On the simulating subject as a quasi-control group in hypnosis research: What, why and how. In E. Fromm & R. E. Shor (Eds.), *Hypnosis: Research developments and perspectives* (pp. 399-443). Chicago: Aldine-Atherton.

Orne, M. T. (1975). Implications of laboratory research for the detection of deception. In N. Ansley (Ed.), *Legal admissibility of the polygraph* (pp. 94–119). Springfield, IL: Charles C. Thomas.

Orne, M. T. (1979). The use and misuse of hypnosis in court. *International Journal of Clinical and Experimental Hypnosis, 27,* 311–341.

Orne, M. T. (1983, October). *Forensic hypnosis.* Presented at the 16th Annual Meeting of the American Academy of Psychiatry and the Law, Albuquerque, NM.

Orne, M. T., Dinges, D. F., & Orne, E. C. (1984). On the differential diagnosis of multiple personality in the forensic context. *International Journal of Clinical and Experimental Hypnosis, 32,* 118–169.

Orne, M. T., Hilgard, E. R., Spiegel, H., Spiegel, D., Crawford, H. J., Evans, F. J., Orne, E. C., & Frischholz, E. I. (1979). The relationship between the Hypnotic Induction Profile and the Stanford Hypnotic Susceptibility Scales, Forms A and C. *International Journal of Clinical and Experimental Hypnosis, 27,* 85–102.

Orne, M. T., Thackery, R. I., & Paskewitz, D. A. (1972). On the detection of deception: A model for the study of physiological effects of psychological stimuli. In N. S. Greenfield & R. A. Sternback (Eds.), *Handbook of psychophysiology* (pp. 743–785). New York: Holt, Rinehart & Winston.

Orpen, C. (1978). Conscious control of projection in the Thematic Apperception Test. *Psychology, 15,* 67–75.

Osborne, D., & Davis, L. J., Jr. (1978). Standard scores for Wechsler Memory Scale subtests. *Journal of Clinical Psychology, 34,* 115–116.

Ossipov, V. B. (1944). Malingering: The simulation of psychosis. *Bulletin of the Menninger Clinic, 8,* 39–42.

Palmer, A. J., & Yoshimura, G. J. (1984). Munchausen syndrome by proxy. *Journal of the American Academy of Child Psychiatry, 23*(4), 504–508.

Pankratz, L. (1979). Symptom validity testing and symptom retraining procedures for the assessment and treatment of functional sensory deficits. *Journal of Consulting and Clinical Psychology, 47,* 409–410.

Pankratz, L. (1981). A review of the Munchausen syndrome. *Clinical Psychology Review, 1,* 65–78.

Pankratz, L. (1983). A new technique for the assessment and modification of feigned memory deficit. *Perceptual and Motor Skills, 57,* 367–372.

Pankratz, L. (1985, May). *The spectrum of factitious post-traumatic stress disorder.* Presentation to American Psychiatric Association, Dallas, TX.

Pankratz, L., Binder, L., & Wilcox, L. (1987). Assessment of an exaggerated somatosensory deficit with Symptom Validity Assessment. *Archives of Neurology, 44,* 798.

Pankratz, L., Fausti, S. A., & Peed, S. (1975). A forced choice technique to evaluate deafness in a hysterical or malingering patient. *Journal of Consulting and Clinical Psychology, 43,* 421–422.

Pankratz, L., & Glaudin, V. (1980). Psychosomatic disorders. In R. H. Woody (Ed.), *Encyclopedia of clinical assessment* (pp. 148–168). San Francisco: Jossey-Bass.

Pankratz, L., & Kofoed, L. (1988). Assessment and treatment of geezers. *Journal of the American Medical Association, 259,* 1228–1229.

Pankratz, L., & Lezak, M. D. (1987). Cerebral dysfunction in the Munchausen syndrome. *Hillside Journal of Clinical Psychiatry, 9,* 195–206.

Pankratz, L., & Lipkin, J. (1978). The transient patient in a psychiatric ward: Summering in Oregon. *Journal of Operational Psychiatry, 9,* 42–47.

Pankratz, L., & McCarthy, G. (1986). The Ten Least Wanted Patients. *Southern Medical Journal, 79,* 613–617.

Parker, N. (1977). Accident litigants with neurotic symptoms. *Medical Journal of Australia, 2,* 318–322.

Parker, N. (1979). Malingering: A dangerous diagnosis. *The Medical Journal of Australia, 1*, 568–569.

Parkin, A. J. (1984). Amnesic syndrome: A lesion-specific disorder? *Cortex, 20*, 479–508.

Parwatikar, S. D., Holcomb, W. R., & Menninger, K. A. (1985). The detection of malingered amnesia in accused murderers. *Bulletin of the American Academy of Psychiatry and Law, 13*, 97–103.

Patrick, C. J., & Iacono, W. G. (1986). The validity of lie detection with criminal psychopaths. *Psychophysiology, 23*, 452–453.

Patterson, G. R. (1982). *Coercive family interactions.* Eugene, OR: Castalia Press.

Pattie, F. A. (1935). A report on attempts to produce uniocular blindness by hypnotic suggestion. *British Journal of Medical Psychology, 15*, 230–241.

Peck, C. J., Fordyce, W. E., & Black, R. G. (1978). The effect of the pendency of claims for compensation upon behavior indicative of pain. *Washington Law Review, 53*, 251–279.

Peck, R. E. (1960). Use of hydroxydione as a truth serum. *Journal of Neuropsychiatry, 1*, 163–166.

People v. Boudin, Ind. No. 81-285 (Sup. Ct. N.Y., Opinion filed March 11, 1983).

People v. Buono, No. 81-A354231 (Cal Super. Ct. November 18, 1983).

People v. Cornell, 52 Cal.2d 99, 338 P.2d 447 (1959).

People v. Ebanks, 117 Cal. 652, 49 P. 1049 (1897).

People v. Harper, 111 Ill. App.2d 204. 250 N.E.2d 5 (1969).

People v. Hughes, 466 N.Y.S.2d 255 (1983).

People v. Hurd, Sup. Ct. N.J. Somerset Cty., April 2, 1980.

People v. Marsh, 17 Cal. App.2d 284, 338 P.2d 495 (1959).

People v. McBroom, 70 Cal. Rptr. 326 (1968).

People v. McNichol, 100 Cal. App.2d 544, 244 P.2d 21 (1950).

People v. Ritchie, No. C-36932 (Sup. Ct. Orange Cty. Cal. April 7, 1977).

People v. Schmidt, (1915). 216 N.Y. 324.

People v. Shirley, 31 Cal.3d 18 641 P.2d 775, 181 Cal. Rptr. 243 (1982).

People v. Thompson, C-12495 (San Mateo Super. Ct. 1983).

People v. Worthington, 105 Cal. 166, 38 P. 689 (1894).

Perry, J. C., & Jacobs, D. (1982). Overview: Clinical applications of the Amytal interview in psychiatric emergency settings. *American Journal of Psychiatry, 139*, 552–559.

Peterson, C. C., Peterson, J. L., & Seeto, D. (1983). Developmental changes in ideas in lying. *Child Development, 54*, 1529–1535.

Pettigrew, C. G., Tuma, J. M., Pickering, J. W., & Whelton, J. (1983). Simulation of psychosis on a multiple-choice projective test. *Perceptual and Motor Skills, 57*, 463–469.

Phillips, M. R., Ward, N. G., & Ries, R. K. (1983). Factitious mourning: Painless parenthood. *The American Journal of Psychiatry, 140*(4), 420–425.

Piaget, J. (1948). *The moral judgement of the child* (M. Gabain, Trans.). New York: Free Press.

Piaget, J. (1968). The mental development of the child. In J. Piaget (Ed.), *Six psychological studies* (A. Tenzer, Trans.) (pp. 3–70). New York: Vintage Books.

Plum, F., & Posner, J. B. (1980). *The diagnosis of stupor and coma* (3rd ed.). Philadelphia: F. A. Davis Company.

Podlesny, J. A., & Raskin, D. C. (1978). Effectiveness of techniques and physiological measures in the detection of deception. *Psychophysiology, 15*, 344–358.

Pollack, S. (1982). Dimensions of malingering. In B. H. Gross & L. E. Weinberger (Eds.), *New directions for mental health services: The mental health professional and the legal system* (pp. 63–75). San Francisco: Jossey-Bass.

Pope, H. G., Jonas, J. M., & Jones, B. (1982). Factitious psychosis: Phenomenology, family history, and long-term outcome of nine patients. *The American Journal of Psychiatry, 139*(11), 1480–1483.

Posey, C. D., & Hess, A. K. (1984). The fakability of subtle and obvious measures of aggression by male prisoners. *Journal of Personality Assessment, 48*, 137-144.

Poulose, K. P., & Shaw, A. A. (1977). Rapidly recurring seizures of psychogenic origin. *The American Journal of Psychiatry, 134*(10), 1145-1146.

Power, D. J. (1977). Memory, identification and crime. *Medicine, Science and the Law, 17*, 132-139.

Pratt, R. T. C. (1977). Psychogenic loss of memory. In C. W. M. Whitty & O. L. Zangwill (Eds.), *Amnesia* (pp. 224-232). London: Butterworths.

Price, G. E., & Terhune, W. B. (1919). Feigned amnesia as a defense reaction. *Journal of the American Medical Association, 72*, 565-567.

Prosser Thomas, E. W. (1937). Dermatitis artefacta: A note on an unusual case. *The British Medical Journal, 1*, 804-806.

Purtell, J. J., Robins, E., & Cohen, M. E. (1951). Observations on clinical aspects of hysteria. *Journal of the American Medical Association, 146*, 902-909.

Putnam, W. H. (1979). Hypnosis and distortions in eyewitness memory. *International Journal of Clinical and Experimental Hypnosis, 27*, 437-448.

Quaglino v. California, cert. denied, --U.S.--, 99 S.Ct. 212, *pet. rehearing denied*, --U.S.--, 99 S.Ct. 599 (1978).

Quinsey, V. L., & Bergersen, S. G. (1976). Instructional control of penile circumference in assessments of sexual preference. *Behavior Therapy, 7*, 489-493.

Quinsey, V. L., & Chaplin, T. C. (1987, January). *Preventing faking in phallometric assessments of sexual preferences*. Paper presented at New York Academy of Sciences meeting. New York, NY.

Quinsey, V. L., Chaplin, T. C., & Upfold, D. (1984). Sexual arousal to nonsexual violence and sadomasochistic themes among rapists and non-sex-offenders. *Journal of Consulting and Clinical Psychology, 52*(4), 651-657.

Quinsey, V. L, Steinman, C. M., Bergersen, S. G., & Holmes, T. F. (1975). Penile circumference, skin conductance, and ranking responses of child molesters and "normals" to sexual and nonsexual visual stimuli. *Behavior Therapy, 6*, 213-219.

Rada, R. T. (1978). *Clinical aspects of the rapist*. New York: Grune & Stratton.

Rada, R. T., Laws, D. R., Kellner, R., Stivastava, L., & Peake, G. (1983). Plasma androgens in violent and nonviolent sex offenders. *Bulletin of the American Academy of Psychiatry and the Law, 11*, 149-158.

Ramani, S. V., Quesney, L. F., Olson, D., & Gumnit, R. J. (1980). Diagnosis of hysterical seizures in epileptic patients. *The American Journal of Psychiatry, 137*(6), 705-709.

Raskin, D. C. (1978). Scientific assessment of the accuracy of detection of deception: A reply to Lykken. *Psychophysiology, 15*, 143-147.

Raskin, D. C. (1982). The scientific basis of polygraph techniques and their use in the judicial process. In A. Trankell (Ed.), *Reconstructing the past*. The Netherlands: Kluwer.

Raskin, D. C. (1986a, August). *Polygraph in the DeLorian case*. Paper presented at the American Psychological Association convention, Los Angeles, CA.

Raskin, D. C. (1986b). The polygraph in 1986: Scientific profession and legal issues surrounding applications and acceptance of polygraph evidence. *Utah Law Review, 1986*, 29-74.

Raskin, D. C., Barland, G. H., & Podlesny, J. A. (1978). *Validity and reliability of detection of deception* (LEAA Report 027-000-00892-2). Washington, DC: National Institute of Law Enforcement and Criminal Justice.

Raskin, D. C., & Hare, R. D. (1978). Psychopathy and detection of deception in a prison population. *Psychophysiology, 15*, 126-136.

Raskin, D. C., & Podlesny, J. (1979). Truth and deception: A reply to Lykken. *Psychological Bulletin, 86*, 54-59.

Rattigan, T. (1973). *The Winslow Boy*. New York: Dramatists Play Services.

Ray, I. (1871). *Treatise on the medical jurisprudence of insanity.* Boston: Little, Brown & Company.

Redlich, F. C., Ravitz, L. J., & Dession, G. H. (1951). Narcoanalysis and truth. *American Journal of Psychiatry, 106,* 586–593.

Regestein, Q. R., & Reich, P. (1978). Pedophilia occurring after onset of cognitive impairment. *The Journal of Nervous and Mental Disease, 166,* 794–798.

Reich, P., & Gottfried, L. A. (1983). Factitious disorders in a teaching hospital. *Annals of Internal Medicine, 99,* 240–247.

Reid, J. E., & Inbau, F. E. (1977). *Truth and deception—The polygraph technique* (3rd ed.). Baltimore: Williams and Wilkins.

Reid, W. H. (1978). *The psychopath: A comprehensive study of antisocial disorders and behaviors.* New York: Brunner/Mazel.

Reid, W. H. (1981). The antisocial personality and related syndromes. In J. R. Lion (Ed.), *Personality disorders: Diagnosis and management* (2nd ed.) (pp. 133–162). Baltimore, MD: Williams & Wilkins.

Reiser, M. (1986). Admission of hypnosis-induced recollections into evidence. *American Journal of Forensic Psychiatry, 7,* 31–40.

Reitan, R. M. (1958). Validity of the Trail Making Test as an indication of organic brain disease. *Perceptual and Motor Skills, 9,* 271–276.

Reitan, R. M., & Davison, L. A. (1974). *Clinical neuropsychology: Current status and applications.* Washington, DC: Witon.

Resnick, P. J. (1984). The detection of malingered mental illness. *Behavioral Sciences and the Law, 2*(1), 21–38.

Resnick, P. J. (1987, October). *The detection of malingered mental illness.* Workshop presented at the American Academy of Psychiatry and Law, Ottawa, Canada.

Rice, M. E., Arnold, L. S., & Tate, D. L. (1983). Faking good and bad adjustment on the MMPI and overcontrolled hostility in maximum security psychiatric patients. *Canadian Journal of Behavioural Science, 15,* 43–51.

Rickarby, G. A. (1979). Compensation-neurosis and the psycho-social requirements of the family. *British Journal of Medical Psychology, 52,* 333–338.

Rieger, W., & Billings, C. K. (1978). Ganser's syndrome associated with litigation. *Comprehensive Psychiatry, 19*(4), 371–375.

Rigler, C. T. J. (1879). Über die folgen der verletzungen auf eisenbahnen. [Concerning the consequences of injuries occurring on railroads] Berlin: Reimer.

Riley, T. L., & Massey, E. W. (1980). Pseudoseizures in the military. *Military Medicine, 145,* 614–619.

Riley, T. L., & Roy, A. (1982). *Pseudoseizures.* Baltimore: Williams and Wilkins.

Ripley, H. S., & Wolf, S. (1947). Intravenous use of sodium amytal in psychosomatic disorders. *Psychosomatic Medicine, 9,* 4–10.

Ritson, B., & Forrest, A. (1970). The simulation of psychosis: A contemporary presentation. *British Journal of Medical Psychology, 43,* 31–37.

Robins, L. N., Helzer, J. E., Croughan, J., & Ratcliff, K. S. (1981). National Institute of Mental Health diagnostic interview schedule. *Archives of General Psychiatry, 38,* 381–399.

Robison, J. C., Gitlin, N., Morrelli, H. F., & Mann, L. J. (1982). Factitious hyperamylasuria. A trap in the diagnosis of pancreatitis. *The New England Journal of Medicine, 306*(20), 1211–1212.

Robitcher, J. B. (1980). *The powers of psychiatry.* Boston: Houghton Mifflin.

Roesch, R., & Golding, S. L. (1986). Amnesia and competency to stand trial: A review of legal and clinical issues. *Behavioral Sciences and the Law, 4,* 87–97.

Rogers, R. (1983). Malingering or random? A research note on obvious vs. subtle subscales on the MMPI. *Journal of Clinical Psychology, 39,* 257–258.

Rogers, R. (1984a). *Rogers criminal responsibility assessment scales (RCRAS) and test manual.* Odessa, FL: Psychological Assessment Resources, Inc.

Rogers, R. (1984b). Towards an empirical model of malingering and deception. *Behavioral Sciences and the Law, 2,* 93–112.

Rogers, R. (1986a). *Conducting insanity evaluations.* New York: Van Nostrand Reinhold.

Rogers, R. (1986b). *Structured interview of reported symptoms (SIRS).* Clarke Institute of Psychiatry: Toronto, Unpublished scale.

Rogers, R. (1987). The assessment of malingering within a forensic context. In D. N. Weisstub (Ed.), *Law and psychiatry: International perspectives* (Vol. 3). New York: Plenum.

Rogers, R., & Cavanaugh, J. L. (1981). Application of the SADS diagnostic interview to forensic psychiatry. *Journal of Psychiatry and Law, 9,* 329–344.

Rogers, R., & Cavanaugh, J. L. (1983). "Nothing but the truth" . . . A re-examination of malingering. *Journal of Law and Psychiatry, 11,* 443–460.

Rogers, R., & Cunnien, A. J. (1986). Multiple SADS evaluation in the assessment of criminal defendants. *Journal of Forensic Sciences, 30,* 222–230.

Rogers, R., & Dickens, S. E. (1987). [Outpatient evaluations of mentally disordered offenders.] Unpublished raw data.

Rogers, R., Dolmetsch, R., Wasyliw, O. E., & Cavanaugh, J. L. (1982). Scientific inquiry in forensic psychiatry. *International Journal of Law and Psychiatry, 5,* 187–203.

Rogers, R., Gillis, R., & Dickens, S. E. (1987). [Pilot data for the development of the SIRS.] Unpublished raw data.

Rogers, R., Thatcher, A. A., & Cavanaugh, J. L. (1984). Use of the SADS diagnostic interview in evaluating legal insanity. *Journal of Clinical Psychology, 40,* 1538–1541.

Rogers, R., & Webster, C. D. (1987). *Assessing treatability in mentally disordered offenders.* Submitted for publication.

Rogers, R., Thatcher, A. A., & Harris, M. (1983). Identification of random responders on the MMPI: An actuarial approach. *Psychological Reports, 53,* 1171–1174.

Rosanoff, A. J. (1920). *Manual of psychiatry.* New York: John Wiley and Sons.

Rosen, R. C. (1973). Suppression of penile tumescence by instrumental conditioning. *Psychosomatic Medicine, 35,* 509–514.

Rosen, R. C., Shapiro, D., & Schwartz, G. E. (1975). Voluntary control of penile tumescence. *Psychosomatic Medicine, 37,* 479–483.

Rosenberg, C. E. (1968). *The trial of the assassin Guiteau.* Chicago: University of Chicago Press.

Rosenfeld, H. M. (1966). Approval-seeking and approval-inducing functions of verbal and nonverbal responses in the dyad. *Journal of Personality and Social Psychology, 4,* 597–605.

Rosenhan, D. L. (1973). On being sane in insane places. *Science, 179,* 250–358.

Rosenthal, R. (1966). *Experimenter bias in behavioral research.* New York: Appleton-Century-Crofts.

Roth, N. (1980). Torsion dystonia, conversion hysteria, and occupational cramps. *Comprehensive Psychiatry, 21,* 292–301.

Rovner, L. I., Raskin, D. C., & Kircher, J. A. (1979). Effects of information and practice on detection of deception. *Psychophysiology, 16,* 197–198. (Abstract).

Rowan, C. (1982). *The Cleveland Plain Dealer,* June 21.

Rubinsky, E. W., & Brandt, J. (1986). Amnesia and criminal law: A clinical overview. *Behavioral Sciences and the Law, 4,* 27–46.

Rubinstein, J. S. (1978). Abuse of antiparkinsonism drugs. *Journal of the American Medical Association, 239,* 2365–2366.

Ruch, J. C., Morgan, A. H., & Hilgard, E. R. (1974). Measuring hypnotic responsiveness: A comparison of the Barber Suggestibility Scale and the Stanford Hypnotic Susceptibility Scale, Form A. *International Journal of Clinical and Experimental Hypnosis, 22,* 365–376.

Rutherford, W. H., Merrett, J. D., & McDonald, J. R. (1977). Sequelae of concussion caused by minor head injuries. *Lancet, 1*, 1-4.

Rutter, M., Tizard, J., & Whitmore, K. (1970). *Education, health and behavior.* New York: John Wiley & Sons.

Sackett, P. R., & Decker, P. J. (1979). Detection of deception in the employment context: A review and critical analysis. *Personnel Psychology, 32*, 487-506.

Sadoff, R. L. (1974). Evaluation of amnesia in criminal-legal situations. *Journal of Forensic Sciences, 19*, 98-101.

Sadoff, R. L. (1978). Personal injury and the psychiatrist. *Weekly Psychiatry Update Series* (Lesson 38). Princeton, NJ: Biomedia.

Sadow, L., & Suslick, A. (1961). Simulation of a previous psychotic state. *Archives of General Psychiatry, 4*, 452-458.

Sandford, D. A. (1974). Patterns of sexual arousal in heterosexual males. *The Journal of Sex Research, 10*(2), 150-155.

Sarbin, T. R., & Coe, W. C. (1972). *Hypnosis: A social psychological analysis of influence communication.* New York: Holt, Rinehart & Winston.

Sarni, C. (1979). Children's understanding of display rules. *Developmental Psychology, 15*, 424-429.

Saxe, L., Dougherty, D., & Cross, T. (1985). The validity of polygraph testing: Scientific analysis and public controversy. *American Psychologist, 40*, 355-366.

Schacter, D. L. (1983). Amnesia observed: Remembering and forgetting in a natural environment. *Journal of Abnormal Psychology, 92*, 236-242.

Schacter, D. L. (1986a). Amnesia and crime: How much do we really know? *American Psychologist, 41*, 286-295.

Schacter, D. L. (1986b). On the relation between genuine and simulated amnesia. *Behavioral Sciences and the Law, 4*, 47-64.

Schacter, D. L., & Crovitz, H. F. (1977). Memory function after closed head injury: A review of the quantitative research. *Cortex, 13*, 150-176.

Schacter, D. L., Wang, P. L., Tulving, E., & Freedman, M. (1982). Functional retrograde amnesia: A quantitative study. *Neuropsychologia, 20*, 523-532.

Schadler, M., & Ayers-NachamKin, B. (1983). The development of excuse-making. In C. R. Snyder, R. L. Higgins, & R. J. Stuky, Excuses, masquerades in search of grace (pp. 159-190). New York: Wiley.

Schafer, E. (1986, October). *Workers compensation workshop.* Presentation at American Academy of Psychiatry and the Law Meeting, Philadelphia.

Schafter, D. W., & Rubio, R. (1978). Hypnosis and the recall of witnesses. *International Journal of Clinical and Experimental Hypnosis, 26*, 81-91.

Schmauk, F. J. (1970). Punishment, arousal, and avoidance learning in sociopaths. *Journal of Abnormal Psychology, 76*, 325-335.

Schneck, J. M. (1967). Hypnoanalytic study of a false confession. *International Journal of Clinical and Experimental Hypnosis, 15*, 11-18.

Schneck, J. M. (1970). Pseudo-malingering and Leonid Andreyev's "The Dilemma." *Psychiatric Quarterly, 44*, 49-54.

Schuman, D. C. (1986). False accusations of physical and sexual abuse. *Bulletin of the American Academy of Psychiatry and the Law, 14*(1), 5-21.

Scoggin, C. H. (1983). Factitious illness. Dramatic deceit versus reality. *Postgraduate Medicine, 74*(5), 259-265.

Scott, M. L., Cole, J. K., McKay, S. E., Golden, C. J., & Liggett, K. R. (1984). Neuropsychological performances of sexual assaulters and pedophiles. *Journal of Forensic Sciences, 29*, 1114-1118.

Scott, P. D. (1965). The Ganser syndrome. *British Journal of Criminology, 5*, 127-134.

Scoville, W. B., & Milner, B. (1957). Loss of recent memory after bilateral hippocampal lesions. *Journal of Neurology, Neurosurgery, and Psychiatry, 20*, 11–21.

Scriven, M. (1976). Maximizing the power of causal investigation: The modus operandi method. In G. V. Glass (Ed.), *Evaluation studies review annual* (Vol. 1) (pp. 101–118). Beverly Hills, CA: Sage Publications.

Seamons, D. T., Howell, R. J., Carlisle, A. L., & Roe, A. V. (1981). Rorschach simulation of mental illness and normality by psychotic and nonpsychotic legal offenders. *Journal of Personality Assessment, 45*, 130–135.

Sears, R. R. (1932). An experimental study of hypnotic anesthesia. *Journal of Experimental Psychology, 15*, 1–22.

Sechrest, L. (1963). Incremental validity: A recommendation. *Educational and Psychological Measurement, 23*, 153–158.

Seigel, R. K., & West, L. J. (Eds.) (1975). *Hallucinations: Behavior, experience and theory.* New York: John Wiley & Sons.

Sgroi, S. M. (1982). *Handbook of clinical intervention in child sexual abuse.* Lexington, MA: Lexington Books.

Shamming insanity (1881, December 5). *New York Times*, p. 4.

Sheehan, P. W. (1971). A methodological analysis of the simulating technique. *International Journal of Clinical and Experimental Hypnosis, 19*, 83–99.

Sheehan, P. W., & McConkey, K. M. (1979). Australian norms for the Harvard Group Scale of Hypnotic Susceptibility, Form A. *International Journal of Clinical and Experimental Hypnosis, 27*, 294–304.

Sheehan, P. W., & Tilden, J. (1985). The consistency of occurrences of memory distortion following hypnotic induction. *International Journal of Clinical and Experimental Hypnosis, 34*, 122–137.

Shennum, W. A., & Bugental, D. B. (1982). The development of control over affective expression in nonverbal behavior. In R. S. Feldman (Ed.), *Development of nonverbal behavior in children* (pp. 101–121). New York: Springer-Verlag.

Sherman, M., Trief, P., & Strafkin, R. (1975). Impression management in the psychiatric interview: Quality, style and individual differences. *Journal of Consulting and Clinical Psychology, 43*, 867–871.

Shipko, S., & Mancini, J. L. (1980). Simulated dystonia [Letter to the editor]. *Annals of Emergency Medicine, 9*, 279.

Schoichet, R. P. (1978). Sodium Amytal in the diagnosis of chronic pain. *Canadian Psychiatric Association Journal, 23*, 219–228.

Shor, R. E. (1959). Hypnosis and the concept of the generalized reality-orientation. *American Journal of Psychotherapy, 13*, 582–602.

Shor, R. E. (1962). Three dimensions of hypnotic depth. *International Journal of Clinical and Experimental Hypnosis, 10*, 23–38.

Shor, R. E., & Orne, E. C. (1962). *Harvard Group Scale of Hypnotic Susceptibility.* Palo Alto, CA: Consulting Psychologists Press.

Shukla, S., Cook, B. L., Mukherjee, S., Godwin, C., & Miller, M. G. (1987). Mania following head trauma. *American Journal of Psychiatry, 144*, 93–96.

Sierles, F. S. (1984). Correlates of malingering. *Behavioral Sciences and the Law, 2*(1), 113–118.

Singer, H., & Krohn, W. (1924). *Insanity and the Law.* Philadelphia: J. Blackiston's Son & Co.

Slater, E. T. O., & Glithero, E. (1965). A follow-up of patients diagnosed as suffering from "hysteria." *Journal of Psychosomatic Research, 9*, 9–13.

Slowick, S. M., & Buckley, J. P. (1975). Relative accuracy of polygraph examiner diagnosis of respiration, blood pressure, and GSR recordings. *Journal of Police Science and Administration, 3*, 305–309.

Small, I. F., Small, J. G., & Andersen, J. M. (1966). Clinical characteristics of hallucinations of schizophrenia. *Diseases of the Nervous System, 27,* 349–353.

Smith, A. (1968). The Symbol Digit Modalities Test: A neuropsychologic test for economic screening of learning and other cerebral disorders. *Learning Disorders, 3,* 83–91.

Smith, B. H. (1967). A handbook of tests to unmask malingering. *Consultant, 7,* 41–47.

Smith, B. M., Hain, J. D., & Stevenson, I. (1970). Controlled interviews using drugs. *Archives of General Psychiatry, 22,* 2–10.

Snowdon, J., Solomons, R., & Druce, H. (1978). Feigned bereavement: Twelve cases. *British Journal of Psychiatry, 133,* 15–19.

Snyder, S. (1986). Pseudologia fantastica in the borderline patient. *The American Journal of Psychiatry, 143*(10), 1287–1289.

Solnick, R. L., & Birren, J. E. (1977). Age and male erectile responsiveness. *Archives of Sexual Behavior, 6*(1), 1–9.

Soniat, T. L. (1960). The problem of "compensation" neurosis. *South Medical Journal, 53,* 365–368.

Spanos, N. P., & Barber, T. X. (1974). Toward a convergence in hypnotic research. *American Psychologist, 29,* 500–511.

Spanos, N. P., Radtke, H. L., Bertrand, L. D., Addie, D. L., & Drummond, J. (1982). Disorganized recall, hypnotic amnesia, and subjects' faking: More disconfirmatory evidence. *Psychological Reports, 50,* 383–389.

Sparr, L. F., & Atkinson, R. M. (1986). Post-traumatic stress disorder as an insanity defence: Medicolegal quicksand. *American Journal of Psychiatry, 143,* 608–613.

Sparr, L. F., & Pankratz, L. D. (1983). Factitious post-traumatic stress disorder. *The American Journal of Psychiatry, 140*(10), 1016–1019.

Spector, R. S., & Foster, T. E. (1977). Admissibility of hypnotic statements: Is the law of evidence susceptible? *Ohio State Law Journal, 38,* 567–611.

Speedie, L. J., & Heilman, K. M. (1982). Amnestic disturbance following infarction of the left dorsomedial nucleus of the thalamus. *Neuropsychologia, 20,* 597–504.

Spencer, C. E. (1929). Methods of detecting guilt: Word association, reaction-time method. *Oregon Law Review, 61,* 158–166.

Spiegel, D., & Spiegel, H. (1984). Uses of hypnosis in evaluating malingering and deception. *Behavioral Sciences and the Law, 2,* 51–65.

Spiegel, D., Detrick, D., & Frischholz, E. (1982). Hypnotizability and psychopathology. *American Journal of Psychiatry, 139,* 431–437.

Spiegel, H., & Bridger, A. A. (1970). *Manual for hypnotic induction profile.* New York: Soni Medica.

Spiro, H. R. (1968). Chronic factitious illness. Munchausen's syndrome. *Archives of General Psychiatry, 18,* 569–579.

Spitzer, R. L. (1974). Critiques of Rosenhan. *Journal of Abnormal Psychology, 84,* 442–452.

Spitzer, R. L., & Endicott, J. (1978). *Schedule of affective disorders and schizophrenia.* New York: Biometric Research.

Spitzer, R. L., Endicott, J., & Robins, E. (1978). Research diagnostic criteria for use in psychiatric research. *Archives of General Psychiatry, 35,* 773–782.

Spitzer, R. L., & Williams, J. B. W. (1986). *Structured clinical interview for DSM III.* New York: Biometric Research.

Spreen, O., & Benton, A. L. (1963). Simulation of mental deficiency on a visual memory test. *American Journal of Mental Deficiency, 67,* 909–913.

Squire, L. R. (1982a). Comparisons between forms of amnesia: Some deficits are unique to Korsakoff's syndrome. *Journal of Experimental Psychology: Learning, Memory, and Cognition, 8,* 560–571.

Squire, L. R. (1982b). The neuropsychology of human memory. *Annual Review of Neuroscience, 5,* 241–273.

Squire, L. R., & Butters, N. (Eds.) (1984). *The neuropsychology of memory.* New York: Guilford Press.

Stalnaker, J. M., & Riddle, E. E. (1932). The effect of hypnosis on long-delayed recall. *Journal of General Psychology, 6,* 429–440.

Starr, A., & Phillips, L. (1970). Verbal and motor memory in the amnesic syndrome. *Neuropsychologia, 8,* 75–88.

State ex rel. Collins v. Superior Court, 132 Ariz. 180, 644 P.2d 1266 (1982), supplemental opinion filed May 4, 1982.

State ex rel. Sheppard v. Koblentz, 174 Ohio St. 120, 187 N.E.2d 40 (1962).

State v. Armstrong, 110 Wis.2d 555, 329 N.W.2d 386 (1983).

State v. Bianchi, No. 79-10116 (Wash. Sup. Ct., October 19, 1979).

State v. Hurd, 86 N. J. 525, 432 A.2d 86 (1981).

State v. Mack, ---Minn.---, 292 N.W.2d 764 (1980).

State v. McClendon, 103 Ariz. 105, 437 P.2d 421 (1968).

State v. McQueen, 295 N.S. 96. 244 S.E.2d 414 (1978).

State v. Papp, No. 78-02-00229 (C. P. Summit Co., Ohio, Lorain Cty. No. 16682, March 23, 1978); *cert. denied,* U.S. Sup. Ct. No. 79-5091 October 1, 1979).

Stefansson, J. G., Messina, J. A., & Meyerowitz, S. (1976). Hysterical neurosis, conversion type: Clinical and epidemiological considerations. *Acta Psychiatrica Scandinavica, 53,* 119–138.

Stephenson, P. E. (1977). Physiologic and psychotropic effects of caffeine on man. *Journal of the American Dietetic Association, 71,* 240–247.

Stern, R. M., Breen, J. P., Watanabe, T., & Perry, B. S. (1981). Effect of feedback of physiological information on responses to innocent associations and guilty knowledge. *Journal of Applied Psychology, 66,* 677–681.

Stern, T. A. (1980). Munchausen's syndrome revisited. *Psychosomatics, 21*(4), 329–336.

Stevens, H. (1986). Is it organic or is it functional: Is it hysterial or malingering? *Psychiatric Clinics of North America, 9,* 241–254.

Stevenson, I., Buckman, J., Smith, B. M., & Hain, J. D. (1974). The use of drugs in psychiatric interviews: Some interpretations based on controlled experiments. *American Journal of Psychiatry, 131,* 707–710.

Stewart, M. A., & DeBlois, C. S. (1984). *Diagnostic criteria for aggressive conduct disorder.* Unpublished manuscript.

Stone, A. A. (1984). The ethics of forensic psychiatry: A view from the ivory tower. In A. A. Stone (Ed.), *Law, psychiatry and morality* (pp. 57–76). Washington, DC: American Psychiatric Press, Inc.

Stone, M. H. (1977). Factitious illness. Psychological findings and treatment recommendations. *Bulletin of the Menninger Clinic, 41*(3), 239–254.

Stouthamer-Loeber, M. (1986). Lying as problem behavior in children: A review. *Clinical Psychology Review, 6,* 267–289.

Sturmann, K., Shoen, T., & Filiberti, A. W. (1985). Factitious arrhythmia. *Annals of Emergency Medicine, 14*(8), 829–830.

Sutcliffe, J. P. (1958). *Hypnotic behavior: Fantasy or simulation.* Unpublished doctoral dissertation, University of Sydney, Sydney, Australia.

Szasz, T. S. (1956). Malingering: "Diagnosis" or social condemnation? *AMA Archives of Neurology and Psychiatry, 76,* 432–443.

Szucko, J. J., & Kleinmuntz, B. (1981). Statistical versus clinical lie detection. *American Psychologist, 36,* 488–496.

Szucko, J. J., & Kleinmuntz, B. (1985). Psychological methods of truth detection. In C. P.

Ewing (Ed.), *Psychology, psychiatry and the law: A clinical and forensic handbook* (pp. 441–466). Sarasota, FL: Professional Resource Exchange.

Talland, G. A., Sweet, W. H., & Ballantine, H. T. (1967). Amnesic syndrome with anterior communicating artery aneurysm. *Journal of Nervous and Mental Disease, 145*, 179–192.

Tesser, A., & Paulhus, D. (1983). The definition of self: Private and public self-evaluation management strategies. *Journal of Personality and Social Psychology, 44*, 672–682.

Tetlock, P. E., & Manstead, A. S. R. (1985). Impression management versus intrapsychic explorations in social psychology: A useful dichotomy? *Psychological Review, 92*, 59–77.

Theodor, L. H., & Mandelcorn, M. S. (1973). Hysterical blindness: A case report and study using a modern psychophysical technique. *Journal of Abnormal Psychology, 82*, 552–553.

Thompson, M. R. (1965). Post-traumatic psychoneurosis—a statistical survey. *American Journal of Psychiatry, 121*, 1043–1048.

Thurber, S. (1981). CPI variables in relation to the polygraph performance of police officer candidates. *Journal of Social Psychology, 113*, 145–146.

Travin, S., Bluestone, H., Coleman, E., Cullen, K., & Melella, J. (1986). Pedophile types and treatment perspectives. *Journal of Forensic Sciences, 31*, 609–620.

Travin, S., & Protter, B. (1984). Malingering and malingering-like behavior: Some clinical and conceptual issues. *Psychiatric Quarterly, 56*(3), 189–197.

Trimble, M. R. (1981). *Post-traumatic neurosis from railway spine to the whiplash.* New York: John Wiley & Sons.

Trivers, R. L. (1971). The evolution of reciprocal altruism. *Quarterly Review of Biology, 46*, 35–57.

United States ex rel. Parson v. Anderson, 354 F.Supp. 1060 (D.Del. 1972), *affirmed*, 481 F.2d 94 (3rd Cir.) (en banc), *cert. denied*, 414 U.S. 1072 (1973).

United States v. Adams, United States v. Pinkerton, 581 F.2d 193 (9th Cir.), *cert. denied*, 439 U.S. 1006 (1978).

United States v. Andrews, General Court-Martial No. 75-14 (N.F. Jud. Cir. Navy-Marine Corps Judiciary, Phila., Pa., October 6, 1976).

United States v. Borum, 464 F.2d 896 (10th Cir. 1972).

United States v. Miller, 411 F.2d 825 (1969).

United States v. Stevens, 461 F.2d 317, (7th Cir.), *cert. denied*, 409 U.S. 948 (1972).

Volow, M. R. (1986). Pseudoseizures: An overview. *Southern Medical Journal, 79*, 600–607.

Wachspress, M., Berenberg, A. N., & Jacobson, A. (1953). Simulation of psychosis: A report of three cases. *Psychiatric Quarterly, 27*, 463–473.

Wade, T. C., & Baker, T. E. (1977). Opinions in use of psychological tests: A survey of clinical psychologists. *American Psychologist, 32*, 874–882.

Waid, W. M., Orne, E. C., Cook, M. R., & Orne, M. T. (1981). Meprobamate reduces accuracy of physiological detection of deception. *Science, 212*, 71–73.

Walker, J. I. (1981). Vietnam combat veterans with legal difficulties: A psychiatric problem? *American Journal of Psychiatry, 138*, 1384–1385.

Ward, L. C. (1986). MMPI item subtlety research: Current issues and directions. *Journal of Personality Assessment, 50*, 73–79.

Ward, N. G., Rowlett, D. B., & Burke, P. (1978). Sodium amylobarbitone in the differential diagnosis of confusion. *American Journal of Psychiatry, 135*, 75–78.

Warrington, E. K., & Weiskrantz, L. (1968). A new method of testing long-retention with special reference to amnesic patients. *Nature, 217*, 972–974.

Warrington, E. K., & Weiskrantz, L. (1974). The effect of prior learning on subsequent retention in amnesic patients. *Neuropsychologia, 16*, 169–177.

Watkins, J. G. (1984). The Bianchi (L.A. Hillside Strangler) case: Sociopath or multiple personality? *International Journal of Clinical and Experimental Hypnosis, 32*, 67–101.

Watson, C. G., & Buranen, C. (1979). The frequency and identification of false positive conversion reactions. *Journal of Nervous and Mental Disease, 167*, 243–247.

Waxman, S. G., & Geschwind, N. (1975). The interictal behavior syndrome of temporal lobe epilepsy. *Archives of General Psychiatry, 32*, 1580–1586.

Weddington, W. W., & Leventhal, B. L. (1982). Malicious abuse of haloperidol [Letter to the editor]. *Journal of Clinical Psychiatry, 43*, 434.

Weighill, V. E. (1983). "Compensation neurosis": A review of the literature. *Journal of Psychosomatic Research, 27*(2), 97–104.

Weiner, I. B. (1977). Approaches to Rorschach validation. In M. A. Ricers-Ousiankina (Ed.), *Rorschach psychology* (2nd ed.). Huntington, NY: Kreiger.

Weingartner, H., Caine, E. D., & Ebert, M. H. (1979). Imagery, encoding, and retrieval of information from memory: Some specific encoding-retrieval changes in Huntington's disease. *Journal of Abnormal Psychology, 88*, 52–88.

Weingartner, H., Grafman, J., Boutelle, W., Kaye, W., & Martin, P. (1983). Forms of memory failure. *Science, 221*, 380–382.

Weingartner, H., Kaye, W., Smallberg, S. A., Ebert, M. H., Gillin, J. C., & Sitaram, N. (1982). Memory failures in progressive idiopathic dementia. *Journal of Abnormal Psychology, 90*, 187–196.

Weinstein, E. A., Kahn, R. L., Sugarman, L. A., & Linn, L. (1953). The diagnostic use of amobarbital sodium ("amytal sodium") in brain disease. *American Journal of Psychiatry, 109*, 789–794.

Weinstein, E. A., Kahn, R. L., Sugarman, L. A., & Malitz, S. (1954). Serial administration of "amytal test" for brain disease. *Archives of Neurology and Psychiatry, 71*, 217–226.

Weinstein, E. A., & Lyerly, O. G. (1966). Conversion hysteria following brain injury. *Archives of Neurology, 15*, 545–548.

Weitzenhoffer, A. M., & Hilgard, E. R. (1959). *Stanford Hypnotic Susceptibility Scales, Forms A and B.* Palo Alto, CA: Consulting Psychologists Press.

Weitzenhoffer, A. M., & Hilgard, E. R. (1962). *Stanford Hypnotic Susceptibility Scale, Form C.* Palo Alto, CA: Consulting Psychologists Press.

Weitzenhoffer, A. M., & Hilgard, E. R. (1963). *The Stanford Profile Scales of Hypnotic Susceptibility: Forms I and II.* Palo Alto, CA: Consulting Psychologists Press.

Weitzenhoffer, A. M., & Sjoberg, B. M., Jr. (1961). Suggestibility with and without "induction of hypnosis." *Journal of Nervous and Mental Disease, 132*, 204–220.

Wells, C. E. (1978). Chronic brain disease: An overview. *American Journal of Psychiatry, 135*, 1–12.

Wells, C. E. (1979). Pseudodementia. *American Journal of Psychiatry, 136*(7), 895–900.

Wells, G. L. (1978). Applied eyewitness-testimony research: System variables and estimator variables. *Journal of Personality and Social Psychology, 36*, 1546–1557.

Wells, L. A. (1986). Varieties of imposture. *Perspectives in Biology and Medicine, 29*(4), 588–610.

Wertham, F. (1949). *The show of violence.* Garden City, NY: Doubleday & Co., Inc.

Whipple, G. M. (1918). The obtaining of information: Psychology of observation and report. *Psychological Bulletin, 15*, 217–248.

White, M. M. (1930). The physical and mental traits of individuals susceptible to hypnosis. *Journal of Abnormal and Social Psychology, 25*, 293–298.

White, R. W. (1941). A preface to the theory of hypnotism. *Journal of Abnormal and Social Psychology, 36*, 477–505.

Whitlock, F. A. (1967). The Ganser syndrome. *British Journal of Psychiatry, 113*, 19–29.

Whitlock, F. A. (1981). Some observations on the meaning of confabulation. *British Journal of Medical Psychology, 54*, 213–218.

Whitlock, R. A. (1967). The aetiology of hysteria. *Acta Psychiatrica Scandinavica, 43,* 114–162.

Whitty, C. W. M. (1977). Transient global amnesia. In C. W. M. Whitty & O. L. Zangwill (Eds.), *Amnesia* (pp. 93–103). London: Butterworths.

Whitty, C. W. M., Stores, G., & Lishman, W. A. (1977). Amnesia in cerebral disease. In C. W. M. Whitty & O. L. Zangwill (Eds.), *Amnesia* (pp. 93–103). London: Butterworths.

Whitty, C. W. M., & Zangwill, O. L. (Eds.), (1977). *Amnesia.* London: Butterworths.

Wicklander, D. E., & Hunter, F. L. (1975). The influence of auxiliary sources of information in polygraph diagnoses. *Journal of Police Science and Administration, 3,* 405–409.

Wiener, D. N. (1948). Subtle and obvious keys for the MMPI. *Journal of Consulting Psychology, 12,* 164–170.

Wiener, D. N., & Harmon, L. R. (1946). *Subtle and obvious keys for the MMPI: Their development.* Advisement Bulletin No. 16, Regional Veterans Administration Office, Minneapolis.

Wiggins, E. C., & Brandt, J. (1988). The detection of simulated amnesia. *Law and Human Behavior, 12,* 57–78.

Wiggins, S. L., Lombard, E. A., Brennan, M. J., & Heckel, R. V. (1964). Awareness of events in case of amnesia. *Archives of General Psychiatry, 11,* 67–70.

Wilson, L., Greene, E., & Loftus, E. R. (1985). Beliefs about forensic hypnosis. *International Journal of Clinical and Experimental Hypnosis, 33,* 110–121.

Wilson, R. S., Koller, W., & Kelly, M. P. (1980). The amnesia of transient global amnesia. *Journal of Clinical Neuropsychology, 2,* 259–266.

Wilson v. United States, 391 F.2d 460 (D.C. Cir. 1968).

Wimmer, H., Gruber, S., & Perner, J. (1985). Young children's conception of lying: Moral intuition and the denotation and connotation of "to lie." *Developmental Psychology, 21,* 993–995.

Winocur, G., Oxbury, S., Roberts, R., Agnetti, V., & Davis, C. (1984). Amnesia in a patient with bilateral lesions to the thalamus. *Neuropsychologia, 22,* 123–143.

Woodruff, R. (1966). The diagnostic use of the amylobarbital interview among patients with psychotic illness. *British Journal of Psychiatry, 112,* 727–732.

Wooten, A. J. (1984). Effectiveness of the *K* correction in the detection of psychopathology and its impact on profile height and configuration among young adult men. *Journal of Consulting and Clinical Psychology, 52,* 468–473.

Worthington, T. S. (1979). The use in court of hypnotically enhanced testimony. *International Journal of Clinical and Experimental Hypnosis, 27,* 402–416.

Wrightson, P., & Gronwall, D. (1981). Time off work and symptoms after minor head injury. *Injury, 12,* 445–454.

Wydra, A., Marshall, W. L., Earls, C. M., & Barbaree, H. E. (1983). Identification of cues and control of sexual arousal of rapists. *Behavior Research and Therapy, 21,* 469–476.

Yankee, W. J., Powell, J. M., II, & Newland, R. (1986). An investigation of the accuracy and consistency of polygraph chart interpretation by inexperienced and experienced examiners. *Polygraph, 16,* 108–117.

Yochelson, S., & Samenow, S. (1976). *The criminal personality, Vol. 1: A profile for change.* New York: Jason Aronson.

Yochelson, S., & Samenow, S. (1977). *The criminal personality, Vol. 2: The change process.* New York: Jason Aronson.

Young, J. (1972). The fakability of the Thematic Apperception Test under conditions of instruction to fake and test clues: Arnold's story sequence analysis scoring for achievement motivation. *Dissertation Abstracts International, 33,* 3379-A.

Yudofsky, S. (1985). Malingering. In H. Kaplan & B. Sadock (Eds.), *Comprehensive textbook of psychiatry* (4th ed.) (pp. 1862–1865). Baltimore, MD: Williams & Wilkins.

Zelig, M., & Beidleman, W. B. (1981). The investigative use of hypnosis: A word of caution. *International Journal of Law and Psychiatry, 4,* 433–444.

Ziskin, J. (1981). *Coping with Psychiatric and Psychological Testimony.* Beverly Hills, CA: Law and Psychology Press.

Ziskin, J. (1984). Malingering of psychological disorders. *Behavioral Sciences and the Law, 2,* 39–50.

Zuckerman, M. (1971). Physiological measures of sexual arousal in the human. *Psychological Bulletin, 75,* 297–329.

Index

Italicized page numbers refer to tables and figures

Robert V. Prescott, Ph.D
Evanston Hospital
(708) 570-2806